WHO
RULES
AMERICA?

THE TRIUMPH OF
THE CORPORATE RICH

SEVENTH EDITION

G. WILLIAM DOMHOFF

University of California, Santa Cruz

Mc
Graw
Hill
Education

WHO RULES AMERICA? THE TRIUMPH OF THE CORPORATE RICH,
SEVENTH EDITION

Published by McGraw-Hill Education, 2 Penn Plaza, New York, NY 10121. Copyright © 2014 by
McGraw-Hill Education. All rights reserved. Printed in the United States of America. Previous editions
© 2010, 2006, and 2002. No part of this publication may be reproduced or distributed in any form or by any
means, or stored in a database or retrieval system, without the prior written consent of The McGraw-Hill
Education, including, but not limited to, in any network or other electronic storage or transmission, or
broadcast for distance learning.

Some ancillaries, including electronic and print components, may not be available to customers outside the
United States.

This book is printed on acid-free paper.

1 2 3 4 5 6 7 8 9 0 DOC/DOC 1 0 9 8 7 6 5 4 3

ISBN 978-0-07-802671-3
MHID 0-07-802671-7

Senior Vice President, Products & Markets: *Kurt L. Strand*	Marketing Specialist: *Alexandra Schultz*
	Editorial Coordinator: *Adina Lonn*
Vice President, General Manager: *Michael Ryan*	Director, Content Production: *Terri Schiesl*
Vice President, Content Production & Technology Services: *Kimberly Meriwether David*	Content Project Manager: *Mary Jane Lampe*
	Buyer: *Nichole Birkenholz*
Executive Director of Development: *Lisa Pinto*	Cover Designer: *Studio Montage, St. Louis, MO*
Managing Director: *Gina Boedeker*	Compositor: *Cenveo® Publisher Services*
Brand Manager: *Courtney Austermehle*	Typeface: *10/12 Adobe Caslon Pro*
Managing Editor: *Sara Jaeger*	Printer: *R. R. Donnelley*

All credits appearing on page or at the end of the book are considered to be an extension of the copyright page.

Library of Congress Cataloging-in-Publication Data

Domhoff, G. William.
   Who rules America? : the triumph of the corporate rich/G. William Domhoff, University of California,
Santa Cruz.—Seventh edition.
      pages cm
   Includes bibliographical references and index.
   ISBN-13: 978-0-07-802671-3 (alk. paper)
   ISBN-10: 0-07-802671-7 (alk. paper)
   1. Elite (Social sciences)—United States.   2. Power (Social sciences)—United States.   3. Social
classes—United States.   4. Corporations—Political activity—United States.   5. United States—Politics
and government.   I. Title.
   HN90.E4D652   2014
   305.5'20973—dc23   2013008437

The Internet addresses listed in the text were accurate at the time of publication. The inclusion of a
website does not indicate an endorsement by the authors or McGraw-Hill Education, and McGraw-Hill
Education does not guarantee the accuracy of the information presented at these sites.

www.mhhe.com

Contents

Preface

This new edition of *Who Rules America?* is completely updated to capture the full sweep of the dramatic changes that occurred in the United States during the first 12 years of the twenty-first century. These changes represent nothing less than the triumph of the corporate rich that own and manage the relative handful of large banks, corporations, agribusinesses, and commercial real estate developments that dominate the American economy and government. The new edition draws on recent studies by sociologists, political scientists, and experts working for public interest groups and government agencies to update information on corporate interlocks, social clubs, private schools, and other institutions that foster elite social cohesion. It also contains new information on the tax-free charitable foundations, think tanks, and policy-discussion groups through which the corporate rich strive to shape public policy.

To update and extend information on the large flow of money from corporations and foundations to think tanks, policy-discussion groups, and opinion-shaping organizations, the new edition draws on the grants section of the *Foundation Directory Online* for invaluable compilations. It presents new evidence based on public opinion surveys that better demonstrates the continuing disjuncture between the liberal policy preferences of low- and middle-income Americans on a variety of economic and foreign policy issues, and the lack of responsiveness to those preferences on the part of the federal government in Washington.

This edition contains a more detailed explanation, rooted in a new study of archival records, of why the moderate conservatives within the corporate community became more conservative on key economic issues in the late 1960s and early 1970s, setting the stage for the Reagan administration and the increasing income inequality that developed from the 1980s onward. It also explains how the rise of the civil rights movement and divisions within the liberal-labor alliance unexpectedly made possible the right turn by a more united corporate rich.

The new edition uses the replacement of Republicans with Democrats in the 2006 and 2008 congressional elections and the election of Barack Obama to the presidency in 2008 and 2012 to show that elections can register citizen discontent with political decisions. It also pays attention to the huge spurt in campaign finance made possible by court decisions and various loopholes in the laws governing campaign finance, which make it possible for the corporate rich to funnel billions of dollars in anonymous donations to political action committees for attack ads. Although the corporate rich have always found ways in the past to circumvent attempts to limit campaign donations and make them more transparent, the 2010 and 2012 elections took these practices to astronomical levels.

In an effort to make the book more accessible to those with no background in the theoretical debates that animate the social science literature, all discussion of alternative theories are confined to a new last chapter. This approach allows readers to see how the empirically based argument unfolds without any brief critical asides that may be confusing or distracting. This change also may make it possible for readers to better form their own judgments about theoretical controversies because they will have seen the full empirical picture. It also allows readers—and instructors—to skip the final chapter without missing any part of the argument and evidence presented in the first eight chapters.

As before, the book is supplemented by a website at whorulesamerica.net. It includes a library of online articles and chapters, and links to methodological tools. The key documents on the site are noted at appropriate points in the book to remind readers that further analyses on particular topics are available. A document providing detailed information on "Wealth, Income, and Power" is regularly updated as new information becomes available. The website www.whorulesamerica.net also houses methodological information on how to do power structure research at both the national and local levels, as well a list of social indicators of upper-class standing that are useful for research on the top 0.3 to 0.5 percent of the adult population that constitute the social upper class. Moving these resources from the book to the Web made it possible to include more detail on methodology for those who want to do their own studies and at the same time have more space in the book for discussing substantive issues of immediate interest to those new to the topic of power.

The lengthy discussions of the origins of the Social Security and National Labor Relations acts of 1935 in previous editions also have been moved to whorulesamerica.net, which allows for in-depth historical discussions of the origins, implementation, and aftermath of these major legislative landmarks, as well as for a discussion of the efforts to expand or eliminate them between the 1940s and 2010. This change makes it possible to provide more focus within the book itself on recent events, such as the legislative failures of the liberal-labor alliance during the 2009–2010 session of Congress.

Several decades ago, there was far more information available on the upper class than there was on the corporate community. That situation is now completely reversed due to the huge increase in the information about corporations available on the Internet, along with the increasing reluctance of the corporate rich to list their private schools and social clubs in *Who's Who in America* and other sources. It therefore makes sense to stress even more than in past editions that the corporate community and the upper class are basically two sides of the same coin, so there is less emphasis on members of the upper class "controlling" the corporate community and greater use of the concept of a "corporate rich" to express this basic unity of corporation and class.

Furthermore, in discussing the upper class in relation to power, the emphasis is on the social cohesion that is generated among the corporate rich by virtue of their participation in long-standing prestigious social institutions, such as prep schools, exclusive social clubs, debutante balls, and elite retreats. In this regard, the new edition continues to emphasize that the social institutions of the upper class also have a role in the power equation through the socialization of the newly rich and their children. They instill feelings of pride and superiority in members of the corporate rich, which can be useful in generating deference on the part of ordinary citizens.

There have been some slight changes in the wording of key phrases. I now refer to the "corporate-conservative alliance" and the "liberal-labor alliance" as the main rivals in the electoral arena, because the term "alliance" seems more accurate than "coalition," the term I previously used. This change also makes it possible to reserve the term "coalition" for the two key voting coalitions in Congress since at least the New Deal, the "conservative coalition" and the "spending coalition." From the late 1930s into the 1990s, the conservative coalition, which most often formed on issues having to do with progressive taxation, unions, and government regulation of business, had great strength in both of the main political parties. But since the 1960s the Southern members of the coalition have gradually moved into the Republican Party, with that process nearing completion in the early 2000s. This is an important point because it means that the Democratic Party of today is a very different party than it was in the past, although it is also still true that the party has a conservative congressional fringe that sides with the Republicans in limiting unions and weakening government regulations, and still depends upon antiunion corporate moderates for a significant percentage of its funding.

As for the spending coalition in Congress, it is and always has been located almost entirely within the Democratic Party. Historically, it delivered government subsidies for plantation owners in the South in exchange for their support for infrastructure and subsidies that were sought after by landowners and real estate developers in urban areas across the nation. In more recent decades it has expanded its spending goals to include a wide range of educational and social insurance programs.

Although this book does not go into great historical detail or provide all the examples and scholarly references that it could, it does not in any way simplify or omit key ideas and concepts. It defines basic terms in an effort to make the book highly accessible to those who are new to the topic. Sometimes it uses familiar terms for concepts that have slightly different labels in the social sciences. It is therefore an in-depth but accessible scholarly presentation that provides new research findings and theoretical insights. More details on many of the issues discussed briefly in this book are provided in other books I have authored or co-authored, which also contain citations to the thousands of important studies by social scientists and historians that make a book such as this possible (e.g., Domhoff 2013; Domhoff and Webber 2011; Gendron and Domhoff 2009). In that regard, this book offers a gateway into the impressive array of scholarship on power in the United States that has been produced by hundreds of historians and social scientists since the end of World War II.

In closing this new preface, I want to extend my deepest thanks to the several colleagues around the country who gave me information and feedback that made it possible to finish this revision in a timely fashion. I am grateful to Amel Ahmed for helping me to better understand her exciting new findings on electoral rules as containment strategies; to Mary Hendrickson, Linda Lobao, and James MacDonald, the latter a member of the Economic Research Service at the Department of Agriculture, who provided me with information and feedback on farming and agribusiness; to David Knoke for his succinct characterization of the organizational theory of the state; to Jeff Manza for answers to my questions on voting and elections; to Craig Reinarman for his insightful perspectives on the Supreme Court; to Benjamin Page for valuable references concerning the impact of public opinion; to Peter Phillips for information on social clubs; to Walter Goldfrank for useful editorial comments; to Adam Schneider for his help with tables and figures; and to Joel Domhoff for his research work. I am also grateful to Richard L. Zweigenhaft for sharing new research findings with me and for his many editorial suggestions on several of the early chapters. I am grateful to the reviewers who provided valuable feedback: Greg Andranovich, California State University, Los Angeles; Nicholas Archer, Middlesex County College; and Kelsey Kretschmer, Southern Illinois University.

Most of all, I want to thank Clifford Staples, Department of Sociology, University of North Dakota, for providing me with his rich new findings from his extensive network analyses of the relationships among the 500 largest corporations and the major foundations, think tanks, and policy-discussion groups, which I have cited at several places in Chapters 2 and 4. His work provides a far more solid and convincing basis for demonstrating how the corporate community and policy-planning network connect with government than anything that has existed in the past. I also thank him for his very helpful editorial suggestions on several sections of Chapters 2 and 4.

Introduction

Do corporations, banks, and other financial institutions have too much power in the United States? Two-thirds to three-fourth of Americans have answered "yes" to that general type of question since the 1980s, with the figure standing at 67 percent in 2011. This book explains why their answers are accurate even though there is freedom of speech, the possibility of full political participation, and increasing equality of individual opportunity due to ongoing efforts by liberal activists to bring full civil rights and fair treatment to everyone whatever their gender, color, or sexual orientation. In other words, the book attempts to deal with a seeming paradox: How is it possible to have extreme corporate domination in a democratic country that can provide many examples of individual advancement from disadvantaged starting points to top positions in business, government, universities, and the arts? This seeming paradox is made all the more striking because corporations do not have as much power in many other democratic countries. The wealth and income differences between people at the top and the bottom are not as large, and the safety net for those who are poor, ill, or elderly is stronger. Why does the richest nation in the world also have the most poverty compared to Canada, Western Europe, and Japan? And why did those differences between the wealthy and other Americans increase between 1980 and 2010 (Alvaredo, Atkinson, Piketty, and Saez 2012; Bernstein 2000; Gallup 2011; Wolff 2012)?

Using a wide range of systematic empirical findings, this book shows how the owners and top-level managers of large companies—the *corporate rich*—work together to maintain themselves as the core of the dominant power group. Their corporations, banks, and agribusinesses form a *corporate community* that shapes the federal government on the policy issues of interest to it, which are issues that also have a major impact on the income, job security, and well-being of most other Americans. At the same time, there is competition within the corporate community for profits, which can lead to highly visible and acrimonious conflicts among rival corporate leaders, which are sometimes fought out in Congress. Nevertheless, the corporate community is cohesive on the policy issues that affect its general welfare, which is often at stake when organized workers, liberals, feminists, communities of color, or strong environmentalists organize sustained political challenges. It is also cohesive when elected officials attempt to raise corporate taxes or place new regulations on business activity. The book therefore deals with another seeming paradox: How can a highly competitive group of business leaders cooperate enough to work their common will in the political and policy arenas?

None of this means the corporate chieftains have complete and total power, or that their success in each new policy conflict is a foregone conclusion, or that they never lose. For example, from the 1960s to the 1980s lawyers and other highly trained professionals with an interest in consumer or environmental issues were able to use lawsuits, lobbying, or publicity to win governmental restrictions on some corporate practices and even to challenge whole industries. They also had considerable success in winning millions of dollars for employees and consumers who suffered from corporate wrongdoing, which led to successful efforts by corporate lawyers and Republicans to put limits on corporate liability. In addition, wage and salary workers, when they are organized into unions and have the right to strike, can gain pay increases and improved social benefits. Even the most powerless of people occasionally develop the capacity to bring about some redress of their grievances through sit-ins, demonstrations, and other forms of disruption.

Moreover, one of the great victories of the civil rights movement, the Voting Rights Act of 1965, began a process that made it possible for liberal black-white-Hispanic-Asian American voting coalitions to challenge the corporate community in the electoral arena. Although this book demonstrates that the corporate community became even more powerful after the 1960s, in part due to a backlash by a significant minority of white Americans against the changes brought about by the civil rights, feminist, gay-lesbian, and other social movements, it also shows that the potential for limiting corporate power developed at the same time.* The Democratic Party has been gradually transformed from the political arm of the Southern rich and urban Democratic organizations (called "machines" in their day because they seemed so powerful and efficient) to the party of corporate moderates, liberals, women, communities of color, religious liberals, and labor unions. And thus another paradox: During the period from 1965 to 2011, when the salaries of chief executive officers (CEOs) of large corporations went from 42 times greater than an average worker's pay to 380 times as much, new political openings for progressive social change nonetheless developed (AFL-CIO 2012). The nature of these openings and the reasons why the liberal-labor alliance has not been able to take full advantage of them are explained throughout the book.

---

* A social movement is best understood as an organized effort to change established rules and customs through a sustained challenge to elite opponents and elected officials by means of actions that are atypical, sometimes unruly, and very often considered illegal. Members of social movements are rule-breakers, even though the laws and customs they thereby seek to change—such as keeping African Americans from sitting at lunch counters, excluding women from using male-only university libraries, or refusing to hire people because of their sexual orientation—are seen as unjust by many members of the society beyond those who are unjustly treated. Social movements are therefore very different from new political campaigns, however liberal or ultraconservative, which simply seek to win office, and traditional "interest groups," which seek to influence specific pieces of legislation of concern to them while playing by conventional rules.

Partly because the corporate rich share great wealth and common economic interests, but also due to the political opposition to their shared interests, they band together to develop their own social institutions—gated neighborhoods, guarded apartment towers, private schools, exclusive social clubs, debutante balls, and secluded summer resorts. These social institutions create social cohesion and a sense of group belonging, a "we" feeling, and thereby mold the owners and top managers in the corporate community into a *social upper class*, which is described in Chapter 3. In addition, the corporate rich supplement their small numbers by financing and directing a wide variety of nonprofit organizations, such as tax-free foundations, think tanks, and policy-discussion groups, to aid them in developing policy alternatives that serve their interests. These organizations are part of a *policy-planning network* that is linked together by shared donors, trustees, and expert advisors. The highest-ranking employees in the policy-planning network, those who serve on the various organizations' boards of trustees, join with leaders from the corporate community and the upper class to form the leadership group for the corporate rich. Collectively, these leaders are called the *power elite;* they derive their power from serving on the governing boards of both the corporations and nonprofit organizations that are controlled by the corporate rich. The composition of the power elite is explained in more detail at the end of Chapter 4.

The corporate rich also attempt to shape public opinion in favor of the policy initiatives they sponsor and against those they dislike. Often drawing on policy positions, rationales, and statements developed within the policy-planning network, the *opinion-shaping network* operates through the public relations departments of large corporations, general public relations firms, and many small opinion-shaping organizations, which direct most of their attention to middle-class voluntary organizations, educational institutions, and the mass media. It is unlikely that the opinion-shaping network is very often successful in altering public opinion, but it is not for lack of trying, and it can claim to have improved the images of specific corporations and to have generated doubt and confusion about what initially appeared to be clear-cut policy changes that would be in the general public interest.

The corporate rich also enter into the electoral arena, first and foremost through their large campaign contributions to candidates in both political parties, with an overwhelming preference for the Republicans. They also have an indirect involvement through providing politicians with lucrative speaking opportunities, lobbying jobs, and well-paid positions on corporate boards before and after their time in government service. Their efforts have led to pro-corporate presidents and a pro-corporate majority in both houses of Congress since corporations became the dominant institutions of American society in the 1870s. Historically, the pro-corporate majority in Congress consisted of a *conservative coalition*, which was defined as a majority of Southern Democrats and Republicans voting together on a legislative proposal in either the House or the Senate (Shelley 1983). However, that arrangement changed gradually after the Voting Rights Act made it possible for African Americans and white liberals to push the most conservative Southern Democrats into the Republican Party, while slowly replacing the few remaining white Democrats in the South with African American legislators in 21 House districts by 2012.* The corporate rich are joined within the Republican Party by a wide range of highly conservative religious organizations concerned with a variety of social issues, including abortion, prayer in schools, and gay marriage. This *corporate-conservative alliance* also includes leaders in the National Rifle Association and other ultraconservative, antigovernment organizations with no religious affiliations. At the same time, the moderate conservatives within the corporate community maintain a significant presence in the Democratic Party, as demonstrated by the major financial backing that they provided to President Barack Obama in his 2004 senatorial campaign and his 2008 and 2012 presidential campaigns.

The ability of the corporate rich to transform their economic power into policy expertise and political access makes them the most important influence on the federal government. Leaders from the corporate community and the policy-planning network have been appointed to top positions in the executive branch in both Republican and Democratic administrations since the last quarter of the nineteenth century, and their allies in Congress listen carefully to the policy recommendations proposed by the experts they employ at foundations, think tanks, and policy-discussion groups. This combination of economic power, policy expertise, and continuing political access makes the corporate rich a *dominant class,* not in the sense of complete and absolute power, but in the sense that they have the power to shape the economic and political frameworks within which other groups and classes must operate, right down to changing the rules that govern elections and who can vote in them. They therefore win far more often than they lose on the issues of concern to them.

Despite their preponderant power in the federal government and the many necessary policies it carries out for them, leaders within the corporate community are constantly critical of the government because of its potential independence and its ability to aid their opponents. They know they need government, but they also fear it. They especially fear it during times of economic crisis when they need it the most, as demonstrated very dramatically in the near meltdown of the financial system in late 2008 and early 2009. Although the corporate community focuses

---

* The South is defined for purposes of this book as the 17 states that had state laws requiring school segregation until the *Brown v. Board of Education* decision by the Supreme Court in 1954: Alabama, Arkansas, Delaware, Florida, Georgia, Kentucky, Louisiana, Maryland, Mississippi, Missouri, North Carolina, Oklahoma, South Carolina, Tennessee, Texas, Virginia, and West Virginia. In addition, all of them were slave states in 1860 with the exception of West Virginia, which was part of the slave state of Virginia until it broke away to become a separate state in 1863, and Oklahoma, a slave territory when the Civil War broke out. This definition emphasizes that "the South" was once much larger and hence much more powerful than it is in people's minds since the 1970s. Today "the South" means what was once called the "Deep South," an area that includes eastern Texas, Alabama, Arkansas, Georgia, Louisiana, Mississippi, South Carolina, and northern Florida.

its complaints on taxes and government spending, the underlying issue usually involves the ongoing struggle between the corporate community and government for dominance on key power issues. In particular, the corporate rich are wary of the federal government due to its capacity to aid average Americans by (1) creating government jobs for the unemployed, which might make people less likely to take low-paying or dangerous positions in the private sector; (2) making health, unemployment, and Social Security benefits more generous, which also might make people less willing to work in low-paying jobs; and (3) helping employees gain greater workplace rights and protections, which would make it more difficult for the corporate rich to control the workplace.

More generally, the corporate rich realize that a liberal-labor majority in Congress could redirect the tax breaks, subsidy payments, research grants, government purchases, and regulations that currently benefit major corporations. Instead, it could invest more tax dollars in schools and employee-owned companies, subsidize renewable energy companies, and raise taxes on coal, oil, and natural gas companies. It could even support publicly controlled enterprises that would compete in the market with private corporations. Corporate leaders are well aware of these possibilities because some of them exist in one or two states. For example, North Dakota has had a state-owned bank and a state-owned flour mill (the largest flour mill in the United States) since progressives temporarily controlled the state government after the 1918 elections. Corporate leaders also know that such possibilities have been proposed by liberals as ways to structure a market system so that it furthers the interests of consumers, workers, environmentalists, and small businesses (e.g., Baker 2011; Carnoy and Shearer 1980).

Most of all, however, corporate leaders oppose any government support for unions, which they see as a primary source of inflation through unrealistic pay raises brought about by collective bargaining agreements. They also dislike union demands for a voice in shaping workplace rules and safety regulations. Even more, they completely oppose unions as a potential organizational base for advocating a whole range of polices that would weaken corporate power. In a phrase, *control of labor markets* is a crucial issue in the eyes of the corporate community.

In the context of the financial crisis and the sudden onset of the Great Recession in late 2007, some of these possibilities seemed to be very real to the corporate rich. They feared that government leaders might take control of the banks, mortgage companies, and automobile manufacturers that were saved from bankruptcy with taxpayer dollars, especially after the Democrats took control of the White House and Congress in the 2008 elections. They knew that government bailouts and financial rescues had occurred in the past—for banks, railroads, and Southern plantations during the 1930s, for example, and for the savings and loan industry in the 1980s. But they worried that the bailouts might grow too large and last too long for them to regain their former degree of dominance. Although their fears proved to be unfounded, they were nonetheless real, and they explain why the corporate rich keep a constant eye on government and react strongly to the slightest hint of any government independence by shouting "Socialism," which is their term for the fact that strong governments can exert more control of the economic sector, as they do in many countries that make use of the market system.*

The corporate community's main opponents—labor unions, liberal university communities, religious liberals, most communities of color, and locally based environmental organizations—sometimes work together on policy issues as a *liberal-labor alliance*. However, this alliance is usually extremely difficult to hold together because its members have divergent and sometimes clashing interests. It also has far less money to spend on political campaigns than the corporate leaders, although this difference has become somewhat smaller because (1) the extreme stances taken by religious conservatives on several issues have made the Democrats more attractive to upper-middle-class professionals and (2) money in small sums can now be raised over the Internet. In addition, despite the fact that unions have represented a declining percentage of wage and salary workers since World War II, they still had nearly 15 million members at the end of 2011 (BLS 2012). Unions therefore remain the largest and best-financed part of the alliance. They also cut across racial and ethnic divisions more than any other sector of American society.

The liberal-labor alliance also includes a few men and women from well-to-do business families that are critical of the corporate community despite their comfortable financial circumstances. This is often because they do not like—and in some cases fear—the alliance that corporate conservatives have forged with religious conservatives within the Republican Party. The presence of people from privileged social backgrounds in the liberal-labor camp suggests that unexpected formative experiences, such as the shock of encountering extreme poverty, religious intolerance, or racial prejudice, can lead to liberal social and religious values that can be as important as class in shaping political orientations. Their opposition to corporate dominance adds another level of complexity to the power equation: There is class domination in the United States, but not all those born into the upper class support class domination.

The liberal-labor alliance enters into the electoral arena through the liberal wing of the Democratic Party, sometimes fielding candidates in party primaries to stake out its policy goals, or more often issuing blueprints for a more liberal economy, as in the case of a booklet called *Prosperity Economics* (Hacker and Loewentheil 2012). Contrary to the strident warnings of ultraconservatives and the fond hopes of liberal commentators, this alliance never has had a major voice

---

* "Socialism" is actually characterized by government ownership of all major income-producing properties and a planned economy that makes little or no use of the market system to determine prices or consumer demand. The economies of the countries called "socialist" in Western Europe by American conservatives are almost entirely privately owned and rely on markets; they differ from the U.S. economy only in that they have tighter regulations on some corporate practices, tax the citizenry (not just the wealthy) at higher rates, and have more extensive government-run social insurance systems (think unemployment insurance, Social Security, and Medicare-for-Everyone as examples). These "social democracies," as they are called, are fairly similar to what liberals in the United States always have sought to achieve.

in the Democratic Party at the national level and never even had the possibility of such a voice as long as the Southern rich were a key element in the party. Despite the potential openings created by the departure of white Southern Democrats from the party, union leaders and liberals had more impact from the late 1930s to the early 1970s than they have had ever since. By the 1990s, unions spent tens of millions of dollars on political campaigns in presidential election years and by 2012 that figure had reached several hundred million if all levels of government are included. They also deploy their paid organizers and members to work at the grassroots level—making telephone calls, stuffing envelopes, and going door-to-door to bring out the vote. However, their political clout has been hurt since the 1960s, not only by a decline in membership, but by the fact that many of their members disagreed with liberals over a variety of issues, such as the integration of neighborhoods, schools, and skilled blue-collar occupations; affirmative action and busing; women in the workplace; and environmental protection laws that they feared might lead to the loss of jobs.

The liberal-labor alliance is sometimes aided by the organizing and social movement skills of political leftists, who in the past played a role as socialists and communists in the struggle for women's suffrage in the Progressive Era, the building of industrial unions in the 1930s, and the development of the civil rights movement in the 1960s. However, the leftists, who now tend to identify themselves as libertarian socialists, anarchists, or anticapitalists, are also strong critics of the liberal-labor alliance because of their grave doubts about the possibility of reforming a market-based economic system to any significant degree. They also criticize the liberals for limiting themselves to an emphasis on improving representative democracy instead of pushing for a more participatory form of democracy, in which people in general are involved in decisionmaking through grassroots councils and other forms of local organization. In addition, they often support left-wing third parties with the hope of replacing the Democrats, a strategy strongly rejected by the liberal-labor alliance. Moreover, a small percentage of them believe that breaking storefront windows, occupying privately owned buildings, tearing down fences, and entering into confrontations with police units are useful tactics in some situations, as last seen in what transpired at the demonstrations and rallies carried out by the anticorporate global justice movement between 1999 and 2001 (e.g., Yuen, Burton-Rose, and Katsiaficas 2001; Yuen, Burton-Rose, and Katsiaficas 2004). As a result of all these disagreements, there is a far larger and more contentious gap between the liberal-labor alliance and the various types of leftists than any differences that exist within the corporate-conservative alliance within the Republican Party.

The major policy conflicts between the corporate community and the liberal-labor alliance are best described as *class conflicts* because they concern the distribution of wages and profits, the rate and progressivity of taxation, the usefulness of labor unions, and the degree to which business should be regulated by government. The liberal-labor side wants corporations to pay higher wages to employees and higher taxes to government. It wants government to strengthen regulations on a wide range of business practices and help employees organize unions. The great majority in the corporate community rejects all these policy objectives, claiming they endanger the freedom of individuals, the efficient workings of the marketplace, and economic growth. The conflicts these disagreements generate can manifest themselves in many different ways: workplace protests, strikes, industry-wide boycotts, massive demonstrations in cities, pressure on Congress, and voting preferences.

Social conflict over abortion, same-sex marriage, gun control, and other social issues supported by liberals and vigorously opposed by strong conservatives are not part of this overall class conflict. They are separate issues related to genuine differences in moral and political values (Lakoff 1996). They also may relate to the very different outlooks toward life in general that characterize strong liberals and strong conservatives (Tomkins 1964). These differences are not reducible to economics or the class structure, and they encompass more than political and social issues (e.g., Altemeyer 2006; Jost and Amodio 2012). The outcomes of conflicts over social issues do not directly affect the power of the corporate community, but they are an important part of the competition between the corporate-conservative and liberal-labor alliances in the electoral arena.

To help familiarize readers with the six main political orientations in the United States, Table 0.1 presents the views of the religious right, ultraconservatives in the corporate community, moderate conservatives in the corporate community, trade unionists, liberals, and leftists on the key issues that differentiate them. The critical issues that separate the three conservative orientations from liberals, leftists, and organized labor are the conservatives' shared opposition to labor unions and their desire for the smallest possible involvement of government in the economy. However, there are some differences between corporate moderates and corporate ultraconservatives on issues such as rent subsidies, federal aid to schools, and Social Security. Moderate conservatives also have more tolerance for women's right to choose and civil and marital rights for gays and lesbians. These differences lead some moderate conservatives to feel more at home in the moderate wing of the Democratic Party, but it bears repeating that they are strongly opposed to unions even though they are Democrats. Thus, for all the tensions between conservatives and ultraconservatives within the Republican Party, the Democratic Party has more profound policy disagreements within it than does the Republican Party.

On the other side of the political fence, the liberal, left, and trade unionist orientations are supportive of unions, seek greater government involvement in the economy, and advocate a liberal social agenda. However, as noted earlier, there is a major disagreement between the liberal-labor alliance and the leftists on the degree to which a private-enterprise system working through markets can be reformed to bring about greater economic equality and on the usefulness of third parties, which lead to very different economic programs and political strategies. These differences can cause conflicts that benefit the Republicans under some circumstances, as discussed in Chapter 6.

Table 0.1 The Policy Preferences on Several Key Issues for Six Political Orientations

	Religious Right	Ultraconservatives	Moderate Conservatives	Trade Unionists**	Liberals	Leftists/Progressives
Favor private ownership and private profit?	yes	yes	yes	yes	yes	no
Oppose unions?	yes	yes	yes	no	no	no
Oppose government regulation?	yes	yes	yes*	no	no	no
Oppose government social benefits?	yes	yes	somewhat	no	no	no
Oppose liberal social agenda?	yes	yes	somewhat	no***	no	no

*With the important exception of environmental regulations, which they now accept.

**Some trade unionists are also liberals or leftists.

***Some trade unionists, especially those in the construction trades, oppose one or more aspects of the liberal social agenda and sometimes vote for Republicans as a result.

Neither the corporate-conservative nor the liberal-labor alliance elicits the strong loyalty of a majority of the American population. They are therefore in constant competition for the allegiance of the general citizenry, most of whom are focused on the positive aspects of their everyday lives when things are running smoothly, such as close personal relationships, the challenges of their jobs, or the enjoyment of a hobby or athletic activity. The typical American usually pays little attention to most policy issues, focuses on political candidates only around the time of elections, and has a mixture of liberal and conservative opinions that seems contradictory—and annoying—to those who have strong conservative, liberal, or leftist orientations. As an analysis based on a 2007 national survey concludes, Americans are "conservative egalitarians." They are wary of big government and they cherish individual freedoms, but they are also supportive of many economic initiatives that are labeled as liberal, and they are willing to pay higher taxes so that everyone has better economic opportunities (Page and Jacobs 2009).

The importance of average centrist citizens in the electoral arena, who usually define themselves as moderate Democrats or independents when it comes to political preferences, can be seen through surveys reporting the percentage of liberals and Democrats in the country. According to periodic surveys by the Pew Research Center for the People and the Press, one of the largest and most reliable nonprofit polling organization in the country, in 2012 only 21 percent of Americans considered themselves liberals, compared to 32 percent who said they were moderates and nearly 43 percent who described themselves as conservatives; this is not very different from how they labeled themselves in 2004 and 2008 (Horowitz 2008; Pew 2012, p. 11). But the mix was a little different at the voting booths: 25 percent of voters described themselves as liberals in exit polls in 2012, while 40 percent said they were moderates and 35 percent said they were conservative. At the same time, just to make things more complicated, these same voters also said they were 38 percent Democrats, 30 percent independents, and 32 percent Republicans, which means that President Obama and other successful Democrats had to gain the support of moderates and independents to win elections, as did any Republicans who won outside the overwhelmingly Republican and conservative states in the South and the Great Plains; moreover, 11 percent of liberals said they voted for the Republican presidential candidate, Mitt Romney, and 17 percent of conservatives said they voted for Obama (Edison Research 2012).

The seeming apathy or ignorance often wrongly ascribed to ordinary citizens actually makes personal sense for several reasons. To begin with, there are time-consuming difficulties in bringing people into agreement on new policy initiatives, which can lead to endless arguments, interpersonal tensions, and frustration for those who attend frequent meetings. Even when there is agreement on a new direction, it can take years to change policies at any level of government. It is therefore hard to maintain enthusiasm and momentum unless the situation is very dire. To most people, it thus seems more sensible and practical to focus on the many necessities and pleasures of everyday life, which have the virtue of leading to feelings of personal accomplishment and satisfaction. Put another way, when social scientists take the time to understand the situations in which different groups and classes find themselves, they find that what people do makes sense, because the pull of everyday life is overwhelming when weighed against the endless hours of effort and trouble that come with political activism (Flacks 1988).

In times of turmoil, however, all bets are off. People pay attention and express themselves clearly. But no one can predict these events or what will happen because of them. The past can be analyzed and trends can be noted, but major events happen when they are least expected—the Great Depression of the 1930s, the resurgence of the civil rights movement in the early 1960s, the sudden collapse of the Soviet Union in the early 1990s, and the Great Recession that began late in 2007. More generally, no one can predict the future. All the experts and media commentators have been wrong about just about everything according to studies of thousands of past predictions (Silver 2012; Tedlock 2005).

1

Power and Class in America

Power and *class* are terms that make Americans a little uneasy. Concepts such as *power elite* and *dominant class* put people on their guard. Even though there is widespread concern about the extent of corporate power, and a strong tendency toward egalitarian values, the idea that a relatively fixed group of privileged people might shape the economy and government for their own benefit goes against the American grain. But what exactly do everyday Americans and social scientists mean when they talk about power and class, and how do their views compare? This chapter answers those two questions. It also explains the methods used to study power and class, as well as providing an outline of how the rest of the book will unfold.

WHAT IS POWER?

American ideas about power had their origins in its colonial history and the struggle for independence from Great Britain, which brought issues of equal treatment and the right to participate in government to the forefront. What is not so well known is that these ideas owe as much to the conflict within each colony over the role of ordinary citizens as they do to the Revolutionary War itself. It is often lost from sight that the average citizens who supported the revolution were making new political demands on their leaders as well as helping in the fight against the British. Before the onset of the anticolonial war called the American Revolution, governments everywhere had been based on the power and legitimacy of religious leaders, kings, self-appointed conventions, or parliaments. The high-status American revolutionary leaders who drafted the constitutions for each of the

13 original states between 1776 and 1780 expected their handiwork to be debated and voted upon by state legislatures, but they did not want to involve the general public in a direct way.

Instead, it was members of the "middling" classes of yeoman farmers and artisans who gradually developed the idea out of their own experience that power is the possession of all the people and is delegated to government with their consent. They therefore insisted that special conventions be elected to frame each colony's constitution, and that the constitutions then be ratified by the vote of all white males without regard to their property holdings. They were steeled in their resolve by their participation in the revolutionary struggle and by a fear of the potentially onerous property laws and taxation policies that might be written into the constitutions by those who were known at the time as their "betters." So the revolutionary idea of the people as the source of legitimate power in the new United States arose from the people themselves (Palmer 1959; Piven 2006, Chapter 3).

In the end, the middle-level insurgents only won the right to both a constitutional convention of elected delegates and a vote on subsequent ratification in Massachusetts in 1780. From that time forth, however, it has been widely agreed that "power" in the United States belongs to "the people." Since then every liberal, leftist, populist, or ultraconservative political group has claimed that it represents the people in its attempt to wrest arbitrary power from the "vested interests," the "economic elite," the "cultural elite," "the media," the "bureaucrats," or the "politicians in Washington." Even the Founding Fathers of 1789, who were far removed from the general population in their wealth, income, education, and political experience, did not try to promulgate their new federal constitution, primarily designed to more fully protect private property and compromise some of their fundamental disagreements, without asking for the consent of the governed. In the process they were forced to add the Bill of Rights to ensure the constitution's acceptance. In a very profound cultural sense, then, no group or class has "power" in America, but only "influence." Any small group or class that has power over "the people" is therefore perceived as illegitimate. This may help explain why those with power in America always deny they have any (see Vogel 1978 for a full analysis of this important point).

THE SOCIAL SCIENCE VIEW OF POWER

Most social scientists believe that the concept of power has two intertwined dimensions. The first involves the degree to which a community or nation has the capacity to perform effectively in pursuing its common goals, which is called *collective power*. Here, the stress is on the degree to which a collectivity has the technological resources, organizational forms, population size, and common spirit to achieve its goals. In that sense, many nations became more powerful in the second half of the twentieth century, including the United States. Moreover, the collective power of the United States grew because of its ability to assimilate immigrants of varying economic and educational levels from all over the world as productive citizens. The gradual acceptance of African Americans into mainstream social institutions also increased the nation's collective power.

The second dimension of power concerns the ability of a group or social class within a community or nation to be successful in conflicts with its rivals on issues of concern to it. Here, the stress is on *power over*, which is also called *distributive power*. When the word "power" is used in the rest of this book, it will always be meant in this distributive sense. Paralleling general American beliefs, most social scientists think of distributive power as meaning great or preponderant influence, not complete and absolute control. More specifically, a powerful group or class is one that can realize its goals even if some other group or class is opposed (Olsen and Marger 1993; Wrong 1995). This definition captures the sense of struggle that is embodied in the everyday meaning of power and it readily encompasses the idea of class conflict. It also fits with the main goal of this book, which is to show how the corporate rich developed the power to institute the policies they favor, even in the face of the liberal-labor alliance's organized opposition to most corporate policies and large majorities that opposed specific policies.

Generally speaking, the ability of a group or class to prevail begins in its control of one or more of the four major social networks—economic, political, military, and ideological—that have been found in historical and cross-national studies to provide the main organizational bases for wielding enduring distributive power in any large-scale society (Mann 1986; Mann 2012; Mann 2013). The economic network consists of a set of organizations concerned with satisfying material needs through the "extraction, transformation, distribution and consumption of the objects of nature" (Mann 1986, p. 24). The political network, which is embodied in "the government" in modern times, regulates activities within the geographical area for which it is responsible, including the movement of people, economic goods, and weapons in and out of its territory. The military network is rooted in organized physical violence that is meant to kill, subjugate, or enslave opponents. The ideology network is most readily understood as a network of organizations that seeks to provide answers to ultimate questions about the meaning and purpose of life, a greater degree of communal closeness, and the alleviation of guilt and suffering for its members, which generates loyal followers, large budgets through freely given donations, and revered leaders. Historically, religious communities, such as churches, mosques, and synagogues, were the primary organizations in this network. However, they were joined in the past several hundred years by messianic political movements on the left and right, groups asserting racial superiority, and highly aggressive nationalistic movements; they give meaning and focus to the lives of their adherents by blaming specific groups or classes for their problems or attacking countries perceived as dangerous and populated by inferior human beings.

Although economic and political networks have been the main power networks in the United States for historical reasons that are discussed in Chapter 8, the four power networks can combine in different ways in different times and places to create widely varying power structures. For example, military force has led to the capture of the government and control of the economic system in many countries, past and present. In other countries, well-organized ideological groups have been able to develop popular support and demonstrate the ability to exercise force if need be in maintaining control over the government. Due to the variety of power outcomes that are found in the historical record, most social scientists believe there is no one ultimate basis for distributive power from which the other types of distributive power can be derived. This means that the concept of distributive power is a fundamental one in the social sciences, just as energy is a fundamental concept in the natural sciences for the same reason: No one form of energy or power is more "basic" than any other (Russell 1938; Wrong 1995).

Although these general ideas provide a good general starting point, they are not specific enough to be useful in deciding how to study distributive power in a complex nation-state such as the United States. How, then, can we decide if the corporate rich have "power"?

THREE POWER INDICATORS

A formal definition of a concept such as distributive power does not explain how the concept is to be measured. In the case of conflicts between groups or classes over desired goals, which are the essence of distributive power, it is seldom possible to observe interactions that reveal its operation even in small groups, let alone to see something as large and diffuse as a social class producing effects on another social class. People and organizations are what can be seen in a power struggle within a community or nation, not rival social classes, although it may turn out that the people and organizations represent the interests of social classes. It is therefore necessary to develop what are called *indicators of power*.

Although distributive power is first and foremost a relationship between two or more contending groups or classes, for research purposes it is useful to think of distributive power as an underlying "trait" or "property" of a specific group or social class. It might make this point more clear to say that the personality traits studied by psychologists and the concept of "magnetism" developed by physicists have a similar logical structure. Thus, whether a theorist is concerned with "magnetism," as in physics, or "friendliness," as in psychology, or "power," as in the case of this book, the nature of the investigatory procedure is the same. In each case, there is an underlying trait whose presence can be inferred only through a series of diagnostic signs that vary in their strength under differing conditions. Because the indicators do not necessarily appear each and every time the trait is manifesting itself, a trait is best measured by a series of indicators, or signs, that bear a probabilistic relationship to it. Research proceeds, in this view, through a series of *if-then* statements based on as many independent indicators as possible. *If* a group is powerful, *then* at least some of the indicators of power should be measurable in some circumstances. (See Lazarsfeld 1966 for a classic statement of this approach.)

Since an indicator of power may not necessarily appear or be measurable in each and every instance in which power is operating, three different types of power indicators are used in this book. They are called (1) who benefits? (2) who governs? and (3) who wins? Each of these empirical indicators has unique strengths and weaknesses. However, the potential weaknesses of each indicator do not present a serious problem if all three of them point to the same group or class as the most powerful.

Who Benefits?

Every society has material objects and experiences that are highly valued, although there is variation from society to society in exactly what is considered valuable. If it is assumed that most people in a society would like to have as great a share of what are believed to be the good things of life as possible, then their distribution can be utilized as a power indicator. Those who have the greatest share of what people want are, by inference, the powerful. Although some value distributions may be unintended outcomes that do not really reflect power, the general distribution of valued experiences and objects within a society still can be viewed as the most publicly visible and stable outcome of the operation of power.

In American society, as most people agree, wealth, high incomes, exotic vacations, and good health are highly valued. Most people would like to own property; to have high-paying, interesting, and safe jobs; to enjoy the finest in travel and leisure; and to live long and healthy lives. All of these "values" are unequally distributed, and all may be utilized as power indicators. In this book, however, the primary focus with this type of indicator is on the wealth and income distributions because there is detailed quantitative information available about them that spans over 100 years of the nation's history. This does not mean that wealth and income are the same thing as power. Instead, high incomes and the possession of great wealth are simply visible signs that a class has power in relation to other classes.

The argument for using value distributions as power indicators is strengthened by studies showing that such distributions vary from country to country, depending upon the relative strength of rival political parties and trade unions. One past study reported that the degree of inequality in the income distribution in Western democracies varied inversely with the percentage of highly liberal candidates who had been elected to the country's legislature in the first three decades after 1945. The greater the liberal presence, the greater the amount of income that went to the lower classes (Hewitt 1977). In a study based on 18 Western democracies in the same era, it was found that strong trade unions and successful social democratic parties were correlated with greater equality in the income distribution and a higher level of welfare spending (Stephens 1979). Thus, there is evidence that value distributions do vary depending on the relative power of contending groups or classes. Information on the wealth and income distributions in the United States will be presented in Chapter 3.

Who Governs?

Power also can be inferred from studying who occupies important institutional positions or takes part in important decision-making groups. If a group or class is highly overrepresented or underrepresented in relation to its proportion of the population, it can be inferred that the group or class is relatively powerful or powerless, as the case may be. For example, if a class that contains 1 percent of the population has 30 percent of the important positions in the government, which is 30 times as many as would be expected by chance, then it can be inferred that the class is powerful. Conversely, if it is found that women are in only a small percentage of the leadership positions in government, even though they make up a slight majority of the population, it can be inferred that women are relatively powerless in that important sector of society. Similarly, if it is determined that a community of color has only a small percentage of its members in leadership positions, even though it comprises 10 to 20 percent of the population in a given city or state, then the basic processes of power—inclusion and exclusion—are inferred to be at work.

This indicator is not perfect because some official positions may not really possess the power they are thought to have, and some groups or classes may exercise power from "behind the scenes." Once again, however, the case for the usefulness of this indicator is strengthened by the fact that it has been shown to vary over time and place. For example, the decline of landed aristocrats and the rise of business leaders in Great Britain has been charted through their degree of representation in Parliament (Guttsman 1969). Then, too, as women, African Americans, Latinos, and Asian Americans joined movements to demand a greater voice in the United States in the 1960s and 1970s, their representation in positions of authority began to increase (Zweigenhaft and Domhoff 2006; Zweigenhaft and Domhoff 2011).

Who Wins?

There are many issues over which the corporate community and the liberal-labor alliance disagree, including taxation, unionization, and business regulation. Power can be inferred on the basis of these issue conflicts by determining who successfully initiates, modifies, or vetoes policy alternatives. This indicator, by focusing on relationships between the two rivals, comes closest to approximating the process of power contained in the formal definition. It is the indicator preferred by most social scientists. For many reasons, however, it is also the most difficult to use in an accurate way. Aspects of a decision process may remain hidden, some informants may exaggerate or downplay their roles, and people's memories about who did what often become cloudy shortly after the event. Worse, the key concerns of the corporate community may never arise as issues on the political agenda because it has the power to keep them in the realm of *nonissues,* that is, most people know there is a problem, but it is never addressed in the political arena because of a variety of barriers that are discussed in Chapters 5 and 6.

Despite the difficulties in using the "who wins?" indicator of power, it is possible to provide a theoretical framework for analyzing governmental decision-making that mitigates many of the methodological problems. This framework encompasses the various means by which the corporate community attempts to influence both the government and the general population in a conscious and planned manner, thereby making it possible to assess its degree of success very directly. More specifically, there are four relatively distinct but overlapping processes (discovered by means of membership network analysis) through which the corporate community tries to control the public agenda and win policy victories on the issues that do appear on it. These processes are based in four influence networks, which are discussed in more detail in later chapters.

1. The *special-interest process* deals with the narrow and short-run policy concerns of wealthy families, specific corporations, and the many different sectors of business. It operates primarily through lobbyists, company lawyers, and trade associations, with a focus on congressional committees, departments of the executive branch, and regulatory agencies (including the Internal Revenue System for purposes of tax avoidance). The lobbyists are often former elected officials or former aides and advisors to elected officials, who can command very large salaries in the private sector because their information and connections are so valuable to wealthy families and corporations. A subsystem of this process is now known as the "wealth defense industry" because the thousands of accountants, tax lawyers, estate planners, and other participants in it spend all their time defending and enlarging the fortunes of the relative handful of families worth $50 million or more (Winters 2011).

2. The *policy-planning process* formulates the general interests of the corporate community. It operates through the foundations, think tanks, and policy-discussion groups that make up the policy-planning network, with a focus on the White House, relevant congressional committees, and the high-status newspapers and opinion magazines published in New York and Washington. It is the place in which corporate leaders meet with academic experts and former government officials to discuss differences and prepare themselves for government appointments.

3. The *opinion-shaping process* attempts to influence public opinion and keep some issues off the public agenda. In addition to the large public relations firms and many small organizations within it, the opinion-shaping network includes a wide variety of patriotic, antitax, and single-issue organizations that celebrate the status quo and warn against "big government." Many advertising executives, former journalists, and former government officials are employed by the organizations in this network. Sometimes they make harsh media attacks on opponents of the corporate community.

4. The *candidate-selection process* is concerned with the election of politicians that are sympathetic to the agenda put forth in the special-interest and policy-planning processes. It operates through large campaign donations and hired political consultants; it is focused on the presidential campaigns of both major political parties and the congressional campaigns of the Republican Party.

Taken together, the people and organizations that operate in these four networks constitute the political action arm of the corporate rich. Building on the structural (economic) power of the corporate community, which is explained in the next chapter, and the status power of the upper class, which is explained in Chapter 3, and then the expert power developed within the policy planning network, which is explained in Chapter 4, this political action arm is the final step on the path to corporate and class domination of the federal government.

WHAT IS A SOCIAL CLASS?

For most Americans, being a member of a "class" implies that people have permanent stations in life, which flies in the face of beliefs about equality of opportunity and seems to ignore the evidence of upward social mobility. Even more, Americans tend to deny that classes might be rooted in wealth and occupational roles. They talk about social class, but with euphemisms like "the suits," "the blue bloods," "Joe Sixpack," and "the other side of the tracks."

American dislike of the idea of class is deeply rooted in the country's colonial and revolutionary history. Colonial America seemed very different to its new inhabitants from European countries because it was a rapidly expanding frontier country with no feudal aristocracy or inherited social statuses. The sense of difference was heightened by the need for solidarity among all classes in the war for freedom from the British. As suggested in the previous section, revolutionary leaders from the higher classes had to concede greater freedom and equality for common people to gain their support. They also had to accept voting rights for all white males that met minimum property qualifications, which could be done with relative ease at the time because land was readily available at reasonable prices (Keyssar 2009). One historian states the trade-off very succinctly: "Leaders who did not fight for equality accepted it in order to win" (Palmer 1959, p. 203). In other words, outside enemies bring a people together out of necessity, at least until they have won their common battle.

Although differences in wealth, income, and lifestyle already existed in the colonial and revolutionary eras, particularly in port cities and the South, these well-understood inequalities were usually explained away or downplayed by members of the middle classes as well as by the merchants, plantation owners, and lawyers who were at the top of the socioeconomic ladder. As shown by a historical study of diaries, letters, newspapers, and other documents of the period, Americans instead emphasized and took pride in the fact that any class distinctions were small compared with Europe. They recognized that there were rich and poor, but they preferred to think of their country "as one of equality, and proudly pointed to such features as the large middle class, the absence of beggars, the comfortable circumstances of most people, and the limitless opportunities for those who worked hard and saved their money" (Main 1965, pp. 239, 284).

The fact that nearly 20 percent of the population was held in slavery and that 100,000 Native Americans lived in the western areas of the colonies was not part of this self-definition as a middle-class, egalitarian society. Instead, the free white majority defined itself in opposition to the potentially dangerous slaves and Native Americans, who were willing to fight for their freedom or to protect their land when they had the opportunity. This recognition of common enemies heightened the American immigrants' shared sense of "whiteness" as a significant part of their social identity. In fact, "race," as defined by the existence of "black," "red," and "white" people, and later people with other skin colors, is another factor that made the class-based nature of American society less salient than it might otherwise be; however, many later immigrant groups originally thought of as racially different became "white" over time as the term became just another way of defining the in-group (Waters 1990; Waters 1999).

Even members of the upper class preferred this more egalitarian view of the class system to what had existed for many centuries in Europe. To emphasize this point, a study of the democratic revolutions in North America and Europe begins with a letter written from Europe in 1788 by a young adult member of a prominent American upper-class family. After the young man registered his disgust with the hereditary titles and pomp of the European class system and with the obsequiousness of the lower classes, he stated his conviction that "a certain degree of equality is essential to human bliss." As if to make sure the limits of his argument were clear, he underlined the words *a certain degree of equality*. He then went on to argue that the greatness of the United States was that it had provided this degree of equality "without destroying the necessary subordination" (Palmer 1959, p. 3). That is, class dominance should be as subtle and reasonable as possible, a principle that is also embodied in the Constitution and the way in which Americans talk about class.

Two hundred years later, in response to sociologists who wanted to know what social class means to Americans, a representative sample of the citizenry in Boston and Kansas City expressed ideas similar to those of the first Americans. Although most people were keenly aware of differences in social standing and judged status levels primarily in terms of income, occupations, and education (but especially income), they emphasized the openness of the system. They also argued that a person's social standing is in good part determined by such individual qualities as initiative and the motivation to work hard. Moreover, many of them felt the importance of class was declining. This belief was partly due to their conviction that people of all ethnic and religious backgrounds were being treated with greater respect and decency, whatever their occupational and educational levels, but even more to what they saw as material evidence for social advancement in the occupations and salaries of their families and friends. In short, a tradition of public social respect for everyone and the belief in social mobility (from which people of color were excluded until the social movements of the 1960s) are also factors in making class less important in the everyday thinking of most white Americans (Coleman, Rainwater, and McClelland 1978). People are very aware of basic economic and educational differences and they can size up social standing fairly well from such outward signs as speech patterns, mannerisms, and style of dress, but the existence of social classes is nonetheless passed over as quickly as possible.

People of the highest social status share the general distaste for talking about social class in an open and direct way. Nevertheless, they are very conscious of the fact that they and their friends are set apart from other Americans. In the study of Boston and Kansas City residents, an upper-class Bostonian said: "Of course social class exists—it influences your thinking." Then she added: "Maybe you shouldn't use the word 'class' for it, though—it's really a niche that each of us fits into" (Coleman, Rainwater, and McClelland 1978, p. 25). In a classic study of social classes in New Haven, a person in the top category in terms of neighborhood residence and educational background seemed startled when asked about her class level. After regaining her composure, she replied: "One does not speak of classes; they are felt" (Hollingshead and Redlich 1958, p. 69). As part of a study of 38 upper-class women in a large midwestern city, a sociologist bluntly asked her informants at the end of the interview if they were members of the upper class. The answers she received had the same flavor of hesitation and denial:

> "I hate [the term] upper class. It's so non–upper class to use it. I just call it 'all of us,' those of us who are wellborn."
>
> "I hate to use the word 'class.' We're responsible, fortunate people, old families, the people who have something."
>
> "We're not supposed to have layers. I'm embarrassed to admit to you that we do, and that I feel superior at my social level. I like being part of the upper crust." (Ostrander 1980, pp. 78–79)

These insights into the social psychology of the upper class, especially the development of a sense of superiority that justifies class dominance, are explored further in Chapter 3.

SOCIAL CLASS ACCORDING TO SOCIAL SCIENTISTS

Social scientists end up with just about the same understanding of social classes as do typical Americans, but only after two important theoretical issues are dealt with first. They begin with a crucial analytical distinction between *economic classes,* which consist of people who have a common position in the economic system, such as "business owners" or "employees," and *social classes,* which consist of people who interact with each other, develop in-group social organizations, and share a common lifestyle, while at the same time excluding people they do not see as similar to themselves. Social scientists also stress that the concept of class includes the relationship between classes as well as a set of positions within the social structure. The idea of a social class is therefore a double-edged or two-dimensional concept, so to speak, denoting both the specific economic or social class people are in as well as the relationships between classes. To use the earlier example once again, business owners and wage earners constitute separate economic classes, but the concept of class also encompasses the relationship between them.

The distinction between economic classes and social classes is important because class as an economic relationship is always operating as part of the social structure, but the people in any given economic position may or may not develop their own social organizations, live in the same neighborhoods, and interact socially. The degree to which a given economic class is also a social class therefore can vary widely from place to place and time to time, which matters because members of an economic class may be limited in the degree to which they can exercise political power if they do not think of themselves as being members of a social class with common interests (Weber 1998; Wright 1998).

Analyzing Social Classes

The systematic study of whether or not people in a given economic position are also members of a social class begins with a search for connections among the people and organizations that are thought to constitute the social class. This procedure is called *membership network analysis,* which boils down to a matrix in which social organizations, such as schools and clubs, are arrayed along one axis and individuals along the other. Table 1.1 provides a hypothetical example of such a matrix.

As can be seen in Table 1.1, the boxes (called *cells*) created by each intersection of a person and an organization are filled in with information revealing whether or not the person is a member of that organization. This information is used to create two different kinds of networks, one organizational, the other interpersonal. An *organizational network* consists of the relationships among

Table 1.1 A Hypothetical Membership Network Using Schools and Clubs

Individuals	Organizations			
	School 1	*School 2*	*Club 1*	*Club 2*
Person 1	X			X
Person 2		X	X	
Person 3	X		X	X
Person 4		X	X	X
Person 5				

Note: Person 5 is an "isolate" with no connections. He or she is not part of the social class.

organizations as determined by their common members. These shared members are usually called *overlapping* or *interlocking* members. An *interpersonal network*, on the other hand, reveals the relationships among individuals as determined by their common organizational affiliations. (These and other methodological issues are explained further with the help of diagrams and tables in the document on "How to Do Power Structure Research" on whorulesamerica.net.)

To provide a more complete example of the type of analysis that appears throughout the book, suppose a researcher had the alumni lists for dozens of private schools and Ivy League universities, along with membership lists for many clubs, as well as guest lists from debutante balls. By determining the names that overlap on two or more of these lists, it would be possible to determine which of these organizations are parts of the same social network. In addition, it could be shown that the most central organizations in the network are determined by the fact that they share members with many other organizations, whereas peripheral organizations might have members in common only with other organizations that are also one or two steps removed from the central organizations. Furthermore, some organizations may have no members in common with any of the others, which reveals they are not part of the social network. In the end, those organizations that are part of the network are the institutional framework for the social upper class.

A membership network analysis is in principle very simple, but it is theoretically important because it contains within it the two types of human relationships of concern in most sociological theorizing: interpersonal relations and memberships in organizations. Thus, these networks contain a *duality of persons and groups* (Breiger 1974). For analytical purposes, the interpersonal and organizational networks are often treated separately, and some social scientists talk of different "levels of analysis," but in the reality of everyday life the two types or levels are always intertwined. Hence the employment of a very useful phrase to explain a complex point: a "duality of persons and groups."

This network-based way of thinking about a social class (as consisting of both organizations and their members) fits well with earlier definitions of social class. For example, in one of the first empirical investigations of social class in America, a study of caste and class in a Southern city in the 1930s, the sociological researchers defined a social class as:

> The largest group of people whose members have intimate access to one another. A class is composed of families and social cliques. The interrelationships between these families and cliques, in such informal activities as visiting, dances, receptions, teas, and larger informal affairs, constitute the structure of the social class. A person is a member of the social class with which most of his or her participations, of this intimate kind, occur. (Davis, Gardner, and Gardner 1941, p. 59n)

A political scientist who did a classic study of class and power in the city of New Haven wrote that similar "social standing" is defined by "the extent to which members of that circle would be willing—disregarding personal and idiosyncratic factors—to accord the conventional privileges of social intercourse and acceptance among equals; marks of social acceptability include willingness to dine together, to mingle freely in intimate social events, to accept membership in the same clubs, to use forms of courtesy considered appropriate among social equals, to intermarry, and so on" (Dahl 1961, p. 229).

As these similar definitions from different disciplines suggest, there is a general agreement among social scientists that there are social classes in America that have separate social organizations, in-group activities, and common lifestyles. Indeed, it may be the only concept on which there is widespread agreement when it comes to studying power. The first problem for power analysts begins with the question of whether the top social class, the upper class, is also an economic class based in the ownership and control of large income-producing properties. This question will be answered in great detail in Chapter 3.

A GUIDE TO WHAT FOLLOWS

Because the analysis presented in this book challenges some basic American beliefs and is met with skepticism by those social scientists who prefer one of the alternative theories discussed in Chapter 9, it is necessary to proceed in a deliberate fashion, defining each concept as it is introduced, and then providing empirical examples of how each part of the system works. By approaching the problem in this manner, readers can draw their own conclusions at each step of the way and decide for themselves if they think the argument fails at some point. Then they can compare their critique of the argument with the theories discussed in Chapter 9.

Using membership network analysis as a starting point, each chapter presents one aspect of a cumulative argument. Chapter 2 provides evidence for the existence of a nationwide corporate community that includes Wall Street banks and stockbrokers, military contractors, agribusinesses, accounting firms, and corporate law firms, as well as large and well-known corporations like ExxonMobil, General Electric, and IBM. It briefly discusses the agricultural sector and small-business to show that they are closely tied to the corporate community and present no challenge to it. It shows that most local businesses are organized into *growth coalitions* that are focused on making local land more valuable, and discusses the ways in which the corporate community and local growth coalitions sometimes come into conflict.

Chapter 3 uses alumni lists, club lists, and memberships in other social organizations to show that the owners and top-level executives in the corporate community form a socially cohesive and clearly demarcated upper class that has created its own social world and a distinctive social psychology. It is this overlap of the corporate community and the upper class that defines those with great wealth in the United States as the corporate rich. The chapter argues that the social bonds developed by the corporate owners and managers combine with their common economic interests to make it easier for them to overcome policy disagreements when they meet in the policy-planning network. In a phrase, *social cohesion helps bring about policy cohesion.*

Chapter 4 demonstrates that the corporate rich finance and direct the network of foundations, think tanks, and policy-discussion groups that provides policies and plans to deal with newly emerging problems faced by the corporate community. It is through involvement in this policy-planning network that corporate leaders gain an understanding of general issues beyond the confines of their own narrow business problems, discuss policy alternatives that are in their interests as a class, and come to know and work with specialists and experts on a wide range of topics. Chapter 5 describes how several of the organizations in the policy-planning network link with the public affairs departments of large corporations, large independent public relations firms, and nonprofit organizations at both the local and national level to form an opinion-shaping network that tries to influence middle-class voluntary groups and reinforce the individualistic and antigovernment dimensions of the American belief system.

Chapter 6 explains the nature of the American electoral system and why it is not as responsive to the preferences of the general public as the electoral systems in other democratic countries. It discusses the nature of the two major political parties and the congressional voting coalitions that shape most major pieces of legislation. In the process it also explains why campaign donations can play an important role in American politics, making support from wealthy donors essential for a successful candidacy at the national level and in highly populated states.

Chapter 7 examines the network-based processes through which corporate leaders are able to dominate the federal government in Washington on issues of interest to them. It begins with a discussion of the special-interest process, providing several examples related to tax cuts, tax havens, and subsidies for specific corporations. The chapter then outlines the several avenues through which the proposals developed in the policy-planning network are incorporated into government policy. It next examines the social, educational, and occupational backgrounds of cabinet appointments and top staff appointments in the White House, showing that they have come disproportionately from the corporate community and policy-planning network.

Chapter 8 outlines the theoretical framework that fits best with these findings, a *class-domination* theory based in an understanding of how the four most important bases of power—the economic, political, military, and ideological networks—relate to one another in the United States. It explains the historical reasons for the ascendancy of the economic network in the United States, which leads to greater power for the corporate community than in other industrialized democracies. Brief comparisons of the relative importance of the four main power networks in the United States and various European countries are used to make this point more clear. Each country has a unique history that makes generalizations across time and place very risky, but the comparisons made in this chapter highlight the fact that the ideological, political, and military networks have been much more important in most European countries than they have been in the United States. Thus, corporate dominance cannot be taken as an inevitable outcome.

Chapter 9 discusses the similarities and differences between the class-dominance theory presented in this book and the three main alternative viewpoints in the social sciences that received the most attention and generated the most empirical studies between 1992 and 2012. It also offers a brief critique of each of these theories based on the empirical information that has been presented in earlier chapters. By that point readers will have enough information of their own with which they can make their own judgments about the usefulness of the alternative theories and the validity of the critiques that are made of them. The chapter concludes with the suggestion that the four-network theory described earlier in this chapter, based on the interactions of economic, political, military, and ideological organizational networks, provides a common meeting ground that does not require the proponents of any of the theories to abandon their key insights.

2

The Corporate Community

It may seem a little strange at first to think about the several thousand big corporations, banks, and other financial companies that sit astride the American economy as any sort of community, but in fact corporations have many types of connections and common bonds. They include shared ownership, long-standing patterns of supply and purchase, and the use of the same legal, accounting, advertising, and public relations firms. Corporations also share common (overlapping) members on their boards of directors, which have the ultimate responsibility for the fate of corporations. Then, too, large corporations share the same goals and values, especially the profit motive. As noted in the Introduction, they also draw closer because they are all opposed and criticized to varying degrees by the labor movement, liberals, leftists, strong environmentalists, and other types of anticorporate activists.

For research purposes, the most objective starting point for grasping the full scope of the corporate community is in the *interlocks* created when a person sits on two or more corporate boards, because interlocks are the most visible and accessible of the ties among corporations. Since membership on a board of directors is public information, it is possible to use membership network analysis to make detailed studies of interlock patterns extending back into the early nineteenth century. The organizational network uncovered in these studies provides a rigorous research definition for the term *corporate community*: It consists of all those profit-seeking organizations connected into a single network by overlapping directors.

The starting point in creating this network since the 1950s has been detailed research by reporters for the business magazine *Fortune*, which leads to a list of the 500 and 1,000 largest publicly owned corporations for each year, which are ranked by their yearly revenues and known as the *Fortune* 500 and *Fortune* 1,000. From this starting point, it is not only possible to determine which of these companies

16

share directors, but to discover the many privately owned companies, financial firms, and corporate law firms that are part of this network, and therefore part of the corporate community, due to sharing common directors with the *Fortune* 500.

However, it is very important not to overstate the actual importance of these interlocks. They are valuable for the dissemination of organizational innovations among corporations, they give the people who are members of several boards a very useful overview of the corporate community as a whole, they contribute to political cohesion, and they seem to have modest effects on some of the financial practices of the interlocked corporations (Burris 2005; Dreiling and Darves 2011; Mizruchi 1996). But for the purposes of this book, corporate interlocks should be thought of primarily as an entry point that outsiders are able to use for learning more about the corporate community. Their importance to how the corporate community functions should not be overestimated because they barely scratch the surface.

Once the outlines of the corporate community are established through an examination of interlocking directorates, it is possible to extend the membership network analysis to find the other types of organizational affiliations maintained by corporate directors. Such studies show that members of the corporate community create two types of organizations for purposes of relating to each other and government. First, they develop trade associations, which are made up of all the businesses in a specific industry or sector of the economy. Thus, there is the American Petroleum Institute, the American Bankers Association, the National Association of Home Builders, and hundreds of similar organizations that focus on the narrow interests of their members and bring their concerns to government through the special-interest process discussed briefly at the end of the previous chapter.

Second, the corporate community is pulled even closer together by several overarching business associations that look out for its general interests and play a role in the policy-planning process discussed in Chapter 4: the National Association of Manufacturers, the U.S. Chamber of Commerce, the Conference Board, the Business Council, the Committee for Economic Development, and the Business Roundtable. In the case of the National Association of Manufacturers and its many state affiliates, for example, its foremost concern since 1903 has been all-out opposition to labor unions in any part of the economy. It also routinely opposes any increase in the minimum wage, unemployment benefits, Social Security payments, or any other legislation that might give more power to its employees. In early 2009, it resisted two bills introduced into the House of Representatives to deal with pay discrimination against women on the grounds that they would "open the floodgates to unwarranted litigation against employers at a time when businesses are struggling to retain and create jobs" (Pear 2009).

The U.S. Chamber of Commerce encompasses all types of American businesses, not just manufacturers, and is therefore much larger in size and reaches into more communities through its state and local affiliates. It shares many views in common with the National Association of Manufacturers. Together, these two associations are the organizational basis for the large "ultraconservative" wing, or faction, within the corporate community.

The Conference Board has a fact-gathering and information-dissemination role in the corporate community, publishing many studies about business conditions and consumer confidence of interest to all members of the community. The Business Council, on the other hand, is primarily an occasion for formal but off-the-record meetings with top appointees in the executive branch of the federal government. On some issues, but not those related to trade unions, its members, all of them past or present chief executive officers (CEOs), have sometimes taken policy positions that are more moderate on various sorts of government social insurance and educational support programs than those of the National Association of Manufacturers and the U.S. Chamber of Commerce. Along with the members of the Committee for Economic Development, a business group started during World War II to plan for the postwar economy, members of the Business Council tend to represent the "corporate moderate" position within the corporate community.

As for the Business Roundtable, with both ultraconservative and corporate moderate members, it is the organization that has usually coordinated the corporate community against a wide range of challenges from the liberal-labor alliance since the 1970s. In 2011, the Business Roundtable, with 209 members, and the Business Council, with 132 members, shared 70 members in common. The Business Roundtable also shared 13 members with the National Association of Manufacturers, 11 with the Chamber of Commerce, three with the Committee for Economic Development, and three with the Conference Board.

The close relationships among these six corporate groups in general has been demonstrated through studies of their shared directors (Burris 2008; Staples 2013). However, the relationships are even closer than individual director interlocks reveal because there are numerous "company-based" interlocks among them as well. That is, one top executive of a corporation may be a director of one organization and another executive may be a director of one of the other organizations. Company-based interlocks show that vice presidents and legal advisors from the largest corporations, especially vice presidents for public relations or government relations, along with chief executive officers in smaller companies, direct the National Association of Manufacturers and the U.S. Chamber of Commerce. In 2011, nine large companies had four or more interlocks with the six groups, including Procter & Gamble with six and Aetna and IBM with five. Overall, 239 of the *Fortune* 500 had at least one link to one of the six groups (Staples 2013).

THE UNEXPECTED ORIGINS OF THE CORPORATE COMMUNITY

Standard historical accounts sometimes suggest that the first American businesses were owned by individual families and only slowly evolved into large corporations with common ownership and many hired managers. In fact, the corporate community had its origins in jointly owned companies in the textile industry in

New England in the late eighteenth and early nineteenth centuries. At that time the common directors reflected the fact that a small group of wealthy Boston merchants were joining together in varying combinations to invest in new companies. By 1845 a group of 80 men, known to historians as the "Boston Associates," controlled 31 textile companies that accounted for 20 percent of the nationwide textile industry. The Boston Associates also had a large role in financing the nation's early railroads. Then, too, 17 of these men served as directors of Boston banks that owned 40 percent of the city's banking capital, 20 were directors of six insurance companies, and 11 sat on the boards of five railroad companies (Dalzell 1987).

Meanwhile, wealthy investors in other major cities were creating commonly owned and directed companies as well. In New York, for example, the 10 largest banks and 10 largest insurance companies in 1816 were linked into one very tightly interlocked network. Most striking, 10 of the companies had from 11 to 26 interlocks and six had six to 10 interlocks; the remaining four had one to five interlocks. In 1836, all but two of the 20 largest banks, 10 largest insurance companies, and 10 largest railroads were linked into one common network, with 12 of the 38 companies having an amazing 11 to 26 interlocks, 10 having six to 10 interlocks, and 16 having one to five interlocks. Even at that time, which is often romanticized as one of small businesses, the 10 largest banks had 70 percent of the bank assets in New York City and 40 percent of the bank assets in the entire state (Bunting 1983).

These big-city networks of financial companies and railroads persisted in roughly their mid-century form until they were transformed between 1895 and 1904 by a massive merger movement, which created a national corporate network that included huge industrial corporations for the first time (Roy 1983). Until that point, industrial companies had been organized as partnerships among a few men or families. They tended to stand apart from the financial institutions and the stock market. Detailed historical and sociological studies of the creation of this enlarged corporate community reveal no economic efficiencies that might explain the relatively sudden incorporation of industrial companies. Instead, it seems more likely that industrial companies adopted the corporate form of organization for a combination of economic, legal, and sociological reasons.

The most important of these reasons seem to have been a need to (1) regulate the competition among them that was driving down profits and (2) gain better legal protection against the middle-class reformers, populist farmers, and socialists who had mounted an unrelenting critique of "the trusts," meaning agreements among industrialists to fix prices, divide markets, and/or share profits (Roy 1997). When trusts were outlawed by the Sherman Anti-Trust Act of 1890 (which was coincidentally followed by a major depression, large wage cuts, and strikes by angry workers), the stage was set for industrialists to take advantage of the increasing number of rights and privileges that legislatures and courts were gradually granting to the legal device called a "corporation." From this point forward the wealthy became the corporate rich, with their fortunes in all business sectors, from agriculture to real estate, protected by their incorporated fortresses.

Several studies show that the corporate community remained remarkably stable after the merger movement ended. Since then it always has included the largest corporations of the era, and until very recently financial companies tended to be at the center. Three changes in the patterns of corporate interlocks between 1904 and the 1970s seem to reflect gradual economic and financial changes, and thereby demonstrate that interlocks often reflect changing power dynamics in the corporate community. First, railroads became more peripheral as they gradually declined in economic importance. Second, manufacturing firms became more central as they increased in economic importance. Third, as corporations became more independent of banks, the banks became less likely to place their top officers on nonbank boards and more likely to receive officers of nonbank corporations on their own boards; this reversal of flow may reflect the gradual transformation of commercial banks from major power centers to places of coordination and communication (Mizruchi 1982; Mizruchi and Bunting 1981).

In short, large American businesses always have been owned and controlled by groups of well-to-do people that share common economic interests and social ties even more than kinship ties. Moreover, the deposits and premiums held by banks and insurance companies for ordinary people were used for investment purposes and the expansion of corporations from the beginning of the nineteenth century. Then, too, control of corporations by a combination of directors and high-level executives is an early feature of the American business system, not a change that occurred when stockholders allegedly lost control of companies to bankers or managers in the first half of the twentieth century (Bunting 1987). Contrary to the traditional claim by many social scientists that corporate growth and restructuring are sensible and efficient responses to changing technology and markets, a claim that leaves no room for any concern with power, research by historians and sociologists suggests that big corporations are a response to legal changes and class conflict, although it is also true that improvements in transportation and communication made such changes possible (Roy 1997).

Before taking a detailed look at the corporate community from the 1970s to 2010, it is necessary to say a few more words about corporate boards of directors.

THE BOARD OF DIRECTORS

The board of directors is the official governing body of the corporation. Usually composed of from 10 to 15 members, it meets for a day or two at a time about 10 times a year and receives reports and other information between meetings. Various board committees meet periodically with top managers as well. A smaller executive committee of the board often meets more frequently, and the most important individual members are sometimes in daily contact with the management that handles the day-to-day affairs of the corporation. The major duty of the board of directors is to hire and fire high-level executives, but it also is responsible for accepting or rejecting significant policy changes. Boards seem to play their most critical role when there is conflict within management, the corporation is in economic distress, or there is the possibility of a merger or acquisition.

The board is the official governing body, but the company executives on the board, who are called *inside directors*, sometimes play the main role in shaping the board's decisions. These inside directors, perhaps in conjunction with two or three of the nonmanagement directors (called *outside directors*), are able to set the agenda for meetings, shape board thinking on policy decisions, and select new outside directors. In those situations, the board may become little more than a rubber stamp for management as long as things are running smoothly, with the top managers having great influence in naming their successors in running the company. When outside directors become displeased with the direction the CEO is taking, however, they often ask him or her to resign with little or no notice, as happened in October 2012 to the CEO of the once-mighty Citibank (the largest financial services company in the world in 2007) because it was not recovering from its near-fatal decline in 2008 as fast as its main rivals (Silver-Greenberg and Craig 2012).

Although the exact role of the board varies from corporation to corporation and with changes in circumstances, boards in general embody the complex power relations within the corporate community. In addition to their role in selecting high-level management and dealing with crises, their importance manifests itself in a number of ways. They speak for the corporation to the rest of the corporate community and to the public at large. New owners demand seats on boards to consolidate their positions and to have a "listening post." Electing the top officers of rival corporations to each other's boards may signal the end of conflicts over hostile merger attempts. Commercial bankers may seek seats on boards to keep track of their loans and to ensure that future business will be directed their way. The CEOs of leading companies often take time from their busy schedules to be on one or two other boards because board membership is a visible sign that their advice is respected outside their home company. Their board memberships also provide them with general intelligence on the state of the business world. Then, too, the presence of investment bankers, corporate lawyers, and academic experts on a board is a sign that the corporations respect their expertise. The presence of a university president, former government official, well-known woman, or prominent person of color is a sign that their high status and respectability are regarded as valuable to the image of the corporation, especially when it is being criticized for racial or gender discrimination (Zweigenhaft and Domhoff 2006, Chapters 2–4).

Boards of directors are pivotal for an important theoretical reason as well. In the broadest sense, they are the interface between corporations and the upper class in the United States. Because of this role, boards of directors are one of the means by which this book attempts to synthesize a class-based theory and insights from organizational theory. From the standpoint of organizational theory, boards are important because they allocate scarce resources, deal with situations in which there is great uncertainty, and link the company to other organizations that are important to the company's future success. The organizational perspective is represented on the board of directors by the inside directors, who are full-time employees of the corporation. They are concerned with organizational survival and therefore make sure that any new initiatives have a minimal effect on routine functioning. They see outside directors as the "ambassadors" of the organization, who help to reduce uncertainty in the organization's environment (DiTomaso 1980).

The outside directors, who are often members of other large-scale profit-making enterprises or wealthy members of the upper class, represent the class perspective on the board. They want to ensure that any given corporation's new policy proposals fit well with their other profit-making opportunities and do not jeopardize general public acceptance in the political realm. Outside directors have a number of "resources" that make it possible for them to represent a class perspective: their own wealth, their connections to other corporations and nonprofit organizations, their general understanding of business and investment, and their many connections to other wealthy people, fundraisers, and politicians. Such resources make it possible for them to have a very real impact when new leadership must be selected or new policy directions must be undertaken (Ostrander 1987). As a former CEO later reflected in regard to the members of Yahoo's board after they replaced her after only one year on the job, "I didn't understand or have the time or take the time—that's a much better thing to say, take the time—to understand the relationships they had between themselves" (Miller 2012, p. B4).

THE CORPORATE COMMUNITY

The American economy is gigantic almost beyond description. In 2012, the estimated value of all the goods and services produced within the country was $15.1 trillion, almost twice the size of the economy as recently as 1984, and a little over six times as large as it was in 1945. However, most of these goods and services were produced by a relatively small number of companies that employ 1,000 or more workers and make the lion's share of the profits. According to a comprehensive survey for the year 2000, which has not been updated, only 8,300 of the estimated 5.5 million corporations, 2.0 million partnerships, and 17.7 million nonfarm proprietorships in the United States, a mere 0.015 percent of the total number of businesses, had 1,000 or more employees. The ownership of economic assets was even more highly concentrated, and the corporations in the *Fortune* 500 earned 57 percent of all profits while employing just 16.3 percent of the private-sector workforce (White 2002).

Several different studies, stretching from 2010 back to the 1970s, all of which focused on the largest corporations, provide a detailed overview of the modern-day corporate community. It is first of all an "extensive" network in terms of corporate interlocks, encompassing 87.5 percent of the *Fortune* 500 in 2010, 84 percent of the 930 largest corporations for 2001, 87.6 percent of 1,029 corporations in

1996, and 90 percent of the 800 largest corporations studied in the early 1970s (Barnes and Ritter 2001; Davis, Yoo, and Baker 2002; Domhoff 1998, pp. 36–40; Mariolis 1975; Staples 2013). Furthermore, most corporations are within three or four "steps" or "links" of any other, but for practical purposes only the first two links are usually apparent to members of the network (even though information and gossip may be passed along to people they don't know) because most directors, like people in any setting, cannot see beyond the "friends of friends" level.

In the case of the 2010 study of the *Fortune* 500, which provides the starting point for further analyses in this chapter and Chapter 4, the large network, with 87.5 percent of the *Fortune* 500 included in it, is not "dense." This is because corporations have relatively few ties with one another as a percentage of all the possible ties in a completely interconnected network. However, the corporate community does have a "core" or "center." It is made up of the corporations with the most interlocks, which tend to be corporations with more frequent interlocks with each other than with other corporations. For 2010, the 30 most central corporations in terms of their total director interlocks included several very familiar names, such as IBM (No. 3), Ford Motor (No. 7), Verizon (No. 9), General Electric (No. 14), McDonald's (No. 15), FedEx (No. 21), and General Mills (No. 30).

When the directors of the six business groups were added to the *Fortune* 500 database, 453 of the 506 organizations (89.5 percent) were part of one large network, which means that adding those groups drew only a few of the "isolates" into the network. It also reveals that there is considerable "redundancy" in the network, which suggests that it would not fall apart if some of the links were broken. It is also noteworthy that five of six general-purpose business groups have the highest centrality rankings, and that 28 of the 30 most central corporations in the first step of the analysis were among the most central 40 organizations in the enlarged network. These results demonstrate in a systematic way what most readers would expect by this point: The large central corporations are closely linked to the business groups (Staples 2013). The results for this analysis are presented in Table 2.1 (on page 24).

The centrality of the Business Roundtable and the Business Council in the corporate community also is demonstrated by determining the extent to which the entire network can be recreated using just the 271 people who are in either or both of those two organizations as a starting point. It shows that 40 percent of the *Fortune* 500 companies and the other four business groups are directly or indirectly connected to the Business Roundtable/Business Council combination. Put another way, even if a significant number of companies lost their direct connections to each other, they still would be linked to each other through the Business Roundtable and the Business Council.

Privately Owned Corporations and Financial Companies

In addition to the thousands of corporations that sell their stocks to the general public through the stock exchanges, there were 212 corporations in 2011 with

Table 2.1 The 40 Highest-Ranking Organizations in the Corporate Community (Numbers in Parentheses Reflect Corporate Rankings **Before** Business Groups Were Added to the Corporation Network)[1]

Ranking	Organization	Ranking	Organization
1	Business Roundtable	21	Eli Lilly (29)
2	Business Council	22	FedEx (21)
3	CED	23	General Electric (14)
4	NAM	24	H. J. Heinz (9)
5	Chamber of Commerce	25	Medtronic (22)
6	Caterpillar (2)	26	Wells Fargo (25)
7	Marathon Oil (5)	27	Alcoa (61)
8	IBM (3)	28	Allstate (18)
9	Ford Motor (7)	29	Boeing (19)
10	3M (1)	30	Corning (28)
11	Deere (6)	31	General Mills (30)
12	American Express (11)	32	Northrop Grumman (24)
13	Conference Board	33	Aetna (60)
14	McDonald's (15)	34	Aon (12)
15	Pfizer (5)	35	Bank of New York Mellon (27)
16	United Technologies (16)	36	Citibank (41)
17	Verizon (9)	37	JPMorgan Chase (32)
18	AT&T (17)	38	McGraw-Hill (94)
19	Abbott Laboratories (10)	39	Northern Trust (23)
20	Chevron (13)	40	PNC Financial (34)

[1] Note that some corporations fell more than six places, and some new ones moved into the Top 40, after the six business groups were added, which reflects the changing dynamics of a network when new organizations are added.

Source: Staples 2013.

$2 billion or more in sales that were privately owned by family members or a few private investors; 65 of them were large enough to be in the *Fortune* 500, and most of them had from 10,000 to 142,000 employees (Forbes 2011). There were also many private financial companies that offer financial services to all corporations and take ownership positions in many of them, and a handful of them are involved in the buying and selling of large corporations ("private equity" firms). Sometimes private equity firms buy companies to take them private, sometimes to turn private companies into publicly held companies, and sometimes to sell off pieces of the newly acquired corporation to other corporations, depending on which of these actions can bring them more profits through tax breaks or through stock purchases by university endowments and government pension funds (Appelbaum, Batt, and Clark 2012; Nanea and Smith 2012). Studies of representative samples of directors of *Fortune* 500 companies and of the members of the Business Council and Business Roundtable suggest that both privately held corporations and financial firms are often part of the corporate community. Some of their owners also participate in the policy-planning network discussed in Chapter 4 and the opinion-shaping network examined in Chapter 5.

Cargill, a producer and marketer of a wide range of foodstuffs, with 142,000 employees in 65 countries, is larger than all but 18 companies on the *Fortune* 500 list. Both its CEO and its president sit on the board of a *Fortune* 500 company, and the CEO is also a member of the Business Council. Three of its five outside directors have numerous directorships in the *Fortune* 500. Five of the 20 largest privately held companies were represented on the Business Roundtable in 2010. To take a privately held company further down the list at No. 84, Carlson, which owns hotels, restaurants, and resorts and employs 52,500 people, one member of the Carlson family is on the board of ExxonMobil. Another director at Carlson Company, the retired CEO of Best Buy, is on the board of General Mills. The CEO of Cargill is also on the board, which gives Carlson a direct link to the Business Council. Members of the Carlson family serve as directors of universities and cultural organizations as well, on which they overlap with directors of *Fortune* 500 companies.

On the other hand, some privately held companies do not have links to the *Fortune* 500 or the six large business groups. Koch Industries, the second-largest of the privately held corporations, which would be 29th on the *Fortune* 500 list, just below Boeing Corporation, if its stock were publicly traded, has no officers who serve on *Fortune* 500 boards. But its two main owners, David H. Koch and Charles G. Koch, who inherited the company from their father and built it into the giant it is now, sit on a wide range of cultural boards with other corporate directors. They also became famous in the 2000s as the major donors to ultraconservative think tanks and the right wing of the Republican Party.

The five largest private equity firms in 2011 (the Texas Pacific Group [aka TPG], Goldman Sachs Principal Investment Area, the Carlyle Group, Kohlberg Kravis Roberts, and the Blackstone Group) are part of the corporate community as owners of *Fortune* 500 firms, corporate directors, and members of the Business Council and Business Roundtable. One of the three founders of TPG is a director of General Motors, Harrah's Entertainment, and Energy Future Holdings. The top partner at Goldman Sachs is a member of both the Business Council and the Business Roundtable, as is the co-founder of the Blackstone Group. The lead partners of the Carlyle Group and Kohlberg Kravis Roberts are members of the Business Council.

Kohlberg Kravis Roberts, the fourth-largest of the private equity firms in 2011, gained notoriety in the late 1980s as the first of the early private equity firms to become involved in hostile takeovers of large corporations. The lead partner, Henry Kravis, who is sometimes listed as a self-made person because it is not generally known that his father was worth tens of millions of dollars, sat on eight corporate boards at one point, including Safeway Stores, RJR Nabisco, and Gillette, companies that he and his partners acquired after 1986. His cousin and partner, George Roberts, joined him on seven of those boards and was on one other board as well. By 2011, Kravis, age 67, was down to one board and Roberts, age 69, had dropped all board affiliations, but their firm still was involved in many companies and the two men were worth $4 and $3 billion, respectively.

This section has only scratched the surface of the corporate community because there are very few systematic studies of it in the social sciences to draw upon. However, there are many other ways that the full extent of the corporate community could be explored. For example, links between the top corporations and the lower portions of the *Fortune* 1,000 could be studied. In the case of corporation No. 1,000, SRA International, one of its directors, who worked for JPMorgan Chase before joining a private equity firm, is also a director of SunGard Data Systems (No. 380 on the *Fortune* list). SunGard, in turn, has one director who is also a director of HCA (No. 77) and another who is a member of the Business Roundtable. Another SRA International director is a partner in Providence Equity Partners, one of the 15 largest private equity firms in the country. This example, picked as the least likely starting point for corporate community connections, might reveal the intricacies and extent of the corporate community if it were studied more fully in the future. This might be especially the case if more financial companies were added.

Are Defense Companies Separate?

Unlike the countries of Europe, which had to have large armies from the sixteenth century onward to expand their territories or defend themselves against their neighbors, the United States did not have a large military establishment until World War II. This fact goes a long way toward explaining the relatively small size of the federal government historically, because military budgets were by far the largest item of state expenditure from the time there is surviving evidence (from the twelfth century) on this issue (Mann 1986; Mann 1993). The relatively small size of the federal government until the 1940s also helps to explain why large corporations were able to have a large role in shaping it, as shown in Chapters 6 and 7. However, the large amount of defense spending since World War II led a few social scientists to argue that there is a separate "military-industrial complex," which is able to win the budgetary allocations it needs and maintain at least some degree of independence from the corporate community. There are three major findings that contradict this notion.

First, several of the largest defense contractors, such as Boeing, General Electric, and United Technologies, which manufactures elevators, escalators, and other industrial products, are also among the largest corporations in the country irrespective of their military contracts. Second, research on the handful of companies that specialized in weapons manufacturing in the years following World War II demonstrated that they were completely integrated into the corporate community through their bank connections and interlocking directors; in addition, their directors went to the same universities and belonged to the same social clubs as other corporate directors (Johnson 1976).

Findings on the top defense contractors' director interlocks in 2010 show they continue to be integrated with the larger corporate community. For example, the largest defense contractor in 2010, Lockheed Martin, had director interlocks with six nondefense companies, including two with Monsanto; Boeing, the second largest, had ties to 12 other nondefense corporations, including two with Abbott Laboratories. Similarly, Northrop Grumman, No. 5 on the list for 2011, had ties to 12 nondefense companies, including a double interlock with Deere. In addition, Lockheed Martin had one director who was on the Business Council, Boeing had two on the Business Council and one on the Business Roundtable, and Northrop had one director who was a member of both the Business Council and the Business Roundtable. More generally, the 21 defense companies large enough to be in the *Fortune* 500 were completely integrated into the corporate network discussed in the previous section, as seen by the fact that a network based strictly on the directors of those 21 companies drew in 119 other companies and five of the six general business groups, with the Business Roundtable and the Business Council once again at the center (Staples 2013).

Third, the idea of a separate military-industrial complex is contradicted by the fact that the defense budget rises and falls as a percentage of the overall economic output (the "gross domestic product," or GDP) in relation to foreign policy crises and military threats. This pattern does not fit with the idea that defense contractors and their Pentagon allies have the power to allocate themselves all the money they would like to have, which would lead to a steady or rising share of the GDP. Budgetary decline as a percentage of economic output was significant after World War II, the Korean War, and the Vietnam War (Goertzel 1985). The drop in defense spending in the decade after the end of the Cold War was substantial as well, although the defense budget continued to grow and to be a major part of the overall federal budget.

Based on these overall findings, it seems likely that the corporate community is a military-industrial complex in and of itself, in addition to being the producer of most of the goods and services purchased by American consumers. For example, Boeing, the second-largest defense contractor in 2011, received 55 percent of its revenues from civilian sales, and Honeywell, No. 10 in defense contracts in that same year, which makes everything from air cleaners to car products and has divisions that deal with oil, gas, healthcare, and fire protection, received 85 percent of its revenues from civilian sales. Only No. 1, Lockheed Martin, with 5 percent civilian revenues and No. 4, Raytheon, with 7 percent civilian revenues were overwhelmingly dependent on military contracts (Defense News 2012).

THE DIRECTOR NETWORK AS A LEADERSHIP GROUP

The interlocks within the corporate community were created by the 18.7 percent of the directors of the *Fortune* 500 companies in 2010 that were members of two or more boards of directors, a percentage that is very similar to what it has been since the early nineteenth century with corporate networks of varying sizes (Bunting 1983; Roy 1983). Based on past studies, the directors who sit on two or more boards do not differ demographically from other directors, but they do tend to be on more nonprofit boards and are appointed more frequently to government positions (Dreiling and Darves 2011, pp. 1542–1543; Useem 1979). They are therefore the core of the corporate leadership for the *Fortune* 500 and the privately owned corporations and financial companies to which the *Fortune* 500 are connected, but it is the 5,044 directors in the full database of *Fortune* 500 firms and the six major business groups that are the general leadership group.

Who are the several thousand directors on *Fortune* 500 boards that were at the heart of the corporate community in 2010? Most were business executives, commercial bankers, investment bankers, and corporate lawyers, but there was also a significant minority of university administrators, foundation presidents, former elected officials, and representatives of ethnic and racial minorities. They were 85 percent men, 87 percent white, 6.7 percent African American, 3.1 percent Latinos, and 2.4 percent Asian American (Zweigenhaft 2013).

Compared to three or four decades earlier, there is greater diversity in the corporate community in terms of the number of women and people of color, which reflects a response to the social movements that emerged in the 1960s. There is irony in this diversity, however, because the social class and educational backgrounds of the women and people of color on corporate boards tend to be similar to those of their white male counterparts, and much less similar to the backgrounds of those who worked in the movements for greater inclusion. They also share the Christian religion and Republican politics of most of the white males. In the case of African American and Latino corporate directors, they tend to have lighter skin color than leaders within their own communities (Zweigenhaft and Domhoff 2006). Based on this and other information, there is reason to believe that white male directors select new women and minority directors that are the most similar to them in class, education, and skin color. There is also evidence that women and minority directors usually share the same perspectives on business and government as the other directors. In a further irony, their presence in highly visible positions shifts the focus of the previously excluded groups from collective action, as in social movements, to a focus on individual advancement (Pettigrew 2008; Wright and Lubensky 2009; Zweigenhaft and Domhoff 2011, pp. 139–141).

The extensive corporate network created by interlocking directors provides a general framework within which common business and political perspectives can gradually develop. It is one building block toward a more general class awareness, which is reinforced by the business associations and in settings that are discussed in Chapters 3 and 4. The understanding gained by studying interlocking directors and the corporate network is therefore a useful starting point in understanding corporate power. But it is no substitute for showing how policy views are formed and how government is influenced on specific issues about which there is conflict with the liberal-labor alliance.

THE CORPORATE LAWYERS

Lawyers specializing in corporate law go back to the beginnings of American corporations. Comprising only a few percent of all lawyers, they generally practice as partners in large firms that have hundreds of partners and even more "associates"—that is, recent law school graduates who work for a salary and aspire to an eventual partnership. Partners routinely earn several hundred thousand dollars each year and top partners make several million, but as corporations began to hire more and more of their own lawyers in the early 2000s, many independent corporate law firms had to tighten their belts and make other adjustments that might trim back their large annual salaries and bonuses (Sorkin 2012).

Corporate law firms grew in size and importance in tandem with the large corporations that developed in the second half of the nineteenth century. Their partners played the central role in creating the state-level laws in New Jersey and Delaware that made the corporate form an attractive and safe haven for companies under pressure from reformers and socialists, who were trying to pass laws at the national level that would break up or socialize large businesses (Parker-Gwin and Roy 1996). During the course of the twentieth century, corporate lawyers made Delaware into a tax and regulatory haven that allows for greater corporate secrecy, has corporate-friendly courts, and makes it easier for a minority of stockholders to maintain control of the corporation, which frees those stockholders to invest a larger portion of their wealth in other ventures. Government officials in other states estimate that it cost them an estimated $9.5 billion in tax revenues between 2002 and 2012 because corporations that do a large amount of business in their states have their official headquarters in Delaware. Liberal critics claim that corporations would have to behave very differently and would have far less power if nationwide corporations had to have federal charters with high standards built into them, but liberal senators have been powerless to bring about any changes (Nader, Green, and Seligman 1976; Wayne 2012). By 2012, 285,000 companies, including 60 percent of the *Fortune* 500, claimed Delaware as their home state (Dyreng, Lindsey, and Thornock 2011).

By the early twentieth century, corporate lawyers prepared briefs for key legal cases, but rarely appeared in court. They advised corporations on how widely or narrowly to interpret requests for information when facing lawsuits over the dangers of their products. They became central to mergers and acquisitions by corporate executives. They also served as important go-betweens with government, sometimes as heads of major departments of the executive branch, sometimes as White House counsel. After government service, they returned to their private practices with new knowledge and contacts that made them even more valuable to their corporate clients. They often sit on corporate boards, and some of them become the heads of corporations at later points in their careers. Thus, many corporate lawyers are part of the corporate leadership group discussed in the previous section.

Despite these close ties with corporations, some social scientists have argued that corporate lawyers are "professionals" with a code of ethics and public-regarding values that set them apart from the corporate community. However, a detailed analysis of four large corporate law firms in Chicago provides convincing evidence that these lawyers are an integral part of the corporate community. They have a strong loyalty to their clients, not to their profession or code of ethics. The sociologist who did this study reports that "lawyers in large firms adhere to an ideology of autonomy, both in their perception of the role of legal institutions in society and the role of lawyers vis-à-vis clients, but that this ideology has little bearing in practice." Instead, when it comes to "the realm of practice these lawyers enthusiastically attempt to maximize the interests of clients and rarely experience serious disagreements with clients over the broader implications of a proposed course of conduct." He concludes, contrary to the claims made by the corporate lawyers for their intermediary role, that the "dominance of client interests in the practical activities of lawyers contradicts the view that large-firm lawyers serve a mediating function in the legal system" (Nelson 1988, p. 232).

Although closely tied to their clients and in that sense not independently powerful, corporate lawyers are nonetheless important in shaping law schools, the American Bar Association, courts, and political institutions. The same author quoted above concludes that corporate lawyers "maintain and make legitimate the current system for the allocation of rights and benefits," and that they do so for the benefit of their clients: "The influence of these organizations in the legal system derives from and can only serve the interests of corporate clients" (Nelson 1988, pp. 264, 269).

The socialization that creates the business-oriented mentality shared by corporate lawyers has been studied in great detail at Harvard Law School, the law school that trained both President Obama and his wife, Michelle Robinson Obama. Based on interviews and classroom observations, the sociological investigator reported that students end up actively participating in building "collective identities" within law school that all but ensure they will become members of the corporate community as a result of a grueling socialization process (Granfield 1992). As a key part of this socialization, students are taught there is no such thing as right or wrong, only differing shades of gray. Summer internships provide the students with a taste of the corporate world. They come to feel they must be special to be attending a high-status law school and to be sought after by powerful law firms that offer starting salaries of $100,000 a year or more. Thus, even though some students enter prestigious law schools with an interest in public interest law, all but a few percent end up in corporate law firms. Mrs. Obama was one of those young corporate lawyers for a year or two after she graduated, working for the most prestigious firm in Chicago. She found the work tedious and left for a career in government and university employment, but not before she met her future husband when he did a summer internship at the firm and she was his mentor (Mendell 2007).

As the careers of Michelle Robinson Obama and Barack Obama show, not all young lawyers from high-status law schools follow the corporate path, and those from lower-status schools are less likely to do so. Some become trial lawyers, who represent aggrieved or injured individuals or groups in cases against corporations. They are often viewed as the major enemies of corporate lawyers, leading Republicans in elected office to propose various changes in the law that end up putting limits on liability. In response to this counterattack by the corporate community, many trial lawyers have become major donors to the Democratic Party. Other young lawyers go to work for the government as prosecutors and public defenders. Still others focus on environmental, civil rights, or labor law, in effect joining the liberal-labor alliance in many instances.

Given this diversity of interests and viewpoints among lawyers, it makes little sense in terms of a power analysis to talk about lawyers in general as part of a profession that is separate from business and other groups in society. Although lawyers share some qualities that make them useful mediators and politicians, as discussed further at the end of Chapter 6, it is important to ascertain what kind of law a person practices for purposes of power studies, and to realize that corporate lawyers are the hired guns of the corporate community.

FROM SMALL FARMS TO AGRIFOOD BUSINESSES

In the second half of the nineteenth century, when the large farm vote was a critical one in state and national elections, farmers often provided major opposition to the rising national corporations. Many angry farmers were part of an anticorporate populist and labor alliance that started the Greenback-Labor Party in the early 1870s and the Populist Party in the 1880s to challenge both Democrats and Republicans. Several of the reforms advocated by the Populist Party—such as a government commission to set railroad rates, the direct election of senators, and the federal income tax—were eventually adopted.

But the day of farmers as challengers to the corporate community ended well over 100 years ago, when the populists were defeated at the turn of the twentieth century by a coalition of prosperous farmers and local business leaders. As the number of farms declined dramatically between 1900 and 2010 from 6.5 million to 2.2 million, and the average size of farms tripled to 450 acres, the remaining farm owners became an interest group rather than a large popular movement. Moreover, the large-scale family farmers of the Midwest and Great Plains increasingly joined with the plantation owners of the South and the ranchers and growers of California as employers of wage labor between the 1930s and 1960s, especially part-time migrant labor, and came to identify themselves as business owners.

The periodic attempts since the 1930s by farmworkers to organize labor unions, often aided and encouraged by liberals and leftists, intensified most farm owners' sense of opposition to the liberal-labor alliance and drew them closer to the ultra-conservatives in the corporate community.

Although nearly 98 percent of the 2.2 million farms in existence in 2010 were still family owned, with cooperatives and a tiny number of corporate-owned farms accounting for the rest, the overwhelming majority of them were extremely small. Roughly 60 percent of farms had less than $10,000 a year in sales, and 66 percent had less than $40,000 in sales. Over 90 percent of their owners' yearly income came from nonfarm sources, mainly jobs in low-wage manufacturing and service firms, many of which relocated to rural areas to escape from unions. At the high end of the farm ladder, just 4,943 farms, with $5 million or more in sales, had 20 percent of all farm sales in 2010, and another 31,600 farms, with sales of $1 million to $4.9 million, accounted for another 31.6 percent, which means that just 50,000 farms, a little over 2 percent of all farms, produced 51.6 percent of sales. More broadly, the 197,000 farms with sales of $250,000 or more, 10.2 percent of all farms, accounted for 83.4 percent of farm sales (Hoppe 2012).

Federal subsidy payments of various kinds, which originated in the Agricultural Adjustment Act of 1933, further increased the importance of large farms. Although only 38 percent of all farms receive subsidies, just 10 percent of that minority of farms received 75 percent of the $277.3 billion in benefits sent out between 1995 and 2011, according to an ongoing database built by the Environmental Working Group after forcing the government to divulge this information through a successful Freedom of Information Act request (Environmental Working Group 2012; Sciammacco 2011; Williams-Derry 2001).

Many farms are part of large "agrifood" systems, a term used by rural sociologists to encompass everything from farms to large supermarket chains. On the production side of the corporate-controlled supply chains, *Fortune* 500 firms such as Monsanto, DuPont, Deere, and Navistar International sell farmers seeds, chemical fertilizers, and farming equipment. Once farmers produce the commodities, another set of large corporations takes over. Nearly 40 percent of farms, most of them with sales of at least $100,000 a year, have either production or marketing contracts with corporations, with great variation from commodity to commodity. For example, 90 percent of sugar beet and poultry production is done on a contract basis, but marketing contracts for corn, soybeans, and wheat cover only 23 to 26 percent of sales (MacDonald and Korb 2011). Contract or no contract, three corporations control 87 percent of corn milling, four control 85 percent of soybean processing, four control 82 percent of beef slaughtering, and four control 63 percent of pork slaughter, and there are similar patterns for other meats and grains, as well as in feedlots for cattle. Cargill, discussed earlier in the chapter as the largest privately owned company in the country, is one of the top four in three of the four specific agricultural sectors mentioned in the previous sentence, and Tyson Foods and JBS, a Brazilian company, are in the top four in two of the four (James, Hendrickson, and Howard 2013, Table 1; Lobao 2013; Lobao and Meyer 2001).

When the time comes to sell food to everyday customers, 10 supermarket chains have 53 percent of all grocery sales (Food & Water Watch 2012, p. 4).

The relatively small numbers of farmers with over $250,000 in yearly sales are organized into a wide variety of "commodity groups," which are made up of those farmers who produce a particular crop, such as the American Soybean Association and the National Corn Growers Association. There are also two or three general farm groups, the most important of which is the American Farm Bureau Federation, which calls itself the "voice of agriculture." The Farm Bureau, as it is known, claims to have six million members, although most of them are people who purchase insurance through one of the several insurance companies owned by the Farm Bureau. The Farm Bureau spent $6 million on lobbying Congress in 2011 and contributed $16 million to congressional candidates between 2001 and 2011 (Shearn 2012). It is usually aligned with the National Association of Manufacturers, the Chamber of Commerce, and business trade associations in the political arena. However, there is one farm organization, the National Farmers Union, with its origins and base in the wheat farmers in the Midwest and Great Plains, that usually sides with the liberal-labor alliance on several key issues.

The National Farmers Union aside, most highly visible farm organizations, such as the Farm Foundation, the National Farm-City Council, and the Center for Food Integrity, have numerous company interlocks with the corporations that sell seeds, fertilizers, and farm equipment, or purchase the commodities produced by farmers. In 2011, for example, the 17-person board of the Center for Food Integrity included officers from Monsanto, Tyson Foods, Novus International (an animal health and nutrition company), and Rabobank (a Netherlands-based financial services company for farmers and agribusinesses), as well as representatives of the trade associations for restaurants and dairy farmers, several farmers, two deans of agricultural schools, and the president of the Farm Bureau. Several of the insurance companies owned by the Farm Bureau have large blocks of stock in the corporations in the agrifood complex (Shearn 2012).

As this brief overview shows, farmers are not a counterweight to the corporate community. They are few in number and most of those few do not have enough income from their farms to have any political impact. At the same time, a significant percentage of the large-scale farmers have production or marketing contracts with the handful of giant corporations that control many facets of food production. In addition, the farmers who produce the great bulk of the cash crops are integrated into the corporate community through serving with executives from large corporations on the boards of directors of organizations in the farm network.

SMALL BUSINESS: NOT A COUNTERWEIGHT

Corporate public relations officers and leaders in the U.S. Chamber of Commerce frequently claim that small businesses, traditionally defined as businesses with less than 500 employees, are a significant counterweight to the corporate community because there are approximately 22 million such businesses in the United States, compared to only 14,000 companies with 500 or more employees. They make about half of all sales and employ half of the private labor force.

Small businesses also have an important place in the American belief system because they are thought to embody the independence and initiative of all Americans. Their advocates claim that they create the majority of new jobs, but they leave out that small businesses, which have a high rate of failure, also are responsible for the most job losses and fare no better than big businesses in terms of net jobs gained. Further, they tend to pay lower wages and are less likely to offer health care and pension benefits.

Moreover, the owners of small businesses are too large in number, too diverse in size, too lacking in financial assets, and too divided in their political opinions to have any collective power that could challenge the corporate community. About one-third of American businesses are part-time operations run from the home or as a sideline from a regular job, and another one-third are solo efforts. Others exist in immigrant ethnic enclaves and have few contacts with business owner outside their community. As a result of these problems, small-business owner have not formed their own associations to lobby for them.

Nonetheless, there is one organization, the National Federation of Independent Business (NFIB), which claims to represent the small-business viewpoint. Created in 1943 by a former Chamber of Commerce employee as a way to make profits on dues and at the same time have a basis for lobbying for his conservative policy preferences, it became a nonprofit organization in the 1970s and has been controlled by a small board of directors made up of wealthy business owners ever since. The NFIB pays its top officers several hundred thousand dollars a year to manage 700 employees and a $170 million budget. In 2012 its president, a former lobbyist for the steel industry, who was employed by the Reagan administration before joining the organization in the early 1990s, earned $743,000.

The organization's 14-member board includes several directors that fit the image of a small-business, such as the owner of a generator repair service in Austin, Texas, with 10 to 20 employees; a member of the family that owns a printing and mailing company in Quincy, Illinois; an accountant in a small town in South Carolina that has her own firm; and a family-owned temporary staffing firm with five offices in Seattle. However, the board also has a multimillionaire aspect to it, such as the chair of the NFIB board, who owns one of the largest independent office supply companies in the country and serves as the vice-chair of the board of Virginia Commerce Bank, which had 30 offices in the Washington metropolitan area in 2011.

Another director of considerable wealth is the chief financial officer of her family's inherited plastering and drywall company, which works with the developers of commercial buildings in the Washington area; another works with her physician brother and her husband, a successful investor, to run one of the largest chains of independent cancer treatment centers in California; and still another had $17 million from venture capitalists to found a company that sells data-storage equipment to medium-sized businesses. Finally, the president of his family-owned and managed food business had 1,500 employees and $250 million in sales in 2011, making it one of nearly 18,000 "small businesses" with 500 or more employees, which account for over half of the employees in all the companies that claim to be small businesses (Small Business Administration 2006, Table 7).

The NFIB had 350,000 members in 2011, less than 2 percent of all small businesses. New members are recruited by traveling sales representatives, who receive a commission for each new member they sign up, but the organization has not been able to grow because there is a 20 percent turnover in membership each year. The NFIB conducts periodic surveys of its members to determine their policy preferences on key issues, but only 20 percent of the surveys are returned each time. The results are then put forth as representative of small business, even though they are usually far more conservative than what is known to be the case from general surveys of small-business owners, who often share the political views of their community or ethnic group (Hamilton 1975, Chapter 7; Kazee, Lipsky, and Martin 2008). In a survey in 2008 of small-business owners with 100 or fewer employees, approximately one-third said they were Republicans, one-third said they were Democrats, and 29 percent said they had no party affiliation, but over 90 percent of the NFIB's campaign donations went to Republicans between 1989 and 2010, even though the organization claims to be nonpartisan (Mandelbaum 2009).

In reality, then, the NFIB is a very potent ultraconservative lobbying organization, which draws most of its leadership and staff from the Republican Party and works closely with other ultraconservative organizations in financing conservative Republican candidates at the state and congressional levels (CMD 2012b; Olson 2006; Shaiko and Wallace 1999). Drawing in good part on large donations from a secretive Republican political action committee (PAC) called American Crossroads GPS, funded by anonymous donations, the NFIB gave over 98 percent of its campaign contributions to Republicans in 2011–2012 (CMD 2012b).

Contrary to the image projected by the NFIB, the small businesses that go beyond the part-time and one-person levels are most often part of trade associations that receive most of their funding and direction from large corporations. They are also part of the two largest general business organizations in the country, the U.S. Chamber of Commerce, which claims over 180,000 companies and 2,800 state and local chambers as members, and the National Association of Manufacturers, which claims 12,500 companies and their subsidiaries as members. These are figures that go well beyond the several hundred companies in the corporate community and the 18,000 companies with 500 or more employees.

Moreover, many small businesses are part of economic networks that have large corporations at the center. The most visible and long-standing examples of small businesses that are part of large corporations are the 747,000 franchise businesses that sell products and services to the general public—convenience stores, fast-food outlets, mall shops, automobile repair shops, and many more (IFA 2012). As for the small manufacturing companies that are sometimes claimed to be major sources of innovation and new jobs, they are often dependent upon their sales of parts and services to large corporations, making them unlikely counterweights to the corporate community. The fact that many of these firms start with 100 or more employees suggests the importance of subcontracts from bigger businesses for their existence and survival; in reality, they are often spin-offs from large corporations attempting to shed unionized workers or obtain a tax break.

Not all small manufacturing firms are directly tied to large corporations, however. Many are part of what one author calls "the minor industrial revolution" that brought small firms into southern states in search of low-wage, nonunionized labor (Browne, Skees, Swanson, Thompson, and Unnevehr 1992, p. 24). Still others owe their origins to discoveries and patents that were developed in large universities, especially in the electronics and biotechnology industries.

When all is said and done, then, there is no "small business community" in the United States to provide any opposition to the corporate community. The relatively few small businesses that are full-time operations and have more than a handful of employees are incorporated into the power networks of the corporate community (1) by belonging to trade associations dominated by larger businesses; (2) as franchise outlets for larger businesses; and (3) as suppliers and service providers for big corporations. These ties place severe market and political constraints on most small businesses in relation to the large corporations. Small business is too fragmented to be a counterweight to the several thousand businesses that control a little over 50 percent of total business assets.

LOCAL BUSINESSES FORM GROWTH COALITIONS

The most important small businesses in the United States are organized into local *growth coalitions*. Members of this coalition share a common interest in intensifying land use in their geographical locale, starting with landowners, developers, and building contractors. Executives from local banks, gas and electric companies, and department stores are part of the growth coalitions as well because they have a strong stake in the growth of the local community. These land-based businesses are not directly involved in the main topic of this book, power at the national level, except in their quest for subsidies through the special-interest process and their support for the spending coalition in Congress on issues concerning urban infrastructure. However, it is useful to consider them briefly in order to understand the complexities of the ownership class and to see the political openings that are created for progressive activists by the occasional conflicts between the corporate community and the growth coalitions, especially on environmental issues. They are also of interest because they are the primary supporters of candidates for local and state offices, and for the House of Representatives as well in large urban areas.

In economic terms, the *place entrepreneurs* at the heart of local growth coalitions are trying to maximize *rents* from land and buildings, which is a little different from the goal of the corporate community, namely, maximizing profits from the sale of goods and services. To emphasize this difference, the concept of rents includes purchases of land and buildings as well as payments that tenants or homebuyers make to landlords, realtors, mortgage lenders, and title companies (Logan and Molotch 2007). More generally, local growth coalitions and the corporate community are different *segments* of the ownership class, meaning that as owners of property and employers of wage labor they are in the same economic class and therefore share more in common with each other than they do with nonowners. The main basis for their cooperation in the past was the fact that the best way for a local growth coalition to intensify land use was to attract corporate investments to its area. The place entrepreneurs were therefore very much attuned to the needs of corporations, working hard to provide them with the physical infrastructure, municipal services, labor markets, and political climate they find attractive. The growth caused by corporate investments, along with investments by universities and government agencies, lead to housing development, increased financial activity, and increased consumer spending, all of which make land and buildings even more valuable.

Still, the relationship between the growth coalitions and the corporate community is not without its conflicts. This is first of all because corporations have the ability to move if they think that regulations are becoming too stringent or taxes and wages too high. The departure of major corporations, which became an increasingly frequent occurrence beginning in the 1970s, has a devastating impact on growth coalitions. Moreover, this ability to move contributes to the constant competition among rival cities for new capital investments, thereby creating tensions among growth coalitions as well as between individual growth coalitions and the corporate community. The net result is often a "race to the bottom" as cities offer tax breaks, less environmental regulation, and other benefits to corporations in order to tempt them to relocate. Ironically, most studies of plant location suggest that environmental laws and local taxes are of minor importance in corporate decisions concerning the location or relocation of production facilities. A union-free environment and low-cost raw materials are the major factors (Bluestone and Harrison 1982; Dreier, Mollenkopf, and Swanstrom 2004).

The longest conflict between the corporate community and local growth coalitions concerns the issue of clean air. From as early as the 1890s local growth coalitions in major cities like Chicago tried to force railroads and manufacturers to control the air pollution problems that developed due to steam engines and smokestacks, but their efforts usually failed in the face of the corporate community's superior power. It was not until Pittsburgh and Los Angeles began to suffer serious blackouts and smog in the 1940s and 1950s that the growth coalitions were able to have some success in these battles, leading to statewide organizations and legislation in California that began to mitigate some of the worst conditions. These conflicts between the corporate community and the growth coalitions are especially notable because they are one basis for the environmental movement that emerged in the 1960s, which capitalized on this disagreement within the ownership class (Gonzalez 2005). Moreover, the concerns of urban landowners were soon shared by suburban homeowners, who saw DDT spraying, threats to the safety of drinking water, and smog as hazardous to their health, turning them into a strong base for the environmental movement by the second half of the 1960s (Sellers 2012).

Local growth coalitions face still another source of potential tension and conflict aside from corporate departures and competition with the growth coalitions in other cities: disagreements with neighborhoods about expansion and development. Neighborhoods are something to be used and enjoyed in the eyes of those who live in them, but neighborhoods are often seen as sites for further development by growth coalitions, which justify new developments with the doctrine of "the highest and best use for land." Thus, neighborhoods often end up fighting against freeways, wider streets, high-rises, and commercial buildings. This conflict becomes the axis of local politics when the downtown interests try to expand the central business district, often at the expense of nearby established low-income neighborhoods, or to build large freeways to encourage suburban dwellers to make use of the downtown area. This kind of expansionist, land-clearing strategy contributed greatly to inner-city tensions from the 1960s onward because African Americans, who were the most frequently displaced group, could not readily find housing in white neighborhoods, forcing them into crowded tenements with high rents and few amenities. The expansion of elite private universities located in urban areas, starting with the University of Chicago and Yale University, continue to contribute to these tensions by buying up housing near their campuses and then taking the land off the tax rolls (Domhoff 2005b; Rossi and Dentler 1961).

The success rate of neighborhoods in conflicts with the growth coalitions is very low. Since the primary focus of residents is on their everyday lives, they usually do not persist in their protests and seldom join larger coalitions with other neighborhoods in the city. There were, however, a few exceptions in the last three decades of the twentieth century, including Burlington in Vermont and Santa Monica in California, along with influential efforts in Berkeley, Boston, Chicago, and San Francisco that generated some changes as well as major counterattacks by leaders of the growth coalitions (Clavel 2010; Domhoff 2005a). Perhaps the most long-lasting and successful effort occurred in Santa Cruz, California, where a coalition of neighborhood leaders, greatly aided by activists from rent control, women's health, socialist-feminist, and environmental organizations, joined with the student voters on the University of California campus located in the city to stop every development proposed by the city's tourist-oriented growth coalition after 1969. The Santa Cruz progressives then won control of city government from 1981 to 2010, instituting numerous small changes aimed at improving the quality of everyday life, while at the same time being blocked in their attempts at larger changes, such as selling home insurance to local homeowners, by pro-growth coalition legislators at the state level (Gendron and Domhoff 2009). (For further information on Santa Cruz and other cities in which neighborhood-based coalitions had an impact between 1960 and 2010, see the documents "Power at the Local Level: Growth Coalition Theory" and "Santa Cruz: The Leftmost City" on whorulesamerica.net.)

STRUCTURAL POWER AND ITS LIMITS

What does all this mean in terms of corporate power? First, the major national-level businesses in the United States are closely interconnected in enough ways to be called a corporate community. Despite the constant competition and deal-making among them, which can lead to intense and long-lasting disagreements and personal animosities, the corporate community is able to maintain cohesion on its common interests through the main organizations that bring it together—the National Association of Manufacturers, the Conference Board, the U.S. Chamber of Commerce, the Business Council, the Committee for Economic Development, and the Business Roundtable. Second, none of the other economic interests discussed in this chapter—small farmers, small businesses, and local growth coalitions—provide the organizational base for any significant opposition to the corporate community at the national level. Third, the directors of the companies in the corporate community, through their numerous interactions at board meetings and in business associations, provide the basis for a cohesive corporate leadership group to emerge.

Corporate leaders exercise a considerable amount of direct power through the way in which they carry out their business operations. For example, they can invest their money when and where they choose. If they feel threatened by new laws or labor unions, they can move or close their factories and offices. Unless restrained by union contracts, they can hire, promote, and replace workers as they see fit, often laying off thousands of employees on a moment's notice. These economic powers give them a direct influence over the vast majority of Americans, who are dependent upon wages and salaries for their incomes and therefore hesitant to challenge corporations directly. Economic power also gives the corporate community indirect influence over elected and appointed officials because the growth and stability of a city, county, or state can be jeopardized by a lack of private investment and job creation.

In short, the sheer economic power of the corporate community often can influence government without any effort on the part of corporate leaders. Because business owner have the legal right to spend their money when and as they wish, and government officials are hesitant to take over the function of investing funds to create jobs, unless it is a time of extreme economic crisis, the government generally has to cater to business. If government officials do not give corporate leaders what they want, there might be economic difficulties that would lead people to desire new political leadership. Since most government officials do not want to lose their positions, they do what they think is necessary to satisfy business leaders and maintain a healthy economy (Lindblom 1977).

Corporate control over the investment function, in conjunction with the right to close factories and lay off workers, provides leaders within the corporate community with a *structural power*, derived from the way in which the economy normally functions, that is independent of any attempts by them to influence government officials directly. While such power is very great, it is not sufficient in and of itself to allow the corporate rich to dominate government, especially in times of economic or political crisis. First, it does not preclude the possibility that government officials might turn to nonbusiness constituencies to support new economic arrangements. For example, there is no necessary relationship between private ownership and markets. Improbable though it may seem to most readers, it is possible for governments to create firms to compete in the market system and thereby revive a depressed economy by giving them money to invest, or to hire unemployed workers in order to increase their ability to spend. In fact, the liberal-labor alliance mounted a legislative effort of roughly this sort shortly after World War II, only to be defeated by the conservative coalition in Congress (Bailey 1950; Domhoff 1990, Chapter 7).

Second, structural power does not guarantee that employees will accept an ongoing economic depression without taking over factories or destroying private property. In such situations, the corporate leaders need government to protect their factories and equipment. They have to be able to call on the government to keep unauthorized persons from entering their plants or to eject workers who refuse to vacate the premises. Just such a situation developed seemingly out of the blue in Chicago in December 2008, when workers refused to leave the Republic Windows and Doors factory (which had been shut down without any notice so it could be moved to a low-wage location in another state) until they were given the severance and vacation pay the company owed them. They also decided not to allow the company to remove the windows they had built over the previous weeks because keeping possession of the windows gave them a bargaining chip.

City officials in Chicago expressed sympathy for the workers, as did President-elect Obama. The city's mayor, Richard M. Daley, did not order the police to force the workers to vacate the premises. The Bank of America, which had just received a $25 billion bailout from the federal government to stave off potential bankruptcy, refused to loan the company the money to make the final payments to the fired employees, but it quickly changed its mind as an outcry developed (Luo and Cullotta 2008). It also turned out that JPMorgan Chase, by then the largest bank in the country, owned 40 percent of the company and agreed to help provide the money owed to the former employees. JPMorgan Chase's chairman for the Midwest region, William M. Daley, the brother of Chicago's mayor and an early backer of President Obama, encouraged a settlement that would end the highly publicized sit-down strike. (Three years later, William M. Daley served as President Obama's White House chief of staff for a year.)

As the sit-down at Republic Windows and Doors clearly demonstrates, structural power primarily concerns the relationship between the corporate community and government officials. It is not able to contain a volatile power conflict between owners and workers, which means that powerful banks and their well-connected executives, such as William M. Daley in this case, have to work out a peaceful settlement if a local government is not willing to employ repressive measures to end a strike. Nor do such confrontations always remain nonviolent in the United States, starting with a strike in 1877 by angry railroad workers in the face of a sudden and unannounced wage cut. The clash that soon followed left over 100 people dead, mostly at the hands of 3,000 federal troops that moved from city to city via train trying to quell the disturbances. Twenty people died in Pittsburgh alone, where angry mobs retaliated against the government's use of violence on them by looting and burning 39 buildings, 104 locomotives, 46 passenger cars, and 1,200 freight cars owned by the Pennsylvania Railroad (Stowell 1999).

The deaths and property destruction were not as extensive during the upheavals of the 1930s, but 15 strikers were killed in 1933 and 40 in 1934, and there were 477 sit-down strikes in 1937 in demand of union recognition (Fine 1969; Piven 2006, p. 88). Significantly, many of those sit-down strikes were carried out by the United Electrical, Radio, and Machine Workers, the same union that decades later represented the workers at Republic Windows and Doors in Chicago, which shows that traditions and organizational memories from the turbulent 1930s still endure as part of working-class culture.

As these examples make clear, there is uncertainty in the relationship between the corporate community and government because there is no guarantee that the underlying population or government officials will accept the viewpoint of corporate owners under all economic circumstances. It is risky for corporate officials to refuse to invest in an attempt to bend government to its will, or to remain passive in the face of an economic depression. Corporate leaders know from past history and from sudden actions such as the one by workers at Republic Windows and Doors that they have to do one of three things. They have to decide if they want to bargain directly with disgruntled employees, encourage the government to make reforms, or call for the use of the police to put down unrest. That is, they have a choice between peaceful compromises and repression. They therefore believe that they need ways to have an influence on both public opinion and government officials, and they have developed a number of organizations in an effort to realize those objectives. As a top corporate leader replied to a sociologist who suggested to him during a research interview that his company probably had enough structural power to dispense with its efforts to influence elected officials: "I'm not sure, but I'm not willing to find out" (Clawson, Neustadtl, and Scott 1992, p. 121).

To fully explain how the owners and top-level managers are able to organize themselves in an effort to create new policies, shape public opinion, elect politicians they trust, and influence government officials, it is first necessary to examine the relationship between the corporate community and the social upper class.

3

The Corporate Community and the Upper Class

This chapter demonstrates that the corporate community and the upper class are closely intertwined. They are not quite two sides of the same coin, but almost. Such a demonstration is important for three reasons. First, it refutes the widely accepted belief that there has been a separation between corporate ownership and control in the United States. According to this view, there is on the one side a wealthy but powerless upper class that is more or less window dressing, consisting of playboys and fashion plates, and on the other a "managerial class" that has power independent of wealthy owners by virtue of its role in running corporations. Due to this division between high-society owners and well-trained independent managers, the argument continues, there is no longer a dominant social class whose general interest in profits transcends the fate of any one corporation or business sector. Instead, corporate managers are reduced to an "interest group," albeit a very potent one.

Contrary to this view, the evidence presented in the final third of this chapter shows that (1) members of the upper class own a large share of the privately held corporate stock; (2) many superwealthy stockholding families in the upper class continue to be involved in the direction of major corporations through family offices, various types of investment partnerships, and holding companies; and (3) the professional managers of middle-level origins are assimilated into the upper class both socially and economically, and share the values of upper-class owners.

Evidence for the overlap of the corporate community and the upper class is important for a second reason in building the case for a class-dominance perspective: Research in social psychology shows that the most socially cohesive groups are the ones that do best in arriving at consensus when dealing with a problem. The members are proud of their identification with the group and come to trust one another through their friendly interactions, so they are more likely to listen to one another and seek common ground. As a classic study of the upper class in New York in the 1930s concluded: "The elaborate private life of the plutocracy serves in considerable measure to separate them out in their own consciousness as a superior, more refined element" (Almond 1998, p. 108).

Social cohesion develops through the two types of relationships found in a membership network: common membership in specific social institutions and friendships based on social interactions within those institutions. Research on small groups in laboratory settings suggests that social cohesion is greatest when (1) the social groups are seen to be exclusive and of high status and (2) the interactions take place in relaxed and informal settings (Cartwright and Zander 1968; Hogg 1992). This chapter shows that many of the social institutions of the upper class provide settings and occasions that fit these specifications very well. From the viewpoint of social psychology, the people who make up the upper class can be seen as members of numerous small groups that meet at private schools, social clubs, retreats, resorts, and social gatherings.

Finally, the fact that the corporate community is closely linked to the upper class adds to a class-dominance analysis because their close ties make it possible to convert economic power into *status power*. Status power operates by creating respect, envy, and deference in others, making them more likely to accept what members of the upper class tell them. Although the more extravagant social activities of the upper class—the expensive parties, the jet-setting to spas and vacation spots all over the world, the involvement with exotic entertainers—are in most ways superfluous trivialities when it comes to the exercise of power, these activities nonetheless can play an inadvertent role in reinforcing the class structure. They make clear that there is a gulf between members of the upper class and ordinary citizens, reminding everyone of the hierarchical nature of the society. They reinforce the point that there are great rewards for business success, helping to stir up the personal envy that can be a goad to competitive striving. For example, in a pamphlet meant for students as part of an economics education initiative, the Federal Reserve Board in Minneapolis specifically wrote that large income differentials in the United States have "possible external benefits" because they provide "incentives for those who are at low- to middle-income levels to work hard, attain more education, and advance to better-paying jobs" (Morris 2004).

So, to the degree that the rest of the population tries to emulate the upper class or defers to it, economic power has been transformed into status power, creating a social psychology of justified entitlement and demand for respect in members of the upper class and a social psychology of envy and deference in those who are outside the charmed circle. However, the importance of status power must not be overstated. In times of social upheaval, respect and deference are often replaced by angry outbursts and mass action, especially if the social upheaval is blamed on members of the upper class.

IS THERE AN AMERICAN UPPER CLASS?

If the owners and managers of large income-producing properties in the United States are also a social upper class, then it should be possible to discover a very large network of interrelated social institutions whose overlapping members are primarily wealthy families and high-level corporate leaders. These institutions should provide patterned ways of organizing the lives of their members from infancy to old age and create a relatively unique style of life. In addition, they should provide settings for socializing both the younger generation and new adult members who have risen from lower social levels. If the class is a sociological reality, the names and faces may change somewhat over the years, but the social institutions that underlie the upper class—the organizations, rules, and customary practices that pattern social order—must persist with only gradual change over several generations.

Four different types of empirical studies carried out several decades ago established the existence of such an interrelated set of social institutions and social activities in the United States, to the point that few social scientists have felt the need to do further studies in recent years: historical case studies, quantitative studies of biographical directories, open-ended surveys of knowledgeable observers, and interview studies with members of the upper-middle and upper classes. Taken together, they suggest that the upper class includes somewhat less than 1 percent of the population, but for purposes of this book the figure 1 percent will be used to keep mathematical analyses simple. These studies not only demonstrate the existence of an American upper class. They also provide what are called "indicators" of upper-class standing, which are useful in determining the degree of overlap between the upper class and the corporate community, or between the upper class and various types of nonprofit organizations. Social indicators can be used to determine the amount of involvement members of the upper class have in various parts of the government as well.

In the first major historical case study, the wealthy families of Philadelphia were traced over the period of 200 years, showing how they created their own neighborhoods, schools, clubs, and debutante balls. Then their activities outside of that city were determined, which demonstrated that there are nationwide social institutions wherein wealthy people from all over the country interact with each other (Baltzell 1958). This study led to the discovery of an upper-class telephone directory called the *Social Register*, published for 13 large cities from Boston to San Francisco between 1887 and 1975. The guide to the 13 city volumes, the *Social Register Locator*, contained about 60,000 families, which made it a very valuable indicator of upper-class standing until many members of the upper class lost interest in it in the 1970s. This loss of interest reminds us that customs can change in the upper class, just as they do in other classes, and that there is always a need for new studies.

Using information on private school attendance and club membership that appeared in 3,000 randomly selected *Who's Who in America* biographies, along with listings in the *Social Register*, another study provided a statistical analysis of the patterns of memberships and affiliations among dozens of prep schools and clubs. The findings from this study are very similar to those from the historical case study (Domhoff 1970, Chapter 1). Still another study asked journalists who cover upper-class social events to serve as informed observers by identifying the schools, clubs, and social directories that defined the highest level of society in their city. The replies from these well-placed informants revealed strong agreement with the findings from the historical and statistical studies (Domhoff 1970, Chapter 1).

A fourth and final method of establishing the existence of upper-class institutions is based on intensive interviews with a cross-section of citizens. The most detailed study of this type was conducted in Kansas City. The study concerned people's perceptions of the social ladder as a whole, from top to bottom, but it is the top level that is of relevance here. Although most people in Kansas City can point to the existence of exclusive neighborhoods in suggesting that there is a class of "blue bloods" or "big rich," it is members of the upper-middle class and the upper class itself whose reports demonstrate that clubs and similar social institutions, as well as neighborhoods, give the class an institutional existence separate from most of the well-trained professionals and successful small-business owners who are part of the upper-middle class (Coleman, Rainwater, and McClelland 1978). (The specific schools and clubs discovered by these and related investigations are listed in the document on "How to Do Power Structure Research" on whorulesamerica.net, but with the caveat that the list needs to be updated to include new schools and clubs if it is to reflect current realities.)

Although the social indicators derived from these studies are a useful tool for research purposes, they are far from perfect for any specific individual. They are subject to two different kinds of errors that tend to cancel each other out with large samples. *False positives* are those people who qualify as members of the upper class according to the indicators, even though further investigation would show that they are not really members. Middle-class and scholarship students at private secondary schools are two examples of false positives. Honorary and performing members of social clubs, who usually are members of the middle class, are another important type of false positive. *False negatives*, on the other hand, are members of the upper class who do not seem to meet any of the criteria of upper-class standing because they do not choose to list their private school or their club affiliations in biographical sources and shun social registries.

Private schools are especially underreported in publicly available biographical sources. Many prominent political figures do not list their private secondary schools in *Who's Who in America*, for example, and future president George H. W. Bush, who held the office between 1989 and 1992, removed Phillips

Andover, the boarding school he attended, from the 1980–1981 edition when he became vice president in the Reagan administration. More generally, studies comparing private school alumni lists with *Who's Who* listings suggest that 40 to 50 percent of corporate officers and directors did not list their graduation from high-prestige private schools in the 1960s and 1970s. Membership in social clubs may also go unreported. In a study of the 326 members of the Bohemian Club in San Francisco who were listed in *Who's Who in America*, 29 percent did not include this affiliation, including presidents Reagan and George H. W. Bush (Domhoff 1983, p. 48). Based on a study of club listings by corporate leaders between the early 1960s and 1996, which showed a considerable decline in the number of clubs mentioned, it is very likely that the percentage who do not mention their social clubs is even higher today (Barnes and Sweezea 2006).

The factors leading to false positives and false negatives raise interesting sociological questions, some of which are given tentative answers in this chapter. Why are scholarship students sought by some private schools, and are such students likely to become part of the upper class? Why don't some members of the upper class list private schools and clubs in biographical sources? Why are some middle-class people taken into upper-class clubs? Merely to ask these questions is to suggest the complex social and psychological reality that lies beneath this seemingly dry catalogue of upper-class indicators. More generally, the information included or excluded in a social register or biographical directory is a *presentation of self* that has been shown to be revealing concerning religious, ethnic, and class identifications (e.g., Zweigenhaft and Domhoff 1982, pp. 92–97).

PREPPING FOR POWER

From infancy through young adulthood, members of the upper class receive a distinctive education. This education begins early in life in preschools that sometimes are attached to a neighborhood church of high social status. Schooling continues during the elementary years at a local private school called a day school. The adolescent years may see the student remain at day school, but there is a strong chance that at least one or two years will be spent away from home at a boarding school in a quiet rural setting. Higher education is obtained at one of a small number of prestigious private universities. Although some upper-class children may attend public high school if they live in a high-status suburb, or go to a state university if there is one of great esteem and tradition in their home state, the system of formal schooling is so insulated that many upper-class students never see the inside of a public school in all their years of education. This separate educational system is important evidence for the distinctiveness of the mentality and lifestyle that exists within the upper class, because schools play a large role in transmitting the class structure to their students (Cookson and Persell 1985; Khan 2010).

The linchpins in the upper-class educational system are the dozens of boarding schools developed in the last half of the nineteenth and the early part of the twentieth centuries, coincident with the rise of a nationwide upper class whose members desired to insulate themselves from inner cities that were becoming populated by lower-class immigrants. These schools become surrogate families that play a major role in creating a national upper-class subculture. The role of boarding schools in providing connections to other upper-class social institutions is also important. As one informant explained to a sociologist doing an interview study of upper-class women: "Where I went to boarding school, there were girls from all over the country, so I know people from all over. It's helpful when you move to a new city and want to get invited into the local social club" (Ostrander 1984, p. 85).

It is within these several hundred schools that a unique style of life is inculcated through such traditions as the initiatory hazing of beginning students, the wearing of school blazers or ties, and participation in esoteric sports such as lacrosse, squash, and crew. Even a different language is adopted to distinguish these schools from public schools. The principal is a headmaster or rector, the teachers are sometimes called masters, and the students are in forms, not grades. Great emphasis is placed upon the building of "character." The role of the school in preparing the future leaders of America is emphasized through the speeches of the headmaster and the frequent mention of successful alumni. Thus, boarding schools are in many ways the kind of highly effective socializing agent called *total institutions*, isolating their members from the outside world and providing them with a set of routines and traditions that encompass most of their waking hours. The end result is a feeling of separateness and superiority that comes from having survived a rigorous education.

Virtually all graduates of private secondary schools go on to college, and most do so at prestigious universities. Graduates of the New England boarding schools, for example, historically found themselves at three or four large Ivy League universities: Harvard, Yale, Princeton, and Columbia. However, that situation changed somewhat after World War II as the universities grew and provided more scholarships. An analysis of admission patterns for graduates of 14 prestigious boarding schools between 1953 and 1967 demonstrated this shift by showing that the percentage of their graduates attending Harvard, Yale, or Princeton gradually declined over those years from 52 to 25 percent. Information on the same 14 schools for the years 1969 to 1979 showed that the figure had bottomed out at 13 percent in 1973, 1975, and 1979 (Cookson and Persell 1985; Gordon 1969).

Since that time, private schools have more than held their own in sending their graduates to Harvard, Yale, and Princeton, as revealed by enterprising journalists, the first of whom ferreted out the 100 high schools that sent the highest percentage of their students to one of those three Ivy League schools between 1998 and 2001. She found that 94 of the 100 were private schools, with 10 that sent more than 15 percent of their students to Harvard, Yale, or Princeton, including such high-status boarding schools as Groton (17.9 percent), Milton Academy (15.8 percent), and Andover (15.7 percent). The difference from the past is that more of the most successful schools are day schools and are located in New York City. For example, Brearley, a girls' school in New York City, had a "Harvard/Yale/Princeton" percentage of 20.9 and the Collegiate School for boys in the same city had a Harvard/Yale/Princeton percentage of 20.0 (Yaqub 2002). A second journalist used admissions to several Ivy League schools, MIT, and Stanford in addition to Harvard, Yale, and Princeton as her criteria for success. She found that 20 private schools, most of them boarding schools whose histories stretch back over 100 years, along with day schools in Boston, Los Angeles, and New York, had an "Ivy/MIT/Stanford pipeline" percentage that ranged from 23 to 41 percent, with an average of about 33 percent (Laneri 2010).

Most private school graduates pursue careers in business, finance, or corporate law, which is further evidence for the close relationship between the upper class and the corporate community. Their business-oriented preoccupations are demonstrated in the greatest detail in a study of all those who graduated from Hotchkiss between 1940 and 1950. Using the school's alumni files, the researcher followed the careers of 228 graduates from their date of graduation until 1970. Fifty-six percent of the sample were either bankers or business executives, with 80 of the 91 businessmen serving as president, vice president, or partner in their firms. Another 10 percent of the sample were lawyers, mostly as partners in large firms closely affiliated with the corporate community (Armstrong 1974).

Due to special recruitment programs, private schools have become a major educational launching pad for a small percentage of low-income African American and Latino students, who frequently go on to graduate from elite universities and work in the corporate world or one of the high-status professions. They are ideal examples of the usefulness of "false positives" (graduates of an elite private school who are not members of the upper class) in understanding the American power structure, because they lead to the discovery that major foundations and wealthy donors have established programs that provide opportunities that allow for a small amount of sponsored upward social mobility. The oldest of these programs, A Better Chance, founded in the 1960s in response to the upheavals of the civil rights movement, had graduated over 12,000 students by 2011 and had 1,900 students—65 percent African American, 20 percent Latino, 6 percent Asian American, 4 percent multiracial, and 4 percent "other"—enrolled in over 300 member schools. The Prep-to-Prep program in New York City and the Steppingstone Foundation in Boston and Philadelphia, both of more recent vintage, have developed programs that identify high-achieving children of color in grade school and help prepare them for private schools with after-school, weekend, and summer instruction. By 2011, 92 percent of Prep-to-Prep's 1,828 students had graduated from "competitive" colleges and about 40 percent from Ivy League schools. The schools with the most graduates were Harvard with 171, Wesleyan with 168, Yale with 148, and Penn with 147 (Zweigenhaft and Domhoff 2011, pp. 123–127).

Deval Patrick, elected as the first African American governor of Massachusetts in 2006 after a long career in corporate law and corporate management, is among the most visible graduates of one of these programs. Raised by his mother in a low-income neighborhood in Chicago, he went to Milton Academy in Milton, Massachusetts, in 1970 as a scholarship student in the A Better Chance program, and then graduated from Harvard and Harvard Law School. He worked for the NAACP's Legal and Educational Defense Fund for three years and joined a prestigious corporate law firm in Boston. From 1994 to 1997 he served in the Clinton administration as the assistant attorney general in charge of the Civil Rights Division of the Department of Justice, then chaired a task force created to ensure fairness and equal opportunity for employees at Texaco after the settlement of a racial discrimination suit. From there it was an executive vice presidency at Coca-Cola from 2001 to 2004. He has served as a corporate director for United Airlines and Reebok. He was an early supporter of Barack Obama's presidential campaign.

However, the most important false positive in terms of private school graduates is President Barack Obama himself, who attended Punahou School in Honolulu, one of the 10 wealthiest private schools in the country, from the fifth through the 12th grades, even though he is not a member of the upper class. He was able to attend Punahou because his maternal grandfather, a furniture salesman, and his maternal grandmother, one of the first female vice presidents in a large Honolulu bank, wanted him to have a good education. In addition, his grandfather's employer, an alumnus of the school, urged the admissions office to accept him (Mendell 2007, p.36). As a result the future president spent eight years mingling with the children of wealthy business leaders and highly educated professionals (90 percent of the students were white) while receiving an excellent education in a setting very similar to prep schools elsewhere in the country. With its impressive theaters and buildings, situated on several acres of green fields surrounded by a fence, largely out of the public view, Punahou is "so idyllic that it resembled a Hollywood set" according to the *Chicago Tribune* reporter who visited the school as part of his research on a biography he wrote of President Obama (Mendell 2007, p. 37).

In addition to an ideal college preparatory education from a school that stands for quality and class in the eyes of college admissions officers, the future president developed valuable "connections" with individuals who possess wealth and other resources. Such connections are now called *social capital* by sociologists because wealthy friends and their parents can be helpful in many ways, such as putting in a good word with an employer, passing on useful information about investment opportunities, or even lending money for an investment. Perhaps even more important, President Obama acquired the style and tastes of the upper class, now called *cultural capital*, because the right sensibilities can be useful in creating a sense of ease and familiarity when meeting members of the upper class (Bourdieu 1986; Khan 2010).

In other words, President Obama's status as a false positive on one upper-class indicator provides useful information on why the son of a Kenyan father (whom he last saw at age 10, for a month, after an eight-year absence) and a white mother (who worked in Indonesia as an anthropologist during his childhood and teen years) could think about a political career. Punahou provided him with the social and cultural capital to interact with members of the corporate community and social upper class in a relaxed and graceful way, and take the possibility of a business or professional career for granted. (In the first year after he finished his undergraduate education at Columbia University he worked for Business International Corporation in Manhattan, which published newsletters on the global economy and provided consulting services to American companies with international operations [Mendell 2007, p. 62].)

Like many private school graduates who decide to pursue a career in politics, President Obama does not list his school in his biographical sketch in *Who's Who in America*. President John F. Kennedy never listed his graduation from Choate Rosemary in Connecticut, and every candidate for president in the first 12 years of the twenty-first century was a graduate of an elite prep school who did not mention that fact. George W. Bush, the Republican candidate in 2004 and 2008, graduated from Andover in Massachusetts. Former vice president Albert Gore, the Democratic candidate for president in 2000, graduated from St. Albans in Washington, D.C. Senator John Kerry of Massachusetts, the Democratic candidate in 2004, graduated from St. Paul's in Massachusetts. Senator John McCain of Arizona, the Republican candidate in 2008, graduated from Episcopal High in Virginia, and Mitt Romney, the Republican candidate in 2012, graduated from Cranbrook School in Michigan.

SOCIAL CLUBS

Private social clubs are a major point of orientation in the social lives of upper-class adults. These clubs also have a role in differentiating members of the upper class from other members of society, in particular those who are "merely" upper-middle class. The clubs of the upper class are many and varied, ranging from family-oriented country clubs and downtown men's and women's clubs to highly specialized clubs for yachtsmen, sportsmen, gardening enthusiasts, and fox hunters. Downtown men's clubs originally were places to have lunch and dinner, and occasionally to attend an evening performance or a weekend party. As upper-class families deserted the city for large suburban estates, a new kind of club, the country club, gradually took over some of these functions. The downtown club became almost entirely a luncheon club, a site to hold meetings, or a place to relax on a free afternoon. The country club, by contrast, became a haven for all members of the family. It offered social and sporting activities ranging from dances, parties, and banquets to golf, swimming, and tennis. Special group dinners were often arranged for all members on Thursday night, the traditional maid's night off across the United States.

Initiation fees, annual dues, and expenses vary from a few thousand dollars in downtown clubs to $100,000 to $250,00 or more in some country clubs, but money is not the only barrier in gaining membership to a club. Each club has a very rigorous screening process before accepting new members. Most require nomination by one or more active members, letters of recommendation from three to six members, and interviews with at least some members of the membership committee (Kendall 2002). Negative votes by two or three members of what is typically a 10-to 20-person committee often are enough to deny admission to the candidate.

Men and women of the upper class often belong to clubs in several cities, creating a nationwide pattern of overlapping memberships. These overlaps provide evidence for social cohesion within the upper class. An indication of the nature and extent of this overlapping is revealed in a study of 20 clubs in several major cities across the country in the late 1960s, when membership lists were more readily available, including the Links Club in New York, the Chicago Club in Chicago, the Pacific Union Club in San Francisco, and the California Club in Los Angeles. There was sufficient overlap among 18 of the 20 clubs to form three regional groupings and a fourth group that provided a bridge between the two largest regional groups. The several dozen men in three or more of the clubs, most of them very wealthy people who sat on several corporate boards, were especially important in creating the overall pattern. The fact that these clubs often have from 1,000 to 2,000 members made the percentage of overlap within this small number of clubs relatively small, ranging from a high of 20 to 30 percent between clubs in the same city to as low as 1 or 2 percent in clubs at opposite ends of the country (Bonacich and Domhoff 1981).

The overlap of this club network with corporate boards of directors provides further evidence for the intertwining of the upper class and the corporate community. In a study in the 1960s for an earlier edition of this book, the club memberships of the chairpersons and outside directors of the 20 largest industrial corporations were counted. The overlaps with upper-class clubs in general were ubiquitous, but the concentration of directors in a few clubs was especially notable. At least one director from 12 of the 20 corporations was a member of the Links Club, which is the New York meeting ground of the national corporate establishment. Seven of General Electric's directors at the time were members, as were four from Chrysler, four from Westinghouse, and three from IBM. In addition to the Links, several other clubs had directors from four or more corporations (Domhoff 1967, p. 26). Another study using membership lists from 11 prestigious clubs in different parts of the country confirmed and extended these findings. A majority of the top 25 corporations in every major sector of the economy had directors in at least one of these clubs, and several had many more. For example, all of the 25 largest industrials had one or more directors in these 11 clubs. The Links in New York, with 79 connections to 21 industrial corporations, had the most (Domhoff 1975).

Elite social clubs came under extreme criticism as bastions of Christian white male privilege in the 1970s, first by wealthy Jewish members of the corporate community, who were incensed by their anti-Semitism, then by civil rights activists that decried the lack of any African American members, and then by feminist groups, which pointed out that the exclusion of women deprived women executives of opportunities to attend business luncheons and develop connections with executives from outside their own workplace (Baltzell 1964; Driscoll and Goldberg 1993; Zweigenhaft and Domhoff 1982). This not only made it more difficult to obtain membership lists for update studies, but it also led to a decline in the listing of membership in such clubs in publicly available sources, such as *Who's Who in America*, because the information was used at confirmation hearings for government appointments to raise questions about the men's fairness. As a result, it has been very difficult to continue to do comprehensive studies on the club network. But a detailed study using *Who's Who in America* for the years 1962, 1973, 1983, and 1995 showed that the corporate executives listed the same clubs over the decades, even though these clubs were mentioned by a declining number of executives in each decade (Barnes and Sweezea 2006).

However, a lack of good membership information has not precluded studies based on other sources of information. For example, a study of social clubs in several Texas cities based on 100 interviews and newspaper articles showed that little if anything has changed in the club world over the decades, except for the huge increase in membership fees and monthly dues for country clubs. The members are still overwhelmingly white Christian men of wealth, wealthy Jews have a parallel club structure, and women are generally excluded from membership, except in country clubs, but they are prohibited from using the clubs' golf course at certain times and excluded from some of the club rooms. The members attach great personal significance to belonging to these clubs and believe they are of value as a source of information, contacts, and support; that is, they remain places to renew social capital. Some clubs have weekend art exhibitions, lecture series, or mini-courses on such topics as "fine wines" that add to the members' cultural capital (Kendall 2008).

An interview study with 47 members of five elite country clubs in a northeastern state that focused on the rationales members used for various forms of exclusionary practices found many of the same patterns. The respondents endorsed greater ethnic and racial diversity, although they were vague about the fact that their clubs had very few minority-group members. Women for the most part accepted their secondary status in country clubs as being due to forces beyond club members' control, such as the fact that they had less wealth and more domestic duties, but some of the women in one of the clubs sued the club because of restrictions on the times they were allowed to play golf (Sherwood 2010). As if to confirm these sociological studies, a rebellious male member of the Phoenix Country Club was expelled from membership in July 2008 for "multiple violations of club etiquette" because he spoke to a *New York Times* reporter about a lawsuit that he and other members had filed against the club for excluding women from the grillroom (Steinhauer 2008).

The Bohemian Grove as a Place of Affirmation and Renewal

One of the central clubs in the club network, the Bohemian Club, is also the most unusual and frequently studied. Its annual two-week retreat in its 2,700-acre Bohemian Grove, 75 miles north of San Francisco, brings together members of the upper class, corporate leaders, celebrities, and government officials for relaxation and entertainment. Several hundred "associate" members, who pay lower dues in exchange for producing plays, skits, artwork, and other forms of entertainment, are also members. There are 50 to 100 professors and university administrators who are members, most of them from Stanford University and campuses of the University of California. This encampment provides a good view of the role of clubs in uniting the corporate community and the upper class. It is a microcosm of the world of the upper class.

Leaders of the Bohemian Club purchased the pristine forest setting called the Bohemian Grove in the 1890s after 20 years of holding the retreat in rented woodland quarters. Bohemians and their guests number anywhere from 1,500 to 2,500 for the three weekends in the encampment, which is always held during the last two weeks in July. However, there may be as few as 400 men in residence in the middle of the week because most return to their homes and jobs after the weekends. During their stay the campers are treated to plays, symphonies, concerts, lectures, and commentaries by entertainers, scholars, corporate executives, and government officials. They also trapshoot, canoe, swim, drop by the Grove art gallery, and take guided tours into the outer fringe of the mountain forest. But a stay at the Bohemian Grove is mostly a time for relaxation in the modest lodges, bunkhouses, and even teepees that fit unobtrusively into the landscape along the two or three dirt roads that join the few "developed" acres within the Grove. It is like a summer camp for corporate leaders and their entertainers. Pranks, story telling, off-color jokes, bragging, and the massive consumption of expensive alcoholic beverages are the order of the day.

The men gather in small camps of 10 to 30 members during their stay, although the camps for the associate members are often larger, a telling reminder of the status differentials that are maintained even during the encampment. Each of the approximately 120 camps has its own pet name, such as Sons of Toil, Pink Onion, Toyland, Woof, and Parsonage. Some camps are noted for special drinking parties, brunches, or luncheons to which they invite members from other camps. One advertises its soft porn collection as an attraction to stop by for a drink. The camps are a fraternity system within the larger fraternity.

There are many traditional events during the encampment, including plays called the High Jinx and the Low Jinx, which sometimes have men dressed as women playing the parts women would take if they were not excluded from the club. The most memorable event, however, is an elaborate ceremonial ritual called the Cremation of Care, which is held on the first Saturday night. It takes place at the base of a 40-foot Owl Shrine, constructed out of poured concrete and made even more resplendent by the mottled forest mosses that cover much of it. According to the club's librarian, who is also a historian at a large university, the event "incorporates druidical ceremonies, elements of medieval Christian liturgy, sequences directly inspired by the Book of Common Prayer, traces of Shakespearean drama and the 17th century masque, and late nineteenth century American lodge rites" (Vaughn 2006). Bohemians were proud that the ceremony has been carried out for 140 consecutive years as of 2012.

The opening ceremony is called the Cremation of Care because it involves the burning of an effigy named Dull Care, who embodies the burdens and responsibilities that these busy Bohemians now wish to shed temporarily. More than 250 Bohemians take part in the ceremony as priests, elders, boatmen, and woodland voices. After many flowery speeches and a long conversation with Dull Care, the high priest lights the fire with the flame from the Lamp of Fellowship, located on the "Altar of Bohemia" at the base of the shrine. The ceremony ends with fireworks, shouting, and a band playing tunes such as "There'll Be a Hot Time in the Old Town Tonight." The attempt to create a sense of cohesion and in-group solidarity among the assembled is complete. (For a detailed account of the Bohemian Grove, along with photographs and posters, see the document "Social Cohesion and the Bohemian Grove" on whorulesamerica.net.)

The retreat sometimes provides an occasion for more than fun and merriment. Although business is rarely discussed, except in an informal way in groups of two or three, the retreat provides members with an opportunity to introduce their friends to politicians and to hear formal noontime speeches, called Lakeside Talks, from political candidates and a wide range of experts. In 2008 a former secretary of state, a retired admiral, a retired university president, and the current librarian of Congress were among the speakers for this occasion.

Every Republican president since the early twentieth century has been a member or guest at the Grove, with Herbert Hoover, Richard Nixon, Gerald Ford, Ronald Reagan, and George H. W. Bush as members. Hoover was sitting in the Grove in the summer of 1927 when Calvin Coolidge announced from Washington that he would not run again, and soon dozens of Hoover's clubmates dropped by his camp to urge him to run and offer their support. Future president Dwight D. Eisenhower made his first pre-nomination political speech in a Lakeside Talk at the Grove in 1951, which was positively received by the previously skeptical West Coast elites around Hoover, including Nixon, who was soon to become Ike's running mate.

Nixon himself wrote in his memoirs that he made his most important speech on the way to the presidency at the Grove in 1967, calling it "the speech that gave me the most pleasure and satisfaction of my political career," and one that "in many ways marked the first milestone on my road to the Presidency" because it was "an unparalleled opportunity to reach some of the most important and influential men, not just from California, but from across the country" (Nixon 1978, p. 284). During that same week he and Reagan had a chat in which Reagan agreed he would not challenge Nixon in the early Republican primaries, and that he would only join the fray if Nixon faltered. Twenty-eight years later, George H. W. Bush used a Lakeside Talk to introduce his son George W. Bush to the members as a potential future president (Vaughn 2006). In 1999 he brought George W. to the Grove to meet more of his friends as he was preparing for the 2000 presidential race:

> In early August, father took son to a private gathering at the secretive and exclusive Bohemian Grove in California. George H. W. Bush had gone to

a meeting there prior to his run, in 1979. He figured it would also benefit George W. to meet his circle of friends there, including corporate heads. The former president was a member of Hill Billies camp, which included William F. Buckley and Donald Rumsfeld as members. (Schweizer and Schweizer 2004, p. 460)

Perhaps the most striking change in the Lakeside Talks since the 1980s has been the absence of any leading Democrats. No Democratic president has ever been a member of the Bohemian Club, but cabinet members from the Kennedy, Johnson, and Carter administrations were prominent guests and Lakeside speakers. In 1990 Jimmy Carter gave a Lakeside Talk, 10 years after his presidency. By the early 1990s, however, there were few Democrats remaining among the regular members (Wehr 1994).

Three studies demonstrate the way in which this one club interweaves the upper class and the corporate community. The first uses the years 1970 and 1980, the second compares 1970 and 1993, and the third focuses on 2008. In 1970, according to the first study, 29 percent of the top 800 corporations had at least one officer or director at the Bohemian Grove festivities as a member or guest; in 1980 the figure was 30 percent. As might be expected, the overlap was especially great among the largest corporations, with 23 of the top 25 industrials represented in 1970, 15 of 25 in 1980. Twenty of the 25 largest banks had at least one officer or director in attendance in both 1970 and 1980. Other business sectors were represented somewhat less (Domhoff 1983, p. 70).

An even more intensive study, which included participant-observation and interviews, along with a membership network analysis, extended the sociological understanding of the Bohemian Grove into the 1990s. Using a list of 1,144 corporations, well beyond the 800 used in the studies for 1970 and 1980, the study found that 24 percent of these companies had at least one director who was a member or guest in 1993. For the top 100 corporations outside of California, the figure was 42 percent, compared to 64 percent in 1970. In terms of what goes on during the encampment, little or nothing changed between the 1970s and early 1990s (Phillips 1994). A study based on several summers of participant-observation in the early 2000s also demonstrated the continuity of the club's culture (Vaughn 2006).

In 2008, there were 101 directors of 116 companies among the 2,259 members. This percentage is lower than in the previous studies because it does not include guests, only members, at the Grove; guest lists were kept under lock and key by the late 1990s, if they were printed at all. In addition, the members in 2008 included many stockbrokers and investment advisors, dozens of retired corporate officials, and several appointees from past Republican administrations, such as two former secretaries of state and two former secretaries of the treasury from the Reagan and George H. W. Bush administrations. Most of the corporate members tended to be located in a few camps, such as Cave Man, where former Republican presidents Hoover and Nixon were members; Owl's Nest, where Reagan was a member; Hill Billies, where former President George H. W. Bush is a member;

and Midway, where Charles G. and David H. Koch, the billionaire ultraconservative brothers who run the family's Koch Industries, mentioned in Chapter 2 as the second-largest privately held company in the United States, are joined by one of the largest commercial builders in the country, a retired CEO of IBM, the former owner of Mondavi Winery, a former CEO of the San Francisco 49ers, several corporate directors, and numerous partners in financial firms, including one who gives generously to the Democratic Party. At Stowaway camp, David Rockefeller, the last remaining grandson of the founder of the Rockefeller fortune, and himself a retired banker, is joined by his son, David Rockefeller, Jr., the main current overseer of the family's billions, real estate investor Paul Pelosi, who is the husband of the top-ranking Democratic leader in the House of Representatives, Nancy Pelosi (D–CA), and corporate directors from CVS and Lockheed Martin. Multimillionaire members of the club who are not in one of the corporate-oriented camps included singer Jimmy Buffett, with an estimated net worth of $300 million, and actor-director Clint Eastwood, with an estimated net worth of $375 million.

As the case of the Bohemian Grove and its theatrical performances rather dramatically illustrates, clubs seem to have the same function within the upper class that secret societies and brotherhoods have in tribal societies. With their restrictive membership policies, initiatory rituals, and great emphasis on tradition, clubs carry on the heritage of primitive secret societies. They create an attitude of prideful exclusiveness within their members that contributes to an in-group feeling and a sense of fraternity within the upper class.

Sociologically speaking, a retreat such as the Bohemian Grove also reaffirms the shared values needed to reinforce class solidarity. There is first of all a ritual separation from the mundane everyday world through the Cremation of Care ceremony, which brings people into the realm of a make-believe time and space that reaffirms a whole range of beliefs that the men hold about themselves and the nature of American society (Vaughn 2006). The encampment also reaffirms another allegedly timeless aspect of the moral universe that the Bohemians want to sustain: male dominance. The very exclusion of women from the Bohemian Grove makes this point, but it is underlined by sexual jokes, dressing up as women for some of the plays and skits, the pornography collection, and frequent verbal put-downs of women. However, the exclusion of women also relates to the larger issue of male bonding: The men are reaffirming that they trust each other by sharing in activities that would be frowned upon if they were carried out in public spaces. They are learning to keep secrets from outsiders, which is also a good part of what is going on when college fraternities force their new initiates to learn a considerable amount of worthless information and take endless amounts of hazing.

In concluding this discussion of the Bohemian Club and its retreat as one small example of the intersection of the upper class and the corporate community, it needs to be stressed that the Bohemian Grove is not a place of power. As the foregoing account makes clear, no business deals or policy plans are made there. Instead, it is a place where people of power relax, make new acquaintances, and enjoy visiting with old friends. It is primarily a place for social bonding and the renewal of traditional values. It could disappear tomorrow without any noticeable change in the upper class.

THE FEMININE HALF OF THE UPPER CLASS

During the late nineteenth and early twentieth centuries, women of the upper class carved out their own distinct roles within the context of male domination in business, finance, and law. They went to separate private schools, founded their own social clubs, and belonged to their own voluntary associations. As young women and partygoers, they set the fashions for society. As older women and activists, they took charge of the nonprofit welfare and cultural institutions of the society, serving as fundraisers, philanthropists, and directors in a manner parallel to their male counterparts in business and politics. To prepare themselves for their leadership roles, they created the Junior League in 1901 to provide internships, role models, mutual support, and training in the management of meetings.

Due to the general social changes of the 1960s, and in particular the revival of the feminist movement, the socialization of wealthy young women changed somewhat during the 1970s. Most private schools became coeducational and their women graduates were encouraged to go to major four-year colleges, where they joined one of the four or five sororities with nationwide social prestige (e.g., Kappa Kappa Gamma, Kappa Alpha Theta, Pi Beta Phi, and Delta Delta Delta). Women of the upper class became more likely to have careers; there were already two or three examples of women who had risen to the top of their family's business by the 1990s.

The most informative and intimate look at the adult lives of traditional upper-class women is provided in four different interview and observation studies from four different regions of the country: East Coast, Midwest, Southwest, and West Coast (Daniels 1988; Kendall 2002; MacLeod 1984; Ostrander 1984). They reveal the similarities in upper-class lifestyles throughout the United States. They show that the women exercise power in numerous cultural and civic organizations, but also take traditional roles at home vis-à-vis their husbands and children. By asking the women to describe a typical day and to explain which activities are most important to them, these sociologists found that the role of community volunteer is a central preoccupation for upper-class women. It has significance as a family tradition and as an opportunity to fulfill an obligation to the community. One elderly woman involved for several decades in both the arts and human services said: "If you're privileged, you have a certain responsibility. This was part of my upbringing; it's a tradition, a pattern of life that my brothers and sisters do too" (Ostrander 1984, pp. 128–129).

The volunteer role is institutionalized in the training programs and activities of a variety of service organizations. This is especially the case with the Junior League, which is meant for women between 20 and 40 years of age, including some upwardly mobile professional women. "Voluntarism is crucial and the Junior

League is the quintessence of volunteer work," explained one woman. "Every-thing the League does improves the situation but doesn't rock the boat. It fits into existing institutions" (Ostrander 1984, p. 113). Quite unexpectedly, many of the women serving as volunteers, fundraisers, and board members for charitable and civic organizations view their work as a protection of the American way of life against the further encroachment of government into areas of social welfare. Some even see themselves as bulwarks against socialism. "There must always be people to do volunteer work," one commented. "If you have a society where no one is willing, then you may as well have communism, where it's all done by the government." Another stated: "It would mean that the government would take over, and it would all be regimented. If there are no volunteers, we would live in a completely managed society, which is quite the opposite to our history of free-dom." Another equated government support with socialism: "You'd have to go into government funds. That's socialism. The more we can keep independent and under private control, the better it is" (Ostrander 1984, pp. 132–137).

Despite this emphasis on volunteer work, the women placed high value on family life. They arranged their schedules to be home when their children came home from school and they stressed that their primary concern was to provide a good home for their husbands. Several wanted to have greater decision-making power over their inherited wealth, but almost all preferred the traditional roles of wife and mother, at least until their children were grown.

Although it comes as a surprise to many people, the debutante season—a series of parties, teas, and dances that culminates in one or more grand balls—remains an important part of the social life of upper-class women. These very expensive rituals, in which great attention is lavished on every detail of the food, decorations, and entertainment, are a central focus of the Christmas social season, but in some cities debutante balls are held in the spring as well. Parents, with the help of upper-class women who work as social secretaries and social consultants, spend many hours planning the details with dress designers, caterers, champagne importers, florists, decorators, and band leaders.

Despite the great importance placed upon the debut by upper-class parents, the debutante season came into considerable disfavor among young women as the social upheavals of the late 1960s and early 1970s reached their climax. This decline reveals that the reproduction of the upper class as a social class is an effort that must be made anew with each generation. Although enough young women participated to keep the tradition alive, the refusal to take part by a significant minority led to the cancellation of some balls and the curtailment of many others. Stories appeared on the women's pages of newspapers across the country telling of debutantes who thought the whole process was "silly" or that the money should be given to a good cause. By 1973, how-ever, the situation began to change again, and by the mid-1970s things were back to normal. As a wealthy young Texas woman told a sociologist in the late 1990s:

> I was very busy while I was in college. On top of my studies, I was presented [as a debutante] in Dallas, Austin, Tyler, and New Orleans. I went to teas and

dinners and parties. It was really fun because some of my sorority sisters were also presented, representing other cities, and we could all be together at these activities away from school. When my parents had my deb party, there were dozens of my [sorority] sisters there. One December my family and I were in New York for my International Debutante Ball presentation. (Kendall 2002, p. 100)

Following graduation, this debutante attended graduate school for a short time and then moved to Washington to take a job in the Bush administration that she obtained through family connections.

The decline of the debutante season and its subsequent resurgence in times of domestic tranquility show very clearly that one of its latent functions is to help perpetuate the upper class from generation to generation. When the underlying values of the class were questioned by some of its younger members, the institution went into decline. Attitudes toward social institutions like the debutante ball are therefore one telltale sign of whether or not adult members of the upper class have succeeded in insulating their children from the rest of society.

For all the changes in traditional gender roles after the 1960s, women of the upper class remain in a paradoxical position. They are subordinate to male members of their class, but they nonetheless exercise important power in some institutional arenas. They may or may not be fully satisfied with their ambiguous power status, but they recognize that they have considerable class power and social standing nonetheless. Both they and their male counterparts realize that they bring an upper-class, antigovernment perspective to their exercise of power. There is thus class solidarity between men and women against the rest of society. Commenting on the complex role of upper-class women, a feminist scholar drew the following stark picture: "First they must do to class what gender has done to their work—render it invisible; next, they must maintain the same class structure they have struggled to veil" (Daniels 1988, p. x).

DROPOUTS, FAILURES, AND CHANGE AGENTS

Not all men and women of the upper class fit the usual molds. Some are dropouts, jet-setters, failures, or even critics of the upper class. Except for a few longstanding exceptions, however, the evidence also suggests that many of the young jet-setters and dropouts eventually return to more familiar pathways. Numerous anecdotal examples show that some members of the upper class lead lives of failure, despite all the opportunities available to them. Although members of the upper class are trained for leadership and given every opportunity to develop self-confidence, some fail in school, become involved with drugs and alcohol, or become mentally disturbed. Once again, however, this cannot be seen as evidence for a lack of cohesion in the upper class, for there are bound to be some problems for individuals in any group.

There are even a few members of the upper class who abandon its institutions and values to become part of the liberal-labor alliance or leftists. They participate actively in liberal or leftist causes and provide financial support. Such people have supported several of the leading liberal and socialist magazines, including *The Nation* and *Mother Jones*. Some of the most visible recent examples of this liberal-to-leftist tendency are part of a national network of 16 change-oriented foundations called the Funding Exchange (FEX). These foundations gave away over $50 million between their founding in the 1970s and the 1990s, and provided over $15 million a year in the early years of the twenty-first century (FEX 2012). They receive money from wealthy individuals and then donate it to feminist, environmentalist, low-income, and minority-group activists. They also set up discussion groups for college-age members of the upper class who are conflicted about issues relating to their privileged class backgrounds and thinking about contributing money to liberal causes. In the case of one of the founding groups in the network, the Haymarket Foundation, the committee that makes the donations (about $400,000 per year) is composed primarily of activists from groups that have been supported by the foundation. This approach provides a way to overcome the usual power relations between donors and recipients (Ostrander 1995).

CONTINUITY AND UPWARD MOBILITY

Americans always have believed that anyone can rise from rags to riches if they try hard enough, but in fact a rise from the bottom to the top is very rare and often a matter of luck—being at the right place at the right time. In the late nineteenth century, a wealthy upper-class Bostonian with a Harvard education, Horatio Alger, became a best-selling author by writing short fictional books about young boys who had gone from penniless adversity to great wealth. In real life, the commentators of his day pointed to three or four actual examples. Subsequent research showed that most of the business leaders of that era did not fit the Horatio Alger myth. As one historian put it, Horatio Algers appeared more frequently in magazines and textbooks than they did in reality (Miller 1949).

Forbes, a business magazine that in 1982 began publishing an annual list of the allegedly 400 richest Americans, has taken up the Horatio Alger story line. "Forget old money," said the article that introduces the 1996 list, a theme that has been repeated since the list was first compiled in 1982. "Forget silver spoons. Great fortunes are being created almost monthly in the U.S. today by young entrepreneurs who hadn't a dime when we created this list 14 years ago" (Marsh 1996). But the Horatio Alger story is no less rare today than it was in the 1890s. In 2011, 21 percent inherited enough money to make the list, another 7 percent inherited $50 million or more, and another 11.5 percent inherited $1 million or more, or received a significant amount of start-up money from a relative to found a company. Another 22 percent had upper-class backgrounds or received start-up money for a business from a relative. Thirty-five percent came from a middle-class or lower-class background (Moriarty, Ali, Miller, Morneault, Sullivan, and Young 2012). As for the immigrants often extolled on the *Forbes* list, they too sometimes come from wealthy families; contrary to the stereotype, not all immigrants to the United States arrive poor (Zweigenhaft and Domhoff 1982; Zweigenhaft and Domhoff 2006).

Even those who seem to come from disadvantaged backgrounds often do not. Consider the social background of Wayne Huizenga, estimated to be worth $1.4 billion in 1996 through the creation of, first, Waste Management Company, and then Blockbuster Video. Huizenga is often depicted as having started out as a mere garbage collector. As *Current Biography* puts it: "The hero of a real-life Horatio Alger story, in his early twenties, Huizenga worked as a garbage-truck driver." But he was born in an elite Chicago suburb, graduated from a private school, and had a grandfather who owned a garbage-collection business in Chicago. His father was a real estate investor. True, Huizenga did start his own garbage company in southern Florida after not showing much aptitude for college, but he also merged it with companies in Chicago that were successors to his grandfather's firm, one of which was headed by a cousin by marriage. This is enterprising behavior, but it is not a Horatio Alger saga.

In another telling example, it is true that the late Sam Walton, the founder of Walmart, was raised in a low-income family and started as a management trainee at J. C. Penney. However, he also had a well-to-do father-in-law who was a small-town banker and rancher. He loaned Walton $20,000 in 1945 to start his first store (the equivalent of $256,000 in 2012 dollars), a sum that surpassed the nonhousing wealth of all but a few percent of American households in 2011 (Wolff 2012). Four of his descendants were in the top 10 on the *Forbes* 400 for 2011.

Forbes also talks about several people on its list as "college dropouts," but people who leave a prestigious institution like Harvard or Stanford to pursue a new opportunity in which timing is everything hardly fit the image of a "college dropout." For example, Bill Gates, the richest person in the United States in 2011, is often described as a college dropout because he left Harvard early to found Microsoft before someone beat him to what was the next logical step in the marketing of computer software. However, he is also the son of a prominent corporate lawyer in Seattle and a graduate of the top private school in that city, and he did go to Harvard.

According to research studies, most upward social mobility in the United States involves gradual changes over three generations for those above the lowest 20 percent and below the top 5 percent of the income ladder. Very few rise from the lowest levels, and very few fall from the top. Most often, over the course of three or four generations, the grandfather is a blue-collar worker, the father has a good white-collar job based on a BA degree, and one or two of the father's children become lawyers or physicians, but most of the father's grandchildren are back to being white-collar workers and middle-level executives. Upward social mobility of this type may be even less frequent for nonwhites. In addition, several recent studies suggest that upward social mobility may be declining since the 1980s (Kerbo 2006, Chapter 12; Mishel, Bernstein, and Shierholz 2009, Chapter 2).

As the conclusions on the rarity of great upward mobility suggest, the continuity of the upper class from generation to generation is very great. This fact conflicts with the oft-repeated folk wisdom that there is a large turnover at the top of the American social ladder. Once in the upper class, families tend to stay there, even while they are joined in each generation by new families and by middle-class brides and grooms who marry into their families. One study demonstrating this point began with a list of 12 families who were among the top wealth-holders in Detroit for 1860, 1892, and 1902. After documenting their high social standing as well as their wealth, the study traced their Detroit-based descendants into the 1970s. Nine of the 12 families still had members in the Detroit upper class; members from six families were directors of top corporations in the city. The study casts useful light on some of the reasons why the continuity is not even greater. One of the top wealth holders of 1860 had only one child, who in turn had no children. Another family persisted into a fourth generation of four great-granddaughters, all of whom married outside of Detroit (Schuby 1975).

A study of listings in the *Social Register* for 1940, 1977, and 1995 revealed the continuing presence of families descended from the largest fortunes of the nineteenth and early twentieth centuries. Using a list of 87 families from one history of great American fortunes and 66 families from another such book, a sociologist found that 92 percent of the families in the first book were still represented in 1977, with the figure falling slightly to 87 percent in 1995. In similar fashion, 88 percent of the families in the second book were represented in 1977 and 83 percent in 1995. Over half of the male heads of households signaled their connection to the founder of the fortune by putting "the 4th," "the 5th," or "the 6th" after their names. Almost half were given the last name of their wealthy mothers as their first name, once again demonstrating the concern with continuity (Broad 1996).

The American upper class, then, is a mixture of old and new members. There is both continuity and social mobility, with the newer members being assimilated into the lifestyle of the class through participation in the schools, clubs, and other social institutions described earlier in this chapter. There may be some tensions between those who are newly arrived and those of established status, as novelists and journalists love to point out, but what they have in common soon outweighs their differences.

IS THE UPPER CLASS AN ECONOMIC CLASS?

It may seem obvious that members of the upper class must have large amounts of wealth and income if they can afford the tuition at private schools, the fees at country clubs, and the considerable expense of an elegant social life. However, it is a difficult matter to demonstrate empirically that they do have greater ownership wealth and higher incomes than other people because the Internal Revenue

Service does not release information on individuals and most people are not willing to volunteer details on this subject. The search has to begin with aggregate information on the wealth and income distributions, followed by the study of lists of rich individuals compiled from the work of journalists and biographers.

In considering the distribution of wealth and income distributions in the United States, it first needs to be stressed that the wealth and income distributions are two different matters. The wealth distribution has to do with the concentration of ownership of *marketable assets*, which in most studies means real estate and financial assets, such as stocks, bonds, insurance, and bank accounts, minus any debts that are owed. The income distribution, on the other hand, has to do with the percentage of wages, dividends, interest, and rents paid out each year to individuals or families at various income levels. In theory, those who own a great deal may or may not have high incomes, depending on the returns they receive from their wealth, but in reality those at the very top of the wealth distribution also tend to have the highest incomes, mostly from interest, dividends and the sale of stocks at higher prices then they paid for them ("capital gains").

Although there were variations between port cities and rural areas, as well as among colonies, the wealth distribution in colonial America was relatively egalitarian because most settlers could purchase land. In 1774, the top 1 percent held about 14 to 16 percent of the wealth after debts are taken into account (Jones 1980). The wealth distribution became far more unequal as the country urbanized and industrialized, to the point that it was as unequal as those in Prussia and Russia in the early twentieth century (Williamson and Lindert 1980, p. 33). In 1916, the first year in which annual information was collected that could be used to calculate the wealth distribution with greater precision, the top 1 percent owned 38.1 percent of all wealth, a figure that reached 40.3 percent in 1930. The share held by the top 1 percent then fell by 12 percentage points by the end of 1932, due to a large decline in the value of their assets caused by the Great Depression. Then the income and estate tax policies enacted by the New Deal, followed by even higher income taxes to help pay for the military buildup during World War II, reduced the top 1 percent's wealth share to 22.6 percent by 1949. It is highly noteworthy that most of the decline between 1930 and 1949 came at the expense of the top 0.1 percent (Kopczuk and Saez 2004, pp. 446, 453, and Table 3). The wealth distribution was then relatively stable between the 1950s and 2010, with a temporary decline for the top 1 percent in the mid-1970s when the stock market took another nosedive.

Despite the decline in the wealth of the top 1 percent due to the multifaceted impacts of the Great Depression, New Deal taxation policies, and the need for the wealthy to help pay for World War II, the overall wealth distribution remained extremely concentrated. This is especially the case for the type of wealth that is the most useful as a power indicator. Called "nonhome wealth" or "financial wealth," it includes stocks, bonds, real estate, and other "liquid" assets, but not owner-occupied housing, which cannot easily be sold unless the family has another source of shelter. According to calculations based on a large-scale triennial survey of households by the Survey of Consumer Finance, an agency of the Federal Reserve Board, the top 1 percent owned 42 percent of all financial wealth as of 2010. The next 4 percent had 30 percent of financial assets, which means that the top 5 percent own 72 percent. In addition, the next 5 percent owned another 13 percent. Thus, the top 10 percent of households, with 85 percent of all financial wealth, basically own the United States, leaving only 15 percent for the bottom 90 percent (Wolff 2012, p. 16; "Wealth, Income, and Power," Table 1, on whorulesamerica.net). These findings may come as a surprise to many readers: A large-scale study of 5,522 participants showed that very few Americans, whatever their gender, age, income level, or political affiliation, have any idea of just how concentrated the wealth distribution is in the United States (Norton and Ariely 2011).

The income distribution provides an even more sensitive power indicator because it changes faster in response to four main factors: (1) increases or decreases in income tax rates; (2) declines in pre-tax income for the top few percent; (3) declines in the value of the minimum wage; and (4) increases in unemployment rates. It thereby reflects any changes in the ability of the corporate rich to lower their taxes, earn a higher share of yearly income, or limit gains in income for average people. In the first year for which there are good estimates, 1913, the top 1 percent received 18 percent of all income when income from capital gains is included. This figure reached 24 percent in 1928 and then fell to the 15 to 17 percent range during the 1930s, primarily because of the precipitous decline in dividend and capital gains income between 1930 and 1932. In addition, there were higher income tax rates on the top brackets after 1932, which were initiated by Republican president Herbert Hoover and augmented by Democratic president Franklin D. Roosevelt (Brownlee 2000; Brownlee 2004, pp. 83–90; Piketty and Saez 2003). Due to continuing high taxation during and after World War II, the income of the top 1 percent gradually declined to the 8 to 9 percent range in the late 1970s, which suggests that the postwar liberal-labor alliance had been able to defend the high tax rates that resulted from the crises of depression and war in the 1930s and 1940s (Piketty and Saez 2003, Table 2, Column 11).

Between 1980 and 2010, however, the top few percent greatly increased their share of income, which implies that the corporate rich had found new ways to improve their power position. As shown in Table 3.1, the income of the top

Table 3.1 Increases in Income Going to Top 10%, 5%, 1%, and .05%, 1980–2010

Year	Top 10%	Top 5%	Top 1%	Top 0.5%
1980	32.9%	21.2%	8.2%	5.5%
2010	46.3%	33.7%	17.4%	13.4%
% increase	40%	50%	110%	140%

Source: Picketty and Saez 2003; Saez 2012.

10 percent increased by 40 percent over that 30-year span while the income of the top 1 percent increased by 110 percent and the income of the top 0.5 percent increased by even more than that. These figures are evidence of a complete triumph for the corporate rich.

Since none of the systematic studies on the wealth and income distributions include the names of individuals, other types of studies had to be done to demonstrate that people of wealth and high income are in fact members of the upper class. The most detailed study of this kind showed that nine of the 10 wealthiest financiers at the turn of the twentieth century and 75 percent of all families listed in a compendium of America's richest families have descendants in the *Social Register*. Supplementing these findings, another study discovered that at least one-half of the 90 richest men in 1900 have descendants in the *Social Register* and a study of 90 corporate directors worth $10 million or more in 1960 found that 74 percent met criteria of upper-class membership (Baltzell 1958; Domhoff 1967; Mills 1956). However, the degree of overlap between great wealth and membership in the upper class has attracted little further research attention because the earlier findings are now generally accepted.

The results from these studies establish that the social upper class is an economic class based in the ownership and control of income-producing assets. However, they do not show that the upper class controls the corporate community, because stock holdings in any one company may be too dispersed to allow an individual or family to control it. The next three sections address this issue.

THE UPPER CLASS AND CORPORATE CONTROL

With the findings on the overall wealth distribution, and the concentration of stock assets in particular, as a backdrop, it can be shown how members of the upper class involve themselves in the ownership and control of specific corporations through family ownership, family offices, holding companies, and investment partnerships. Their general involvement in the corporate community was also examined in the 1960s and early 1970s through large-scale studies of the social backgrounds of corporate directors, showing a large overrepresentation for upper-class directors on the "who sits?" indicator of power, but those studies have never been updated, so they can no longer be considered relevant (Domhoff 1967, pp. 51–57; Dye 1986, p. 194).

Family Ownership

As shown by the early history of the corporate community discussed in the previous chapter, it has never been the case that American corporations were primarily owned by separate families, but instead they were usually owned by groups of investors, banks, and other types of financial companies. However, there are nonetheless many family-owned firms in the United States today that are often overlooked when talking about the separation of ownership and control. As discussed in Chapter 2, they include 212 privately owned firms that have $2 billion or more in sales, many of which would be in the *Fortune* 1,000 if they were publicly owned.

The way in which these privately held companies can be part of larger family empires is seen in the case of the Pritzker family in Chicago, who provide a useful example because several members of the family became strong financial backers of future president Barack Obama when he first ran for the Senate from Illinois in 2004, as discussed in Chapter 6. Building on their core property, Hyatt Hotels, which had been in the family for three generations and is now called Global Hyatt because it has over 200 hotels around the world, the Pritzkers also own an industrial conglomerate; Encore Senior Living, which is a network of assisted living centers; and Royal Caribbean Cruises, in which they have a 25 percent ownership stake. In addition, the family has a real estate arm, Pritzker Realty, and owns a majority interest in the Parking Spot, which operates parking lots near airports.

In 2008, the family leaders had to sell a major share of their industrial conglomerate to Warren Buffett, the second-richest person in America in 2011, and a minority share of Global Hyatt to Goldman Sachs, one of the largest financial companies in the country, in order to settle a lawsuit filed by two younger members of the family, who felt their father, uncles, and older cousins had misused their trust funds. The suit revealed that the family was then worth $15 to $20 billion, which was wrapped up in over 1,000 trust funds, some of which were held in offshore locations (Andrews 2003; Savage 2008a).

Even in the case of publicly controlled corporations, three different studies provide detailed evidence of the extent of family involvement in the largest American corporations. The first used both official documents and the informal—but often more informative—findings of the business press as its source of information. It concluded that 40 percent of the top 300 industrials were probably under family control in the 1960s, using the usual cutoff point of 5 percent of the stock as the criterion (Burch 1972). Analyzing the official records that became available in the 1970s, a team of researchers at Corporate Data Exchange provided detailed information on the major owners of most of the top 500 industrials for 1980, showing that significant individual and family ownership continued for all but the very largest of corporations. One individual or family was a top stockholder, with at least 5 percent of the stock, in 44 percent of the 423 profiled corporations that were not controlled by other corporations or foreign interests. The figures were much lower among the 50 largest, however, in which only 17 percent of the 47 companies included in the study showed evidence of major family involvement (Albrecht and Locker 1981). The relatively small percentage of the very largest industrials under individual or family control concurs with findings in a third study, which focused on the 200 largest nonfinancial corporations for 1974–1975 (Herman 1981).

The Family Office

A family office is an informal organization through which members of a family or group of families agree to pool some of their resources in order to hire people to provide them with advice on investments, estate planning, charitable giving, and even political donations in some cases. Family offices often handle all financial transactions and legal matters as well as personal needs such as theater tickets and car rentals (White 1978). One office has kept track of $840 million for four families for three generations (Konigsberg 2008). In the 1990s, multifamily offices began to appear, usually serving an average of 50 families with $10 million or more in assets. One survey concluded that there were 80 such offices handling $305 billion in assets in 2006 (Hawthorne 2008). There were an estimated 3,000 to 4,500 family offices in 2012, most of them managing $500 million or more (Ahmed 2012).

In terms of the issue of corporate control, the relevance of family offices is their potential for maintaining control of corporations founded by an earlier generation of the family, or to take over other corporations. Such offices contradict the belief that corporate control is necessarily lost due to the inheritance of stock by a large number of descendants. They often serve as a unifying source for the family as well. They sometimes have employees who sit on boards of directors to represent the family. In 2010, one collection of family offices teamed up to create a $1.2 billion fund for investment in clean tech (Ahmed 2012).

The most detailed account of a family office was provided by a sociologist as part of a study in the 1970s of the Weyerhaeuser family of Saint Paul, Minnesota, and Tacoma, Washington, whose great wealth is concentrated in the lumber industry. By assembling a family genealogy chart that covered five generations and then interviewing several members of the family, he determined that a family office called Fiduciary Counselors Inc. helped the family to maintain a central role in two major corporations. He demonstrated that there were members of the family on the boards of these companies whose last names are not Weyerhaeuser and that the stock holdings managed by the family office were large enough to maintain control (Dunn 1980).

Fiduciary Counselors Inc. also housed the offices of two Weyerhaeuser holding companies (meaning companies created only to own stock in operating companies). These holding companies were used to make investments for family members as a group and to own shares in new companies created by family members. Although the primary focus of the Weyerhaeuser family office was on economic matters, it served other functions as well. It kept the books for 15 different charitable foundations of varying sizes and purposes through which family members gave money and it coordinated political donations by family members all over the country.

The status of a family office is fluid in that it can be transformed into another type of investment fund through more formal legal arrangements if it decides to invest other people's money as well. Conversely, investment funds can be changed back to family offices. This is what the billionaire investor and large Democratic Party campaign donor George Soros did with his Soros Fund Management in 2011 by returning money to nonfamily investors. Several other once-famous hedge fund operators had already done the same thing in the previous two years. The new Soros family office manages $24 billion (Ahmed 2011; Ahmed 2012).

Holding Companies and Investment Partnerships

Holding companies, briefly defined in the previous section as companies that merely hold the stock of other companies, can serve the economic functions of a family office if the family is still small and tight-knit. They have the added advantage over a family office of being incorporated entities that can buy and sell stock in their own names. Because they are privately held, they need report only to tax authorities on their activities.

The Crown family of Chicago, estimated to be worth over $4 billion in 2012, operates through a combined holding and investment company, Henry A. Crown and Company, which manages investments in banking, transportation, oil and gas, cellular phones, home furnishings, and resort properties. The company is a useful example because several family members became financial supporters of President Obama's political career in the early 2000s, as discussed in Chapter 6. Starting with a company that sold building supplies, the two brothers who founded the dynasty in 1921 used that company to take control of General Dynamics, one of the largest defense contractors, in 1959 (Zweigenhaft and Domhoff 1982, pp. 27–29). In addition, the family owns part of JPMorgan Chase, Hilton Hotels, and the Rockefeller Center. Its private holdings include Crown Golf Properties, which operates golf courses in seven states. The current family leader, James S. Crown, a grandson of the founder of the Crown empire, is on the boards of JPMorgan Chase, General Dynamics, and Sara Lee; he is also the chair of the board of trustees of the University of Chicago. His sister, Susan Crown, who manages the family's charitable foundation, is a director of Northern Trust Bank and Illinois Tool Works, and a trustee of Yale.

The cumulative findings on the importance of family ownership, family offices, holding companies, and investment partnerships in large corporations suggest that a significant number of corporations continue to be controlled by major owners. In the case of the private equity firms discussed in Chapter 2, their takeover bids show that firms allegedly controlled by their managers can be acquired by groups of rich investors whenever they so desire, unless of course they are resisted by a rival group of owners (Bruck 1988; Stewart 1991).

However, the very largest corporations in several sectors of the economy show no large ownership stake by individuals or families, whether through family offices, holding companies, or other devices. Their largest owners, in blocks of a few percent, are bank trust departments, investment companies, mutual funds, and pension funds. Interview studies suggest that bank trust departments and investment companies do not take any role in influencing the management of the corporations in which they invest (Herman 1975; Herman 1981). As for any possible governance role for pension funds, those controlled by corporations and other private entities also have taken a hands-off role. For a brief time in the late 1980s and early 1990s, however, several public employee and union pension funds, whose assets account for less than 20 to 25 percent of all pension assets, seemed to be flexing their muscles in corporate boardrooms. Their actions raised the possibility of an "investor capitalism" in which government employees and unions could challenge the prerogatives of the traditional owners and executives (Useem 1996). However, this fledgling challenge met with little or no success, and it faded in the late 1990s. By 2003, the *New York Times* called this effort a "Revolution That Wasn't" based on interviews with its disheartened leaders (Deutsch 2003). (For a detailed history of the rise and fall of the pension fund movement and of the losses many public pension funds incurred through their involvement with private equity funds and other financiers, see "Pension Fund Capitalism" on whorulesamerica.net.)

As has been the case for many generations, the largest corporations in the United States are still controlled by a combination of their high-level executives, the for-profit financial institutions that are concerned with the price of their stockholdings, and top individual stockholders, all of which are often represented on the board of directors. However, the power to run such corporations on a day-to-day basis belongs to the CEO and his or her handful of supporters on the board. The CEOs and other top corporate executives are the topic of the next two sections.

WHERE DO CORPORATE EXECUTIVES COME FROM?

There have been many studies reaching back to the nineteenth century on the class origins of the top executives in very large corporations. They most frequently focus on the occupation of the executive's father. These studies show that "between 40% and 70% of all large corporation directors and managers were raised in business families, which are only a small percentage of all families, especially before the 1960s" (Temin 1997; Temin 1998; Useem and Karabel 1986; Zweigenhaft and Domhoff 2011, pp. 2–4).

However, even though most corporate executives at large corporations come from business backgrounds, the fact remains that many high-level managers come from middle-level origins and work their way up the corporate ladder. The number may be exaggerated somewhat because people tend to deny their privileged backgrounds and relevant information on schools and clubs is not always available, but their role within the corporate community is a large one even by conservative estimates. Today, few chief executive officers at the largest corporations were born into the upper class. This raises the possibility that professional managers are distinct from upper-class owners and directors, which suggests there might be some degree of separation between the corporate community and the upper class.

Before turning to this issue, the fact that members of the upper class are not more frequently found at high-level executive positions in large corporations can be addressed briefly. While it may seem surprising that members of the upper class have their least involvement at the executive level in the very largest corporations, the reasons have nothing to do with lack of education, ability, or expertise. Simply put, the sons and daughters of wealthy parents usually are not interested in a career that requires years of experience climbing the corporate ladder in a large bureaucratic organization when there is no incentive for them to do so. They prefer to work in finance, corporate law, or their own family businesses, or they spend their time managing their own large fortunes and following the stock market. All of these pursuits give them greater personal autonomy and more opportunities to exercise power. After the 1980s, they were especially attracted to Wall Street, where there was more money to be made than in the 45 years after the New Deal put some constraints on highly risky financial deals. In a word, many members of the upper class become financiers who strive to make a profit by investing their funds, not corporate managers who have to deal with the day-to-day problems of keeping an organization together.

THE ASSIMILATION OF RISING CORPORATE EXECUTIVES

The evidence presented in this section shows how rising corporate executives are assimilated into the upper class and come to share its values, thereby cementing the relationship between the upper class and the corporate community rather than severing it. The aspirations of professional managers for themselves and for their offspring lead them into the upper class in behavior, values, and style of life.

Whatever the social origins of top managers, most are educated and trained in a small number of private universities and business schools. The results from several different studies reveal that about one-third of those who manage the nation's largest firms graduated from Harvard, Yale, or Princeton, and two-thirds studied at one of the 12 most heavily endowed schools (Useem 1980). It is in these schools that people of middle-class origins receive their introduction to the values of the upper class and the corporate community, mingling for the first time with men and women of the upper class and sometimes with upper-class teachers and administrators who serve as role models. This modeling continues in the graduate schools of business that many of them attend before joining the corporation. People of color who are not from wealthy families show the same educational patterns as other upwardly mobile corporate executives in terms of attendance at these same schools (Zweigenhaft and Domhoff 2006; Zweigenhaft and Domhoff 2011).

The conformist atmosphere within the corporations intensifies the rising executives' socialization into upper-class styles and values. The great uncertainty and latitude for decision-making in positions at the top of complex organizations creates a situation in which trust among leaders is absolutely essential. "That need for trust is what creates a pressure toward social conformity," according to a classic study by sociologist Rosabeth Kanter (1993, p. 49). "It is the uncertainty quotient in managerial work, as it has come to be defined in the large modern corporations," she continues, "that causes management to become so socially restricting; to develop tight inner circles excluding social strangers; to keep control in the hands of socially homogeneous peers; to stress conformity and insist upon a diffuse, unbounded loyalty; and to prefer ease of communication and thus social certainty over the strains of dealing with people who are 'different.'"

In this kind of atmosphere, it quickly becomes apparent to new managers that they must demonstrate their loyalty to the senior management by working extra hours, tailoring their appearance to that of their superiors, and attempting to conform in their attitudes and behavior. Rightly or wrongly, they come to believe that they have to be part of the "old-boy network" in order to succeed in the company. Although there are competence criteria for the promotion of managers, they are vague enough or hard enough to apply that most managers become convinced that social factors are critical as well.

Executives who are successful in winning acceptance into the inner circle of their home corporations are invited by their superiors to join social institutions that assimilate them into the upper class. The first invitations are often to charitable and cultural organizations in which they serve as fundraisers and as organizers of special events. The wives of rising executives, whose social acceptability is thought to be a factor in managers' careers, experience their first extensive involvement with members of the upper class through these same organizations. Then, too, the social clubs discussed earlier in the chapter are important socializing agents for the rising executive.

Upwardly mobile executives also become personally connected to members of the upper class through the educational careers of their children. As their children go to day schools and boarding schools, the executives take part in evening and weekend events for parents, participate in fundraising activities, and sometimes become trustees in their own right. The fact that the children of successful managers become involved in upper-class institutions also can be seen in their patterns of college attendance. This is demonstrated very clearly in an early study of upwardly mobile corporate presidents. Whereas only 29 percent of the presidents went to an Ivy League college, 70 percent of their sons and daughters did so (Hacker 1961).

Rising executives are assimilated economically at the same time as they are assimilated socially. One of the most important of these assimilatory mechanisms is called a "stock option," which grants employees the right to buy company stock at any point within a future time period at the price of the stock when the option is granted. If the price of the stock rises, the executive purchases it at the original low price, often with the help of a low-interest or interest-free loan from the corporation. In the 1990s and early 2000s, the gains from purchasing and selling stock under these arrangements were taxed at a lower rate—15 percent—than was ordinary income above $250,000, which was the starting point for the 35 percent tax bracket. Stock-option plans, in conjunction with salaries and bonuses in the millions to tens of millions of dollars, allow some top executives to earn hundreds of times more than the average wage earner each year. These high levels of remuneration enable upwardly mobile corporate leaders to become multimillionaires in their own right and important leaders within the corporate community.

The assimilation of professional executives into the upper class also can be seen in the emphasis they put on profits, the most important of ownership objectives. This manifests itself most directly in the performance of the corporations they manage. Several past studies that compared owner-controlled companies with companies that have professional managers at the top showed no differences in their profitability. Corporations differ in their profitability, but this fact does not seem to be due to a difference in values between upper-class owners and rising corporate executives (Useem 1980).

By any indication, then, the presence of upwardly mobile executives does not contradict the notion that the upper class and the corporate community are closely related. In terms of their wealth, their social contacts, their values, and their aspirations for their children, successful managers join the corporate rich as they advance in the corporate hierarchy.

CLASS AWARENESS

The institutions that weave the owners and high-level executives of corporations into a national upper class transcend the presence or absence of any given person or family. Families can rise and fall in the class structure, but the institutions of the upper class persist. Not everyone in this nationwide upper class knows everyone else, but everybody knows somebody who knows someone in other areas of the country, thanks to a common school experience, a summer at the same resort, membership in the same social club, or membership on the same board of directors. The upper class at any given historical moment consists of a complex network of overlapping social circles linked by the members they have in common and by the numerous bonds of trust created by common cultural styles and values that emerge from a similar upbringing, education, and lifestyle. Viewed from the standpoint of social psychology, the upper class is made up of innumerable face-to-face small groups that are constantly changing in their composition as people move from one social setting to another.

Involvement in these institutions usually instills a class awareness that includes feelings of superiority, pride, and entitlement, and a sense that they are fully deserving of their station in life. This class awareness is in effect a social psychology of justified privilege, which is reinforced by shared social identities and interpersonal ties. More important, the fact that the upper class is based in the ownership and control of profit-producing investments in stocks, bonds, and real estate shows that its members are collectively a corporate rich. They are not concerned simply with the interests of the corporations they own or any one business sector, but with such matters as the "investment climate," the health of the stock and bond markets, the "rate of profit," and the overall "political climate."

With the exception of those few who join the liberal-labor alliance or a leftist movement, members of the upper class have a conservative outlook on issues that relate to the well-being of the corporate community as a whole. As noted in the introductory chapter, they may be liberal or conservative on social issues, and they vary somewhat on the degree to which they are wary of government, but they are nearly unanimous in their opposition to labor unions, which they see as the major potential challengers to their wealth and power. This tendency toward a general class perspective is utilized and reinforced within the policy-planning network discussed in the next chapter. The organizations in that network build upon the structural (economy-based) power explained in Chapter 2, supplemented by the social cohesion demonstrated in this chapter, in reaching consensus on complex policy issues about which the potential for misunderstanding and disagreement is great.

In other words, developing a common policy outlook is not automatic for the corporate rich. Their leaders have to create plans that satisfy as many different sectors of the corporate community as possible, or at least minimize the damage to those that cannot be fully accommodated. Then they have to develop access to government. At the same time, they have to contend with the possible objections of everyday working people who have little or nothing except a job, a house, and the opportunity to obtain educational credentials that might help them move up the occupational ladder.

4

The Policy-Planning Network

Shared economic interests and social cohesion provide the starting point for the development of policy consensus, but they are not enough in and of themselves to lead to agreed-upon policies without research, consultation, and deliberation. The issues facing the corporate community are too complex and the economy is too large for new policies to arise naturally from common interests and social cohesion alone. That is why a set of nonprofit, ostensibly nonpartisan organizations is a necessary feature of the corporate landscape. These organizations are the basis for a policy-planning process through which the corporate community articulates its general policy preferences and then conveys them to the two major political parties, the White House, and Congress. They take the form of charitable foundations, think tanks, and policy-discussion groups, which are defined shortly.

Members of the corporate community and the upper class involve themselves in the policy-planning process in four basic ways. First, they finance the organizations at the center of these efforts. Second, they provide a variety of free services, such as legal and accounting help for some of these organizations. Third, they serve as the trustees of these organizations, setting their general direction and selecting the people that will manage the day-to-day operations. Finally, they take part in the daily activities of some of the groups in the network or send their assistants to keep them abreast of new developments.

The policy-planning network also shows how seemingly independent experts, who often provide new policy ideas, fit into the power equation. They do their work as employees and consultants of key organizations in the network. These organizations give them financial support, confer legitimacy on their efforts, and provide the occasions for them to present their ideas to decision-makers. Although the corporate community has a near monopoly on what is considered respectable or legitimate expertise by the mass media and government, this expertise does not go unchallenged. There also exists a small group of think tanks and advocacy groups financed by liberal foundations, wealthy liberals, unions, and direct mail appeals. Some of these liberal policy organizations also receive funding from major foundations controlled by moderate conservatives, to the great annoyance of ultraconservatives. In addition, there are many academic experts at university research institutes that try to remain above the fray, but most of them are more marginal on power issues than they are portrayed to be in the media and in biographical accounts of their lives, which focus too readily on individuals who wrote articles or registered protests after the new initiatives were well under way.

As the annoyances expressed by the ultraconservatives reveal, the corporate-financed policy network is not totally homogeneous. Reflecting differences of opinion within the corporate community, the moderate and ultraconservative subgroups have long-standing disagreements. The ultraconservative organizations are the ones most often identified with "big business" in the eyes of many social scientists and the general public. In the past they opposed the expansion of trade with Europe and Asia, as well as any type of government regulation or increases in various types of government social insurance. The fact that they are generally nay-sayers who lost on several highly visible spending issues in the turmoil of the 1960s and early 1970s is one reason media commentators and some social scientists doubt that the corporate community is the dominant influence in shaping government policy. However, most of these differences were smoothed over between 1975 and 2012 because the ultraconservatives accepted the need for an expansion of trade and the moderate conservatives decided that cutbacks in government spending on social programs were necessary.

Since the late 1990s, the two groups have developed new differences over foreign policy. The internationally oriented moderate conservatives, who long held sway in this issue area, are *multilateralists* when it comes to foreign policy; they favor working closely with allies and making use of the United Nations whenever possible. They think they won the Cold War by patiently containing the Soviet Union and waiting for its nonmarket economy to fail, all the while working with Soviet leaders on arms control and other issues. The ultraconservatives, who have tendencies to ignore what is happening in other countries and shun foreign aid, are *assertive nationalists* when they do engage one or another part of the world, as seen in the unilateralism and the disdain for the United Nations that were visible in George W. Bush's administration. Assertive nationalists, ignoring the fact that Soviet premier Mikhail Gorbachev knew full well that the country's economy needed major adjustments, believe they won the Cold War by increasing defense spending in the early 1980s and arming the mujahideen to fight the Soviets in Afghanistan, thereby forcing the Soviets into an unwinnable arms race that ruined their economy and contributing to their defeat in Afghanistan. They thought that the kind of bold initiatives allegedly taken during the Reagan administration would work in Iraq, Iran, and North Korea, but all of them backfired (Daalder and Lindsay 2003).

No one factor has been shown by systematic studies to be the sole basis for the division into moderates and ultraconservatives within the corporate community. The basis for their differences therefore remains an unsolved puzzle. There is a tendency for the moderate organizations to be directed by executives from the very largest and most internationally oriented of corporations, but there are numerous exceptions to that generalization. Moreover, there are corporations that support policy organizations within both policy subgroups. Then, too, there are instances in which some top officers from a corporation will be in the moderate camp and others will be in the ultraconservative camp. There is clearly a need for much more research on this issue while avoiding any attempts to reduce the divisions to differences in economic interests. For all their disagreements, however, leaders within the two clusters of policy organizations have a tendency to search for compromise policies due to their common membership in the corporate community, their social bonds, and the numerous interlocks among all policy groups. When compromise is not possible, the final resolution of policy conflicts often takes place in legislative struggles in Congress, which are discussed in Chapter 7.

In considering the information that follows, it is important not to be overly impressed with the outcome of these efforts at policy planning. For all their education, financial backing, and media attention, the experts involved in this network are wrong far more than they are right. They are as likely to screen out information that does not fit with their biases and sense of self-importance as anyone else. They are also as susceptible to subtle social pressures to arrive at a consensus as any other group of people. There is no better evidence for these points than the certitudes that were expressed by most foreign policy experts within the policy-planning network about the ease with which Iraq could be transformed, or the certainty with which most economists in the network said that the economy could prosper without much government oversight because of the self-regulating nature of markets.

Nor were there any prominent experts within the policy-planning network that listened to the warnings by several liberal economists about the dangers of the rapid rise in housing prices in the early years of the twenty-first century. Based on historical experience with housing and stock market bubbles, as well as sound economic analyses based on mainstream theories, the liberal economists predicted that the bubble was certain to burst and create a huge drop in consumer demand, which would bring about a serious recession, if steps were not taken to deflate the bubble gradually (Baker 2009; Krugman 2012).

AN OVERVIEW OF THE POLICY-PLANNING NETWORK

The policy-planning process begins in corporate boardrooms, social clubs, and informal discussions, where problems are identified as "issues" to be solved by new policies. It ends in government, where policies are enacted and implemented. In between, however, there is a complex network of people and institutions that plays an important role in sharpening the issues and weighing the alternatives. This network has three main components—foundations, think tanks, and policy-discussion groups.

Foundations are tax-free institutions created to give grants to both individuals and nonprofit organizations for activities that range from education, research, and the arts, to support for the poor and the upkeep of exotic gardens and old mansions. They are an upper-class adaptation to inheritance and income taxes, that is, another strategy in the effort to keep government as small as possible. In effect, they provide a means by which wealthy people and corporations can decide how to spend what otherwise would have been tax payments, the expenditure of which are decided by elected officials. From a small beginning at the turn of the twentieth century, foundations have become a very important factor in shaping developments in higher education and the arts, and they play a significant role in policy formation as well. Although the grants they give to think tanks and policy-discussion groups each year are essential to the functioning of those organizations, the amount of money involved is small compared to what they provide to education, research, charity, and cultural organizations. "To a Wall Streeter, intellectuals are pretty cheap," a senior fellow at one policy-discussion group told a *New York Times* reporter. "There are wedding rings that cost more than I do" (Bumiller 2008, p. A12).

Historically, the Rockefeller Foundation, based in an oil fortune; the Carnegie Corporation, based in a steel fortune; the Ford Foundation, based in the Ford family's automotive fortune; and the Sloan Foundation, based in a General Motors fortune, were the most influential. After the 1970s they were joined by a new set of heavily endowed liberal and moderate-conservative foundations as well as by several somewhat smaller, but highly coordinated ultraconservative foundations. Beyond these several dozen large foundations, there are tens of thousands of small family foundations that allow wealthy individuals to provide support for charities and high culture at the local and state levels, and they sometimes give modest gifts of $50,000 to $500,000 to national-level nonprofits on whose boards they serve.

Think tanks are nonprofit organizations that provide settings for experts in various academic specialties to devote all of their time to the study of policy alternatives, free from the teaching, committee meetings, and departmental duties that are part of the daily routine for most members of the academic community. Supported by foundation grants, corporate donations, donations from wealthy individuals, and government contracts, think tanks are a major source of the new policy prescriptions discussed in the policy-planning network. In the language of sociology, they are "intermediate organizations" because they incorporate aspects of "academia, politics, business, and the market" (Medvetz 2012a, p. 113; Medvetz 2012b).

The *policy-discussion organizations* are nonpartisan groups that bring together corporate executives, lawyers, academic experts, university administrators, government officials, and media specialists to talk about general problems such as foreign aid, international trade, and environmental policies. Using discussion groups of varying sizes, these organizations provide informal and off-the-record meeting grounds in which differences of opinion on various issues can be aired and the arguments of specialists can be heard. In addition to their numerous small-group discussions, they encourage general dialogue by means of luncheon speeches, written reports, and position statements in journals and books. Taken as a whole, the several think tanks and policy-discussion groups are akin to an open forum in which there is a constant debate concerning the major problems of the day. Their conclusions are publically available for anyone to read because they are summarized in newspaper stories and published in annual reports, pamphlets, and books.

The organizations in the policy-planning network are interlocked with one another and the corporate community in terms of both common trustees and funding. Figure 4.1 presents an overview of the network, with linkages expressed in terms of (1) trustee interlocks, (2) money flows, and (3) the flow of ideas and plans. Anticipating the discussion of how the corporate community shapes government policy in Chapter 7, the figure shows some of the ways in which the "output" of the policy-planning network reaches government.

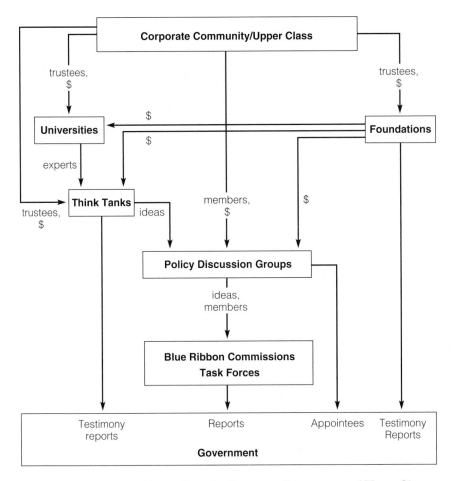

Figure 4.1   The Flow of Policy from the Corporate Community and Upper Class to Government through the Policy-Planning Network

For purposes of this chapter, the main emphasis in terms of money flows is on foundation grants, but it is important to underscore that they provide only one-third to two-thirds of the annual budgets for most of the think tanks and policy-discussion groups in the network (Staples 2012a). This is because the support provided by wealthy individuals and corporate treasuries is not as easily traced as foundation grants, which have to be reported to the Internal Revenue Service and are usually summarized in a foundation's annual reports. In recent decades the IRS filings have been cumulated and made available to everyone by the Foundation Center in New York by means of its *Foundation Directory Online*, which is usually available without charge at local community foundations. Thus, information on foundation grants is invaluable in developing a systematic understanding of the policy-planning network because this information is both governmentally mandated and readily accessible in a highly useful format.

No one type of organization in the network is more important than the others. It is the network as a whole that shapes policy alternatives, with different organizations playing different roles on different issues. It is also the case that new crises spawn new organizations and that established organizations can decline in importance if they outlive their usefulness. One such fading group, the Committee for Economic Development, is discussed later in the chapter. New archival findings on the conflicts that divided its members between 1970 and 1975 shed light on the more conservative direction that many moderate conservatives took in the early 1970s. This general "right turn" reduced the impact of the Committee for Economic Development because the CEOs of the largest corporations transferred their time and money into other organizations in the policy-planning network (Domhoff 2013).

CORPORATE INTERLOCKS WITH THINK TANKS AND POLICY GROUPS

The extent of the overlap between the corporate community and the policy-planning network implied in Figure 4.1 is demonstrated by a three-step analysis that builds on the *Fortune* 500 database used in Chapter 2 to study the corporate community. In the first step, the directors of 46 think tanks and specialized policy-discussion groups, such as the Council on Foreign Relations, were added to the *Fortune* 500 database. As part of this step, the members of the six major business groups were purposely excluded in order to see if think tanks and specialized policy-discussion groups have direct connections to *Fortune* 500 firms. This first step showed that nine think tanks and specialized policy-discussion groups were among the 15 most central organizations in the network, with most ultraconservative and liberal think tanks more peripheral, or absent from the network altogether (Staples 2013).

In the second step, the six major business groups, several of which double as discussion groups within the policy-planning network, were reinserted into the database. As might be expected from the results in Chapter 2, three of them (the Business Roundtable, the Business Council, and the Committee for Economic Development) were the most central organizations in the enlarged database. They were joined in the top 25 by the other three general business groups, the nine think tanks and specialized policy-discussion groups from the first step, and 10 large corporations. More generally, 497 of the 552 organizations (90 percent) of the organizations in the combined corporate community and policy-planning network were connected to each other either directly or indirectly, which is slightly higher than the figure for the *Fortune* 500 by themselves (87.5 percent), as reported in Chapter 2 (Staples 2013). Thus, the first two steps in the study made it possible to establish that the corporate community and the policy-planning networks are almost completely integrated into one larger network. The 40 highest-ranking organizations in the complete database of *Fortune* 500 firms, business groups, and think tanks are listed in Table 4.1.

Table 4.1 The 40 Highest-Ranking Organizations in the Combined Corporate and Policy-Planning Networks

Ranking	Organization	Ranking	Organization
1	Business Roundtable	21	National Bureau of Economic Research
2	Business Council	22	Chevron
3	Committee for Economic Development	23	Deere
4	Brookings Institution	24	Eli Lilly
5	Center for Strategic and International Studies	25	General Electric
6	Institute for International Economics	26	Pfizer
7	National Association of Manufacturers	27	3M
8	Atlantic Council	28	AT&T
9	Chamber of Commerce	29	American Express
10	Council on Foreign Relations	30	Boeing
11	Aspen Institute[1]	31	FedEx
12	Marathon Oil	32	Medtronic
13	American Enterprise Institute	33	Aetna
14	Caterpillar	34	Coca-Cola
15	IBM	35	ConocoPhillips
16	RAND Corporation	36	General Mills
17	United Technologies	37	McDonald's
18	Alcoa	38	Verizon
19	Conference Board	39	Wells Fargo
20	Ford Motor	40	Abbott Laboratories

[1] Although the Aspen Institute is usually listed as a think tank, it does not issue specific policy recommendations with a corporate imprimatur, and it is best described as a general discussion center and a training ground for future leadership.

Source: Staples 2013.

The centrality of the business groups in relation to the think tanks and corporate community was demonstrated in the third step of the study. It used the members of the Business Council and Business Roundtable as the starting point for an "egonet" to determine the extent to which the combined corporate community and policy-planning networks could be reproduced with just the 271 people who were in one or both of those groups. It revealed that 40 percent of the organizations were connected directly or indirectly to the Business Council and the Business Roundtable (Staples 2013). This is strong testimony to the centrality of these two business groups and to the integration of the corporate community and the policy-planning network at the director level.

These several findings are consistent with studies of corporate directors from the 1970s, 1990s, and early 2000s, which obtained similar results using a smaller number of corporations as a starting point (Dolan 2011, Chapter 4; Moore, Sobieraj, Whitt, Mayorova, and Beaulieu 2002; Salzman and Domhoff 1983). They are also consistent with two studies focused exclusively on the trustees of 12 think tanks and policy groups for 1973, 1980, 1990, and 2000 (Burris 1992; Burris 2008).

With the overlap between the corporate community and the policy-planning network documented for a period of several decades, it is possible to look at foundations, think tanks, and policy-discussion groups in more detail to show how they shaped major new policies throughout the twentieth and early twenty-first centuries.

FOUNDATIONS

Among the 65,000 to 75,000 foundations that exist in the United States, with some going out of business each year and new ones being added, only a few dozen have the money and interest to involve themselves in funding programs that have a bearing on national-level public policy. Foundations are of four basic types:

1. According to the authoritative *Guide to U.S. Foundations*, published by the Foundation Center, there were about 8,300 *independent* foundations among the largest 10,000 foundations in 2010–2011, all of which were created by families to serve a wide variety of purposes. Most were relatively small and local. Only about 10 percent of them donated over $500,000 a year, led by the Gates Foundation in 2011, based on a Microsoft fortune, with $2.5 billion; the Walton Family Foundation, based on a Wal-Mart fortune, with $1.5 billion; the Ford Foundation, with $424.7 million; and the Robert Wood Johnson Foundation, based on a medical supplies fortune, with $359.2 million. Another 21 family foundations gave $100 million or more.

2. There were 884 major *corporate* foundations for the same two-year period, which are mostly funded on a year-by-year basis by the corporations that sponsor them. Their number and importance increased greatly after the 1970s, and they provided $4.7 billion in donations

in 2010. The Bank of America Foundation headed the list with $190.7 million, followed by the Wal-Mart Foundation ($164.1 million), the JPMorgan Chase Foundation ($133.8 million), the GE Foundation ($112.2 million), and the ExxonMobil Foundation ($72.2 million).

3. There were 446 *community* foundations at the local level, which are designed to aid charities, voluntary associations, and special projects in their home cities. They receive funds from a variety of sources, including independent foundations, corporate foundations, and wealthy families. Boards that include both corporate executives and community leaders usually direct them. In some cities, such as Cleveland, the community foundation is an integral part of the local power structure (Tittle 1992). The community foundation in New Orleans, directed by leaders in the city's growth coalition, proved to be a useful conduit for outside donations to help the city after Hurricane Katrina in 2005, and in the rebuilding process the city was reconfigured more to the liking of major landowners, developers, and the tourism industry (BondGraham 2011). A few of the larger community foundations give money outside of their local area, usually at the direction of a wealthy donor that has set up a separate fund within the foundation, thereby saving administrative costs.

4. Finally, there were 291 foundations that used their money to finance a particular museum, garden project, or artistic exhibit. They are called *operating* foundations and are not of concern in terms of the policy-planning process. Operating foundations contribute to the control of the fine arts and high culture by the corporate rich.

The general importance of foundations to the other organizations in the policy-planning network is revealed in summary figures brought together and analyzed by sociologist Clifford Staples (2013) using the *Foundation Directory Online.* Between 2003 and 2011, 1,260 foundations gave $1.9 billion via 10,549 individual grants to the 41 most prominent think tanks and specialized policy-discussion groups. However, the 25 largest foundations alone accounted for over 71 percent of the total donations.

The first extensive study of the relationship of policy-discussion groups to foundations and think tanks, carried out with information from the late 1970s, started with a sample of 77 large foundations, which included 20 that had over $100 million in assets and gave over $200,000 in public policy grants. These 20 foundations led to a group of 31 think tanks and policy-planning groups that received grants from three or more of these foundations (Colwell 1980; Colwell 1993). This analysis also demonstrated that a set of policy groups and think tanks identified with ultraconservative programs were linked to a separate set of foundations. The findings on the ultraconservative foundations were confirmed in another study that used tax returns to reveal that 12 foundations provided half the funding for the American Enterprise Institute as well as 85 percent or more of the funding for the other prominent ultraconservative think tanks (Allen 1992). Corporate foundations also supported some of these groups, but they gave donations to the moderate-conservative groups as well. The continuing nature of this relationship was demonstrated in a study of an even large number of ultraconservative foundations that provided donations to a wide range of ultraconservative think tanks between 2003 and 2011 (Staples 2013).

Upper-class and corporate representation on the boards of the large general-purpose foundations that give policy-oriented grants to the most central think tanks and policy groups has been documented in several past studies. In a study of the 12 largest foundations in the 1960s, for example, it was found that half the trustees were members of the upper class (Domhoff 1967, pp. 64–71). A study of corporate connections into the policy network in the 1970s showed that 10 of these 12 foundations had at least one connection to the 201 largest corporations; most had many more than that (Salzman and Domhoff 1983). Since that time, due to a combination of factors, including smaller boards, an effort to diversify on the basis of gender and color, and the addition of a few directors from other countries, the director links between the largest foundations and the corporate community declined somewhat, as shown by a quick look at the board of trustees for 2011 for the Ford and Rockefeller foundations.

At the Ford Foundation, the only corporate executives on the 13-person board were a senior director of Goldman Sachs, who also sat on the board of the State Street Corporation (a financial company) and taught at the Harvard Business School; the CEO of Sonic Corporation, a drive-in restaurant company headquartered in Oklahoma City, with 3,500 outlets in 43 states; and the co-founder of Infosys Technologies, an international software services firm in India. There were also two investment advisors, one a former senior advisor at Morgan Stanley. The board also included two corporate lawyers, a professor at MIT, and the presidents of Planned Parenthood, the Japanese American National Museum in Los Angeles, and the University of Texas at Brownsville. The foundation's president rounded out the board; he was formerly a director of McKinsey & Company, a management consulting firm. As for the Rockefeller Foundation, nine of the 13 trustees are active in the corporate world, seven as directors on a dozen *Fortune* 500 boards and one as the founder and CEO of a major Internet and cellular company in South Africa. The ninth trustee active in the corporate world is also the chair of the foundation's board, David Rockefeller Jr., the son of the former chair of Chase Manhattan Bank, one of the banks that became part of JPMorgan Chase. In 1991 Rockefeller Jr.'s cousins elected him as president of the family's Rockefeller Financial Services, a $3 billion holding company that manages the family's stockholdings, real estate interests, and other assets. Another trustee is the minister of finance for Nigeria. The remaining three are the president of the University of Texas at El Paso, a former Harvard professor of microbiology and molecular genetics who became a senior associate in biology at the California Institute of Technology when she retired, and a retired Supreme Court justice, Sandra Day O'Connor.

Foundations often become much more than sources of money when they set up special programs that are thought to be necessary by their trustees or staff. Then they create special commissions within the foundation itself or search out appropriate organizations to undertake the project. A few foundations have become so committed to a specific issue that they function as a policy-discussion organization on that topic. The Ford Foundation provides the best example of this point because it became involved in two of the main issues of the 1960s, environmentalism and the tensions that arise when downtown business districts attempt to expand into nearby low-income neighborhoods, which have persisted ever since.

First, it played a major role in creating and sustaining the mainstream organizations that have been the leaders of the environmental movement for many decades. Its conference on resource management in 1953 and subsequent start-up funding led to the founding of the first and most prominent environmental think tank, Resources for the Future. This organization broke new ground by incorporating market economics into thinking about conservation work. Economists at Resources for the Future and other think tanks showed that resource substitution could be managed through the price system and that it was a myth to claim there is a trade-off between jobs and environmental regulation. They also pointed out that there was money to be made in cleaning up the air and water. Their work reassured moderate conservatives that most environmental initiatives were completely compatible with the current economic system, contrary to the angry outcries of ultraconservatives (Alpert and Markusen 1980; Goodstein 1999).

In the early 1960s, the Ford Foundation spent $7 million over a three-year period developing ecology programs at 17 universities around the country, thereby providing the informational base and personnel infrastructure for efforts to control pesticides and industrial waste. At the same time, the foundation put large sums into the land-purchase programs of Nature Conservancy and the National Audubon Society. It also encouraged environmental education and citizen action through grants to municipal conservation commissions and the nationwide Conservation Foundation, the latter founded by the Rockefeller family as a combined think tank and policy-discussion group (Robinson 1993). The new militant wing of the environmental movement soon moved beyond the purview envisioned by the moderate conservatives, inspired in part by Rachel Carson's book *Silent Spring* (1962), but the fact remains that much of the early grassroots movement was encouraged and legitimated by major foundations and some of the established environmental groups funded by them. As an Audubon Society biologist who read Carson's book in galleys later said, "She had it right," but he also added, "It's a fabrication to say that she's the founder of the environmental movement. She stirred the pot" (Griswold 2012, p. 39).

In the 1970s the Ford Foundation aided environmentalists in another way by backing several new environmental law firms that used the legal system to force corporations and municipal governments to clean up the water, air, and soil. Leaders at the foundation actually created one of these organizations, the Natural Resources Defense Council (NRDC), by bringing together several Wall

Street corporate lawyers with a group of young Yale Law School graduates who wanted to devote their careers to environmental law. Ford then gave the new organization $2.6 million between 1970 and 1977. Between 1971 and 1977, it also gave $1.6 million to the Center for Law in the Public Interest in Los Angeles, $994,000 to the Environmental Defense Fund, and $603,000 to the Sierra Club Legal Defense Fund. Many of the young leaders in these organizations became senior spokespersons for the environmental movement in later decades (Mitchell 1991; NRDC 1990).

Appointees to the Nixon administration from the mainstream environmental groups helped secure tax-exempt status for the environmental law firms. They then presided over the creation of the federal government's Council on Environmental Quality and the Environmental Protection Agency. Indeed, the origins of these agencies provide an ideal example of how moderate conservatives create policies that are later reinterpreted as setbacks for the corporate community. At the same time, these organizations are often criticized by strong environmentalists as being too cautious and for "selling out" via compromises on key issues (Dowie 1995). Although the Ford Foundation continued to give environmental grants, mostly to organizations in other nations, its support for American environmental groups was more modest after these organizations were firmly established. However, several dozen major foundations, including corporate foundations, picked up the slack.

Second, the Ford Foundation became the equivalent of a policy group on the issue of urban unrest in the late 1950s, creating a wide range of programs to deal with the problems generated by urban renewal and racial tensions in cities. One of these programs, called the Gray Areas Project, became the basis for the War on Poverty declared by the Johnson administration in 1964. Once the War on Poverty was launched, the Ford Foundation donated tens of millions of dollars to support for community-action organizations and groups formed by communities of color in the inner cities, with a strong focus on the millions of African Americans who were being displaced (Domhoff 2013, Chapters 6 and 7). These investments were seen at the time as a way of encouraging insurgent groups to take a nonviolent and electoral direction in addressing the obstacles they encountered. By the 1970s, when the social disruption had subsided, ultraconservatives began to criticize the Ford Foundation for its support for what they called "liberal experiments." However, the foundation persisted in this support, which was seen by moderate conservatives in the corporate community as a sensible way to incorporate people of color into the larger society. (For a detailed account of the Ford Foundation's leadership on urban issues, see the document "The Ford Foundation in the Inner City" on whorulesamerica.net.)

Foundation funding was also essential for three Mexican American advocacy organizations: the National Council of La Raza, the Mexican American Legal Defense and Educational Fund, and the Industrial Areas Foundation's network of city-level organizations in Texas. All three developed during the turmoil of the 1960s and continued their work thereafter. A study of their income statements filed with the Internal Revenue Service over the 10-year period from 1991 to 2000 showed that most of them received virtually all of their money from a handful of foundations, led by the Ford Foundation, the Rockefeller Foundation, and the Mott Foundation (based on a General Motors fortune). Furthermore, the Ford Foundation took an active role in the establishment of the National Council of La Raza and the Mexican American Legal Defense and Educational Fund to begin with (Marquez 1993).

The absence of any local or membership fundraising in the case of the Industrial Areas Foundation affiliates came as a surprise. The inspiration for its efforts, Saul Alinsky, emphasized that outside funding should be used only at the outset of an organizing effort to ensure that local volunteer leadership controlled the grassroots groups. With only two or three exceptions in the seven cities in which the project operated, most of their monies came from large foundations and local businesses, and none had a majority of its funding from neighborhood members. The funding for these organizations increased greatly after they set up an Interfaith Education Fund, which became a conduit for foundations. In effect, organizers paid by foundations were the people that managed the Industrial Areas Foundation affiliates in Texas, even though local volunteer leadership nominally controlled them (Marquez 2003).

The ongoing importance of large foundations to these groups is demonstrated by the fact that the Mexican American Legal Defense and Educational Fund received $27.1 million in donations from 56 foundations between 2003 and 2011, with 70 percent of it coming from the Ford Foundation ($10.2 million), BP ($3.8 million), the Marguerite Casey Foundation ($1.5 million), the Gates Foundation ($1.3 million), and three other foundations that gave $1 million or more. In the case of the National Council of La Raza, which received $96.5 million from 79 foundations, 85 percent of it came from the 22 foundations that gave $1 million or more, led by the Gates Foundation ($16.2 million), the Bank of America ($12.2 million), Pepsico ($9.2 million), the Annie Casey Foundation ($5.5 million), and the Wal-Mart Foundation ($4.8 million) (Staples 2013). The intermediary role of the Interfaith Education Fund for the Industrial Areas Foundation in Texas continued in an expanded form, as shown by a listing of its seven top donors in Table 4.2 (on page 87).

Foundations funded several other major advocacy groups between 2003 and 2011 in varying patterns and degrees of intensity. For example, the Ford Foundation was a strong supporter of the NAACP Legal Defense and Educational Fund with donations totaling $13.2 million. It was joined by several other family foundations with total grants in the million-dollar range, as well as the New York Community Trust, which gave $3.8 million, but by very few corporate foundations. On the other hand, corporate foundations were frequent donors of $1 million or more to two other organizations that advocate for African Americans, the United Negro College Fund and the Urban League, although their donations were dwarfed in the case of the United Negro College Fund by $61.1 million from the Gates Foundation, $11.4 million from the Andrew Mellon Foundation

Table 4.2 Foundations Donating over $600,000 to the Interfaith Education Fund, 2003–2011

Foundation Name	No. of Grants	Total Donations
Ford Foundation	5	$ 4,600,000
Mott Foundation	12	$ 3,200,000
Marguerite Casey Foundation (UPS family)	7	$ 1,380,000
Annie Casey Foundation (UPS family)	10	$ 1,285,000
Gates Foundation	1	$ 954,216
Open Society[1]	3	$ 750,000
Cummings Foundation (founder of Sara Lee Corporation)	3	$ 637,500
All Foundations = 16	55	$14,519,716

[1] This organization, funded by a billionaire investor George Soros, was called the Open Society Institute until 2011, and then renamed the Foundation to Promote Open Society.

Source: Foundation Grants Directory Online (2012).

(the 10th-largest family foundation), and $10.7 million from the Kresge Foundation (the 12th-largest family foundation).

Corporate foundations also steered clear of advocacy groups for women, which received most of their foundation support from family foundations. The Ford Foundation gave $13.3 million to the Ms. Foundation, and the Kellogg Foundation (the sixth-largest family foundation) provided another $3.8 million. When it came to Planned Parenthood, which is under incessant pressure from ultraconservatives, four family foundations were at the forefront, starting with the ninth-largest family foundation, the Susan Thompson Buffett Foundation, named after the late wife of investor Warren Buffett and chaired by their daughter. Large contributions also came from the fifth- and seventh-largest family foundations, the Hewlett Foundation and the Packard Foundation. Both of these foundations derive from the large fortunes made by William Hewlett and David Packard as the founders of Hewlett-Packard, ranked No. 11 on the *Fortune* 500 list in 2011. The Gates Foundation, the largest family foundation in the country by many orders of magnitude, also provided large donations. The specific amounts provided by these four family foundations to Planned Parenthood at the national level (the Susan Thompson Buffett Foundation also gave tens of millions to Planned Parenthood's state, local, and international affiliates) are presented in Table 4.3 (on page 88).

The Ford Foundation's support for disadvantaged people of color, low-income children, women, and the environmental movement led to the claim that it became a "liberal" organization in the 1960s, despite its corporate-dominated board of trustees at the time, including the chairman of the Ford Motor Company, Henry Ford II. However, this conclusion confuses liberalism with a moderate

Table 4.3 Donations to Planned Parenthood by Four Large Family Foundations

Foundation	Family Foundation Ranking	Total Donations
Buffett Foundation	No. 9	$184,900,000
Hewlett Foundation	No. 5	$41,000,000
Gates Foundation	No. 1	$33,500,000
Packard Foundation	No. 7	$16,100,000

Source: Foundation Directory Online (New York: The Foundation Center, 2012).

conservatism that is supportive of changes that do not challenge the class structure. Incorporation into the current system is one thing; altering power balances between the corporate community and its main rivals is another.

This difference is demonstrated by the fact that the Ford Foundation took a very different stance on issues that involve class conflict, as seen in the foundation's support for opposition to unionization efforts. In 1967, for example, the Ford Foundation entered into an emerging conflict over public employee unions by financing a think-tank study that was very negative toward unions. Then, in 1970, it provided $450,000 to three associations of government managers—the U.S. Conference of Mayors, the National League of Cities, and the National Association of Counties—to establish the Labor-Management Relations Service, an organization intended to help government managers cope with efforts at union organizing. One year later this organization set up the National Public Employer Labor Relations Association with money from the Ford Foundation and other foundations (Miller and Canak 1995). Publications from these two organizations provided advice on defeating organizing drives and surviving strikes. They suggested contracting out public services to private businesses to avoid unions and decrease wage costs. This opposition to public employee unions is consistent with the distance that all major foundations have kept from the labor movement (Magat 1999).

As shown by both the systematic data and the several mini–case studies presented in this section, foundations are an integral part of the policy-planning process as sources of funds and as program initiators. Contrary to the usual perceptions, they are not merely donors of money for charity and value-free academic research. They are extensions of the corporate community in their origins, leadership, and goals.

THINK TANKS

The most sustained research and brainstorming within the policy-planning network usually takes place in various think tanks. Experts bring any new initiatives that survive criticism by other experts to the policy-discussion groups for discussion, modification, and possible use by the corporate leaders. Among the relative handful of major think tanks, some highly specialized in one or two topics, the most important are The Brookings Institution, the American Enterprise Institute, the Urban Institute, the National Bureau of Economic Research, the RAND Corporation, the Atlantic Institute, and the Center for Strategic and International Studies. Their efforts are sometimes augmented by advice from professors at institutes and centers connected to universities, especially in the area of foreign relations, but these university institutes are one step removed from the policy-planning network, as explained in the next section.

Three highly visible general-purpose think tanks—The Brookings Institution, the American Enterprise Institute (AEI), and the Heritage Foundation—vie for attention and influence in Washington. The Brookings Institution, the oldest and generally most respected of the three, was founded in 1927 from three institutes that go back as far as 1916. Virtually all of its early money came from foundations, although by the 1930s it was earning income from a small endowment provided by the Rockefeller Foundation and other sources. Centrist in its orientation, it ranked No. 4 in centrality in the combined corporate community and policy-planning networks in 2010, received $164.2 million in grants from foundations between 2003 and 2011, and had a budget of about $90 million in 2010. By comparison, the ultra-conservative AEI ranked No. 13 in centrality, received $56.2 million in foundation grants between 2003 and 2011, and had a budget of about $30 million in 2010. Finally, the even more ultraconservative Heritage Foundation ranked No. 321 in the overall network, but received much more money by way of foundation grants ($77.8 million) and had a far larger budget ($80 million in 2010) than did its ultra-conservative rival, the AEI (Staples 2013).

The Brookings Institution is sometimes said to be a liberal think tank, but that is a misperception generated by the presence of a few liberal members and overblown media complaints by ultraconservatives. The fact that Keynesian economists from Brookings advised the Kennedy and Johnson administrations also contributed to this stereotype.* In fact, the Brookings Institution always has

---

* For purposes of this book, the essence of "Keynesian economics" is that governments need to temporarily spend more money, run larger deficits, and/or lower interest rates in times of recession and depression because (1) consumers are not able to generate sufficient demand through their purchases and (2) businesses are unwilling to make investments because consumers do not have the money to buy new products. Conversely, when the economy is strong and inflation might develop, Keynesian economics suggests that the government should move closer to a balanced budget, impose higher taxes on the wealthy and well-to-do, and/or raise interest rates. This is not "liberalism," but an economic model based on economic analysis and historical experience. The originator of this theory, British economist John Maynard Keynes, thought that it had moderately conservative implications. As explained later in the chapter in the discussion of the Committee for Economic Development, even corporate moderates rejected most of the theory because they did not like the idea of government spending (for political reasons) and did not like the prescription of higher taxes on them to balance the budget and restrain demand when the economy is at risk for higher inflation. Instead, they preferred the aspect of Keynesian theory that relies strictly on changes in interest rates by the Federal Reserve Board, which is the government agency they shape and trust the most through their service on the boards of directors for the 12 Federal Reserve Banks throughout the country.

been in the mainstream or on the right wing. Although some of its economists were important advisors to the Democrats in the 1960s, they were also among the most important advisors to the corporate moderates in the Committee for Economic Development as well, and by 1975 these same economists were criticizing government initiatives in ways that later were attributed to the employees of the American Enterprise Institute (Peschek 1987).

The Brookings Institution's most noteworthy effort in the mid-2000s, the Hamilton Project, named after the first secretary of the treasury, Alexander Hamilton, was aimed at influencing future Democratic administrations. It brought together leaders in various types of financial companies, economists, and policy experts from several think tanks in 2006 to write reports on such topics as economic growth, the federal budget, and international trade. It was sponsored by one of The Brookings Institution's most prominent trustees at the time (a former chair of Goldman Sachs and the secretary of the treasury for four years in the Clinton administration). Several of its participants did end up consulting for President Obama's 2008 economic transition team, and two economists in the group were appointed to the new president's White House staff.

The American Enterprise Institute, formed in 1943 as an adjunct to the U.S. Chamber of Commerce, had little money and no influence until the early 1970s, when a former chamber employee began selling the need for a new think tank to corporate executives by exaggerating the liberal inclinations of the Brookings Institution. His efforts received a large boost in 1972 after the Ford Foundation gave him a $300,000 grant (the equivalent of a grant of $1.7 million in 2012). But as already shown, the AEI still received less money from foundations than did The Brookings Institution, and its budget was only one-third as large as the Brookings budget in 2010.

The Heritage Foundation, created in 1974, is the most recent and famous of the Washington think tanks. It is wrongly thought to reflect current wisdom in the corporate community, but it is actually the product of a few extremely conservative men of inherited wealth. The most important of these founding ultraconservatives were members of the Coors family, which then owned the beer company that bears their name (Bellant 1991). Richard Mellon Scaife, a major inheritor of a huge aluminum, steel, and banking fortune, which was assembled by the Mellon family of Pittsburgh beginning in the nineteenth century, served on the board of trustees of the Heritage Foundation and was close behind the Coors family in his donations.

Unlike the AEI, the Heritage Foundation usually made no effort to hire established experts or build a record of respectability within the academic or policy communities. Instead, it hired young ultraconservatives that were willing to attack all government programs and impugn the motives of all government officials as bureaucratic empire builders. While this approach did not endear the Heritage Foundation to its counterparts in Washington, it did lead to second-level staff positions in the Reagan, George H. W. Bush, and George W. Bush administrations, which needed people to carry out their antigovernment objectives. Ironically, a substantive idea from a Heritage Foundation report in the early 1990s concerning health insurance was built into the health insurance program that Mitt Romney signed while he was governor of Massachusetts in 2006. It mandated the purchase of insurance by all adults as a necessary ingredient in making a universal private insurance program feasible and profitable for insurance companies. This mandate then became a key feature, insisted upon by the insurance companies, in the Patient Protection and Affordable Care Act ("Obamacare") passed in 2010, but by that time all ultraconservatives had rejected the idea and opposed the bill (Quadagno 2012).

THE MIXED ROLE OF UNIVERSITIES IN AMERICAN POWER CONFLICTS

The thousands of research institutes at the top 100 or so American universities, which range from a few members to hundreds of members, train many of the experts who become employees at think tanks. Some of the professors in these university institutes advise think tanks or take part in policy-discussion groups. Thus, it may seem that universities should be considered a part of the policy-planning network, but that would not take into account the complex role that universities have in the American power structure. In a very general sense, yes, universities are part of the power equation because they educate future leaders and train the experts who work for the think tanks discussed in the previous section. This is especially the case for the handful of prestigious private schools such as Harvard, Yale, Stanford, and the University of Chicago, which have very large endowments to support their programs and students. It is also true that the trustees of the top private universities, as well as many large state universities, are disproportionately from the corporate community and upper class, as demonstrated by numerous investigations stretching back to the early twentieth century (e.g., Barrow 1990; Pusser, Slaughter, and Thomas 2006).

Nevertheless, universities are not part of the policy-planning network because only specific institutes within them are directly involved in it in any way. Furthermore, both the faculty and student bodies at many universities are too diverse in their intellectual and political orientations to be considered part of the power structure unless corporations or organizations in the policy formation network employ them. Then, too, a significant minority of faculty in some social science and humanities departments supports the liberal-labor alliance or are leftists of various kinds, and many more professors have come to give campaign donations to the Democrats because of the criticisms of science and universities by a large number of Republican leaders and ultraconservative grassroots activists. In addition, the institution of tenure, which protects senior faculty members from arbitrary dismissal in order to encourage academic freedom, gives the faculty some degree of independence from trustees and administrators. The nationwide American Association of University Professors and other faculty organizations zealously guard this tenure system and other faculty rights.

Nor are all students who graduate from high-status universities uniformly destined to join the corporate community or the policy-planning network. A small minority become leading activists in the liberal-labor alliance, sometimes immediately after graduation, sometimes after a career in business. Longtime consumer activist Ralph Nader is a graduate of Princeton University and Harvard Law School, for example. The person who provided much of the money in the early 1960s to start the Institute for Policy Studies, a left-leaning think tank in Washington, was a wealthy graduate of Harvard, who worked as an investment banker on Wall Street before beginning his journey to liberalism (Warburg 1964). David Dellinger, the son of a corporate lawyer and a pacifist who led many major antiwar efforts from the 1950s through the 1980s, entitled his autobiography *From Yale to Jail* (1993), a title that provides a useful reminder of the extent to which some graduates of Ivy League universities become leaders on the American left. John Wilhelm, the president of UNITE HERE, a service workers union with about 230,000 members in 2011, began his career in the union movement in the late 1960s by trying to organize employees at his extremely antiunion alma mater, Yale University.

Put another way, universities provide resources and recruits for both the corporate community and its opponents. In recent decades corporations have come to fund or benefit from the research carried out on university campuses in the natural sciences, information sciences, and engineering to the point at which "campus capitalism" and "University, Inc." are used in the titles of books examining the near takeover of many research areas by corporations (Greenberg 2007; Washburn 2005). However, universities are a far more important political base for activist liberals and leftists, whether on the faculty or in the student body, than they are for the corporate community. Indeed, the educational system in general, including public high schools and libraries, may be the most important institutional home for liberalism in the United States. The educational system also is the basis for two of the largest unions in the liberal-labor alliance, the National Education Association with 3.2 million members and the American Federation of Teachers with 2.0 million members in 2011, which is one reason why ultraconservatives came to favor charter schools and vouchers as a possible way to undercut teachers' unions.

Based on these complexities, it seems more useful to see the universities as a training ground for people on both sides of class and social-issues conflicts in the United States. Thus, only those experts from universities who work for think tanks or consult for policy-discussion groups in the policy-planning networks are relevant to the corporate side of the power equation. Even then, many of them may have very temporary roles out of personal choice or because they are not seen as helpful by corporate leaders. Only those who come to have major roles within the policy-planning network become part of the leadership group for the corporate rich, which is discussed in the final section of this chapter.

THE POLICY-DISCUSSION GROUPS

The policy-discussion groups are in many ways the linchpins in the policy-planning network because they serve several important functions for the corporate community.

1. They provide a setting in which corporate leaders can familiarize themselves with general policy issues by listening to and questioning the experts from think tanks and university research institutes.

2. They provide a forum in which conflicts between moderate conservatives and ultraconservatives can be discussed and compromises can be reached, usually by including experts of both persuasions within the discussion group, along with an occasional liberal or university professor on some issues.

3. They provide an informal training ground for new leadership. It is within these organizations that corporate leaders can determine in an informal fashion which of their peers are best suited for service in government and as spokespersons to other groups.

4. They provide an informal recruiting ground for determining which policy experts may be best suited for government service, either as faceless staff aides to the corporate leaders who take government positions or as high-level appointees in their own right.

In addition, the policy groups have three useful roles in relation to the rest of society:

1. These groups legitimate their members as serious and expert persons capable of government service. This image is created because group members are portrayed as giving of their own time to take part in highly selective organizations that are nonpartisan and nonprofit in nature.

2. They convey the concerns, goals, and expectations of the corporate community to those young experts and young professors who want to further their careers by receiving foundation grants, invitations to work at think tanks, and invitations to take part in policy discussion groups.

3. Through such avenues as books, journals, policy statements, press releases, and speakers, these groups try to influence the climate of opinion both in Washington and the country at large. This point is developed when the opinion-shaping network is discussed in the next chapter.

The remainder of this section and the next sketches the origins and activities of five major policy-discussion organizations. They are discussed in chronological order to show how they often arose in response to new issues, especially in times of crisis. In effect, an accounting of their activities and successes provides a history of the main power struggles within the United States between 1900 and the early 2000s from the perspective of the corporate rich. Discussing these organizations in chronological order also helps to explain the nature of the policy disagreements between the moderates and the ultraconservatives in the corporate community.

The National Association of Manufacturers and the U.S. Chamber of Commerce

The National Association of Manufacturers (NAM), founded in 1895, was the first nationwide organization that encompassed a large part of the newly emerging corporate community of that era. Its primary purpose was to encourage the marketing of American products overseas. To that end, its first president tried to avoid any discussion of management-labor issues. However, when antiunion employers took over the association in 1903 in a three-way race for the presidency, it quickly turned into the largest and most visible opponent of trade unions in the United States. It then provided coordination and strategic advice for the many industrial sectors that renewed their battles with union organizers after a brief but failed attempt to create an "Era of Good Feelings" through collective bargaining agreements. It next created a staff to provide advice and draft reports for committees of trustees, which made it possible for the organization to take stands (usually very conservative) on a wider range of policy issues. At this point it became a policy-discussion group as well as a trade association. As part of this ultraconservative direction, the trustees abandoned their efforts to expand sales overseas, turning their attention to developing American markets for the member corporations.

The Chamber of Commerce was initiated in 1911 as a way to coordinate the interests of a wider range of business owners than simply manufacturers, with special attention to the needs of retailing companies. Its early orientation is reflected in the concerns of one of its key founders, the liberal owner of William Filene & Sons, a major department store in Boston. Like the NAM, it developed a range of committees to discuss specific policy issues, some of which were supportive of President Franklin D. Roosevelt's first attempts to deal with the Great Depression. However, the chamber was in all-out opposition to Roosevelt's New Deal by the spring of 1934, against the wishes of its liberal founder, who remained highly committed to the New Deal. With occasional exceptions, the Chamber of Commerce has adopted positions much like those of the NAM ever since it turned against the New Deal.

The Council on Foreign Relations

With the NAM turning inward and looking out for the interests of industrial corporations, and the Chamber of Commerce increasingly focused on local businesses and retailing, internationally oriented bankers and leaders in large corporations established the Council on Foreign Relations (CFR) in 1921. Lawyers, diplomats, and academic experts interested in fostering a larger role for United States in world affairs joined them. The CFR was created in part because of its leaders' disappointment with the terms of the peace settlement after World War I. However, they also wanted to counter the nationalistic, even isolationist orientation that had developed within the NAM, which by the 1920s supported high tariffs to protect American industrialists from foreign competition. The CFR's desire to expand American financial and corporate interests in Europe was opposed by the NAM, thereby creating a policy division within the corporate community that lasted for another 50 years. After losing most battles over trade and tariffs in the 1920s, the CFR and other internationalist organizations achieved their first major success with the Trade Act of 1934, which gave the executive branch the authority to negotiate trade agreements that would then be approved or disapproved by Congress (Dreiling and Darves 2011; Woods 2003).

The council exerts its influence through policy statements that are created by study groups with 15 to 25 members, which bring together business executives, government officials, scholars, and military officers for detailed consideration of specific topics. Usually meeting about once a month, their work revolves around discussion papers by a visiting research fellow (financed by a foundation grant) or a regular staff member. The goal of such study groups is a statement of the problem and a set of policy recommendations by the scholar leading the discussion. Any book that eventuates from the group is understood to express the views of its academic author, not of the council or the members of the study group, but the books are nonetheless published with the sponsorship of the CFR. The names of the people participating in the study group are usually listed at the outset of each book. In addition, the CFR conducts an active program of luncheon and dinner speeches in New York and Washington, and encourages dialogue and disseminates information through books, pamphlets, and articles in its influential periodical, *Foreign Affairs*. Hundreds of its members have been appointed to government positions in the executive branch of the federal government since the 1940s, including virtually every secretary of state.

The CFR's most successful set of study groups created the framework for the post–World War II international economy. Beginning in 1939 with financial support from the Rockefeller Foundation, its War-Peace Studies developed the postwar definition of the national interest through a comprehensive set of discussion groups. These groups brought together approximately 100 top bankers, lawyers, executives, economists, and military experts in 362 meetings over a five-year period. The academic experts within the study groups met regularly with officials of the State Department. In 1942, the experts became part of the department's new postwar planning process as twice-a-week consultants, while at the same time continuing work on the War-Peace project. As all accounts agree, the State Department had little or no planning capability of its own at the time.

Although the study groups sent hundreds of reports to the State Department, the most important one defined the minimum geographical area that was needed for the American economy to make full utilization of its resources and at the same time maintain harmony with Western Europe and Japan. This geographical area, which came to be known as the "Grand Area," included Latin America, Europe, the colonies of the British Empire, and all of Southeast Asia. Southeast Asia was necessary as a source of raw materials for Great Britain and Japan and as a consumer of Japanese products. The American national interest was then defined in terms of the integration and defense of the Grand Area, which led to plans for the United Nations, the International Monetary Fund, and the World Bank, and eventually to the decision to defend Vietnam from a communist takeover at all costs. The goal was to avoid both another Great Depression and increased government control of what was at the time a very sluggish economy. This work provided the framework within which American economic dominance of the world unfolded over the next 30 years (Domhoff 1990, Chapters 5, 6, and 8; Shoup 1974).

Among many dozens of policy studies that had an impact after that time, a report on America's relationship with Iran in 2004 (*Iran: Time for a New Approach*), calling for negotiations instead of continuing confrontation, provides one good example. The co-leader of the 2004 study group, Robert M. Gates, a former CIA official, then serving as the president of Texas A&M, went on to be a key member of the bipartisan Iraq Study Group authorized by Congress, which made a similar recommendation in 2006 for negotiations, as well as for a phased withdrawal of American troops from Iraq and negotiations with Syria and Iran to end the war. Although American policy toward Iran and Iraq did not change for several more years, Gates was appointed secretary of defense shortly after the study group's report appeared and then was reappointed to that position by President Obama. He retired in 2010.

Several past studies demonstrated the organization's connections to the upper class and the corporate community. For example, 22 percent of the members in 1969 served on the board of at least one of *Fortune*'s top 500 industrials, and a study that included the directors of 201 large corporations found that 125 of those companies had 293 interlocks with the CFR; 23 of the very largest corporations and banks had four or more directors who were members (Domhoff 1983; Salzman and Domhoff 1983).

The 37-member board of directors in 2011 reflected the ongoing ties of the CFR to the corporate community and the rest of the policy-planning network with a ranking of No. 10 in the combined corporate/policy database (Staples 2013). Sixteen of its members were on one or more corporate boards, linking the council to 14 companies across the country, including two interlocks with FedEx, IBM, and MetLife. It also had ties to three financial firms, including Goldman Sachs and the Carlyle Group. Reflecting its central location in the overall policy-planning network, four of its members were also trustees of the Committee for Economic Development, three were members of the Business Council, and one was a member of the Business Roundtable. It had several trustee interlocks with think tanks as well: four with the Institute for International Economics and three with

The Brookings Institution and the Center for Strategic and International Studies. The board also included two former secretaries of state, one from the Clinton administration, one from the George W. Bush administration, along with a former secretary of the treasury in the Clinton administration and several scholars.

The council grew from several dozen to several hundred members in its first 30 years of existence, but then grew much larger in the 1970s in response to criticism from the left and right by including a larger number of government officials, especially Foreign Service officers, politicians, and aides to congressional committees concerned with foreign policy, which also made it possible to include many more women members than in the past. By the early 2000s, the council had approximately 4,500 members, most of whom do little more than receive reports and attend large banquets. It is therefore far too large for its members to issue policy proclamations as a group. Moreover, its usefulness as a neutral discussion ground that can help mediate disputes that break out in the foreign policy establishment would be diminished if it tried to do so.

The Business Council

The Business Council is a unique organization in the policy-planning network because of its close formal contact with government. It was created as the Business Advisory Council during the 1930s as a quasi-governmental advisory group to give advice in relation to many policy issues. Led by the presidents of General Electric and Standard Oil of New Jersey (now named ExxonMobil), its members had a central role in the creation of two of the most important pieces of legislation of the twentieth century, the National Labor Relations Act and the Social Security Act, both passed in 1935. In the case of the labor relations act, Business Advisory Council leaders suggested a meeting with union leaders in 1933 to deal with an unexpected surge in union organizing generated by the arrival of the New Deal, then proposed the creation of a National Labor Board that would consist of six business executives, six union leaders, and a leading liberal senator of the day, Senator Robert F. Wagner of New York (McQuaid 1979; McQuaid 1982).

The new National Labor Board had several successes in its first few weeks in ending strikes by using a five-step procedure drafted by the president of General Electric: (1) the strike would end immediately; (2) the employers would reinstate strikers without discrimination; (3) the board would supervise a secret election by workers to determine whether or not they wished to have a union as their representative; (4) the employer would agree to bargain collectively with the representatives of those workers who voted to be represented by a union; and (5) all differences not resolved by negotiation would be submitted to an arbitration board or the National Labor Board itself. But several large industrial companies managed by ultraconservative leaders of the National Association of Manufacturers soon defied the board's authority, leading Senator Wagner to instruct the reform-oriented corporate lawyers and Ivy League law professors temporarily staffing the National Labor Board to draft a tougher version of the original provisions.

The proposed legislation included a clause stating that a majority vote for a union would be sufficient for it to have the right to represent all of the workers in the company, a change that was unanimously rejected by all members of the Business Advisory Council, because they wanted to be able to deal separately with craft and industrial unions, as they had in the past. However, the new law passed over their vehement objections and lobbying efforts, opening the way for the growth of unions for the next three decades (Domhoff and Webber 2011, Chapter 4). The later fate of the National Labor Relations Act is discussed in Chapters 7 and 8.

In the case of the Social Security Act, the Business Advisory Council, once again spearheaded by the presidents of General Electric and Standard Oil of New Jersey, was successful in creating an old-age insurance program that was completely to its liking. Based on corporate experience with private pensions over the previous 15 years and with the help of social insurance experts from the leading labor relations think tank of that era, the leaders of the Business Advisory Council based their program on three principles considered essential by all corporate moderates: Benefits levels were tied to salary levels to preserve values established in the labor market, there were no government contributions from general tax revenues, and both employers and employees contributed to the system in order to limit the tax payments by corporations. In addition, corporate contributions to the system were not to be taxed (Domhoff and Webber 2011, Chapter 5). (The origins, implementation, and aftermath of the Social Security Act, including the way in which the corporate moderates worked to restrict it after 1980, can be found in the document "How Corporate Moderates Created Social Security" on whorulesamerica.net.)

After arguments with the Kennedy administration's secretary of commerce, a fellow businessman, the Business Advisory Council withdrew from its quasi-governmental standing in 1962 and changed its name to the Business Council. It became a private organization that made itself available to consult with any part of the federal government, not just the White House. Many of its regular meetings with government officials since that time have been held in the relaxed and friendly atmosphere of an expensive resort hotel 60 miles from Washington. During the meetings Business Council members hear speeches by government officials, conduct panels on issues of the day, receive reports from their staff, and talk informally with each other and the government officials in attendance. Business sessions are alternated with social events, including golf tournaments, tennis matches, and banquet-style dinners for members, guests, and spouses. Corporate leaders pay the expenses for the meetings, reports, and social events. The Business Council also meets with the president and his staff from time to time in the White House (Kubey 1973; McQuaid 1982).

THE COMMITTEE FOR ECONOMIC DEVELOPMENT

The shortcomings of the Business Council, including its inability to create fully developed policy statements on a wide range of issues, led its leaders to play the major role in establishing the Committee for Economic Development (CED) in the early 1940s to help plan for the postwar world. They had two major concerns in doing so: (1) There might be another depression after World War II ended, and (2) if they did not have a viable economic plan for the postwar era, the liberal-labor alliance might be successful with plans that would not be acceptable to the corporate community.

As a result, the CED supported a business-oriented version of Keynesian economics that allowed for tax cuts, government deficits, and increased government spending through unemployment insurance and welfare benefits in the face of recessions. These prescriptions went against the NAM and the Chamber of Commerce's insistence on cutting government spending and balancing the budget as the way to deal with recessions, which widened the already existing divisions between corporate moderates and ultraconservatives created by disagreements over international trade and the Social Security Act. On the other hand, the CED trustees firmly rejected the liberal version of Keynesianism favored by the liberal-labor alliance, which wanted to manage economic downturns through government employment of unemployed workers and increases in government spending for infrastructure projects.

Despite their partial acceptance of Keynesian policies for dealing with depressions and recessions, the CED trustees nonetheless continued to favor the most conservative way to deal with inflation, increases in interest rates by the Federal Reserve Board, which led to higher unemployment rates in the process of reducing demand. They thereby put themselves in opposition to the liberal Keynesian view advocated by the liberal-labor alliance, which thought that periods of inflation should be handled by raising taxes on the wealthy and the well-to-do while at the same time reducing government expenditures. In other words, the liberal-labor leaders wanted to reduce demand by decreasing the purchasing power of those with large incomes, not by increasing unemployment. The liberal-labor advocates further claimed that their approach also would provide extra tax money that would enable the government to pay down the federal debt. It thus seems clear that the conflict between the corporate moderates in the CED and the liberal-labor alliance concerned power, not simply economic policies.

In its early years the CED's membership consisted of 100 to 200 corporate leaders. Later it added a small number of university presidents. In addition, leading economists and public administration experts served as advisors and conducted research for it; many of them went on to serve in advisory roles in both Republican and Democratic administrations, especially with the Council of Economic Advisors in the White House (Domhoff 1987). In the 1960s the leadership became even more moderate on domestic issues in the face of turmoil and disruption in inner cities across the country and antiwar protests on university campuses. By 1970, CED reports were calling for campaign finance reforms to make the system more transparent and for many improvements in social benefit programs, including a plan for a guaranteed annual income for families without any employed adults (CED 1968; CED 1970a; CED 1970b).

However, at the same time that CED trustees were taking a supportive stance toward various kinds of government social benefit programs, they were renewing their attack on unions and the National Labor Relations Board. They became hardliners on labor issues because they blamed unions for "cost-push inflation," which is defined as inflation caused by factors that lead to higher costs for corporations, not by too much consumer demand for too few available goods and services. Higher prices for raw materials, for example, can lead to cost-push inflation, but rising labor costs were by far the most important cause of cost-push inflation according to the CED. At the same time, the trustees divided sharply on the use of voluntary government wage-price guidelines for dealing with inflation, because the more conservative members feared that such guidelines might lead to government control over wages and prices. The trustees also differed over proposals to create a small planning agency controlled by the White House, which the most conservative trustees rejected as a potential foot in the door for the liberal-labor alliance if it gained more power.

As a result of these internal conflicts, funding for the CED was reduced or withdrawn by many corporations in the early 1970s. Its president retired a year early rather than continuing to deal with the tensions. The hardliners made highly personal criticisms of some of the hired experts, even accusing one of them of being soft on communism. Soon thereafter, few if any liberal experts were invited to participate in policy discussions. The hardliners rejected wage-price guidelines in future policy statements and reaffirmed that increases in interest rates were the only acceptable way to control inflation. They also called for the end of cost-of-living adjustments in union contracts, which meant in effect that their employees would absorb the costs of inflation through decreases in the purchasing power of their wages (Domhoff 2013, Chapters 9 and 10).

The difference between the CED at the beginning and the end of the 1970s is demonstrated by a comparison of policy statements issued in 1971 and 1979. In the first report, the emphasis was on the social responsibility of corporations and the need for corporations to work in partnership with government on social problems. The report at the end of the decade stressed the need to limit the role of government in a market system. The second report ignored all the social issues the CED had addressed before 1974. This change occurred even though almost half of the 40 members of the Research and Policy Committee in 1979 were on the committee in 1971 and had endorsed the earlier policy statement (Frederick 1981). This is strong evidence that the moderate conservatives had come to agree with ultraconservatives on many issues in the changing circumstances of the 1970s.

The Business Roundtable

The strong differences of opinion within the CED, along with the need for greater coordination with the White House and the conservative coalition in doing battle with unions, led to the creation of the Business Roundtable in 1972. Drawing from the leadership of the Labor Law Reform Committee and the Construction

Users Anti-Inflation Roundtable (two corporate groups that had been formed in the 1960s to challenge organized labor on a variety of issues), the new Business Roundtable was composed of CEOs from a cross-section of the corporate community, with many hardliner CED trustees taking the lead (Domhoff 2013, Chapter 10; Gross 1995, pp. 234–239). At this point the CED became little more than an auxiliary to the Business Roundtable with instructions from corporate leaders to develop in-depth policy statements on a few specific topics, although it remained close to the center of the overall corporate and policy-planning network (Domhoff 2013, Chapter 11).

As demonstrated in network studies, the Business Roundtable was at the center of the policy-planning network by 1973 (Burris 1992; Burris 2008). Reflecting the globalization of the largest corporations in all major countries, by 2000 the Business Roundtable also included the chief executives of the American subsidiaries of a number of foreign-based companies, and it played a key role in creating greater coordination between North American and European countries. In 2005, it joined with similar CEO groups in Australia, Canada, Mexico, Europe, and Japan to create a new 500-member transnational organization, World Business Leaders for Growth, to monitor and lobby the World Trade Organization (WTO) (Staples 2012b).

Decisions on where the Business Roundtable will focus its efforts are determined by a policy committee that meets every two or three months to discuss current policy issues, create task forces to examine selected issues, and review position papers prepared by task forces. Task forces are asked to avoid focusing on problems in any one industry and to concentrate instead on issues that have a broad impact on business. With a staff of less than a dozen people, the Business Roundtable does not have the capability to develop its own information. However, this presents no problem because the organization has been designed so that task force members will utilize the resources of their own companies as well as the information developed in other parts of the policy network.

The Business Roundtable began its more public efforts by coordinating a successful lobbying campaign against a liberal-labor proposal for a new governmental Office of Consumer Representation in the mid-1970s. It created a Clean Air Working Group that battled the environmental-labor coalition to a standstill from 1980 to 1990 on proposed tightening of the Clean Air Act, agreeing to amendments only after several standards were relaxed or delayed and a plan to trade pollution credits in market-like fashion was accepted by environmentalists (Gonzalez 2001). On a less conservative note, it helped reign in the ultraconservatives in the Reagan administration by calling for tax increases in 1982 and 1983, which began to reduce the huge deficits the administration's earlier tax cuts had created. In 1985 it called for cuts in defense spending as well. Along with other business organizations, it quietly opposed the attack on affirmative action by the ultraconservatives in the Reagan administration, pointing out that the policy had proven to be very useful for corporate America. It supported a mild extension of the Civil Rights Act in 1991, putting it at odds with the U.S. Chamber of Commerce (Belz 1991; Vogel 1989).

During the Clinton administration, the Business Roundtable joined with the U.S. Chamber of Commerce and the National Federation of Independent Business in defeating a proposal for national health care reform in 1994 (Mintz 1998). Then it organized the grassroots pressure and forceful lobbying for the corporate community's victory in 1994 on the North American Free Trade Agreement (NAFTA) (Dreiling 2001). In 2000 it successfully lobbied Congress to give China the legal status called "permanent normal trade relations," which is the government's term for free trade with a nation. For both of the trade agreements, the Business Roundtable organized the corporate community on a state-by-state basis and contacted members of Congress. Sophisticated network studies that made thousands of dyadic comparisons using a method called quadratic assignment procedure demonstrated the impact of the Business Roundtable's efforts (Dreiling 2001; Dreiling and Darves 2011).

According to public opinion polls at the time, both the 1994 and 2000 trade agreements were strongly resisted by the majority of citizens. Organized labor, environmentalists, and many of their liberal allies also vigorously opposed both agreements, because "trade" was intended in good measure to make it easier for American corporations to move their production facilities to low-wage countries. Although supporters of the two initiatives claimed that they were meant to bring lower-cost goods to American consumers and help raise living standards in less-developed countries, the initiatives also undercut what remained of the industrial union movement and ensured larger profits for transnational corporations.

THE LIBERAL-LABOR POLICY NETWORK

There is also a small liberal-labor policy network. It suggests new ideas and perspectives to liberal political organizations, unions, and liberals in government for their attempts to challenge the corporate community. Because the organizations in it are small in comparison to the corporate-backed organizations, some of them also serve as advocacy groups as well as think tanks. Most of them are focused on domestic economic policy. Several organizations in the liberal-labor network receive some of their financial support from labor unions, but the sums are seldom more than a few hundred thousand dollars per year. It is difficult to know the exact figures because the donations come from different unions and the AFL-CIO is not motivated to compile the totals. The liberal policy groups also receive grants from liberal foundations and a few mainstream foundations.

The liberal-labor alliance also includes two ostensibly independent think tanks, the Progressive Policy Institute and the Center for American Progress, which in reality serve as adjuncts to the Democratic Party in the same way that most ultraconservative think tanks are adjuncts to the Republican Party. The Progressive Policy Institute began as the policy arm of the Democratic Leadership Council (DLC), an organization of centrist Democrats founded in the early 1980s in an attempt to counter the party's liberal wing and bring the party's image back into what its leaders defined as the mainstream. Many of these moderates were

Southern Democrats, including future president Bill Clinton and future vice president Albert Gore, both of whom had leadership roles in the group in the 1980s and developed strong connections with funding sources for their future campaigns through it (Baer 2000). Members of the congressional staffs of DLC members became the staff for the DLC itself, the same kind of smooth blending of government and private staffs found on the Republican side of the aisle, and then became second-level advisors in the Clinton and Obama administrations.

The Center for American Progress was founded in 2003 by a former chief of staff for President Clinton, John Podesta, after he grew restive working for trade groups such as the Nevada Resort Association and the American Insurance Association as a partner in a lobbying firm he co-founded with his brother. Major Democratic donors provided most of its early funding, but it soon received support from a large number of foundations. By late 2008 the center had a staff of 180 and a budget of $25 million a year. It was positioned as a counterweight to the Heritage Foundation. Most of its policy analysts had worked in the Clinton administration, and Podesta was in charge of President Obama's transition team in 2008 (Savage 2008b). Table 4.4 presents the major foundation support for the

Table 4.4 Four Liberal Groups and Six of Their Main Foundation Funders between 2003 and 2011

Foundations[2]	Think Tanks[1]			
	Center on Budget and Policy Priorities	Center for American Progress	Economic Policy Institute	New America Foundation
Annie Casey Foundation	$10,473,240	$1,066,500	$1,224,110	$1,969,600
Ford Foundation	$28,305,000	$7,084,600	$7,510,000	$9,111.000
Mott Foundation	$5,755,000	$70,000	$1,200,000	$2,175,000
Open Society[3]	$9,753,000	$6,609,991	$4,860,000	$4,256,875
Rockefeller Foundation	$10,520,270	$4,228,400	$5,605,054	$5,463,000
Gates Foundation	$17,829,037	$2,998,809	0	$4,100,000
Donations/Percent of all donations from these six foundations	$82,635,547 (56.4%)	$22,058,300 (36.1%)	$20,399,164 (77.8%)	$22,975,475 (35.3%)
Total Donations, All Foundations	$146,400,000	$60,940,847	$26,214,050	$65,010,632

[1] These groups received funding from other sources as well.
[2] These foundations gave to many other groups as well.
[3] This organization, funded by a billionaire investor, George Soros, was called the Open Society Institute until 2011, and then renamed the Foundation to Promote Open Society.

Source: Foundation Directory Online (New York: The Foundation Center, 2012).

Center for American Progress and three other, more independent liberal think tanks between 2003 and 2011.

Although several of the organizations in the liberal-labor policy network receive grants from large centrist foundations as well as liberal ones, their distance from the center of the combined corporate/policy-planning network is shown by the fact that the one with the highest centrality ranking, the New America Foundation, was No. 122, followed by the Economic Policy Institute at No. 271 and the Center for American Progress at 356. The Center on Budget and Policy Priorities, the liberal think tank that receives the most money from foundations, is not part of the overall network.

Several liberal think tanks have excellent media connections, in part because some of their members are prominent journalists. However, the extent of the coverage for liberal think tanks should not be exaggerated. In 2011, they received only 20 percent of all media mentions of think tanks, compared to 47 percent for the moderates and 33 percent for the ultraconservative groups. For example, The Brookings Institution was first in the top 25 with 2,475 mentions, the Heritage Foundation was second with 1,540 mentions, and the Economic Policy Institute was 10th with 602 (Dolny 2012).

Although the liberals' reports are not featured as often as those of their centrist and ultraconservative rivals, they nonetheless receive coverage as a counterbalance to corporate policy proposals. This media visibility is further enhanced by ultraconservative claims about the allegedly great power of the liberal-labor alliance in the alarmist letters they send to their sympathizers as part of their fundraising drives. However, as explained in Chapters 6 and 7, the liberals' ability to distribute their message to a wide audience translated into very few successes between 1939 and 2012.

THE POWER ELITE

In concert with the large corporations and financial institutions in the corporate community, the foundations, think tanks, and policy-discussion groups in the policy-planning network provide the organizational basis for the exercise of power on behalf of the owners of all large income-producing properties. The leaders of these organizations are therefore the institutionalized leadership group for the corporate rich; they work to preserve the governmental rules and regulations that make possible the inequality in the wealth and income distributions.

This leadership group is called the *power elite*. The power elite are those people who serve as directors or trustees in profit and nonprofit institutions controlled by the corporate community through stock ownership, financial support, involvement on the board of trustees, or some combination of these factors. This precise definition of who is and who is not in the power elite includes the top-level employees who are asked to join the boards of the organizations that employ them. It is useful for research purposes in tracing corporate involvement in voluntary associations, the media, political parties, and government. Although the power elite are a leadership group, the phrase always is used with a plural verb in this book to emphasize that the power elite are also a collection of individuals who have some internal policy disagreements. They also have personal ambitions for the same government appointments and bitter rivalries that receive detailed media attention and often overshadow the general policy consensus. In other words, the power elite are not a monolithic leadership group.

The concept of a power elite makes it possible to integrate class and organizational insights in order to create a more complete theory of power in America. Once again, as in the case of corporations, the key point is that any differences in perspective between class and organizational concerns are worked out in meetings of the boards of trustees in which wealthy owners and CEOs from major corporations meet with the top employees of the policy-network organizations. This integration of class and organizational theories is discussed further in Chapter 9, when the main alternative theories are compared with the one that is unfolding in this book.

The corporate community, the upper class, and the policy-planning network provide the organizational basis and social cohesion for the creation of a power elite. A person can be a member of one of the three, or two of the three, or all three of these networks. This point can be visualized in terms of the three intersecting circles presented in Figure 4.2, which are referred to as "Venn diagrams" in mathematics and have many useful properties for illustrating complex relationships among several sets of people or objects (Ruskey and Weston 2012). In this instance, the diagram shows that not all the people in these three overlapping networks are part of the power elite. The distinctions presented in the next paragraph clear up a point that can be confusing when first encountering a class-domination theory: Not all members of the dominant class are involved in governing and not all members of the power elite are part of the dominant class.

First, there are upper-class people who are only socialites and sit on no boards of directors in the corporate community or the policy-planning network. Except for their financial support for policy-discussion groups and think tanks, and their campaign donations to political candidates, they play no part in the exercise of power. Second, there are corporate leaders just below the board level who are neither upper class nor involved in policy planning; they focus exclusively on their roles in the corporate community. Finally, there are policy experts who are neither members of the upper class nor on boards of directors of corporations; they are simply employees of the power elite who spend all their time doing research and writing reports.

As a practical matter, the interrelations among these three sectors are somewhat closer than the image of three intersecting circles would indicate. Although most male members of the upper class do not serve on a major board of directors, a majority of them that are between 45 and 65 are part of the corporate community as active investors, financiers, corporate lawyers, officers of privately held companies, or titled executives. Second, as discussed in Chapter 3, many rising

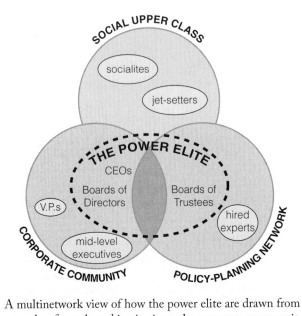

Figure 4.2   A multinetwork view of how the power elite are drawn from three overlapping networks of people and institutions: the corporate community, the social upper class, and the policy-planning network. The power elite are the members of the three overlapping circles that sit on the board of directors of a corporation in the corporate community or the board of trustees of a nonprofit organization in the policy-planning network. They are encompassed by the dotted line within the Venn diagram.

corporate executives become involved in some upper-class social activities, such as charitable events and parent meetings for private schools. Finally, some members of the policy network become involved in the corporate community as consultants and advisors, even though they do not rise to the level of corporate directors. In other words, the corporate community becomes the common sector that encompasses many of the older men within the three overlapping circles, along with a small (and slowly increasing) number of women.

THE POLICY-PLANNING NETWORK IN PERSPECTIVE

Although this chapter provides evidence for the existence of a network of policy-planning organizations that is an extension of the corporate community in its financing and leadership, it does not claim there is a completely unified power elite policy outlook that is easily agreed upon. Instead, it shows that the upper class and the corporate community have created a complex and only partially coordinated set of institutions and organizations that often disagree among themselves about what policies are most compatible with the primary objectives of the corporate community. From their point of view, it is their differences that vex and annoy them, because they take their many shared assumptions—and common enemies—for granted when they argue among themselves.

Nevertheless, the emphasis from a social-science perspective has to be on the considerable similarity in viewpoint among institutions that range from moderately conservative to highly conservative in their policy suggestions. In addition, the many policy successes for the Ford Foundation, the Council on Foreign Relations, the Business Council, the Committee for Economic Development, and the Business Roundtable should not be overlooked, even though the ultraconservatives grumbled about most of them. In fact, policy suggestions from corporate moderates shaped Social Security, the framework for international economic expansion after World War II, the early environmental movement, and many other programs, although the unexpected creation of a strong National Labor Relations Act was an unpleasant sore spot for all members of the corporate community.

Moreover, even though they were not able to agree completely among themselves, the corporate rich accomplished an equally important task that is often forgotten because of their constant bickering: They marginalized the few experts with a more liberal perspective. This point cannot be stressed enough, but there is not much more that can be said about it. Liberal experts received grants from foundations, appeared on talk shows, and published books, but even in Democratic administrations there was barely a sign of their existence. Instead, centrists were appointed by elected Democrats to carry out whatever liberal correctives were thought to be necessary to deal with the problems supposedly caused by ultraconservative policies inherited from Republican administrations.

This chapter thus provides evidence for another form of power exercised by the corporate rich through the power elite—expertise. *Expert power* is an important supplement to the structural power and status power discussed in the previous two chapters. Since government officials with only small policy-planning staffs must often turn to foundations, policy groups, and think tanks for new ideas, expertise is once again a form of power that can be exercised without any direct involvement in government.

Structural power, status power, and expertise are formidable independently of any participation in politics and government, but they are not enough to make owners and top executives a dominant class because they do not ensure domination of government. It still could be possible for the liberal-labor alliance to elect a liberal Congress and president, and then to use government legislation to bring about some redistribution of the country's wealth and income in a democratic way through higher estate taxes and more steeply progressive income taxes. In addition, a liberal government could pass laws that hinder profit making, or it could collect and utilize tax funds in such a way as to discourage economic growth.

It also could take on greater involvement in corporations when the economy is in crisis, as liberals called for in 2008 and 2009.

Given the great stakes involved when the economy faces unexpected collapse or high inflation, or if a foreign policy crisis arises, there is too much uncertainty in the relationship between the corporate community and the government for the power elite to rely solely on structural power, status power, and expertise to ensure that their interests are realized. They therefore try very hard to shape public opinion, influence elections, and determine government policy on the issues of concern to them. The next three chapters examine the nature of these efforts and the degree to which they are successful.

5

The Role of Public Opinion

Due to the constitutional protections surrounding free speech and the right of assembly, there is the potential for the opinions that people develop based on their own experiences and discussions with friends to have an influence on government policies. For example, citizens can organize into pressure groups to run newspaper ads and lobby Congress in order to communicate their preferences on specific policy issues. They also can register their opinions by exercising their right to vote, a topic that is discussed in Chapter 6.

Furthermore, the results of several decades of public opinion surveys suggest that people develop opinions that make sense in the context of the situations in which they find themselves, and that their opinions often differ from those expressed by corporate leaders, experts within the policy-planning network, and elected officials. The great majority favor more social support from government on health, education, and employment issues, and they advocate a foreign policy that is more cooperative with other nations and less militaristic (Gilens 2012; Moore 2007; Page 2008; Page and Jacobs 2009).

However, surveys asking about people's views on specific legislation under discussion in Congress, or about the stances adopted on legislative proposals by elected officials, reveal that most people pay little attention to politics, have a limited understanding of the options being considered, do not know how their representatives are likely to vote, and do not develop specific opinions on impending legislation, even when it has received much attention in the media. These findings suggest it is unlikely that public opinion is focused enough on any specific issue to have a direct effect (Delli Carpini and Keeter 1996; Zaller 2006, Chapter 5).

Although most studies suggest that public opinion rarely has any direct impact on policy debates, members of the power elite are nonetheless very fearful that it might in some cases lead to policies they do not like. Since they are well aware, due to opinion polls and their own past experience, that a majority of citizens disagree with them on many foreign and domestic issues, they spend hundreds of millions of dollars each year trying to shape public opinion in order to guarantee the success of the policies they favor. They do so through an opinion-shaping network that started with the creation of public relation firms in the 1920s and slowly developed into a complex network. This network operates at many different levels and reaches into many middle-class voluntary and charity organizations that do not at first seem to be relevant to the issue of public opinion.

AN OVERVIEW OF THE OPINION-SHAPING NETWORK

The most important think tanks and policy-discussion groups at the heart of the policy-planning network also have a central role in the opinion-shaping network. They generate many of the ideas on how their policy positions should be presented to the general public. In this network, however, it is large public relations firms and the public affairs departments of the major corporations that carry out the tasks of coordination and execution. Both have large staffs and the ability to complement their efforts with financial donations from the corporate foundations discussed in the previous chapter. In addition, they are connected to a widespread dissemination network that includes special committees to influence single issues, corporate-financed advertising councils, local advertising agencies, and the mass media. In contrast to the policy-planning process, in which a relatively small number of organizations do most of the work, there are hundreds of small organizations within the opinion-shaping process that specialize in public relations or persuasion on virtually every issue. Thus, the opinion-shaping network is extremely diverse and diffuse at its point of direct contact with the general public. Figure 5.1 provides a general picture of the opinion-shaping network.

The policy-discussion groups at the center of this network do not enter into the opinion-shaping process directly, except through releasing their reports to newspapers and magazines. Instead, their leaders set up special committees to work for changes in public opinion on specific issues. Sometimes it is not possible to illustrate this close connection until historical archives are available. For example, three of the most important opinion-shaping committees of the post–World War II era denied any connection to the Council on Foreign Relations, but studies by historians of the papers and correspondence in historical archives revealed otherwise (Wala 1994).

To create an atmosphere in which the general public more readily accepts policy changes, these committees attempt to portray the situation as one of great crisis. For example, this is what the Committee on the Present Danger did in the mid-1970s in order to gain public support for increased defense spending, claiming that government estimates of Soviet defense spending and military capability were far too low. Both claims proved to be patently false (Sanders 1983). Similarly, the perception

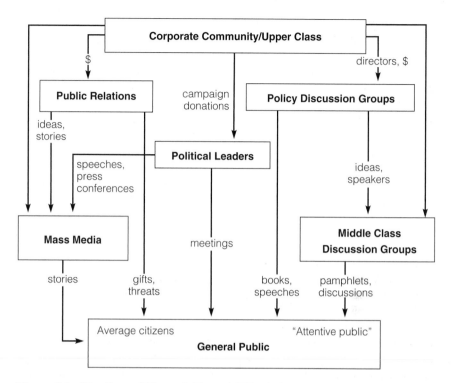

Figure 5.1 The General Network Through Which the Power Elite Attempt to Shape Public Opinion

of a health care crisis in the late 1980s was in good part the product of corporate concern about the rising costs of their health benefit plans (Bergthold 1990).

One of the most important goals of the opinion-shaping network is to influence public schools, churches, and voluntary associations by establishing a supportive working relationship with them. To that end, organizations within the network have developed avenues into these institutions by offering them movies, television programs, books, pamphlets, speakers, advice, and financial support. However, it is important to stress that the schools, churches, and voluntary associations are not part of the opinion-shaping network. They are independent settings within which the power elite must constantly contend with spokespersons from the liberal-labor alliance and the religious right. To assume otherwise would be to ignore the social and occupational affiliations of the members of these groups, along with the diversity of opinion that often exists within them. In the attempt to prevent the development of attitudes and opinions that might interfere with the acceptance of policies created in the policy-planning process, leaders within the opinion-shaping process also attempt to build upon and reinforce the underlying principles of the American belief system.

Academically speaking, these underlying principles are called *laissez-faire liberalism*, and they have their roots hundreds of years ago in the work of several European philosophers, such as John Locke and John Stuart Mill, and the American Founding Fathers. These principles emphasize individualism, free enterprise, competition, the fairness of economic markets, equality of opportunity, and a minimum of reliance upon government in carrying out the affairs of society. This classical liberal creed had no serious rivals in a small new nation that did not have a feudal past or an established state church (Hartz 1955; Lipset 1963). More generally, and viewed from a sociological angle, classical liberalism deals with the tension between liberty and democracy by trying to maximize freedom within the context of the necessary minimum of government regulation. Liberty is in good part dependent upon markets and private property, but government is needed to protect markets, private property, and freedom. Government, while suspect, can be controlled through representative democracy (Flacks 1988, pp. 9–12, 51–53).

However, by the early twentieth century there were serious disputes among liberals over (1) the increasing exclusion of African Americans in the 17 segregationist states and (2) the refusal by traditional liberals to extend the right of association to unions, which they saw as a violation of basic property rights and a hindrance to the proper functioning of markets. Liberals soon divided into rival camps over these issues, with traditional, nineteenth-century liberals (who came to call themselves "conservatives" in the 1950s) on the one side and modern, twentieth-century liberals (who have called themselves "liberals" or "progressives" since the 1930s) on the other. The twentieth-century liberals also reluctantly, but firmly, concluded that the scope of the federal government would have to be extended to ensure that basic individual freedoms and the right to vote would be available to everyone who lived in the segregationist states and that unions could develop in the states that were completely dominated by antiunion property owners (Starr 2007, Chapters 4–6). These disputes over the interpretation of basic liberal principles then became one aspect of the ongoing battles between the corporate-conservative and liberal-labor alliances that are discussed throughout this book.

The conflicts between the corporate-conservative and liberal-labor alliances express themselves in the arena of public opinion as a struggle to define the meaning of "Americanism," a general belief system rooted in basic liberal values, which is thought by most Americans to be part of human nature or the product of good common sense. Thus, the organizations that make up the opinion-shaping network strive to define good Americanism in terms of traditional liberalism, stressing individualism and "small government" (i.e., "states' rights"), while at the same time criticizing the "collectivism" and sympathy for "big government" that they attribute to spokespersons for the liberal-labor alliance. More generally, the organizations in the opinion-shaping network try to defeat the liberal-labor alliance by becoming the accepted arbiters of which policies and opinions are in keeping with good Americanism and which are not.

The efforts of the opinion-shaping network sometimes reach a more subtle level as well. Even though many people do not accept the overt messages presented in ads, speeches, and booklets, they often accept the implicit message that their problems lie in their own personal inadequacies. The strong emphasis on personal effort and responsibility in the individualistic liberal belief system not only rewards the successful, it in effect blames the victims of how the economic system operates. Educational failure and other social problems, which are best understood in terms of the way in which a class system encourages some people and discourages others, are turned into reproaches of the victims for their alleged failure to correct personal defects and take advantage of the opportunities offered to them (Lane 1962; Ryan 1971). A classic study based on in-depth interviews explains how an individualistic belief system leaves many working people with a paralyzing self-blame for their alleged failures even though they know the social system is not fair to them:

> Workingmen intellectually reject the idea that endless opportunity exists for the competent. And yet, the institutions of class force them to apply the idea to themselves: If I don't escape being part of the woodwork, it's because I didn't develop my powers enough. Thus, talk about how arbitrary a class society's reward system is will be greeted with general agreement—with the proviso that in my own case I should have made more of myself. (Sennett and Cobb 1973, pp. 250–251)

This self-blame is important in understanding the reluctant acquiescence of wage earners in a hierarchical system with extreme economic inequalities:

> Once that proviso (that in my own case I should have made more of myself) is added, challenging class institutions becomes saddled with the agonizing question, Who am I to make the challenge? To speak of American workers as having been "bought off" by the system or adopting the same conservative values as middle-class suburban managers and professionals is to miss all the complexity of their silence and to have no way of accounting for the intensity of pent-up feeling that pours out when working people do challenge higher authority. (Sennett and Cobb 1973, p. 251)

There is a further problem for most Americans: It is very hard to imagine that the overall socioeconomic system, with all its many integrated parts, could be the problem because the world is fair and sensible—it's a "just world" (Jost, Chaikalis-Petritsis, Abrams, Sidanius, and van der Toorn 2012; Jost and Major 2001). Since the system is mostly fair, the average American ends up in the conflicted position of having many critical observations about how things work, but the criticisms are mixed with an overall attitude of acceptance. The result is usually a grumbling acceptance of the political status quo and an even greater focus on the pleasures of everyday life that are available.

It is only when people are part of collective efforts that they overcome their tendency to blame themselves. But the liberal-labor alliance, as explained in Chapters 6 and 8, has not been able to develop an organizational base in either unions or a political party from which it could advocate a more communal, coop-erative, and pro-government alternative in which government is portrayed as a way to solve common societal problems.

Public Relations/Public Affairs

Public relations is a multibillion-dollar industry created by the power elite in the 1920s for the sole purpose of shaping public opinion (Ewen 1996). There are hundreds of important independent firms, but a few large ones do the major work, taking in hundreds of millions of dollars in fees each year. Advertising companies of even greater size in turn own most public relations firms. Public relations firms usually do not run general campaigns aimed at shaping overall public opinion. Instead, they are hired to work on very specific issues and are asked to focus on relatively narrow target audiences. The goal is not to change general public opin-ion, but to block any activities that might harm the image or profits of their cli-ents, sometimes by claiming there are contending voices, sometimes by attacking the critics as unreliable.

For example, Burson-Marsteller, one of the largest of these firms, created the National Smokers Alliance in the early 1990s for the tobacco industry, sending its paid canvassers into bars to find members and potential activists. Another firm, National Grassroots and Communications, specializes in creating local organiza-tions to oppose neighborhood activists. Still another, Nichols-Dezenhall Com-munications Management Group, concentrates on helping corporations by trying to expose and discredit their critics (Stauber and Rampton 1995). Its founder is the author of *Rules for Corporate Warriors: How to Fight and Survive Attack Group Shakedowns*, which was published by the Center for the Defense of Free Enter-prise in 2001 (CMD 2012a).

Public relations sometimes operates through the mass media, so it is not surprising that one-third of its nearly 200,000 practitioners are former journalists and that about half of current journalism school graduates go into one form of public relations work or another. Some public relations experts with journalism backgrounds put their contacts to work by trying to keep corporate critics from appearing in the media. One company keeps files on practicing journalists for possible use in questioning their credibility. Public relations experts use their skills to monitor the activities of groups critical of specific industries, everyone from animal rights groups opposed to the use of animals in testing cosmetic products to antilogging groups. Some of the actions taken against these groups, which include infiltration of meetings and copying materials in files, add up to spying (Stauber and Rampton 1995). (See www.prwatch.org for regularly updated accounts of campaigns organized by public relations firms.)

Public affairs, on the other hand, is a generally more benign form of pub-lic relations, which is practiced by departments within the large corporations themselves. Here the emphasis is on polishing the image of corporations rather than criticizing journalists and opposition groups. Women and minorities more frequently staff these departments than other corporate departments in order to provide the company with a human face more reflective of the larger community. In one large corporation, the employees in public affairs used to refer to their department as the "velvet ghetto" because the job is a pleasant one with an excellent salary and expense account, but one that rarely leads to positions closer to the top of the corporation (Ghiloni 1987).

The first task of employees in public affairs departments is to gather newspaper stories and radio-TV transcripts in order to monitor what is being said about their own corporation at the local level. They then try to counter any negative commentary by placing favorable stories in local newspapers and giving speeches to local organizations. They also join with members of other public affairs departments in an effort to shape public opinion in the interests of local corporations in general. "Looking good" and "doing good" is the goal set for themselves by public affairs personnel (Himmelstein 1997).

The efforts of the public affairs departments are supplemented by the financial gifts they are able to provide to middle-class charitable and civic organizations through the corporations' foundations. About one-third of this money goes to educational institutions and programs, including funding for the programs for low-income students of color at elite private schools, which were discussed in Chapter 3 (Zweigenhaft and Domhoff 2011, Appendix 3). Another quarter is given to health and charitable services, and the rest to community and cultural organizations. The emphasis on improving the image of the corporation and cultivating goodwill is seen most directly in the fact that since the 1970s it has been cigarette and alcoholic beverage companies, along with corporations with poor environmental and product safety records, that give the most money to sporting events, the arts, and other organizations and events that might burnish their image (Chen, Patten, and Roberts 2008; Ermann 1978).

Public relations specialists backed by corporate largesse have not been able to overcome negative opinions toward corporations in general. However, they usually have been successful in creating a positive attitude toward specific corporations in the communities in which they are located, or at least reluctance to bite the hands that feed local voluntary associations. They thereby make it difficult to mobilize average citizens against local corporations on a particular grievance. People may be critical of corporations in opinion polls, but they usually do not want to confront the corporations in their own cities. This is one example of why general public opinion often does not lead to any specific actions, which is an acceptable outcome for corporations. Corporations may not be loved, but their top executives did not have to endure any sustained criticism between 1975 and 2008, except by small liberal and leftist advocacy groups that were not able to gain any widespread public support. Following the crash of the housing market in 2007 and the federal bailout of the financial sector that soon followed, large banks were subject to scathing criticism, but the large commercial banks that survived—JPMorgan Chase, Bank of America, Citibank, and Wells Fargo—did not suffer any loss of customers. In fact, all but Citibank grew much larger through the takeover of banks, mortgage companies, and stock brokerages that failed during the meltdown.

Corporations, their public affairs departments, and their corporate foundations also have a strong voice in nationwide organizations that reach into thousands of cities and communities to help low-income families and their children. More generally, it is clear from reading through the list of grants to highly visible voluntary organizations in the *Foundation Directory Online* that few if any of these nonprofit organizations could survive without the financial support that large corporations provide through corporate, family, and community foundations. Most often the support for any one nonprofit is from a range of foundations, but some foundations supply a large portion of the support for their favorite nonprofit organizations.

For example, Big Brothers Big Sisters of America, which works with disadvantaged children, depends on corporate partnerships for much of its funding, including partnerships with the corporate foundations for Arby's Restaurants, the Bank of America, Cargill, Comcast, MetLife, and UPS. In 2011, its board of directors included the CEO of Cargill, the chief financial officer of Comcast, the retired president of Koch Industries, and senior executives from Jack in the Box Restaurants and JPMorgan Chase. Between 2003 and 2011, its national office received $18 million from the Clark Foundation in New York (based on an Avon Products fortune), $3.9 million from the Goizueta Foundation (based on the fortune built by a former CEO of Coca-Cola), $3.6 million from MetLife Foundation, $2.6 million from the Annie Casey Foundation (based on a UPS fortune), and $1.1 million from the Jack in the Box Foundation, along with many smaller grants from 40 other foundations. Many Big Brother Big Sister affiliates throughout the country also received hundreds of donations, including $1.4 million from JPMorgan Chase for the Greater Lowell, Massachusetts, chapter and $1.1 from the Dallas Foundation for the North Texas chapter.

Perhaps the best evidence for the essential role that corporations play in most nationwide nonprofit groups can be seen in the funding of United Way of America and its 1,200 local offices, which raise a significant share of the money spent by charities and other nonprofit groups throughout the country. In addition to their foundation grants to United Way, the corporations organize campaigns to collect money from their employees, which is often included as part of the corporate foundation's contribution. As Table 5.1 shows, 17 family, corporate, and community foundations gave a million dollars or more between 2003 and 2011, with the largest donations coming from the UPS Foundation ($52.5 million), the GE Foundation ($37.7 million), Nationwide Insurance Foundation ($21.6 million), the Lilly Endowment ($21 million), and the Gates Foundation ($15.7 million).

By way of thanks, United Way runs full-page ads in major newspapers each year to acknowledge the help provided by corporations and trade associations, which is also a form of goodwill advertising for the corporate community. In 2007, for example, the ad listed 117 companies in rank order that raised $15 million or more, which added up to "more than $1 billion to improve lives and strengthen

Table 5.1 Foundations That Gave $1 Million or More to United Way of America, 2003–2011

Foundation	No. of Grants	Total Amount
The UPS Foundation	12	$52,542,993
GE Foundation	6	$37,714,899
Nationwide Insurance Foundation	5	$21,617,077
Lilly Endowment Inc.	3	$21,000,000
Bill & Melinda Gates Foundation	4	$15,701,263
The Bank of America Charitable Foundation Inc.	10	$14,721,000
The Wal-Mart Foundation Inc.	4	$ 7,064,063
Best Buy Children's Foundation	10	$ 5,740,755
The Annie E. Casey Foundation	18	$ 3,566,279
Intel Foundation	1	$ 2,567,373
Xcel Energy Foundation	2	$ 2,148,143
Doris Duke Charitable Foundation	1	$ 1,835,585
The Columbus Foundation and Affiliated Organizations	2	$ 1,533,888
MetLife Foundation	1	$ 1,125,000
Caterpillar Foundation	27	$ 1,092,454
AT&T Foundation	3	$ 1,025,000
The Weaver Family Foundation	1	$ 1,000,000

Source: *Foundation Directory Online* (New York: The Foundation Center, 2012).

communities" (*New York Times*, December 11, 2007, p. A6). At the top of the list were UPS, Microsoft, IBM, Bank of America, Publix Supermarkets, General Electric, Wells Fargo, AT&T, and Pfizer. In 2010, the United Way's board chair was the chairman emeritus of a worldwide advertising agency that has 180 offices in 120 countries. The CEO of Eli Lilly and Company, the retired CEO of Southern Bancorp, and executives from UPS, Nationwide Insurance, and over 15 other firms joined him on the board, along with three union representatives.

At the least, then, foundations provide a stable funding base for most nonprofit organizations, along with the discretionary money that makes it possible for them to test new programs. They provide the seed money for any fundraising that reaches out to the general public, and they ensure that the officers of the largest and most visible nonprofits will receive high salaries. (For a detailed account of the full range of donations provided by 3,300 corporate-sponsored foundations and 1,700 corporate giving programs, see the *National Directory of Corporate Giving* [Grabois 2012].)

The corporate attempts to establish good relationships with a wide range of voluntary organizations through public relations departments, board memberships, and foundation grants reinforces the ethic within these organizations to steer clear of conversations about politics. They therefore rarely if ever play any role in creating a political debate concerning new ways to deal with the social problems their organizations are meant to overcome. It therefore seems doubtful that very many voluntary associations carry out the important function of political socialization that has been claimed for them by theorists of democracy since the nineteenth century. Instead, they now encourage the avoidance of politics for a variety of reasons (Eliasoph 1998).

Creating Doubt About Scientific Findings

Neither the negative attacks often used by public relations firms nor the soft sell and financial gifts of corporate public affairs departments are effective for corporations that use dangerous chemicals in their production process or sell products that are detrimental to people's health. In these cases, the opinion-shaping process plays a major role in resisting any changes opposed by corporations by casting doubt on the credibility of scientific findings. Since science involves the gradual development of a consensus through a wide range of rigorous experimental and epidemiological studies by different investigators, the goal of the corporations that want to maintain the status quo is to generate uncertainty about the consensus that has in fact developed about the dangers of asbestos, lead, tobacco, vinyl chloride, and many other substances. Building on the principles of spreading confusion and creating cover, they admit that "doubt is our product," as one tobacco company executive wrote in a memo to public relations specialists in 1969, "since it is the best means of competing with the 'body of fact' that exists in the public mind" (Michaels 2008, p. 80). The tobacco companies' campaign was so successful that every corporation that faced similar challenges adopted its methods, including health insurance companies (Potter 2010).

The way in which these campaigns are carried out by nonprofit think tanks and advocacy groups can be seen in the case of ExxonMobil's reaction to calls for legislation to slow global warming. Between 1998 and 2005 the company donated $16 million to a mixture of ultraconservative think tanks and opinion-influencing organizations with the expressed goal—stated in memos that were leaked to media outlets—of creating doubt about the emerging consensus on the role of fossil fuels in bringing about global warming and extreme weather. Many of the smaller organizations funded by ExxonMobil had overlapping boards of directors and staff members; they all hired the same few contrarian scientists and free-market economists—who usually had little or no training or expertise on climate change—to write their reports and appear in forums arranged by the nonprofit groups. Staffers and consultants from these groups also testified before Congress and worked as lower-level appointees in government agencies during the George W. Bush administration (Union of Concerned Scientists 2007). (For greater detail on the ExxonMobil network, see "Map Exxon's Network" at www.exxonsecrets.org.) By the end of 2008, however, the top executives at ExxonMobil were acknowledging the existence of human-generated global warning.

The Advertising Council

Although it is not feasible to discuss more than one of the numerous small organizations that attempt to shape public opinion on a wide range of issues, the Advertising Council, usually called the Ad Council, provides an ideal example of how they operate. Whether the mission of one of these organizations is to encourage, criticize, or cast doubt, they have three basic uses: They provide think-tank forums in which academics, journalists, and other cultural experts can brainstorm with corporate executives about the problems of shaping public opinion on a specific issue; they help create a more sophisticated corporate consciousness on social problems through forums, booklets, speeches, and awards; and they disseminate their version of the national interest and good Americanism to the general public on issues of concern to the corporate rich.

In the case of the Ad Council, it sells the free-enterprise system through public-interest advertising that is presented from a corporate point of view that builds on individualism and Americanism. It began its institutional life as the War Advertising Council during World War II, founded as a means to support the war effort through advertising in the mass media. Its work was judged to be so successful in promoting a positive image for the corporate community that corporate leaders decided to continue it into the postwar period. Since then it has been enlisted by the American Red Cross, Big Brothers Big Sisters of America, the Girl Scouts of the USA, the National Urban League, the American Cancer Society, the Department of Homeland Security, and the United States Army to conduct ad campaigns on their behalf.

With an annual budget of only a few million dollars, the Ad Council nonetheless places over $1.5 billion worth of free advertising each year through radio, television, magazines, newspapers, billboards, and public transportation. In 2011, its various "PSAs" (public-service announcements) were viewed a little over 168,000 times on YouTube. After the council leaders decide which campaigns they want to undertake, the specifics of the program are given to one or another Madison Avenue advertising agency, which does the work without charge.

Corporations provide much of the Ad Council's funding. Like the United Way, the Ad Council uses full-page ads to thank its corporate sponsors and remind newspaper readers that corporations are good citizens ("we made a difference, you made it possible"). Topping the list of 260 contributors in 2008, which ranged from American Express to Facebook to NASCAR, were six donors of $150,000 or more: Coca-Cola, Johnson & Johnson, Microsoft, Pepsico, Time Warner, and Yahoo. Between 2003 and 2011, the Ad Council also received $2.5 in grants from 17 corporate foundations, with the largest coming from Johnson & Johnson ($570,000), Alcoa ($285,000), Ford Motor Company ($275,000), and MetLife ($255,000). The chair of the Ad Council's board of directors in 2011 was the global brand-building officer for Procter & Gamble, and the chair of its finance committee was the chief financial officer for Viacom. A majority of the members of the Ad Council's large board of directors were vice presidents for advertising, marketing, or public relations at large corporations.

Most Ad Council campaigns seem relatively innocuous and in a public interest that nobody would dispute. Its best-known figure, Smokey the Bear, who was recognized by 98 percent of adults and had 60,000 "likes" on Facebook in 2011, has been the centerpiece of the council's ongoing campaign to prevent forest fires since 1944. In addition to preventing forest fires, its major campaigns in 2011 included efforts to convince people without a high school education to earn a GED, to educate the general public on food safety issues, and to increase awareness of autism. In the face of the turmoil triggered by the Vietnam War and inner-city tensions in the late 1960s, it brought together over 100 famous Americans of all races, ethnicities, creeds, and walks of life in 1970 to sing "Let the Sunshine In" from the musical *Hair* as the capstone for that year's theme, "Love" (Hirsch 1975, pp. 75–76).

At the same time, many of the Ad Council's campaigns have a strong slant in favor of corporations. Its environmental ads, for example, suggest that "people start pollution, people can stop it," thereby putting the responsibility on individuals rather than on a system of production that allows corporations to avoid the costs of disposing of their waste products by dumping them into the air or water. A special subcommittee of the council's Industry Advisory Committee gave very explicit instructions about how that particular ad campaign should be formulated: "The committee emphasized that the advertisements should stress that each of us must be made to recognize that each of us contributes to pollution, and therefore everyone bears the responsibility" (Hirsch 1975, p. 69). Thus, the Keep America Beautiful campaign is geared to show corporate concern about the environment while at the same time deflecting criticism of the corporate role in pollution by falling back on the individualism of the American creed.

The effectiveness of specific campaigns is open to question. It is doubtful that they have any influence on very many opinions. At best, they reinforce already existing opinions. Even when an ad campaign can be judged a failure in this limited role, however, it has filled a vacuum that might have been used by a competing group. This is especially the case with television, because the Ad Council is able to capture a significant percentage of the public-service advertising time that television networks provide (usually late at night). Thus, the Ad Council has the effect of reinforcing existing values while simultaneously preventing groups with a different viewpoint from presenting their interpretation of events. (For more on the Ad Council, its history, and its current campaigns, see www.adcouncil.org.)

With the information provided in this section about how the opinion-shaping network generally operates, it is now time to see how the network functions on specific issues that have the potential to impact government policies.

STRIVING TO SHAPE OPINION ON FOREIGN POLICY

The opinion-shaping network can be seen most clearly in the area of foreign policy because it is based in a handful of organizations. Several opinion polls show that the general public has more liberal and less militaristic views than the members of the policy-planning network that focus on foreign policy (Jacobs and Page 2005; Moore 2007; Page 2008). Despite these differences, foreign policy experts believe that the general public agrees with them, has little knowledge of specific issues, and is likely to accept new foreign policy initiatives out of patriotism or a general wariness about the actions of other countries. Opinion leaders in the area of foreign policy therefore focus their major efforts on a small stratum of highly interested and concerned citizens with a college education who might become a thorn in their side.

The Foreign Policy Association

There are several organizations that attempt to influence the opinions of upper-middle-class Americans on foreign affairs, including the World Affairs Council and the United Nations Association. However, the Foreign Policy Association (FPA), founded in 1918 and based in New York, is the most prominent among them. About one-third of the trustees on its governing council are also members of the Council on Foreign Relations. Although the FPA does some research and discussion work, its primary focus is on shaping opinion outside the power elite, a division of labor with the Council on Foreign Relations that is well understood within foreign-policy circles. The FPA's major effort is an intensive program to provide literature and create discussion groups in middle-class organizations and on college campuses, working closely with local World Affairs Councils. Both independent and corporate foundations support its general activities. Between 2003 and 2011, it received $6.4 million through 86 grants from 30 different foundations, the largest of which ($2.2 million) came from the Starr Foundation, founded by an insurance magnate, and the Annenberg Foundation, created by the family that owns *TV Guide* and many other publications ($1.5 million).

Presidents, Wars, and Public Opinion

Although the efforts of the Foreign Policy Association, the World Affairs Councils, and the United Nations Association are important in shaping opinions among the most attentive publics, the actions of the president and his top foreign-policy officials are the strongest influences on public opinion in general on specific foreign policy issues. Public opinion polls conducted before and after an escalation in the war in Vietnam still provide one of the most dramatic examples of this point. Before the bombing of Hanoi and Haiphong began in late spring of 1966, the public was split fifty-fifty, but when asked in July 1966, after the bombing began, if "the administration is more right or more wrong in bombing Hanoi and Haiphong," 85 percent supported the bombing. After President Johnson announced a partial bombing halt in April 1968, only 26 percent favored continued bombing (Mueller 1973, pp. 70–73).

However, there are limits to the shaping of public opinion on foreign policy when social stability is threatened, the lives of young Americans in the military are at risk, and there is potential for social protest. Opposition to both the Korean and Vietnam wars grew consistently as the number of American casualties continued to mount. Demonstrations and teach-ins at universities in the mid-1960s helped consolidate a large minority against the Vietnam War by 1967 and probably played a role in halting the escalation of the ground war. At the same time, opinion polls showed that the general public disliked the antiwar protestors even more than they disliked the war (Mueller 1973, pp. 164–165; Mueller 1984).

Despite a massive public relations effort on the part of the Bush administration after its invasion of Iraq in 2003 and a generally supportive press, public opinion turned against the war by 2005 as the military's death toll mounted. There was only one difference from the past, according to a political scientist who has done sustained work on public opinion concerning American involvement in wars since World War II: This time the critical attitudes developed much faster (Mueller 2005). Nevertheless, it was not until late September 2006, shortly before the midterm congressional elections, that it seemed likely that this growing disapproval of the war might affect the election. Even with the last-minute warnings, many analysts were still surprised when people reported in exit polls that their number one concern was the war and that they had voted to put the Democrats back in charge of both houses of Congress for the first time since 1994.

TRYING TO SHAPE OPINION ON ECONOMIC POLICIES

Corporate leaders find the generally liberal opinions held by a majority of people on economic issues to be very annoying and potentially troublesome. They blame these opinions in good part on a lack of economic understanding. They label this alleged lack of understanding *economic illiteracy*, a victim-blaming term, which implies that people have no right to their opinions because of their educational deficiencies. They claim these ill-informed liberal opinions would change if people had the facts about the functioning of corporations and the economy. As a result, they have spent tens of millions of dollars trying to present the facts as they see them. However, attempts to shape public opinion on economic policy are even less successful than on foreign policy because people have their own experience and observations to draw upon, as well as those of friends and neighbors they trust.

These points can be demonstrated by a look at the central organization in the field of economic education, the Council on Economic Education (CEE). It is only one of many organizations that attempt to shape public opinion on domestic economic issues, but its efforts are typical in many ways. Founded in 1949 by leaders within the Committee for Economic Development, who wanted to counter the strident ultraconservative economic educational efforts of the National Association of Manufacturers, the CEE received much of its early funding from the Ford Foundation. Most of its financial support now comes from corporations and corporate foundations. The CEE's website lists the following corporate foundations that have given $100,000 or more to support its efforts: 3M Foundation,

Allstate Insurance Company, American Express Foundation, Ameritech, AT&T, Bank of America, HSBC, International Paper, McGraw-Hill, Merrill Lynch, Moody's, State Farm Insurance, UPS, Verizon, and Wells Fargo. The Business Roundtable, the Mortgage Bankers Association, NASDAQ, the federal government's Department of Education, and three family foundations round out the list.

The CEE's board reflects the fact that it is part of the opinion-shaping network. In 2011 it included Harold Burson, the co-founder of the public relations firm Burson-Marsteller, along with the managing director of Burson-Marsteller. Senior vice presidents from State Farm Insurance, Verizon, and Well Fargo Bank; several partners and officers in financial firms; and professors of economics from Harvard and George Washington University also served on the board. The president in 2011, Nan J. Morrison, earned a BA at Yale, an MBA at Harvard Business School, worked as a middle-level executive at General Electric and Morgan Stanley, and was a partner at Accenture, a major accounting and consulting firm, before she joined CEE. In response to a new grant from the Department of Education in 2010, she said in a news release, "The economic turbulence of the past few years has certainly heightened the importance of economic and financial literacy" (Morrison 2010).

The CEE attempts to influence economic understanding by means of books, pamphlets, videos, and press releases. Its most important effort is aimed at elementary and high schools through its "Economics America" program. This program provides schools with curriculum plans and materials to introduce basic economic ideas at each grade level. To prepare teachers to carry out its general curriculum, the CEE has created a network of state councils and several hundred university centers to coordinate the training of teachers in the nation's colleges and universities. The CEE claims that it reaches 150,000 teachers who serve 15 million students each year.

After the near implosion of the economy when the housing bubble deflated in 2007–2008, the CEE quickly developed an eight-lesson packet named "Teaching Financial Crisis." It also launched another campaign against economic illiteracy that had a strong victim-blaming quality toward both individuals and schools through its claim that there is a "lack of understanding of the importance of saving and investing," as well as an "inability to discern the consequences of powerful international economic changes." Moreover, the fact that many people do not "even know the meaning of 'profit,'" is "evidence that we as a nation can no longer afford to make economics an option in our schools" (CEE 2009; Wikipedia 2012). AT&T, 3M, the Bank of America, Wells Fargo, the Business Roundtable, and many other corporations and business groups donated $100,000 or more for the campaign.

As this brief overview shows, the CEE's program began in corporate boardrooms and a policy-discussion group, is financed by corporate and family foundations, is carried out through affiliated councils and university centers, and ends up in teacher-training programs and public school curricula. In that regard, it is an ideal example of the several steps and organizations that have to be studied to understand how the corporate community and policy-discussion organizations attempt to shape public opinion on any domestic issue of concern to their leaders. However, despite all this effort, the level of "economic illiteracy," according to CEE polls, remained as high in the 2000s as it was in earlier decades.

The CEE's survey results fit with a large-scale national survey conducted by political scientists in 2007. It showed that Americans agree with the corporate community that private enterprise is a good way to run an economic system, and they share the opinion that government can grow too large. But everyday Americans also want far more job-creation programs, financial support for college educations, and social insurance programs than most wealthy individuals think is sensible. This contrast once again suggests that a majority of Americans are conservative egalitarians, and pragmatic as well, but their views are economically illiterate from the corporate point of view (Page and Jacobs 2009). In 2010, for example, a majority of average Americans thought that creating jobs was far more important than reducing the federal deficit, but wealthy Americans in the top 1 percent, with a median net worth of $7 million, strongly disagreed on this and several other economic issues (Page, Bartels, and Seawright 2011).

The power elite's inability to engineer support for their views on economic issues reveals the limits of the opinion-shaping process in general. As emphasized throughout this chapter, these limits are in good part created by the work experiences and general observations of average citizens, which lead them to be skeptical about many corporate claims. Then, too, the alternative analyses advocated by liberals, trade unionists, and the religious right also have a counteracting influence on elite efforts at opinion-shaping.

Although the power elite are not able to alter the liberal views held by a majority of Americans on a wide range of economic issues, this does not necessarily mean that the liberal opinions have had any influence. To the contrary, a large body of evidence suggests that the majority's opinion is often ignored. This point is demonstrated historically by the conservative directions taken by the Carter and Reagan administrations from 1978 to 1983, despite strong evidence that the public remained liberal on the issues under consideration: "Throughout that period the public consistently favored more spending on the environment, education, medical care, the cities, and other matters, and it never accepted the full Reagan agenda of 'deregulation'" (Page and Shapiro 1992, p. 117). Another detailed analysis of survey data relating to the alleged rightward shift in that time period found little support for the claim, except on issues related to crime. It concluded that Democratic and Republican leaders embraced conservatism in the 1970s, but that the American electorate did not follow their lead (Gold 1992).

These past findings were reinforced by a new analysis of questions drawn from several hundred opinion surveys carried out primarily between 1981 and 2002, augmented by questions from surveys from 1964–1968 and 2005–2006. It concluded that the American government was responsive to the "most affluent citizens" on issues of taxes, economic regulation, and social welfare, which meant a responsiveness to the top 10 percent, because there are too few high-income respondents in standard survey to make more refined analyses. In contrast, "the preferences of the vast majority of Americans appear to have essentially no impact on which policies the government does or doesn't adopt" on these issues (Gilens 2012, p. 1). These results are supported by a smaller study of three general social surveys from the past that compared the top 4 percent of income earners with the remaining 96 percent (Page and Hennessy 2010).

It is usually possible to ignore public opinion on domestic economic issues because the nature of American political parties makes it difficult to influence policy through the electoral process, as explained in Chapter 6. In particular, most liberal initiatives that made it to the floor of Congress were blocked between 1939 and 1996 by the conservative coalition of Northern Republicans and Southern Democrats. As most of the remaining conservatives found their home in the Republican Party between 1996 and 2012, there were always enough of them in the House or Senate to block domestic spending programs that were favored by a majority of the public.

THE POWER ELITE AND SOCIAL ISSUES

Highly charged social issues have received great attention in the mass media and figured prominently in political campaigns since the 1960s. Some of these issues are now history, such as busing; some were still burning hot in the early 2000s, including abortion, gun control, protection against discrimination for gays and lesbians, and same-sex marriage. Despite the time and energy that goes into these issues, they are not of direct concern to the power elite. There is no power elite position on any of them. Some individuals within the power elite may care passionately about one or more of them, but these issues are not the subjects of discussion at the major policy groups or of position papers from the mainstream think tanks because they have no direct bearing on the corporate community.

Nonetheless, these issues are very important in election campaigns because many people care passionately about them. They are therefore front and center in battles between the Democrats and Republicans due to the fact that liberals support progressive changes on all of them and social conservatives resist such changes. Although the religious right is deeply and genuinely concerned about moral issues as a matter of principle, they are seen by most conservative political consultants as "cross-cutting" issues that can be used as "wedges" in trying to defeat liberal-labor candidates in the electoral arena. This point is revealed extremely well in a tell-all memoir of his years in the Office of Faith-Based Initiatives in the White House by a disenchanted Christian conservative, who was surprised by the cynicism of the George W. Bush administration's political advisors (Kuo 2006). These issues are thought to be useful to conservative political candidates because voters who agree with the liberal-labor alliance on economic issues often disagree with it on one or more social issues, which provides an opportunity for conservatives to win their allegiance.

Although a majority of Americans were liberal or tolerant on most of these issues by the 1980s, conservative political consultants nonetheless continue to stress them because they hope to gain support from a few percent of the most emotional opponents of each of the liberal social initiatives, people who might otherwise vote Democratic. If each of these issues can win over just 1 to 2 percent of voters, the cumulative effect can make a large difference in close elections. Social issues therefore have been an integral part of the Republicans' electoral strategy since the mid-1960s.

Ultraconservative foundations, think tanks, and opinion-shaping groups contribute to the effective use of social issues in the electoral arena by running a variety of media campaigns. In the process they link their dislike for gender equality, abortion, greater sexual freedom, and gay rights with economic issues such as poverty and welfare spending. They do so, for example, by claiming that childhood poverty and youth violence are caused by an alleged decline in family values and responsible fatherhood, not by low incomes and unemployment (Coltrane 2001).

THE ROLE OF THE MASS MEDIA

Ownership and control of the mass media—newspapers, magazines, books, radio, movies, television, and increasingly, the Internet—are highly concentrated. Members of the upper class own all of the large media companies and these companies have extensive interlocks with other large corporations. In addition, the media rely on corporate advertising for the lion's share of their profits, making them dependent on other corporations (e.g., Bagdikian 2004; Klinenberg 2007).

The large media play their most important role in the power equation by reinforcing the legitimacy of the social system through the routine ways in which they usually accept and package events. Their style and tone generally take the statements of business and government leaders seriously, treating any claims they make with great respect. This respectful approach is especially noticeable and important in the area of foreign policy, which the media cover in such a way that America's diplomatic aims usually seem honorable, and corporate and government involvement overseas is portrayed as necessary and legitimate. However, beyond these very general influences, which can fall by the wayside in times of social or economic disruption, the media are a secondary part of the opinion-shaping process because their message is often ambiguous or ignored.

Moreover, studies of media influence provide conflicting results, especially between what is found in experimental studies as compared to studies in more natural settings and to surveys of what people remember from news stories. Laboratory studies on "agenda setting" by political scientists and social psychologists suggest that the placement of a story first on a doctored version of the evening news, or repeating it several times during the course of a week, leads people to think of those issues as more important (Iyengar and Simon 2000). On the other hand, a detailed analysis of how people in focus groups react to various media stories suggests that "a) people are not so passive, b) people are not so dumb, and c) people negotiate with media messages in complicated ways that vary from issue to issue" (Gamson 1992, p. 4). Adding to doubts about strong influence from the media, there is also evidence that the news is often not watched even though the television is on, and that people don't remember much of what they do see. An authoritative textbook on public opinion concludes its chapter on the mass media by saying there is no clear evidence that this relationship is more than minimal (Erikson and Tedin 2011, Chapter 8).

The limits on the owners and managers of the mass media in shaping public opinion were demonstrated dramatically in 1998 by the unwillingness of the public to endorse the impeachment of President Bill Clinton for sexual indiscretions and his failure to tell the truth about them, even though it was enthusiastically advocated by most of the Washington pundits who appear on television. In addition, over 140 newspapers called for his resignation. However, to the surprise of media leaders, a strong majority of Americans opposed impeachment, despite their highly negative opinion of the president's personal behavior. They made their own distinction between job performance and personal morality. One polling expert concluded that the campaign against President Clinton might have increased public resentment toward the media. He also thought that this event "proves just the opposite of what most people believe: how little power the media elite have over public opinion" (Schneider 1998, p. 2350).

In the case of television, any influence on public opinion it might have had in the past declined because the audience for the relatively few serious news programs that used to be carried by the three main television empires (ABC, CBS, and NBC) all but disappeared after the rise of cable TV and the new social media in the 1990s. As a result, television stations put even more emphasis on human interest stories, usually starting with local crime news, because people use sites on the Internet, talk radio, and late-night comedy news shows to keep up with the news. The rise of the ultraconservative Fox News channel and other conservative media led to much concern and commentary, but their main influence was to reinforce the views of the already convinced and to help mobilize them for grassroots political action (Skocpol 2012, pp. 50–54, 69).

Despite the generally conservative biases of newspaper owners, systematic past studies of the socialization of journalists and of how the news is gathered and produced conclude that every effort was made to present both sides of a story (Gans 1985; Schudson 1995; Schudson 2011, Chapters 1–2). The relative independence of journalists was first of all seen in the many newspaper and magazine stories on corporate and government wrongdoing within the long tradition of investigative journalism, which is the aspect of journalism that may be disappearing due to cost cutting and the further concentration of media into the few remaining conglomerates (Klinenberg 2007).

Then, too, there is evidence that what appears in the media is most importantly shaped by forces outside of them, which means that the corporate leaders, politicians, experts, and celebrities with the ability to make news have as much impact as, or more than, owners, editors, and reporters. A political scientist who specializes in media studies concluded that the media are "to a considerable degree dependent on subject matter specialists, including government officials among others, in framing and reporting the news" (Zaller 2006, p. 319). He made his point with examples from the natural sciences, psychology, and psychiatry, but it can be generalized to all specialized fields once liberal and conservative experts come to agreement on the steps that need to be taken. As a result of the ensueing consensus, journalists tend to adopt what is taken to be the accepted viewpoint in framing their stories.

It is precisely at this juncture that the policy-planning and opinion-shaping networks play their most important roles in terms of the foreign and domestic issues of concern to the corporate rich. Their organizations provide bipartisan written reports by established experts, often with representatives from past Democratic and Republican administrations. The think tanks and policy-discussion groups also make the experts available to journalists for background interviews or television appearances. Such experts include those corporate leaders who have been legitimated as statesmen on specific issues on the basis of their long-time involvement in policy-discussion groups. This process constrains any inclination on the part of journalists to inject their personal views, although it remains the case that they have some leeway to pick the spokespersons they want to feature.

In addition, the generally objective nature of newsgathering often leads to instances in which the media print or broadcast stories that create major problems for the power elite. For example, political leaders, corporate executives, and policy experts are unable to stop or even shape stories when there are unexpected accidents, scandals, or leaks, which lead to stories that tell readers and listeners about corporate wrongdoing, illegal payments to government officials, torture of prisoners by the American military, and much else. In 2005, for example, there was no way to hide the fact that the George W. Bush administration had been slow to respond to Hurricane Katrina when it destroyed parts of New Orleans. Nor could the public relations employees at British Petroleum (BP) disguise the fact that the company was cutting corners and risking its employees' lives when one of its oil wells exploded in the Gulf of Mexico in April 2010, killing 11 men working on the rig and creating the largest marine disaster in the history of the oil industry.

In these unexpected and usually uncontrollable situations, the general public learns through the media how the power structure actually operates. Most of all, people are reminded to take the claims by politicians and the public relations industry with a huge grain of salt (Molotch 2004; Molotch and Lester 2004). Then, too, the media played a role in the successes that small clusters of reformers enjoyed in past decades on a few specific issues. These lawyers, experts, and activists developed information on the issues of concern to them, found ways to present that information at just the right moment in one or another governmental setting, such as congressional hearings, and then depended on press releases, press conferences, and staged events to encourage the media to spread their stories. In short, their formula for success was information plus good timing plus use of the media.

Generally speaking, then, the media can amplify the message of the people that have the power to gain access to them, starting with government officials, corporate leaders, and experts from the policy-planning network, and they can sometimes marginalize, trivialize, or ignore the concerns of the less powerful. But the messages the media provide sometimes aid the liberal-labor alliance. In many cases, media messages are ambiguous or confusing to their half-attentive audiences and are often ignored (see Schudson 2011 for a detailed and balanced perspective of the role and influence of the mass media in American society).

ATTEMPTS TO "ENFORCE" PUBLIC OPINION

There are limits to the tolerance within the power elite for the general public's disagreements about public issues, although these limits vary from era to era depending on the degree of strife generated by social movements, and they are never fully clear until they are tested. Members of the power elite therefore utilize a range of coercive measures to limit changes in public opinion that they see as threatening, which means there can be serious personal costs for the people who begin to criticize the general consensus. These attempts to enforce the limits on disagreement begin with strong criticism from their employers or in stories planted in the media by public relations firms, which carry warnings through the angry use of labels such as "extremist" or "un-American" or "anti-American." The next steps are exclusion from events and dismissal from jobs. Such punishments are relatively minor for activists who are extremely committed to their viewpoint, but most people are very uncomfortable when they are in any way excluded or criticized by their peers.

The use of scorn, isolation and other sanctions is seen most directly in the treatment of "whistle-blowers," employees of corporations or government agencies who expose wrongdoing by their superiors. Contrary to the impression that they are rewarded as good citizens for stepping forward, they are relieved of their responsibilities by higher authority figures in the organization, and then shunned by peers out of fear of guilt by association. Their lives are often turned upside down. Many regret they took the action they did, even though they thought it was the honest or moral course to take. Their fate serves as a warning for others that speaking out is personally risky (Miethe 1999; Rothschild and Miethe 1994). Those who become prominent public critics of some aspect of conventional wisdom receive similar harsh treatment. Their motives are questioned and negative stories appear in the media, which attempt to demonstrate that they are acting from irrational psychological motives. They and any organizations they lead become subject to spying, intimidation, and the disruption of their meetings. The tactics used against the opponents of lumber, chemical, and meat companies have been especially harsh (Stauber and Rampton 1995).

WHEN PUBLIC OPINION CAN AND CANNOT BE IGNORED

A majority of Americans have moderate opinions on foreign policy and liberal ones on economic issues that are often opposed by the corporate rich. However, it is unlikely that any focused public opinion exists on very many of the complicated legislative issues of concern to the corporate community or on the volatile foreign policy issues that often arise suddenly and are shaped by grim warnings from the president, the secretary of state, and the secretary of defense, with a large assist from scare stories in major media outlets. More generally, under the umbrella of crisis talk, confusion, and doubt, which are in part generated by organizations in the opinion-shaping network, the power elite and elected officials enjoy a great deal of leeway on many domestic economic and social welfare questions as well. Furthermore, public opinion usually can be ignored because people's beliefs do not lead them into opposition or disruption if they have stable roles to fulfill in the society or see no clear organizational path to social change. Routine involvement in a compelling and enjoyable daily round of activities, the most crucial of which involve family, jobs, friends, and forms of relaxation and entertainment, are more important in understanding people's acquiescence than attempts by the power elite to shape public opinion (Flacks 1988).

What happens in the economy and in government therefore has far more impact on how people act than what is disseminated through the opinion-shaping network and the mass media. This point is demonstrated by the fact that the George W. Bush administration lost favor with the great majority of the American people because of the rising American casualties in Iraq after 2005 and the rapid decline of the economy in late 2007, in spite of massive attempts by power elite spokespersons and organizations with complete access to the mass media to claim that the war was going well and that the economy was on the right track.

But there are limits to the actions the power elite and elected officials can take without generating a reaction from a significant number of Americans of one political persuasion or another. Public opinion can have an impact when people are forced out of their routines by economic upheaval, wars, and other forms of social disruption. In those cases, public opinion can have an impact because it leads to large-scale election setbacks for the incumbent political party, or disruption of corporate and government activities, or social movements that challenge one or another aspect of the established order. Historically, disruptive social movements motivated members of the power elite to seek solutions—sometimes reformist, sometimes repressive—that would restore social stability.

Government spying and intimidation can become very important in the face of such instances of extreme upheaval, as seen by FBI and CIA actions during the civil rights and antiwar movements in the 1960s, which is another reason why the corporate rich want to be sure they control government (Cunningham 2004; Davis 1992).

Although this chapter suggests there is usually a large amount of latitude for the power elite and elected officials to operate as they wish to, this conclusion is incomplete in one important respect. It has not considered the possible impact of public opinion through the electoral process. It is now time to see if and when elected officials respond to majority public opinion, or if they instead adopt policies advocated by the corporate community within the special-interest and policy-planning processes.

6

Parties and Elections

Elections hold the potential for citizens to shape public policy through support for candidates that share their policy preferences. But have elections delivered on their promise in the United States? To provide perspective on this question, it is useful to begin with a brief discussion of how the expansion of voting rights in most Western countries in the nineteenth and early twentieth centuries was hedged in by changes in the way elections were organized.

ELECTORAL RULES AS CONTAINMENT STRATEGIES

Although historical studies of voting and elections usually focus on the gradual acquisition of voting rights by the large percentage of people who previously were not allowed to vote, it is also the case that already established political parties and their well-to-do backers were at the same time creating containment strategies as "safeguards" that would limit the impact of expanded electorates on legislative bodies (Ahmed 2010, p. 1060). These safeguards primarily concerned the nature of the rules under which elections would be held. Would there be one representative elected from each of many specific geographical areas, as has been the case in most states in the United States for most of its history, or would there be several representatives from each geographical district, or even legislative representatives selected by the country as a whole?

The nature of the debate and its eventual outcome depended on many factors that varied from country to country. But they always included the extent to which the established parties felt they could work together to defend the status quo, along with the degree to which they feared that political parties supported by the new voters might pose a major threat to economic elites (Ahmed 2013b). Generally speaking, leaders from the established parties, after much arguing within and between parties, decided on one representative for each geographical district if they thought that the new voters and their parties could be easily contained. In other countries, the powerful and their parties opted for a more radical containment strategy because they felt sure the new labor-based parties would win large majorities and change the socioeconomic system. Called "proportional representation," this system abandons districts for nationwide elections in which each party receives representation in the legislature roughly in proportion to its overall percentage of the vote once a minimum threshold is reached.

In Belgium, Denmark, and Sweden, by way of striking examples, the established parties opted for a system of proportional representation because they saw it as the only possible way to limit the burgeoning leftist parties. These new labor and socialist parties generally opposed this change very vigorously because they, too, thought that they would win large majorities under the current rules. Ironically, the proportional representation system, which was instituted in all three countries despite the protests of the leftist parties, is now seen as a very fair and open system, and perhaps it is. But the fact remains that it was promulgated as a defensive measure to ensure that pro-business and conservative constituencies would have at least a strong minority representation in the legislature that could limit systemic changes. In that regard, proportional representation is the outcome of a power struggle, a containment strategy that very much succeeded.

ELECTORAL CONSTRAINTS AND VOTER SUPPRESSION IN AMERICA

The brief history of electoral containment in the previous section might seem to have little relevance to the United States. After all, the right to vote spread fairly quickly before and after the Constitution was passed. Sometimes states used the right to vote as a way to attract more settlers, and sometimes rival political parties were eager to enfranchise those portions of the underlying population that they thought would be sympathetic to them for religious, ethnic, or regional reasons. Still, the Constitution itself did include containment strategies, which the Founding Fathers thought were necessary to "filter popular influence," such as the election of senators by state legislatures and the creation of the Electoral College to select the president (Piven 2006, p. 52).

Single-member districts seemed well established in the United States by the early nineteenth century, but the fact that the Constitution left it to the states to decide how they would elect members to the House of Representatives led to problems. By the 1830s, a few states were electing multiple representatives from a few large districts. Furthermore, 10 of the 26 states, mostly smaller states in both the North and South, were using statewide elections to fill all their House seats in an attempt to send one-party delegations to Washington to maximize their impact. This strategy soon led to the realization that if just three or four of the largest states in the North adopted this approach, then one party could dominate the entire House. These problems were compounded by the formation of a Workingmen's Party in 61 cities by 1834, and then by the development of pro-worker factions within the Democratic Party in some states. Faced with the possibility of "mob rule," conservative members of both parties narrowly passed congressional legislation in 1842 that reaffirmed the need to elect just one representative from a specific district for each House seat allotted to a state (Ahmed 2013a, Chapter 4).

Conflicts over electoral rules then declined in the face of the increasing strife between the North and South in the 1840s and 1850s, and the ensuing Civil War. However, the same tensions returned in the 1870s due to the growth of the Greenback-Labor Party, an anticorporate farmer-labor alliance, which won 13 of the 293 seats in the House in 1878. There was even a small group of worried conservatives who thought that proportional representation might be necessary. However, the collapse of the Greenback-Labor Party because of mutual suspicions between its farmer and labor wings ended any discussion of changing the electoral rules (Ahmed 2013a, Chapter 4). Both parties decided they could contain any potential threats that might develop from African American voters in the South or from the fast-growing working class in the North by manipulating the boundaries of House districts ("gerrymandering") and by engaging in various types of voter suppression.

The impact of gerrymandering can be seen very clearly in the results of the redistricting based on the 2010 census, which changed outcomes in as many as twenty-five districts in the 2012 elections and helped Republicans win six seats in the House they might otherwise have lost. The full impact of gerrymandering for both parties can be seen in the finding that Republican candidates won 53 percent of the vote and 72 percent of the seats in states controlled by Republicans, while Democratic candidates won 56 percent of the vote and 71 percent of the seats in states controlled by Democrats. By way of contrast, in states in which the courts, an independent commission, or both parties reconfigured the districts, Democrats won a little over half the vote and 56 percent of the seats, whereas Republicans won 46 percent of the votes and 44 percent of the seats. Most districts shaped by Republicans included such a high percentage of likely Republican voters that their party may be able to control the House until the redistricting after the 2020 census. For example, voters in Pennsylvania cast 83,000 more votes overall for Democratic congressional candidates in 2012, but Republicans won thirteen of the state's eighteen House seats (Palmer and Cooper 2012).

As for voter suppression, Southern Democrats used poll taxes, literacy tests, and violence between the 1880s and 1965 to keep African Americans from voting, and in the process disenfranchised many low-income white voters as well

(Kousser 1974). Beginning in the 1970s, Republicans made frequent accusations of voter fraud, demanded proof of citizenship, mandated picture IDs, and arbitrarily purged voter rolls to suppress voting by low-income people from communities of color in the states they controlled, although state-level courts blocked some of these efforts shortly before the 2012 elections (Davidson, Dunlap, Kenny, and Wise 2004; Hasen 2012; Piven, Minnite, and Groarke 2009, Chapter 6). The result of these combined party efforts to suppress voting by some groups, which included several other stratagems besides those already mentioned, such as rejecting same-day voter registration and weekend voting, is a constricted electorate that is skewed toward white and higher-income citizens.

HOW GROWTH COALITIONS CHANGED ELECTORAL RULES

Lest any reader think that containment strategies have never been implemented in the United States, the manipulation of electoral rules can be seen very directly and dramatically at the local level in reaction to serious challenges. These challenges began in the 1880s when ethnically based political machines, usually affiliated with the Democratic Party and strongly dependent upon the votes of craft and industrial workers, came to dominate many city governments. In the early twentieth century, a further threat arose from the newly formed Socialist Party, which elected 1,200 members in 340 cities across the country in 1912, including 79 mayors in 24 different states (Weinstein 1967, pp. 93–118).

The local growth coalitions reacted to these challenges in 1894 by creating a national-level policy-planning organization, the National Municipal League, at a meeting that included 150 city developers, lawyers, political scientists, and urban planners from 21 cities in 13 states. The organization gradually developed a number of potential changes in electoral rules (called "reforms") that added up to a containment strategy. These changes were presented as efforts to eliminate corruption, reduce costs, and improve efficiency, but each of them lowered voter turnout and thereby made it more difficult for Democrats and Socialists to win elections (Alford and Lee 1968). Three of the reforms were especially important:

1. *Off-year elections.* It was argued that local elections should not be held in the same year as national elections because city issues are different, which obscured the many policy connections between local and national levels;

2. *Nonpartisan elections.* It was claimed that parties should not play a role at the local level because the citizens of a community have common interests that should not be overshadowed by partisan politics. This reform made it necessary for candidates to increase their name recognition because voters could no longer rely on the labels "Democrat" or "Socialist" to identify the candidates with whom they sympathized.

3. *Citywide elections.* It was argued that districts do not have the same usefulness that they do at the congressional level because the problems facing members of a city council involve the city as a whole and not separate neighborhoods. The elimination of city electoral districts made it more difficult for neighborhood leaders, whether Democrats, Socialists, or ethnic and racial minorities, to hold their seats on city councils, because they did not have the money and name recognition to win citywide elections.

The National Municipal League's efforts did not produce many successes until it was able to take advantage of the fear and patriotism created during World War I, branding the Socialists as antiwar traitors. By 1919, it had been able to implement its ideas in 130 cities, and it continued to make gains in the next several decades (Schiesl 1977). By 1991, 75 percent of American cities had nonpartisan elections and 59 percent used citywide elections. The successful resistance to the package of reforms came from large cities with strong Democratic Party organizations (Renner and DeSantis 1994).

Despite the partial failures in large cities, the larger goals of the growth coalitions' containment efforts were achieved. The direct connections between local and national government were now less obvious and the local branches of the two major parties were eliminated from local politics in half of all American cities, thereby reducing the usefulness of city councils as a training ground for liberal-labor candidates and making it harder to create a comprehensive liberal-labor program. By the 1940s, business owners, often legitimated for elected office by service on well-publicized committees of the local Chamber of Commerce, were the overwhelming presence on most city councils, which demonstrates once again that all segments of the ownership class have to be constantly involved in efforts to control government in a country in which citizens have the right to vote.

HOW ELECTIONS NONETHELESS MATTER

Despite the success of the various efforts to contain and suppress the voting power of average Americans, elections nonetheless made it possible for them to have some impact on government. At the least, elections allow citizens to determine which of the rival parties plays the lead role in government. In practice, this means that different occupational, religious, and ethnic groups become part of rival corporate-led coalitions that contend for office on a wide range of appeals. For example, white Protestants of all classes in all regions of the country are far more likely to vote for Republicans than either Catholics or Jews, although Catholics became more sympathetic to the Republicans after the 1960s (Manza 2012; Manza and Brooks 1999). In 2006, for example, 62 percent of white Protestants voted Republican, compared to 49 percent of white Catholics and 12 percent of Jews. In 2012, 70 percent of white Protestants, 60 percent of white Catholics, and 29 percent of Jews (who are less than 2 percent of the electorate) voted for Romney (Edison Research 2012). Religion is a major factor in party preferences in many other countries as well (Nieuwbeerta, Brooks, and Manza 2006).

Then, too, elections provide the opportunity to register disapproval of government policies. This role was demonstrated when voters replaced the Republican Party, which had been dominant throughout the 1920s, with Democrats in the 1930, 1932, 1934, and 1936 elections in the face of the Great Depression, reducing the Republicans to a very small minority in Congress. Conversely, Republicans replaced Democrats in the White House and the Senate in 1980 at least in part due to the frustrating combination of high inflation and rising unemployment in the late 1970s.

The importance of elections in rejecting current policies was demonstrated again in 2008 when a majority of voters took a decisive turn to Senator Obama in late September after the financial turmoil made the perilous state of the economy by far the overriding issue in most people's minds. According to weekly polls, the change was especially pronounced among those whites most concerned about the state of the economy, 54 percent of whom came to favor Obama, compared to a mere 10 percent of whites not worried about the economy (Balz and Cohen 2008). Although the Obama campaign rallied many new voters to the polls, a study utilizing both voter turnout figures and a survey of voters in 2008 estimated that 23.6 percent of Bush supporters in 2004 either did not vote, or else voted for Obama or a third-party candidate, which was enough for Senator Obama to win the election without the new voters (Lupia 2010, Table 3).

Finally, elections matter as a way to introduce new policies in times of social upheaval caused by extreme domestic problems. In the nineteenth and early twentieth centuries, this role was often fulfilled by third parties that appeared suddenly on the scene, such as the new parties of the 1840s and 1850s that first advocated the abolition of slavery. Beginning in the second decade of the twentieth century, primary elections gradually became the main electoral arena for the introduction of new ideas.

Even after taking various containment strategies into account, however, elections have yielded far fewer successes for the liberal-labor alliance than might be expected on the basis of liberal-labor victories in most Western democracies. The reasons for this difference are explained in the remainder of this chapter.

WHY ONLY TWO MAJOR PARTIES?

In sharp contrast to countries that use proportional representation to elect their legislatures, in which there are always four or more substantial political parties, there have been only two major parties for most of American history. The lone exceptions were a brief one-party era from about 1812 to 1824, after the Federalist Party collapsed, and a few years in the 1850s, when the conflict over extending slavery into Kansas and Missouri led to the breakup of the short-lived Whig Party. Due to the very rapid disintegration of the Whigs between 1852 and 1856, the Republican Party that developed in 1854, based on its uncompromising stance toward the extension of slavery westward, does not really qualify as a third party because it replaced the Whigs so quickly.

Why are there only two major parties despite the country's tumultuous history of racial, regional, religious, and class rivalries? Two fundamental features of American government lead to a two-party system. The first is the use of an electoral system that everyone takes for granted in the United States, namely, the selection of senators and representatives from states and districts in elections that require only a plurality of votes, not a majority. This system is called a "single-member-district plurality system," and it has led to two-party systems in most of the countries that use it (Lipset and Marks 2000; Rosenstone, Behr, and Lazarus 1996). The exceptions tend to be in countries in which a third party has some strength in a single region for ethnic or religious reasons.

The second reason for the American two-party system is a relatively unique one: The election of a president creates a very different dynamic from that of the parliamentary systems of government in Canada and most of Western Europe. The election of a president is in effect a strong version of the single-member-district plurality system, with the nation serving as the only district. By way of contrast, a parliamentary system, even when based in single-member districts, provides some room for third parties because a prime minister is selected by the parliament after the elections. As a result, there is less pressure toward the two pre-electoral coalitions that are called the Democratic and Republican parties in the United States. Thus, the enormous power of the presidency makes the tendency toward two parties even greater. Third parties are therefore far less likely to develop and much smaller than third parties in other countries with district/plurality elections.*

The simple fact that only one person can win the presidency or be elected to Congress from a given state or district leads to a two-party system by creating a series of "winner-take-all" elections. A vote for a third-party candidate of the right or left is in effect a vote for the voter's least-favored candidate on the other side of the political spectrum. Because a vote for a third-party candidate of the left or right is a vote for "your worst enemy," the usual strategy for those who want to avoid this fate is to form the largest possible pre-election coalition, even

---

* As shown dramatically in the 2000 elections, the president is selected by the Electoral College, within which each state has a number of electors equal to the size of its congressional delegation. The minimum number of electors a small state can have is three—two senators plus one House member. Electors cast their ballots for the candidate that wins in their state. The focus on electoral votes forces candidates to concentrate on winning a plurality in as many states as possible, not simply on winning the most votes in the nation overall. This system creates a further disadvantage for third parties.

if numerous policy preferences must be abandoned or compromised. The result is two coalitional parties.*

Third parties of the left or right therefore seldom last for more than one or two elections and rarely receive more than 1 to 2 percent of the vote when they do persist, but they can have dramatic impacts on the overall results. In 2000, Ralph Nader and the Green Party contributed to President Bush's victory by taking just enough votes from Democrat Albert Gore in New Hampshire and Florida to give their electoral votes—and the presidency—to Bush. It was the first time in history that a leftist party had any major influence on the outcome of a presidential election, which led to deep and lasting anger toward Nader and the Green Party on the part of liberals, feminists, environmentalists, and civil rights activists, and to the near-total exclusion of Nader from any liberal-labor forums for many years.

What is less known is that the tiny Libertarian Party to the right of the Republicans cost the Republicans a Senate seat in Nevada in 1998, a Senate seat in Washington in 2000, a Senate seat in South Dakota in 2002, a Senate seat in Montana in 2006, and the governorships of Oregon and Wisconsin in 2002 by winning far more votes than the margin by which the Republican candidates lost to their Democratic opponents (Miller 2002). It is also likely that Libertarian candidates made it possible for Democrats to win the governorship and retain a senatorial seat in Montana in 2012 by winning nearly 17,000 votes in a governor's race that was decided by a margin of just 8,300 votes and by winning nearly 30,000 votes in a senatorial race decided by 18,000 votes. In addition, another third party to the right of the Republicans, the Constitution Party, helped to defeat the incumbent Republican senator in Oregon in 2008 by winning 5.2 percent of the vote in an election that the Democrat won by 48.9 percent to 45.6 percent.

Although the American system of single-member congressional districts and presidential elections generates an enormous pull toward a two-party system, it was not designed with this fact in mind. The Founding Fathers purposely created a system of checks and balances that would keep power within bounds, especially the potential power of an aroused and organized majority of farmers and artisans. However, a party system was not among their plans. Parties are the result of the fact that the Founding Fathers decided that the country needed the office of the president to create some unity among the rival states and that it needed a Congress based in geographical elections so that every state was sure to have representation in Congress. In fact, the Founding Fathers disliked the idea

---

* This analysis is not contradicted by the 19 percent of the vote that H. Ross Perot received in 1992, running as the candidate of his Reform Party, because his party was positioned between the two major parties. As a centrist party, it drew votes from independents as well as partisans of both parties, and hence was not more threatening to one than the other. Perot's vote was also unusual because he spent $72 million of his own money to promote his candidacy in 1992, which was the equivalent of $118.8 million in 2012.

of parties, which they condemned as "factions" that are highly divisive. Parties are a major unintended consequence of their deliberations, and it was not until the 1830s and 1840s that a new generation of political leaders finally accommodated themselves to the idea that the two-party system was not disruptive of rule by the wealthy few (Hofstadter 1969).

Historically, a two-party system did not foster parties that articulate clear images and policies, in good part because rival candidates attempt to blur their differences in order to win the voters in the middle. It causes candidates to emphasize personal qualities rather than policy preferences. Moreover, there is evidence that a two-party system actually discourages voting because those in a minority of even 49 percent receive no representation for their efforts. Voting increases considerably in countries in which districts have been replaced by proportional representation (Lipset 1963).

For all these reasons, then, the American two-party system leads inadvertently to a very important opening for the corporate rich: There need not be a close relationship between politics and policy. Candidates can say one thing to be elected and then do another once in office, which of course gives people with money, access, and information an opportunity to shape legislation. However, none of this fully explains why the liberal-labor alliance has not been able to create a party of its own. The historic differences between the Northern and Southern economies, one based in free labor, the other in slavery and segregation, provides the explanation for this unusual situation.

REPUBLICANS AND DEMOCRATS

Two contrasting claims predominate in popular discussions of the Republican and Democratic parties. "There's not a dime's worth of difference between them" according to some Americans, which reflects the parties' need to appeal to the centrist voters in a two-party system. "Republicans represent big business and the Democrats represent liberals, unions, and people of color" according to other Americans, a belief that derives in about equal amounts from the scare tactics used by ultraconservatives and the mythmaking by liberals about their party's allegedly progressive past. In fact, neither of these common images is correct. There always have been differences between the two parties along regional, racial, religious, and class dimensions, and the Democratic Party did not even have a chance to be a liberal-labor party until after the 1960s.

Although there are many differences between the two parties, the most important point in terms of articulating a class-domination theory of power is that different segments within the ownership class controlled both parties for most of their history, as discussed further in Chapter 8. After the ratification of the Constitution in 1789 settled the major issues between the Northern and Southern segments of the ownership class, at least until the 1850s, it did not take long for political parties to develop. From the day in 1791 when wealthy Virginia plantation owners made contact with landowners in upstate New York to create what was to become the first incarnation of the Democratic Party, the two parties represented different economic interests within the upper class. For the most part, the Democrats were originally the party of agrarian wealth, especially in the South, the Republicans the party of bankers, merchants, industrialists, and small farmers in the North (Domhoff 1990, Chapter 9).

As with all generalizations, this one needs some qualification. The Democratic-Republican Party, as it was first known, also found many of its adherents in the North among merchants and bankers of Irish origins, who disliked the English-origin leaders in the Federalist Party for historical reasons. Then, too, religious dissenters and Protestants of low-status denominations often favored the Democratic-Republicans over the "high church" Federalist Party. These kinds of differences persist down to the present. In terms of social status, the Federalist and Republican parties have been the party of the secure and established, the Democrats the party of those who were in the out-group on one dimension or another. The characterization of the Democratic Party as a coalition of out-groups even fits the wealthy slaveholders who dominated the party in its first 69 years because they were agrarians in an industrializing society, slaveholders in a land of free labor. Although they controlled the presidency in 32 of the first 36 years of the country's existence by electing famous slave owners such as Thomas Jefferson, James Madison, and Andrew Jackson, the planters were on the defensive, and they knew it.

Following the Civil War, the Democratic Party became even more completely the instrument of the Southern segment of the ownership class because all wealthy white Southerners became its strong supporters to be sure that a coalition between populist small farmers and black sharecroppers could not develop within the confines of the two-party system. At this time they also gained new allies in the North with the arrival of millions of ethnic Catholic and Jewish immigrants, who were often treated badly and scorned by the Protestant Republican majority. When some of these new immigrants grew wealthy in the first half of the twentieth century, they became major financial backers of local Democratic machines, which soon worked closely with the "courthouse gangs" that predominated in the South. Working together, the Northern machines and Southern courthouse gangs became the core of the spending coalition that flourished during and after the Great Depression. The liberal-labor alliance that developed within the Democratic Party in the 1930s was no match for the well-established Southern rich and their wealthy urban ethnic allies, which already had secured the allegiance of their fellow Irish, Italian, and Eastern European Jewish immigrants (Shefter 1994; Webber 2000).

There is, of course, far more to the story of the Democratic Party. But enough has been said to explain why the liberal-labor alliance does not have a party of its own, as it does in most democratic countries. The electoral rules leading to a two-party system, in conjunction with control of the Democrats by wealthy Southern whites until the 1970s, left the liberal-labor alliance with no good options. It could not form a third party without assuring the election of even more Republicans, who are its sworn enemies, but it was not able to win control of the Democratic Party.

The Spending Coalition

Based on analyses that search for issue-focused patterns of voting, political scientists identified a large cluster of legislators that were willing to support most government spending initiatives, which is best understood as a "spending coalition." For the most part, the spending coalition consisted of a majority of Southern and non-Southern Democrats who were interested in providing subsidies and benefits for their main constituents, namely, planters, ranchers, and growers in the South, Southwest, and California, and urban real estate interests across the country (Clausen 1973; Sinclair 1982). The nature of their bargain was very explicit. A majority of the non-Southern Democrats supported agricultural subsidies and price supports that greatly benefited plantation owners and other agribusinesses. The Southerners in turn were willing to support government spending programs for roads, urban redevelopment, public housing, hospital construction, school lunches, and even public assistance. Although some of these spending programs are thought of as "liberal," in fact many of them benefited the urban real estate interests that financed the urban Democratic political machines in the North and were used to the benefit of Southern Democrats as well. Then, too, the construction unions that are dependent upon urban growth for their livelihoods were highly supportive of these programs (Logan and Molotch 2007).

However, Southern support for the spending sought by urban Democrats, growth coalitions, and construction unions was conditional, based on the acceptance of three provisos. The spending programs would contain no attacks on segregation, they would be locally controlled so the Southerners could limit benefits for African Americans to programs for low-income people, and they would differentially benefit Southern states, even on such matters as hospital spending and urban renewal funds (Brown 1999, pp. 182–200). In other words, the spending coalition was premised on excluding African Americans from many of its policy benefits. This exclusionary alliance was one of the main reasons why African Americans took to the streets in large Northern cities between 1963 and 1967 to force government agencies staffed by traditional Democrats to change their rules and give them access to programs related to jobs, housing, and education (Quadagno 1994; Sugrue 2008).

The basic core in this spending coalition was the approximately 100 Democrats from the segregationist states and the 50 to 60 machine Democrats from major urban areas outside the South, which together controlled the House and Senate committees of concern to them through their seniority and their shared interest in government spending. However, after World War II this core coalition had to be augmented by some of the 100 liberal non-Southern Democrats who were supportive of government spending programs. For the most part, the liberal Democrats received nothing in return on two of their most important issues, unions and civil rights. Instead, they had to settle for incremental improvements on economic and welfare issues crucial to the lives of average Americans, which they were often able to win when they could attract the support of machine and Southern Democrats. These victories included increases in the minimum wage, increases in old-age pensions, the addition of disability insurance to the Social Security Act, and increases in unemployment and welfare payments, food stamps, and rent subsidies.

The Conservative Coalition

Despite the mutual back-scratching that bound the Democrats on many issues, they differed among themselves on the issues of greatest concern to the corporate rich: union rights, the regulation of business, progressive taxation, and the limitation of civil rights for African Americans. These are precisely the issues that defined class conflict before 1965 because the limitation of civil rights was essential to planters for the coercive control of their low-wage African American workforce (Patterson 1967; Potter 1972). As a result, the Southern Democrats and Republicans formed a conservative coalition in 1938 that voted together on anywhere from 15 to 40 percent of the votes that were taken in any given two-year session of Congress and was generally successful, as shown by detailed studies of roll call votes (Shelley 1983). The coalition gradually became less important because of the growing number of Southern Republicans in Congress. As late as 1996, however, with conservative white Southern Democrats accounting for less than 30 votes in the House, the conservative coalition still formed on 11.7 percent of the congressional votes and was successful 98.9 percent of the time. The Southern Democratic votes were essential to 33 of 51 conservative victories in the House in that year, offsetting defections by the handful of moderate Republicans from the Northeast that were still in office (CQ 1996).

More generally, the conservative coalition was able to block, water down, or turn to its own advantage every initiative put forward by the liberal-labor alliance between 1939 and 2012 that was also opposed by a united corporate community. Two of the most prominent apparent exceptions, the Civil Rights Act of 1964 and the addition of Medicare to the Social Security Act in 1965, demonstrate this point. In the case of the Civil Rights Act, it was not opposed by the corporate community, which had been preparing for its enactment for several years (Delton 2009; Golland 2011, Chapter 2). It finally passed after the longest filibuster (defined as an indefinite extension of debate) in Senate history because the Republicans deserted their Southern allies, at least in part because of pressure from the corporate community (Whalen and Whalen 1985). As for Medicare, for which the liberal-labor alliance deserves much of the credit, it also had the tacit support of the American Hospital Association because its members were losing money through increasingly expensive treatments of growing numbers of low-income patients (Quadagno 2005). This issue is discussed in more detail in Chapter 7.

Thus, the fact that Democrats formally controlled Congress for most of the years between 1932 and 1994, when many present-day government practices and programs became deeply entrenched, is therefore largely irrelevant in terms of understanding the domination of government policy by the corporate rich. The important point is that a strong conservative majority was elected to Congress, some of whom were Republicans, some of whom were Democrats. They always voted together on the issues that related to class conflict, while at the same time limiting the inclusiveness and cost of social insurance programs for lower-income people.

Nor were the disagreements over unions and civil rights between Southern Democrats and machine Democrats as divisive for the party as they might at first appear to be. Machine Democrats, who were regularly returned to the House and thereby attained considerable seniority, backed the Southern Democrats on issues of party leadership and the retention of the seniority system. At the same time, they were able to maintain liberal voting records by supporting the tepid labor, civil rights, and social welfare legislation that did come up for a vote, thereby satisfying their labor and liberal constituencies. "By voting right," concluded a reporter who covered Congress for the *Wall Street Journal* in the 1960s, "they satisfied liberal opinion at home; by doing nothing effective, they satisfied their Southern allies in the House" (Miller 1970, p. 71). This reporter's observations are supported by a systematic quantitative study based on all committee roll call votes from 1970 to 1980 (Unekis 1993, pp. 96–97).

The control of both major political parties by members of the power elite reinforces the worst tendencies of a two-party system: avoidance of issues and an emphasis on the character and personality of the candidates. This is the main reason why the electoral system is best understood from a class-domination perspective as a "candidate-selection process." Its primary function is one of filling offices with the least possible attention to the policy aspects of politics, which provides openings for the policies developed within the special-interest and policy-planning networks.

However, this does not mean that rival candidates are without at least some personal policy preferences that they would like to see enacted. To the contrary, elected official from both parties employ a variety of strategies so that they can vote their policy preferences, even when they are opposed by a majority of voters, and at the same time win reelection (Jacobs and Shapiro 2000). Nor does an emphasis on the influence of large economic interests in both parties deny that elections are fiercely competitive, not least because the rival candidates would very much like to win, a personal competitiveness that is heightened by the strong policy differences between the rival parties on some issues. Thus, there is a great deal of complexity and detailed maneuvering at the intersection between the power elite, political candidates, and ordinary citizens within the candidate-selection process. It is at this intersection that crafting the right strategies and using the most emotionally salient media images can matter. This is the province of the political consultants that advise candidates and try to assess the factors that will lead to success in specific elections. Many of these consultants double as corporate lobbyists, as discussed later in the chapter.

PARTY PRIMARIES AS GOVERNMENT STRUCTURES

The inexorable two-party logic of the American electoral system led to another unique feature of American politics, the use of primary elections regulated by state governments to determine the parties' candidates. The system was first legislated in 1903 by reformers in Wisconsin, who were convinced there was no hope for third parties (Lovejoy 1941). About the same time, a system of white primaries was adopted in the segregationist Southern states as a way for rival white candidates to challenge each other within the Democratic Party without allowing African Americans to vote (Key 1949).

As primaries grew in frequency, they gradually became an accepted part of the overall electoral system due to pressures from liberal reformers. By the 1970s it reached a point at which the use of government-regulated primaries, when combined with long-standing governmental control of party registration, had transformed the two major parties into the official office-filling agencies of the government. From a legislative and legal point of view, the party primaries labeled *Republican* and *Democratic* can be seen as two different pathways legitimated by the government for obtaining its elected officials. Thus, government-sponsored primaries reinforce the point that American politics is a candidate-selection process.

Put another way, parties are not fully independent organizations that control membership and choose their own leaders, as they are in most other democratic countries and once were in the United States. Since anyone can register with the government to be a member of a party, party leaders cannot exclude people from membership based on political beliefs. Furthermore, people registered in the party can run in its primaries for any office, so party leaders and party conventions have very little influence on the policies advocated by its candidates. In effect, a party stands for what the successful candidates in primaries say it stands for. Party leaders can protest and donors can withhold crucial campaign funds, but the winners in the primaries, along with their many political consultants and fundraisers, are the party for all intents and purposes. This is a major difference from political parties in most other countries.

As a result of these changes, American voters gained the opportunity to decide which individuals from rival groups and classes would have the opportunity to compete in the general elections. Primaries force candidates to mingle with everyday people and pay attention to them. In the process, even incumbents are graphically reminded that they can be deposed if they are not attentive. The need for political candidates to interact with individuals from the general public puts limits on the degree to which money, advertising, and name recognition can shape the outcome of elections.

The use of primaries by insurgents also led to some surprising victories for them in the twentieth century. In 1934, in the midst of the Great Depression, the most famous leftist of his day, the prolific author Upton Sinclair, switched his party registration from Socialist to Democrat. He then announced that he would run for governor of California on a detailed program to End Poverty In California (EPIC), which featured a mixture of socialist and self-help ideas. He organized his supporters into EPIC clubs, thereby giving them an identity that distinguished them from other Democrats, with whom his leftist supporters did not want to be associated. He proceeded to win the primary with 51 percent of the vote in a field of seven candidates. After an extraordinary campaign in which the incumbent Republican governor promised to embrace many New Deal programs, Sinclair lost the general election with 37 percent of the vote. But the Democratic Party was forever changed in California because many young liberal and socialist activists ran for other offices as part of Sinclair's campaign, and later started a set of liberal California Democratic Clubs throughout the state that transformed the party (Carney 1958; Mitchell 1992).

In 1968, antiwar liberals entered Democratic presidential primaries to register their strong opposition to the Vietnam War and did so well that the incumbent president, Lyndon B. Johnson, chose not to run again (Rising 1997). A major civil rights leader from the 1960s to early 2000s, Jesse Jackson, ran solid presidential campaigns in the 1984 and 1988 primaries. In fact, he received more votes in the 1988 primaries than either future president Bill Clinton or future vice president Albert Gore, thereby establishing his credibility with white Democratic politicians that previously ignored him. However, the suspicions and tensions between him and the leftist activists who temporarily joined him were too great for them to build a lasting organization (Barker and Walters 1989; Celsi 1992).

And yet, it was ultraconservatives that made by far the most successful use of party primaries, taking their platform and strong separate social identities as "Young Americans for Freedom" into Republican primaries in 1964 to secure the presidential nomination for Senator Barry Goldwater of Arizona. Although Goldwater lost badly in the regular election, his "state's rights" platform (a code word signifying that the Republicans would not try to end segregation in Southern states) started the movement of the solid Democratic South into the Republican Party in response to the Civil Rights Act of 1964. His campaign also recruited a new cadre and steeled the determination of his followers to take over the party at the grassroots level over the next three decades.

THE BIG, NOT DETERMINATIVE, ROLE OF CAMPAIGN FINANCE

In an electoral system in which party differences often become blurred, and the emphasis on the character and image of each candidate looms large, the corporate rich can play an important role through large campaign contributions used to raise name recognition and craft a winning image. The role of wealthy donors and fundraisers is especially crucial in determining which candidates enter primaries and do well. In particular, it is the need for a large amount of start-up money—to travel around a district or the country, to send out mass mailings, to schedule television ads in advance—that gives the corporate rich and their employees in lobbying and public relations a very direct role in the process right from the start. In a detailed study of campaign finance in the 1950s, well before primaries were as important as they came to be later, they were called a "choke point" in American politics (Heard 1960, p. 34).

With glaring exceptions that receive much publicity, big donors rarely try to tie specific strings to their donations. Nonetheless, they are able to make their views known to the candidates in a strong and direct way, and to work against candidates they do not consider sensible and approachable. At a more psychological level, their donations create a sense of obligation in the recipients because candidates experience them as a "gift." In fact, there is evidence that people everywhere feel a sense of "debt" upon receiving a gift, which leads them to want to reciprocate to rid themselves of the burden (Gordon 2005; Mauss 1924/1969).

All that said, the candidate with the most money does not always win, and there is a long history of failed candidates that far outspent the winners, including many instances of major "self-funders" that lost in 2012 (OpenSecrets 2012c). Moreover, incumbents and those running in safe districts often have more money simply because big donors want to be on the side of sure winners, so the high correlation between having the most cash and winning can be deceptive. The important point is to have the necessary minimum to compete, which is why a few large donors can matter.

The failed history of campaign finance reforms over many decades shows just how important big donations are to candidates. The saga began in the 1970s when a coalition of liberals and corporate moderates seemed to be successful in limiting the impact of big donors by restricting the size of donations and creating a system of optional public financing for both primaries and regular elections at the presidential level. But the reforms did not diminish the influence of the corporate community because big donors became "bundlers," who collected many hundreds of checks for candidates by organizing receptions, luncheons, and dinners at which their colleagues and friends gave a few thousand dollars each. Then the restrictions on the size of individual donations were circumvented in 1979 when the Federal Election Commission ruled that unrestricted donations to state parties for "party building" were permissible, although the money could not be used to support a particular candidate. This "soft money" for attack ads and get-out-the-vote efforts climbed to $46 million for both parties combined in 1992, then jumped to $150 million in 1996 and to over $250 million in 2000 (the equivalent of $335.8 million in 2012). Then another cycle of (failed) reforms began. Still, the "hard" money of regular donations remained much larger.

Corporate leaders also borrowed a page out of organized labor's playbook by forming political action committees (PACs), thereby making it possible for their stockholders and executives to give another several thousand dollars each year through a side door. Corporations could not give money to a PAC from their own funds, but they could pay for the costs of administering a PAC. Similarly, unions could only solicit funds from their members, but they could use their own monies to pay for administrative costs. In addition, trade associations and professional societies organized PACs. It became a full-time job to figure out the networks through which political money flows, as shown by the existence of nonpartisan Internet sites hosted by the Center for Responsive Politics (http://www.opensecrets.org) and the Campaign Finance Institute (http://www.cfinst.org/), which post and analyze government reports as well as information they develop based on a variety of other sources.

Although the corporate community and the growth coalitions are the largest donors to Democratic as well as Republican candidates, analyses of PAC donation patterns at the congressional level provide strong evidence that the differences between the corporate community and the liberal-labor alliance nonetheless manifest themselves in the electoral process. These studies show that corporate PACs usually support one set of candidates and liberal and labor PACs a different set. Not all corporate PACs give to the same candidates, but they seldom give to two different candidates in the same race (Neustadtl, Scott, and Clawson 1991). These conclusions, based on sophisticated statistical analyses, were bolstered by interviews with PAC executives, which revealed there is a large amount of coordination among corporate PACs. Furthermore, candid interviews with corporate PAC managers by the same researchers revealed that they sometimes support Democrats for one or more of three atypical reasons: (1) because the Democrat is a moderate or conservative, usually from a rural area; (2) to maintain access to a Democrat who sits on a congressional committee important to the corporation; or (3) as a favor to another corporation that wants to maintain access to the Democrat (Clawson, Neustadtl, and Weller 1998).

Moreover, there is systematic evidence from an exhaustive quantitative analysis of thousands of roll call votes in the House of Representatives between 1991 and 2006 that the corporate and trade association PACs have a larger influence than the union PACs. A comparison of the degree to which legislators voted the same way with the degree to which they received money from the same pro-business or pro-labor PACs, based on tens of thousands of statistical comparisons between pairs ("dyads") of donors and recipients, showed that business PACs had a significant impact in every two-year session during that 16-year time span. However, labor PACs had an influence in only a few sessions; in addition, the business influence was greater than the labor influence in the few instances in which the labor PACs had any influence at all (Peoples 2007). The credibility of these findings is strengthened by a more general causal analysis of PAC effects during the same time period (Peoples 2010). It is further supported by a study of campaign donations and voting patterns in the Canadian House of Commons in the late 1990s, which revealed that neither business nor labor donations had any impact. This cross-national comparison demonstrated that the House of Representatives is more susceptible to outside influences than its Canadian counterpart (Peoples and Gortari 2008).

Donations by business PACs continued to be large in 2012, with business giving $329.7 million to candidates in both parties, 63 percent of which went to Republicans. Unions, by contrast, contributed less than one-fifth that amount, $58.3 million, 90 percent of which went to Democrats. Even within the Democratic Party, business PACs contributed 2.3 times as much as labor PACs, $122.6 million to $52.4 million (OpenSecrets 2012d).

The escalation in corporate-related funding reached heights that would not have been believed possible early in 2010. A 5–4 majority of the Supreme Court ruled in *Citizens United v. Federal Elections Commission* to uphold a challenge to legal restrictions on donations from corporate funds for "independent expenditures" as a violation of the free-speech rights granted to all persons by the First Amendment. This decision was followed shortly thereafter by a Court of Appeals ruling that PACs that did not give to parties or candidates could collect as much money as they wished from corporations and unions. Based on these two rulings, a number of "super PACs" that could mount very large independent campaigns for or against candidates quickly developed. Further, the lawyers for super PACs soon figured out that they could create front groups to give unlimited and undisclosed donations to super PACs. They did so by incorporating purported "social welfare" organizations, which do not have to disclose their donors as long as they can plausibly claim that political issues are not their primary purpose. At this point the corporate rich could enter into the political arena with the full force of both their personal fortunes and their corporate treasuries, and they could do so anonymously.

The result was a large number of secretive money sources known as "501(c)(4)'s," which is the section in the federal tax code that allows for their existence. Through them, undisclosed contributions could be passed on to the super PACs without anyone knowing the source or extent of individual, corporate, or union donations. The new situation provided a stark contrast with past requirements for disclosure, which led to a detailed understanding of the wealthy financial backers of the two parties going back to the 1920s and 1930s (e.g., Alexander 1971; Overacker 1932; Webber 2000). Legally, the super PACs could not coordinate with party campaigns, but in practice there was usually close coordination, with former aides to the candidates managing the super PACs.

Large donations to the new 501(c)(4)/super PAC combinations led to a fourfold increase in spending by nonparty organizations between 2006 and 2010, from $68.9 million to $294.2 million. The Chamber of Commerce alone spent $31.2 million in undisclosed funds to help Republican candidates in 2010, with much if not most of it coming from corporate leaders who believed that the chamber would never violate its promise to them (Public Citizen 2011, pp. 9–11). Some indication of what is going on is revealed by an inadvertent disclosure by Aetna Insurance, which accidently reported to one government agency in 2011 that it had given $4 million to the Chamber of Commerce for campaign donations

(Riley 2012). One of the newly minted pro-Republican 501(c)(4) social welfare organizations, the American Action Network, headed by a former senator from Minnesota and with the billionaire founder of Home Depot as the most prominent person on its board, provided 27 percent of the 501(c)(4) funds that supported Republicans, with $3 million of that total coming from Aetna (Beckel 2012). With the Republican 501(c)(4) groups outspending those sympathetic to Democrats by $78 million to $16 million in 2010, a ratio of nearly 5 to 1, the Republican challengers had an overwhelming financial advantage, even adding in spending by traditional Democratic Party organizations.

This advantage may have contributed to the Democrats' loss of six seats in the Senate and 63 in the House, although the decline of turnout between 2008 and 2010 from 60 to 40 percent of the electorate was a big factor in the Democrats' loss.

Wealthy liberals initially refused to support secretive funding groups, based on their principled objections to both secrecy and unlimited donations. Republican donors therefore seemed likely to have a large edge in undisclosed funding once again in 2012. However, as the ultraconservative attack ads escalated, many liberals decided that their only hope for any reform in campaign finance would necessitate the election of more Democrats. The result was equally secretive groups on the Democratic side in 2012, such as Patriot Majority USA, which ran ads criticizing Romney for several of the business deals carried out by his private equity firm in the 1990s, and for keeping tens of millions of his estimated $250 million in overseas tax havens; it also criticized specific ultraconservative billionaires for running self-serving ads against President Obama and other Democrats (Draper 2012). Democrats also created several other secretive super PACs, such as the Majority PAC and the House Majority PAC, to help out with Senate and House races. The three Democratic super PACs were mostly supported by wealthy liberals, but in the last two weeks of the campaign they were unexpectedly given $9.7 million by several unions (Choma 2012). Although the pro-Democratic money machines did not come close to matching the funds provided by Republican super PAC supporters, they did help provide the necessary minimum to compete, especially for last-minute efforts to turn out Democratic voters.

Senate candidates supported by the pro-Democratic Majority PAC mostly won, as did a majority of those that received donations from the House Majority PAC. Planned Parenthood Votes, an independent super PAC, which provided partial disclosure of donors, spent $1.1 million supporting Democrats and $6 million opposing Republicans and was on the winning side in most instances. American Crossroads/Crossroads GPS, a super PAC and 501(c)(4) combination, spent $195.2 on Republicans at the presidential and congressional levels and mostly lost. The Chamber of Commerce PAC spent $36.2 million supporting Republicans in 48 House and Senate races, but was on the winning side only seven times (Lichtblau 2012; OpenSecrets 2012c).

As this brief overview of campaign finance indicates, it takes a very large minimum to be a viable candidate. However, as stressed at the beginning of this section and as shown by the many losses for pro-business super PACs, money is only one part of the equation. "Money is a necessary condition for electoral success," concluded one of the campaign finance experts at the Center for Responsive Politics. "But it's not sufficient, and it's never been" (Confessore and Bidgood 2012). The executive director of the Campaign Finance Institute described the 2012 elections as "an arms war fought to a standstill." He added, "Unilateral disarmament is not an effective strategy when the other side shoots" (Campaign Finance Institute 2012). By 2012, candidates usually needed $2 to $3 million to compete for a House seat and $9 to $11 million to fuel a campaign for the Senate. And it takes much, much more to run for president, as shown in the next section.

THE OBAMA DONOR NETWORK: A CASE HISTORY

President Obama's network of donors was similar to those of most other successful national-level candidates in that it built on wealthy contributors from the growth coalitions on up to the corporate community. The gradual development of the president's campaign-finance network and its transformations along the way provide a case study in how such networks are constructed in a step-by-step fashion, which is all the more useful in this instance because he won a Senate seat from Illinois in 2004 and presidential elections in 2008 and 2012.

President Obama's original donor network developed after he received his law degree from Harvard in 1992 and returned to the South Side of Chicago (where he had been a community organizer from 1985 to 1988) to take charge of a voter registration project in African American neighborhoods. This effort brought him into contact with middle-class African Americans and well-to-do white liberals, who would later become his political supporters. For example, Bettylu Saltzman, an heir to a large real estate fortune, was impressed with his political skills. She introduced him to as many wealthy donors as she could and sang his praises to a veteran campaign manager, David Axelrod, who ended up several years later managing his campaigns for the Senate and the presidency (Becker and Drew 2008). She told her political friends from the day she met Obama that he had the potential to be president, and many of them came to agree with her (Yearwood 2008).

At the same time, the future president strengthened his ties to black executives and financiers through his wife, who grew up on the South Side. As mentioned in Chapter 2, she left corporate law and took a job for a few years in city government, before going to work for the University of Chicago's medical school as a liaison to the surrounding community. While employed by the city, she worked for another African American lawyer that had abandoned corporate law, Valerie Jarrett. With degrees from Stanford and Michigan, Jarrett also had many well-to-do friends throughout the Hyde Park neighborhood around the University of Chicago, because her father was among the first black professors in the medical school. Obama's financial network soon included the founder of the largest black-owned money management firm in the country, the chief executive officer of a commercial real estate development firm, black executives in major Chicago corporations, and not least, an African American vice president in the Pritzker Realty Company and the Parking Spot, two of the many companies owned by the Pritzker family briefly discussed in Chapter 3.

However, support from the Pritzkers and other large corporate owners was still in the future when Obama ran for the state senate from the Hyde Park area in 1996 with the help of donations from his African American business friends, a few wealthy white liberals such as Saltzman, and most importantly at the time, the developers who were in the process of gentrifying part of the area encompassed by his state senate district. As Obama explained to a reporter in the late 1990s, after he won the seat in the state senate, the developers, brokerage houses, and law firms supported political candidates that in turn helped them gain government contracts for urban renewal: "They do well, and you get a $5 million to $10 million war chest" (Lizza 2008, p. 58; Murray 2008). His own war chest was never that big, but developers were a key ingredient in his success.

Obama's financial network expanded after Democratic victories in 2000 made it possible for him to ask the Democratic leader in the state senate to redraw his district so that it included the wealthy Gold Coast district along Chicago's lakefront as well as Hyde Park and parts of the impoverished black neighborhoods to its south. At this point Saltzman took him to meet the Ladies Who Lunch, a group of 19 women executives and heiresses "who see themselves as talent scouts and angel investors for up-and-coming liberal candidates and activists" (Lizza 2008, p. 61). One of them, Christie Hefner, who ran Playboy Enterprises at the time, after inheriting it from her father, later said that "I was very proud to be able to introduce him during the Senate race to a lot of people who have turned out to be important and valuable to him, not just here but in New York and L.A." (Lizza 2008, p. 61). He also came to know members of the billionaire Crown family, discussed briefly in Chapter 3. In particular, he gained the confidence of James S. Crown, the president of the family holding and investment company, who sat on the boards of General Dynamics and JPMorgan Chase.

When Obama brought his group of African American friends together to surprise them with the news that he intended to run for the U.S. Senate in 2004, and that he was sure he could win if he could raise several million dollars, they agreed to back him as best they could. But they also knew that he would have to tap much deeper pockets as well. It was at this point that the black vice president of Pritzker Realty arranged for Obama and his wife to spend two days with Penny Pritzker and her husband, an eye surgeon, at the Pritzkers' weekend home 45 minutes east of Chicago. Although Pritzker told one of Obama's biographers that she and her husband had met the Obamas previously, the visit was in many ways an audition, during which she asked the candidate many questions about his general philosophy and campaign plans. By the end of the weekend, she had agreed to help raise money for him (Mendell 2007, p. 155). Pritzker, who ranked 135th on the 2007 Forbes list of the richest 400 in America, with an estimated net worth of $2.8 billion, gave the campaign immediate credibility in the Chicago business community, in part because she defined herself as a centrist who provided financial support to candidates in both parties.

Other Obama fundraisers reached out to the national level, starting with his friend Jarrett, whose cousin is married to one of the most prominent African Americans in the corporate community, Vernon Jordan. A former civil rights lawyer and president of the Urban League, Jordan later became a corporate lawyer and the chief White House counsel to President Bill Clinton. He was on the boards of five corporations at the time he was approached by the Obama campaign (American Express, Asbury Automotive Group, J. C. Penney, Sara Lee, and Xerox) and his wife, Ann Dibble Jordan, was on three: Automatic Data Processing, Citibank, and Johnson & Johnson. The result was a fundraiser in Washington at which Obama gained new financial backers and first met people that subsequently became members of his administration (Silverstein 2006). With the help of Pritzker, Saltzman, Crown, Jordan, and many other wealthy donors, the campaign raised over $5 million, half of which came from just 300 people (Street 2008, p. 15).

The same network was in place as Senator Obama prepared to enter the presidential primaries in 2007. This time Pritzker was the national campaign finance chair. The senator also raised money on Wall Street through a friend from Harvard Law School who worked as an executive for Citibank from 1999 through 2008 after serving in the Treasury Department during the Clinton administration. In addition, Obama received large donations from wealthy donors in Los Angeles and Hollywood that he met through other mutual friends. By March 2008, his 79 top money raisers, five of them billionaires, had collected at least $200,000 each (Mosk and MacGillis 2008).

As the campaign picked up steam late in the summer, the Obama forces set up a special party committee, the Committee for Change, so that donors that had given the maximum to the candidate ($2,300) and to the Democratic National Committee ($28,500) could provide money that would go directly to state-level parties in 18 battleground states. The new funds made it possible to pay for transportation, lodging, and meals for the large army of young get-out-the-vote activists that had been recruited through e-mail, Facebook, YouTube, and text messaging (Melber 2008). Individual checks for $5,000 to $66,000 poured in from the financial sector, lawyers, corporate leaders, and celebrities. Members of the Crown family, who already had raised $500,000 and donated $57,000 to the Obama Victory Fund, gave another $74,000 to the Committee for Change (Mosk and Cohen 2008).

President Obama disappointed many liberals in 2008 when he decided to be the first presidential candidate in either party since 1976 to forgo public financing for his campaign, even though he had promised a year earlier to continue this reformist innovation if his opponent also agreed to do so. As a result, he outspent his Republican opponent by nearly three to one from September 1 to election day, and in the process "ran more negative ads than any presidential candidate in modern history" (Lizza 2012, p. 39). He justified his decision to abandon public financing in part with the claim that his campaign had created a parallel public financing system of small donors (defined as people who give $200 or less) via the Internet and door-to-door campaigning. Although he did raise approximately $200 million in donations from these small donors and had more donors (3.1 million) than any previous campaign, his dependence on small donors turned out to be exaggerated. Subsequent close scrutiny of the final campaign finance reports showed that many of the seemingly small donors gave $200 or more several times in the course of the campaign. Only 26 percent of his donations actually came from people who gave $200 or less, which was about the same as the percentage of small donors for George W. Bush in 2004. Almost half of the money donated to Obama came from people who gave $1,000 or more (Luo 2008b; Malbin 2008).

President Obama's basic donor network remained largely intact in 2012, although there was turnover for a variety of reasons, including disappointments with the administration's approach to some issues and the appointment of about one-third of his 556 bundlers for 2008 (or their spouses) to governmental positions and committees. Most striking, close to 80 percent of those that collected $500,000 or more received high administrative positions (Public Citizen 2012; Schulte, Farrell, and Borden 2011). According to estimates by the Center for Responsive Politics, about 25 percent of his 2012 funding was raised by 758 bundlers, which is 202 more than he had in 2008. They were led by 178 lawyers that raised $41.8 million, 90 members of the financial services industry ($21.9 million), 41 in the entertainment industry ($11.4 million), and 26 in the computer industry ($6.6 million). Thirty-seven of his bundlers raised $1 million or more, including Penny Pritzker ($1.1 million) and James Crown ($1 million), although they were not as active and visible as they were in his campaign in 2008 (OpenSecrets 2012a; OpenSecrets 2012b).

This time the president received 28 percent of his funds from small donors, around $215 million, compared to 12 percent for Romney, by means of the same aggressive outreach program through social media and door-to-door campaigning that he used in 2008 (Campaign Finance Institute 2013). He also received support from the "education industry," consisting mainly of universities, which gave $19.5 million to him and only $3.1 million to Romney because of the Republicans' changing stance toward federal support for education and the skeptical comments some of them make about the value and validity of scientific research. For example, 85 percent of $2 million contributed by employees of Harvard University went to Democrats, as did 76 percent of $1.7 million from Stanford employees, 82 percent of $721,600 from employees of the University of Texas, and 96 percent of $599,000 from employees of the University of Chicago. (Between 1990 and 2012, professors, administrators, and staff at universities increased the percentage of their donations going to Democrats from 59 to 76 percent.) (OpenSecrets 2012c).

There was one major difference with the 2008 campaign: The president received far less support from Wall Street, which gave him $14.5 million in 2008 with much of it coming after September 1, when his Republican opponent was limited in his private fundraising efforts by his acceptance of public spending. In sharp contrast to 2008, the president received only 39 percent as much, $5.5 million. Romney, on the other hand, with many connections to the financial community through his past membership in it as the owner of a private equity firm, raised $18.3 million there. However, it was not simply past relationships with Romney that influenced many high-profile financiers' donation decisions. They already had expressed their public disapproval of the president for criticizing their role in events leading up to the 2008 meltdown and for supporting the financial reform legislation passed in 2010 against their strong objections (OpenSecrets 2012g).

When the dust finally settled, the president and the Democratic National Committee had raised $835.7 million through traditional means with open disclosure and received about $124.5 million in support from outside spending for a total of about $1.1 billion. By contrast, the Republican campaign raised $958.7 million through traditional open channels. Moreover, it had outside support of $454.5 million from nondisclosing super PACs for a total of about $1.4 billion, about $300 million more than the Democratic total (OpenSecrets 2012a). More generally, the same gap between Democratic and Republican spending at the presidential level persisted when all political spending at the federal level is considered. The Democrats spent about $2.1 billion and the Republicans about $2.6 billion, a difference of $500 million. To remain competitive, it seems that Democrats can't allow Republicans to outspend them by too much. By the same token, it appears that Republicans have to hold on to their financial advantage if they are going to win outside of their Southern, Great Plains, and Rocky Mountain strongholds.

Although President Obama's 2008 and 2012 campaigns demonstrated that large sums of money could be raised in small amounts, the fact remains that a relative handful of large donors in the Chicago growth coalition and the national corporate community were essential to his political career. He proved to be an excellent politician and he was able to attract many small donors and enthusiastic campaign workers, but he had to have wealthy backers, too: It is the combination that counts. As if to underscore this point, his decision to abandon public financing for his presidential campaign in 2008 put an end to the public financing of presidential campaigns as a feasible option for future candidates, and thus to the general reform thrust that began in the 1970s. He thereby reinforced his image among campaign advisors in both parties, based on decisions he made to advance his past campaigns, as a tough and ruthless politician (Lizza 2012, pp. 38–40).

OTHER CORPORATE SUPPORT FOR CANDIDATES

As important as large campaign donations are in the electoral process, there are also numerous other methods by which the corporate rich provide support to the politicians they favor. One of the most direct is to purchase property from them at a price well above the market value. Back in 1966, for example, just this kind of favor was done for a future president, Ronald Reagan, shortly after he became governor of California. Twentieth-Century-Fox purchased several hundred acres of his land adjacent to its large outdoor set in Malibu for nearly $2 million, triple its assessed market value and 30 times what he had paid for it in 1952. The land was never utilized and was later sold to the state government. It was this transaction (which netted $14.3 million in 2012 dollars) that gave Reagan the financial security that made it possible for him to devote full time to his political career (Horrock 1976).

A very direct method of benefiting the many politicians who are lawyers is to hire them or their law firms as legal consultants or to provide them with routine legal business. Corporations can be especially helpful to lawyer-politicians when they are between offices. For example, the chairman of Pepsico retained former vice president and future president Richard M. Nixon as the company's lawyer in 1963, while Nixon was out of office. He thereafter paid for every trip Nixon made overseas in the next two years. This made it possible for Nixon to remain in the political limelight as a foreign-policy expert while he quietly began his campaign to become president in 1968 (Hoffman 1973, p. 106).

Members of the corporate rich help political candidates by hiring them to give highly paid speeches at corporate and trade association events. They also provide large donations to foundations, scholarship funds, and charities that elected officials set up in their home congressional district or state. They further help candidates in both parties by lending them corporate lobbyists to serve as political strategists, campaign managers, and fundraisers. The 2008 Republican presidential candidate, the multimillionaire senator from Arizona, John McCain, emphasized that he was an opponent of lobbyists and of the favors won by them. Still, his primary campaign was financed and managed by several of the most important lobbyists in Washington. His chief political strategist, who had worked in Republican presidential campaigns since the 1980s, had a client list that included AT&T, Alcoa, JPMorgan Chase, United Technologies, and US Airways. Similarly, Senator McCain's campaign manager was the co-founder of a lobbying firm that worked for Verizon and other telephone companies. His top fundraiser worked as a lobbyist for Saudi Arabia, Toyota, Southwest Airlines, and the pharmaceutical manufacturers' trade association. Seventeen of the 106 people that collected $100,000 or more for the primary campaign were lobbyists (Luo and Wheaton 2008; Shear and Birnbaum 2008).

Elected officials also know from following the career trajectories of older colleagues that the corporate rich can reward them after their tenure in office if they are seen as reasonable and supportive. As of 2011, 373 former members of Congress were senior advisors or lobbyists for corporations, or worked for lobbying firms or public relations firms (OpenSecrets 2012e). To take a dramatic example, a Southern Democrat-turned-Republican from Louisiana was mainly responsible as chair of the key House committee for a provision in the amendments to Medicare in 2004 that prohibited the federal government from bargaining about the prices of the prescription drugs it purchases. When he retired the next year, he was appointed president of the Pharmaceutical Research and Manufacturing Association, the industry's trade group. His initial salary was reported to be $2 million a year; he received $4.6 million in 2009 and $11.6 million in his final year with the trade group in 2010 (Albert 2011). Former president Bill Clinton, who had little or no money before he became president, earned tens of millions of dollars from speeches to business associations and foreign governments after he left office. He also was included in investment opportunities by a few of his wealthy backers in exchange for opening doors for them. By 2012 he was worth an estimated $200 million and Hillary was worth $34 million.

THE LIBERAL-LABOR ALLIANCE IN ELECTORAL POLITICS

Although the liberal-labor alliance had very little independent influence at the presidential level by the early twenty-first century, it still played a huge role in electing the Democratic candidates that emerged from Democratic presidential primaries in key swing states that still had a significant union presence, such as Wisconsin, Illinois, Michigan, Ohio, and Pennsylvania. Fearing the antiunion and antiliberal stance of the Republican Party, the liberal-labor alliance ended up trying desperately to turn out voters for the centrists and moderate conservatives who had the money to compete in Democratic Party presidential primaries. It played a similar large role in helping Democrats in congressional campaigns in many states, including New York, California, and Massachusetts, as well as the Midwestern swing states.

This point was on display in the 2012 elections, thanks in part to the Supreme Court decision on *Citizens United v. Federal Elections Commission*, which opened two new avenues for unions. First, the decision permitted unions to give unlimited donations from their own funds to super PACs and to mingle those contributions with unlimited contributions from well-to-do professionals and rich liberals, as revealed by the $9.7 million unions gave the three pro-Democratic super PACs just before the elections (Choma 2012). Second, and possibly even more important, it allowed unions to contact nonunion households personally and on the telephone. At this point, organized labor also established closer coordination with MoveOn.org, the NAACP, and Planned Parenthood, which led to very large get-out-the-vote efforts in Pennsylvania, Ohio, and Wisconsin. The liberal-labor alliance thus served as the foot soldiers for the Democrats, which is a useful metaphor because the alliance had little influence on the generals at the top of the party.

However, even though it only had a secondary role at the presidential level, the liberal-labor alliance always was able to elect a significant number of supporters to both the House and Senate between 1948 and 2012, even in times of Republican ascendancy. According to studies of congressional voting records by the liberal Americans for Democratic Action (ADA), the percentage of

Democratic representatives with liberal voting records grew steadily from the late 1990s to 2010. Using the organization's standard that voting liberal 80 percent of the time on liberal legislative proposals is what defines a "liberal," nearly half the members of the Democratic caucus in the House were liberals in 2007 and perhaps as many as 40 percent in the Senate (Riddiough and Card 2008). For 2010, the figures were at or near an all-time high for both houses, with 86 percent of 56 Senate Democrats and 77 percent of 253 House Democrats having liberal voting records (ADA 2010). The presence of such a large contingent of liberals in Congress during the brief interlude before control of the House returned to the Republicans in 2010 demonstrates the limits on the influence of the corporate rich in the electoral arena, despite their financial advantage and the many favors they can do for candidates.

THE RESULTS OF THE CANDIDATE SELECTION PROCESS

What kinds of elected officials emerge from a candidate selection process that narrows down to two political parties and puts great emphasis on campaign finance, personal image, and name recognition? The answer is available from numerous studies. First, politicians come from the top 10 to 15 percent of the occupational and income ladders, especially those who hold the highest elective offices. Only a small minority is from the upper class or corporate community, but in a majority of cases they share a business or legal background in common with members of the power elite. Between 1950 and 2010, the 10 percent of the workforce in business or law contributed 75 percent of the members of Congress, whereas less than 2 percent of the members of Congress were former blue-collar workers or union officials (Carnes 2012, p. 6). Nonetheless, politicians feel a need to stress the humble nature of their social backgrounds whenever it is possible.

The emphasis on modest origins and pedestrian work early in their lives begins at the top with presidential candidates, but most presidents since the country's founding were wealthy, or connected to wealth by the time they became president. George Washington was one of the richest men of his day, partly through inheritance, partly through marriage. Andrew Jackson, allegedly of humble circumstances because his father died before he was born, was raised in a well-to-do slave-holding family and became even wealthier as an adult. He "dealt in slaves, made hundreds of thousands of dollars, accumulated hundreds of thousands of valuable acres in land speculation, owned racehorses and racetracks, bought cotton gins, distilleries, and plantations, was a successful merchant, and married extremely well" (Pessen 1984, p. 81). Abraham Lincoln became a corporate lawyer for railroads and married into a wealthy Kentucky family.

Few presidents after 1900 were from outside the very wealthiest circles. Theodore Roosevelt, William H. Taft, Franklin D. Roosevelt, John F. Kennedy, George H. W. Bush, and George W. Bush are from upper-class backgrounds. Herbert Hoover, Jimmy Carter, and Ronald Reagan were millionaires before they became deeply involved in national politics. Lyndon B. Johnson was a millionaire several times over through his wife's land dealings and his use of political leverage to gain control of a lucrative television license in Austin. Even Richard M. Nixon, whose father ran a small store, was a rich man when he was elected president in 1968, after earning high salaries as a corporate lawyer between 1963 and 1968.

Bill Clinton, elected president in 1992 and 1996, tried to give the impression he was from an impoverished background, claiming he was just a poor boy from the tiny town of Hope, Arkansas, born of a widowed mother. But Clinton was gone from Hope, where he lived in comfortable circumstances with his grandparents, who owned a small store, by the age of six. At that time his mother married Roger Clinton, whose family owned a car dealership in the nearby tourist town of Hot Springs. He grew up playing golf at the local country club and driving a Buick convertible. His mother sent him money throughout his years in college. Clinton was not wealthy or from the upper class, but he had a very solid middle-class upbringing and education that he artfully obscured.

The second general finding about elected officials is that a great many of them are lawyers. Between 50 and 60 percent of congressional members have been lawyers, and 28 of the 44 American presidents earned law degrees, including Democratic presidents Clinton (Yale Law School) and Obama (Harvard Law School) (Eulau and Sprague 1984; Miller 1995). The large percentage of lawyers in the American political system is highly atypical compared with other countries, where only 10 to 30 percent of legislators have a legal background. Comparing the United States with a deviant case at the other extreme, Denmark, where only 2 percent of legislators are lawyers, provides insight into this overrepresentation. The class-based nature of Danish politics since the late nineteenth century, along with the fact that political careers are not pathways to judicial appointments, are thought to discourage lawyer participation in that country. The Danish situation thus suggests that the marginalization of class issues by the two main American political parties, combined with the intimate involvement of the parties in the judicial system, creates a climate for strong lawyer involvement in the political system (Pederson 1972).

Whatever the reasons for their involvement in politics, which may vary from person to person and party to party, lawyers are the occupational grouping that by training and career needs are ideal go-betweens and compromisers. The lawyers who become politicians have developed the skills necessary to negotiate the complicated relationship between the corporate rich, who finance them, and average citizens, who vote for them. They are the supreme "pragmatists" in a nation that prides itself on a pragmatic and can-do ideology. Despite the public hyperbole and histrionics that many of them use to reassure their constituents that they are in touch with their sentiments, they generally have an ability to be dispassionate about "the issues" and they are usually respectful of the process by which things are done. They are also masters of timing, small gestures, and symbolism, which are essential skills in diffusing the tension that is inherent in politics because it is at bottom a contest for power between rival groups or classes.

Whether elected officials are from business or law, the third general result of the candidate-selection process is a large number of very ambitious people who are eager to "go along to get along." To understand the behavior of politicians, one political scientist concluded after studying many political careers in the first half of the twentieth century, it is more useful to know what they aspire to be than how they made it to where they are at any given point in their careers (Schlesinger 1966). This conclusion was reinforced 30 years later by another close observer (Ehrenhalt 1991). Their great ambition, whether for wealth or higher office, leads politicians to become involved with people who can help them realize their goals. Such people are often members of the corporate community or upper class with money to contribute and connections to other districts, states, or regions in which striving candidates need new friends. Thus, even the most liberal or ultraconservative of politicians may develop a new circle of moderate supporters as they move from the local to the congressional to the presidential level, gradually becoming more and more involved with leading figures within the power elite.

The Chicago *Tribune* reporter assigned to follow Barack Obama's political career on a daily basis from 2002 to 2008 was struck by his overwhelming ambition: "He is an extraordinarily ambitious, competitive man with persuasive charm and a career reach that seems to know no bounds; he is, in fact a man of raw ambition so powerful that even he is still coming to terms with its full force" (Mendell 2007, p. 7). Indeed, keeping his ambition under wraps and suppressing his "privately haughty manner" was his most difficult problem, a problem that was remarked about frequently in the media during the 2012 presidential campaign because he had alienated some of his 2008 financial supporters (Mendell 2007, pp. 353–354). Ambition aside, President Obama also fit the general pattern because he moderated his liberal positions on many issues when he ran for the Senate in 2004 and then for the presidency in 2008. Some of the liberal activists in Hyde Park who helped him win his first campaign resigned themselves to the fact that he took more moderate positions when he started to raise money in wealthy financial circles, but others became disillusioned and no longer supported him (Becker and Drew 2008; Lizza 2008).

The fourth generalization about most successful political candidates is that they try to straddle the fence or remain silent on the highly emotional social issues. Basically, very few candidates can win if they challenge the limits that have been set by the actions and media advertising sponsored by ultraconservatives on one or another social issue. As long as a majority of people say they believe in the death penalty or oppose gun control, for example, it is unlikely that anyone who openly opposed those positions could be elected to any office except in a few liberal districts and cities. Here, then, is an instance in which public opinion has a direct effect on the behavior of candidates and elected officials.

The fifth general finding, alluded to earlier in the chapter, is that the majority of elected officials at the national level have been pro-business moderates and conservatives. For most of the twentieth century, as explained earlier in the chapter, this conservative majority consisted of Republicans and Southern Democrats.

Starting in the 1960s, and accelerating in the 1980s and early 1990s, Republicans replaced Southern Democrats in both the House and the Senate, which contributed heavily to the Republican takeover of Congress in 1994. It also contributed to the image that American politics became more "polarized" than it had been in the past, but much of this seemingly new polarization consists of the replacement of liberal and moderate Republicans in the Northeast with liberal and moderate Democrats and of ultraconservative Democrats in the South and Great Plains with Republicans that are even more conservative on most issues.

By 2000, most strong conservatives were part of the Republican Party, and the two parties had become very different on a wide range of issues. The only wealthy people that remained in the Democratic Party were those who depended on the spending coalition for their wherewithal, or felt offended or threatened by ultraconservative Republican positions on gay rights, religion, immigration, or abortion, or feminist issues more generally. With the exception of union issues, these rich Democrats were willing to make common cause with the other "outgroups" that differentially favor the Democrats—people of color, single women of all colors and ages, members of the LGBT community, low-income whites, and white middle-class liberals.

BUT THERE'S STILL UNCERTAINTY

Although most elected officials at the national level have been supported by and feel sympathetic toward the corporate rich, there is always the possibility that some of them may be inclined at some point to side with the liberal-labor alliance on specific issues. This possibility once again shows, as emphasized at the end of Chapters 2 and 4, that there is too much uncertainty and volatility in the workings of government for the corporate rich to leave anything to chance. They therefore have to be able to influence government policy. They do not want to risk the possibility that the liberal-labor minority in Congress might be able to create coalitions with moderates that could defeat them on key issues, especially in times of crisis.

7

How the Power Elite Dominate Government

The corporate rich and the power elite build on their structural power, their status power, their storehouse of policy recommendations, and their success in the electoral arena to dominate the federal government on the issues they care about. Lobbyists from corporations, law firms, and trade associations, working through the special-interest process, play a crucial role in shaping government policies on narrow issues of concern to wealthy families, specific corporations, or business sectors. At the same time, the policy-planning network supplies new policy directions on major issues, along with top-level governmental appointees to implement those policies.

However, these victories within government are far from automatic. The power elite face opposition from a significant number of liberal elected officials and their supporters in labor unions and in liberal, civil rights, feminist, and environmental advocacy groups. These liberal-labor opponents are sometimes successful in blocking the social initiatives advocated by the religious right, such as making abortions almost impossible to obtain, but the corporate community and its supporters in Congress seldom lost in the years between 1877 and 2012 on any issue on which they were in agreement.

There is only one major issue that does not fit that generalization, labor legislation, which is discussed briefly in the middle of the chapter. This issue is ancient history from the perspective of the twenty-first century because the corporate rich ultimately triumphed on it, but the rise of union power between 1935 and the 1970s was once the most important reason why the great majority of social scientists doubted a class-domination theory.

THE ROLE OF GOVERNMENTS

Governments are potentially independent because they have a unique function: regulating what goes on within the territories they govern. They set up and guard boundaries and then regulate the flow of people, money, and goods in and out of the area they control. They also have regulatory functions inside the territory itself, such as settling disputes through the judicial system and setting the rules that make it possible for markets to function. In a world in which one country is prone to invade and conquer another, governments also have the crucial function of protecting the home territory and fending off rival states, and they often take advantage of opportunities to expand their own territories as well.

Neither business, the military, or ideological groups are organized in such a way that they can provide these necessary functions. The military sometimes steps in—or forces its way in—when a government is weak or collapsing, but it has a difficult time carrying out routine regulatory functions for very long. Nor can competing businesses regulate themselves. As thousands and thousands of illegal actions between the 1960s and 2012 clearly demonstrate, with new examples appearing virtually every day on the business pages of major newspapers, there is always some business that will try to improve its market share or profits by adulterating products, reducing wages, colluding with other companies, or telling half-truths. As most economists and all other social scientists agree, a business system could not survive without some degree of market regulation by government. Contrary to any assertions about markets being "free," historical and sociological research shows that markets are historically constructed institutions that are dependent upon governmentally sanctioned enforcement of property and contract rights (e.g., Massey 2005). When government regulatory agencies are captured by the corporate community, as they very often are, the result is often the kind of speculative frenzy in financial markets that led to the bankruptcy of several large companies in the early 2000s and then again in 2008–2009, as well as accounting scandals, insider dealing among stockbrokers, bid-rigging by private equity funds, excessive charges to customers by mutual funds, kickbacks by insurance companies, false applications by mortgage companies, and fraudulent ratings of stocks and bonds by stock analysts and credit rating companies.

Governments are also essential in creating money, setting interest rates, and shaping the credit system. Although private bankers tried to manage the monetary system without a government central bank for much of the nineteenth century, the problems caused by a privately controlled money system were so great that the most powerful bankers of the early twentieth century worked together to create the Federal Reserve System in 1913 (Greider 1989; Livingston 1986). The system was improved during the 1930s and has been an essential institution in keeping a highly volatile business system from careening off in one direction or another. When the stock market crashed in 1987, for example, the Federal Reserve made sure that stockholders would not lose their wealth by instructing large New York banks to keep making loans to temporarily insolvent debtors. Similar bailouts were carried out in the 1990s due to problems in Mexico, Korea, and a Wall Street investment firm, Long Term Capital Management, which could have caused large-scale bankruptcies (Woodward 2000). Only massive efforts by the Federal Reserve System, this time in conjunction with the Department of Treasury and Congress, staved off a potentially disastrous meltdown of the financial system in late 2008.

The federal government also is essential in providing subsidy payments to groups in trouble, whether it's well-off growers or low-income workers, and it needs to do so in ways that bolster the market system and benefit large corporations. For example, and as already mentioned in Chapter 2, 38 percent of all farms receive tens of billions in direct payments and government crop insurance, which adds up to half of all farm income in some years. As for low-income employees that work full time, they receive tens of billions of dollars (ranging from about $500 for a married couple without children to $6,000 for a parent or parents with three or more children) through a program called "Earned Income Tax Credits." The Earned Income Tax Credits serve as an offset to payroll taxes for individuals and as a subsidy for corporations that pay low wages, which is why most corporate leaders and Republicans supported them back in the 1970s as preferable to welfare payments. From their point of view, this type of income support also increases the size of the labor pool and reinforces the work ethic. As of 2012, 26 states also had Earned Income Tax programs, including several Republican-dominated states.

Nor is government any less important in the context of a globalizing economy. If anything, it is even more important because it has to enforce rules concerning patents, intellectual property, quality of merchandise, and much else in an unregulated international arena. The film industry, publishers, and pharmaceutical companies, among several, are absolutely dependent on the government to protect them against cheaply produced copies and knock-offs. Furthermore, the international economy simply could not function without the agreements on monetary policy and trade that the governments of the United States, Japan, Canada, and Western Europe uphold through the International Monetary Fund, World Trade Organization, and other international agencies. For all these reasons, domination of the federal government on domestic and international economic issues is vital for the corporate community.

THE SPECIAL-INTEREST PROCESS

The special-interest process, as noted at earlier points in the book, consists of the many and varied means by which wealthy families, individual corporations, and business sectors gain the tax breaks, favors, regulatory rulings, and other governmental assistance they need to realize their narrow and short-run interests. The process is based on frequent personal contact with elected officials and their staffs, but its most important ingredients are the information and financial support that the lobbyists have to offer. It is carried out by people with a wide range of experiences: former elected officials, experts who once served on congressional staffs or in regulatory agencies, employees of trade associations, corporate executives whose explicit function is government liaison, and an assortment of lawyers and public relations specialists (Goldstein 1999; Luger 2000). In reaction to the growing number of women in elected and appointed government positions, there are also a number of women lobbyists, many of them experts on taxes and finance (Benoit 2007).

Intricate and arcane tax breaks are one of the most important aspects of the special-interest process, starting with a variety of legal loopholes that save individuals and families many millions in taxes each year (Johnston 2003; Johnston 2007). However, corporations also benefit from similar strategies. Due to successful efforts in 1993 to relax rules concerning minimum corporate taxes, and then changes in 1997 making it possible for corporations to spread tax breaks over several years, 12 of 250 profitable large firms studied for the years 1996–1998 paid no federal income taxes. Seventy-one of the 250 paid taxes at less than half the official rate during those three years (Johnston 2000). The trend to increasingly large tax breaks continued during the administration of George W. Bush. Forty-six of 275 major companies studied for 2003 paid no federal income taxes, a considerable increase from a similar study in the late 1990s (Barshay and Wolfe 2004; Browning 2004; McIntyre 2004).

Although President Obama and his Republican opponent agreed during the 2012 election campaign that the tax rates on corporations were too high, 26 large companies, including Boeing, General Electric, DuPont, and Verizon, paid no taxes at all between 2008 and 2011 (CTJ 2012a). Another study by Citizens for Tax Justice, a Washington tax research group, found enough information on 290 *Fortune* 500 companies to determine that they kept $1.6 trillion in earnings in offshore tax havens for an estimated tax savings of $433 billion; just 20 companies were sheltering half of that income, and the next 30 had another 24 percent of it (CTJ 2012b). According to a study for the *New York Times*, the effective tax rate on corporations in general was 23 percent in 2011, well below the official top rate of 35 percent (Duhigg and Kocieniewski 2012; NYT 2012).

Corporations spend far more money on lobbying than their officers give to political candidates or to their company's political action committee. In 2000, for example, the tobacco industry, facing lawsuits and regulatory threats, spent $44 million on lobbyists and $17 million on the Tobacco Institute, an industry public relations arm, but gave only $8.4 million to political campaigns through political action committees (deFigueiredo and Snyder 2003). A study of the top 20 defense contractors showed that they spent $400 million on lobbying between 1997 and 2003, but only $46 million on campaign contributions (POGO 2004). The top pro-business lobbying organization in 2012, the Chamber of Commerce, spent $95.7 million, compared to $36.2 million on campaign donations.

In achieving their successes, individual corporations and trade associations deploy many thousands of former congressional staffers and employees in departments and agencies of the executive branch. In 2012, for example, 521 worked for the TV/movie/music industry, 423 for the automotive industry, and 279 for finance and credit companies (OpenSecrets 2012e). At the same time, a large number of lobbyists were part of a few big firms that were major businesses in and of themselves, bringing in from $100 to $500 million each year (OpenSecrets 2012f). Several of these firms, in turn, are owned by the public relations firms that have a major role in the opinion-shaping network discussed in Chapter 5.

Still, even though far more money is spent on lobbying, the important point is that corporate lobbying and campaign donations go hand-in-hand, as seen in a case study of the 30 most successful companies in seeking large tax breaks. This study showed that in addition to the $476 million they spent on lobbying Congress between 2008 and 2010, they also contributed $41 million to 98 percent of the members of Congress, with the largest donations going to the leaders of both parties and the chairs of key congressional committees (PIRG/CTJ 2012). Strikingly, these 30 corporations received $10.6 billion in tax rebates during the same time period, so it is not surprising that many corporations view their Washington offices as another "profit center" within the corporation (Clawson, Neustadtl, and Weller 1998).

Special interests and their lobbyists work through Congress to hamstring regulatory agencies or reverse military purchasing decisions they do not like. For example, when the Federal Communications Commission tried to issue licenses in 2000 for over 1,000 low-power FM stations for schools and community groups, Congress blocked the initiative at the behest of big broadcasting companies, setting standards that restricted new licenses to a small number of stations in the least populated parts of the country (Labaton 2000). Sometimes the lobbyists go directly to the relevant government agency for possible redress. Pfizer paid one firm $400,000 to work against a National Transportation Safety Board proposal to ban the use of antihistamines by truck drivers. The Magazine Publishers of America paid another firm $520,000 to oppose a possible 15 percent increase in magazine postal rates (Zeller 2000).

Some special-interest conflicts pit one sector of business against another, such as when broadcasters jockey for advantage against movie or cable companies. Sometimes the arguments are within a specific industry, as occurred when smaller insurance companies moved their headquarters to Bermuda in 1999 and 2000 to take advantage of a tax loophole worth as much as $4 billion annually. Since the bigger insurance companies could not easily avail themselves of this opportunity, they hired a lobbying firm, several law firms, and a public relations firm to advocate bipartisan legislation to end the tax benefits that derive from creating a mail drop in Bermuda. The small companies countered by hiring a different set of law firms and public relations companies (Stone 2000). The loophole stayed open and the bigger companies continued to fight it, but in 2012 Bermuda still was advertising itself as the ideal place for insurance companies to incorporate (Forbes 2012; Johnston and Treaster 2007).

The special-interest process often is used to create loopholes in new legislation that was accepted in principle by the corporate community. "I spent the last seven years fighting the Clean Air Act," a corporate lobbyist in charge of PAC donations for his company told researchers. He then went on to explain why he gave money to elected officials who voted for the strengthening of the Clean Air Act in 1990: "How a person votes on the final piece of legislation is not representative of what they have done." Most members of Congress voted for the act, he continued. "But during the process some of them were very sympathetic to some of our concerns" (Clawson, Neustadtl, and Weller 1998, p. 6). Translated into results, this means there were 40 pages of exceptions, extensions, and other loopholes in the 1990 version of the act after a 13-year standoff between the Business Roundtable's Clean Air Working Group and the liberal-labor alliance's National Clean Air Coalition. For example, the steel industry was given 30 years to bring 26 large coke ovens into compliance with the new standards. Once the bill passed, lobbyists went to work on the Environmental Protection Agency to win the most lax regulations possible for implementing the legislation.

Although most studies of the special-interest process recount the success of one or another corporation or trade association in gaining the tax or regulatory breaks it seeks, or discuss battles between rival sectors of the corporate community, there are occasional defeats for corporate interests at the hands of liberals and labor within this process, but most of them were long ago. In 1971, for example, environmentalists convinced Congress to end taxpayer subsidies for construction of a supersonic transport. In 1977, a relatively strong anti–strip mine bill was adopted over the objections of the coal industry. Laws that improved auto safety standards were passed over automobile industry objections in the 1970s, as were standards of water cleanliness opposed by the paper and chemical industries (Luger 2000; Vogel 1989).

The special-interest process is the most visible and frequently studied aspect of governmental activity in Washington. It also consumes the lion's share of the attention devoted to legislation by elected officials. Although the special-interest process is very important to wealthy families and the corporate community, it is not the heart of the matter when it comes to a full understanding of corporate power in the United States. Moreover, there is general agreement among a wide range of theorists about the operation of this dimension of American politics: everyone concludes that wealthy families and organized business groups have great power in this arena. But as far as most social scientists are concerned, as explained further in Chapter 9, this is not enough to demonstrate corporate dominance of the federal government in general. They note that the special-interest process is too narrow to explain the adoption of important new foreign and domestic polices of a more general nature, even while agreeing that many departments and regulatory agencies are dominated by the business sectors with the greatest interest in their activities and rulings. Although corporate domination of many specific parts of the government is no trivial matter as evidence for a class-dominance theory, this point about general policies means that the policy-making process discussed in the next section is not only important to the corporate community, but pivotal in theoretical arguments among social scientists as well.

THE POLICY-MAKING PROCESS

Domination of the federal government on issues of concern to the corporate community as a whole is the culmination of work done in the policy-planning network described in Chapter 4. However, the differences between moderate conservatives and ultraconservatives within the policy-planning network sometimes lead to major conflicts between them within the executive branch or Congress over new policies. In addition, at this point the power elite have to fend off alternative legislative proposals put forward by the liberal-labor alliance.

The recommendations developed by organizations in the policy-planning network reach government in a variety of ways. On the most general level, elected officials and their staffs read the reports, news releases, and interviews that emanate from the think tanks and policy-discussion groups. Members of the policy organizations appear before congressional committees and subcommittees that are writing legislation or preparing budget proposals. However, the most important contacts with government are more direct and formal in nature. They include service on federal advisory committees, service on specially appointed presidential and congressional commissions, and direct exchanges of viewpoints between government officials and corporate leaders through regularly scheduled meetings with the Business Council and the Business Roundtable. Representatives of the corporate community and the policy-planning network are also appointed to important government positions, which places them in a position to endorse the policy recommendations put forward by their colleagues and former employees in the policy-planning network.

Federal Advisory Committees

Corporate executives and experts from the policy-planning network are often members of the many unpaid committees that advise specific departments of the executive branch on a wide range of policies. Building on a 2006 database that included the 100 largest corporations as well as foundations, think tanks, policy-discussion groups, and federal advisory committees, sociologist Scott Dolan (2011, Chapter 6; Dolan and Moore 2013) discovered that many of the top 100 corporations and several of the policy-planning groups had one or more members on advisory groups. The corporations were most likely to have representatives on advisory committees in the departments of defense, commerce, energy, and state, along with Homeland Security, the Federal Communications Commission, and the Office of Science and Technology. Similarly, think tanks and policy-discussion groups had their most frequent connections to the defense, commerce, energy, and state departments. On the other hand, neither corporations nor organizations in the policy-planning network are involved in health and human services, education, or the arts, in which advisory committee members are overwhelmingly from the medical, scientific, university, and arts communities.

These findings are consistent with a study of advisory committee linkages to the profit and nonprofit sectors for the mid-1990s: 72 percent of the 100 largest corporations and 83 percent of 12 think tanks and policy-planning groups had members on federal advisory committees (Moore et al. 2002). For example, the Defense Policy Advisory Committee on Trade within the Department of Defense came primarily from the defense industry, while the National Security Tele-communications Advisory Committee in the Department of State came from telecommunication, information, and electronic companies. CEOs made up the entire membership of some of these advisory committees. The findings also fit with the close connection between the Business Roundtable and key federal advi-sory groups in the Department of Commerce during the conflicts over the passage of NAFTA in 1994 and permanent normal trade relations with China in 2000. In both cases the advisory committees were especially important because consulta-tion with advisory committees in the Department of Commerce was made man-datory by legislation passed in 1974 (Dreiling and Darves 2011). (For detailed earlier information on these advisory committees, see the document on "Federal Advisory Committees" on whorulesamerica.net.)

Presidential and Congressional Advisory Commissions

Corporate executives and experts from the policy-planning network have been prominent on the presidential and congressional commissions that have been appointed from time to time since World War II to make recommendations on a wide range of issues from highway construction to changes in Social Security to a new missile defense system to, during the first Obama administration, deal-ing with the federal debt. The recommendations of these commissions have met with varying degrees of success, and sometimes they are meant as no more than window dressing, but they reinforce and legitimate corporate policy positions even when they do not lead to immediate changes.

President Obama's National Commission on Fiscal Responsibility and Reform, appointed in 2010, was meant to lead to a "grand bargain" on how to deal with the federal debt through fiscal reform, with tax increases on the one hand and cuts in spending on the other. It consisted of 18 presidential appointees, start-ing with three Democrats, two Republicans, and an independent from outside of government. In addition, there were six congressional Democrats and six con-gressional Republicans. After months of deliberations, no official report could be issued because seven commissioners would not support it. Four liberal members (three from Congress and a former union leader) rejected cuts in Social Security benefits and three ultraconservative members (all from the House) rejected tax increases on dividends and capital gains, even though the overall plan called for cuts in the top personal and corporate rates from 35 percent to 28 percent that far outweighed the dividend and capital gains increases.

Five of the six non-governmental appointees were a classic cross-section of the corporate rich and the power elite. The Republican co-chair of the com-mission was a graduate of an elite prep school and a wealthy former senator from Wyoming, who retired from the Senate in 1997 at age 66, taught at various centers at Harvard for three years, and then returned to Wyoming to practice corporate law. The other Republican appointee was the CEO of Honeywell, a director of JPMorgan Chase, and a member of the Business Roundtable and the Business Council. The Democratic co-chair, whose father ran a large family-owned wholesale food distribution company in North Carolina, graduated from an elite private school, the University of North Carolina at Chapel Hill, and the Columbia University Business School. He worked as a partner at Morgan Stanley for several years, later founded his own investment firm, and served as President Clinton's White House chief of staff from 1997 to 1998. Another Democratic appointee was a graduate of an elite women's prep school, Bryn Mawr College, and Harvard, where she received a Ph.D. in economics. She was a fellow of The Brookings Institution, a former head of the Office of Management and Budget in the Carter administration, and a former vice chair of the Federal Reserve Board during the Clinton years. The third Democrat from outside government, the former president of the Service Employees International Union, represented the labor movement. The independent member was raised in a middle-class African American family in Washington, DC, attended Catholic high schools, and received a BA from Simmons College and an MBA from Harvard. She was a long-time high executive at General Mills and Kraft Foods, and retired from business in 2007 as the chair of Young & Rubicam, one of the largest public relations and marketing firms in the world. She was a director of General Electric, Novartis, and Unilever, and a trustee of the Rockefeller Foundation, the Council on Foreign Relations, and The Brookings Institution.

Although no official report could be submitted to the president, the draft approved by the majority became the basis for a new corporate lobbying effort, the Campaign to Fix the Debt, made up of 70 CEOs, over half of whom were members of the Business Roundtable and/or Business Council. The Fix the Debt effort, led by the Republican and Democratic co-chairs of the Obama debt commission, began with a press conference in Washington in November 2012, which emphasized that the CEOs' were now willing to pay a higher personal tax rate to facilitate a resolution to a stalemate between the White House and the Republicans over whether to let the Bush-era tax cuts expire and trigger automatic spending cuts on January 1, 2013, or create a compromise (the "fiscal cliff" drama). The lobbying effort consisted of a huge advertising blitz, at a cost of over $50 million, in Washington and in the congressional districts of top Republicans in the House, along with personal visits with members of Congress by CEOs.

In a last-minute compromise in the early days of 2013, President Bush's tax cuts were preserved on all income up to $400,000, with any income over that figure taxed at the rate of 39.6 percent, and the tax rate on income from dividends and capital gains was raised from 15 to 20 percent for those with incomes over $400,000. Most important for the corporate rich, gifts and estates of up to $5 million per person (indexed for inflation) were exempted from taxes, and anything over that amount was taxed at a maximum rate of 40 percent, which means that major fortunes can be passed on to children largely intact. In exchange,

Republicans agreed to extend unemployment benefits for one year and the Earned Income Tax Credit, the child tax credit, and certain education tax credits for five years. But a temporary decease in the payroll tax was not extended, which meant that there was a decline in take-home pay for most employees in 2013.

Until archival records and oral histories become available, the extent to which the highly publicized efforts of the presidential debt commission and the lobbying by the leaders of the Campaign to Fix the Debt played a significant role in bringing about the compromise will not be known. It is likely that the Republican CEOs had an impact in swaying congressional Republicans to agree to some tax increases, but it is also the case that the CEOs and other corporate lobbyists could not convince the congressional Democrats to accept the cuts in Social Security they had hoped to bring about through a decrease in yearly inflation adjustments and an increase in the age at which a full pension could be collected.

Government Consultations with the Business Council and Business Roundtable

Corporate leaders have personal contact with both appointed and elected officials as members of the two policy organizations with the most access to government, the Business Council and the Business Roundtable. Although the Business Council has taken a back seat to the Business Roundtable since the mid-1970s, its members are straightforward in presenting their recommendations to the White House and cabinet officials on a wide range of issues, including support for tax cuts in the early 1960s and tax increases in 1967 to help pay for the Vietnam War (Domhoff 2013; McQuaid 1982). In one particularly striking instance in 1971, Business Council members were adamant in pressuring the Nixon administration for a wage-price freeze in an effort to reign in rising construction costs that corporate leaders blamed on overly generous concessions to construction unions in the face of major strikes.

At a moment when President Nixon was not yet prepared to institute a wage-prize freeze, partly because of strong divisions within his administration over taking that step, the Business Council decided that it did not want to wait any longer for action, especially because it already had sent the president a "message of censure" for his failure "to check excessive wage and price increases." In a meeting at the White House with the president in May 1971, the president of a major corporation "espoused the immediate adoption of wage and price controls." Then the Business Council as a whole took "the unprecedented step of taking a straw vote on the issue, subsequently conveying to the president an expression of discontent at the administration's failure to secure smaller wage and price increases" (Marchi 1975, pp. 326, 340). Strikes in several different industries in the summer of that year, which resulted in large wage hikes, including a 30 percent wage increase over a three-year period for the United Steel Workers, finally forced Nixon's hand (Matusow 1998, p. 110).

Although the Business Council is assertive behind the scenes, the Business Roundtable usually takes a more public stance. As shown in Chapter 4, it mobilized the corporate community to pass the legislation that created the Canada–United States–Mexico free trade zone in 1994 (NAFTA) and permanent normal trade relations for China in 2000 (Dreiling 2001; Dreiling and Darves 2011).

The Creation of New Government Agencies

Proposals developed in the policy-planning network led to new government agencies throughout the twentieth century, usually in response to specific crises and pressures. This process began with corporate involvement in the creation of the Federal Trade Commission in 1914 and the Bureau of the Budget (now called the Office of Management and Budget to reflect its expanded duties) in 1919. Both agencies were responses to challenges generated by corporate critics during the Progressive Era (Kahn 1997; Weinstein 1968). The role of organizations in the policy-planning network in recommending—and helping establish—new government agencies continued during the New Deal with the creation of the Agricultural Adjustment Administration and the Social Security Administration (Domhoff and Webber 2011, Chapters 2 and 4). As explained in the discussions of the Council on Foreign Relations and the Committee for Economic Development in Chapter 4, members of the policy-planning network also created the framework for American foreign policy and trade policy for the post–World War II era. Here it can be added that members of the policy-planning network had a major role in reorganizing the Department of Defense after World War II and then establishing the National Security Council and the CIA (Huntington 1961).

The Great Exception: Labor Policy

There is one major exception to the general rule: The labor policy that fostered the development of the liberal-labor alliance was not the product of the policy-making process and does not seem to fit the idea that there is class domination. The National Labor Relations Act of 1935 passed in spite of intensive lobbying by the entire corporate community. It then played a role, along with the need for harmony between the corporate-conservative and liberal-labor alliances during World War II, in leading to a fivefold increase in union membership from 3 million in 1933 to 15 million in 1945. At that juncture, 35.4 percent of all wage and salary workers were represented by a union, and the sky seemed to be the limit. This dramatic growth made the liberal-labor alliance a significant force in American politics until the 1980s, though never the force that it wanted to be or that it was constantly claimed to be by the corporate community. In addition to winning wage increases and health benefits for their members, unions developed sufficient clout to aid in the election of enough liberal and moderate Democrats to maintain the high tax rates on the top income brackets that were legislated during the New Deal and World War II.

The passage of legislation supportive of unions is often interpreted as an unalloyed victory for the liberal-labor alliance. However, the involvement of leaders in the Business Council in establishing the original National Labor Board and some of its procedures, as discussed briefly in Chapter 4, is often overlooked. Moreover, there was another crucial ingredient in addition to labor militancy and a large number of liberals in Congress. The liberal-labor alliance accepted the exclusion of agricultural and domestic workers from the purview of the legislation in order to win the support of the Southern plantation owners, as represented by the Southern Democrats. In effect, the corporate rich lost on this issue because they were divided. This analysis is supported by the fact that they were able to limit the effectiveness of the National Labor Relations Board when Northern industrialists and Southern plantation owners united against it just three years after it passed (Gross 1981).

Most surprising, the corporate community never lost on any issue related to unions after World War II ended. In the process, it halted the growth in the percentage of wage and salary workers in unions; 1945 turned out to be the high point. Contrary to what members of the invigorated liberal-labor alliance expected in 1946, the corporations' string of successes began in 1947 and included a major triumph in 1978. These victories, along with rulings against unions by the Republican-dominated National Labor Relations Board in the early 1970s and throughout the 1980s, accelerated the decline of unions and the loss of power by the liberal-labor alliance. The National Labor Relation Act's usefulness to union organizers was all but gone by the end of the Reagan administration in 1988, when the number of workers in unions was down to 17 million from 21 million in 1979, and the percentage of wage and salary workers in unions fell to 16.2 percent, less than half of its all-time high in 1945 (Mayer 2004, Table A1). The corporate rich won again in 2009 in defeating a union-sponsored initiative that might have revived union organizing, which is discussed briefly in the final section of this chapter. The percentage of employees in unions was down to 11.8 percent in 2011 and even lower in the private sector, 6.9 percent, which is what matters the most to the corporate community; in addition, total union membership fell to 14.8 million (BLS 2012). (A detailed account of the pitched battles over labor legislation from the 1830s to 2011, with a special focus on the origins, implementation, and dismantlement of the National Labor Relations Act, can be found in the document on "The Rise and Fall of Labor Unions in the United States" on whorulesamerica.net.)

The Role of Congress in Major Policy Changes

Congressional approval of large-scale policy proposals put forth by organizations in the policy-planning network does not mean that congressional voting coalitions develop any more quickly and easily on policy legislation than they do on special-interest issues. Instead, each coalition has to be carefully constructed by elected officials with the help of corporate lobbyists and grassroots publicity.

It is here that the political leaders do their most important work in terms of major policy changes that generate strong disagreements and receive media attention. They are specialists in arranging trades with other politicians for votes and in being sensitive to the electoral risks for each colleague in voting for or against any highly visible piece of legislation. They are also experts at sensing when the moment is right to hold a vote, often keeping the final outcome hanging in the balance for weeks or months at a time. Sometimes they wait until a lame-duck session shortly after elections have been held, or slip controversial legislation into omnibus bills that are hard for voters to fathom. Finally, their constant interaction with constituents and the media gives them the experience and sensitivity to use the rhetoric and metaphors needed to make the new legislation palatable to as many people as possible.

APPOINTEES TO GOVERNMENT

The final way to see if and how the corporate rich have shaped the federal government is to look at the social, educational, and occupational backgrounds of the people that are appointed to important positions in it. If the corporate rich are as important as this book claims, such appointees should come disproportionately from the upper class, the corporate community, and the policy-planning network.

There have been numerous studies of top-level governmental appointees under both Republican and Democratic administrations. They are unanimous in their conclusion that the majority in both Republican and Democratic administrations have been corporate directors and their corporate lawyers, or members of boards of trustees in the policy-planning network, and hence members of the power elite (Salzman and Domhoff 1980). For example, 64 percent of the appointees to major cabinet, diplomatic, and court posts were members of the corporate community from 1934 to 1980, but only 47 percent during the New Deal, and most of them had connections to the policy-planning network (Burch 1980). A second study, which focused more narrowly on the 205 individuals that served in presidential cabinets between 1897 and 1972, reported that 60 percent were members of the upper class and 78 percent were members of the corporate community. There were no differences in the overall percentages for Democrats and Republicans or for the years before and after 1933 (Mintz 1975). By contrast, there were very few top appointees from liberal organizations and virtually none from labor organizations.

Reflecting the different coalitions that make up the two parties, however, there were often striking differences between the second-level and third-level appointees in Republican and Democratic administrations in the years between 1932 and 2008. Republicans appointed ultraconservatives to agencies that they thoroughly disliked, such as the Environmental Protection Agency, the Occupational Safety and Health Administration, the National Highway Traffic Safety Commission, and the Office of Civil Rights. These appointees proceeded to do everything they could to limit the effectiveness of these agencies. Democrats, on the other hand, often placed liberals in the same agencies. The Clinton administration's lower-level appointments to the Office of the Attorney General, for example, were far more vigorous in using the antitrust laws to challenge monopolistic corporate practices than those of the Reagan and George H. W. Bush administrations.

The many pre-1980 studies were updated for the Reagan, Clinton, and George W. Bush administrations for previous editions of this book. They show the same patterns as the earlier studies (Domhoff 1983, pp. 139–141; Domhoff 1998, pp. 251–255; Domhoff 2006, pp. 167–170). For example, the four people who served as secretaries of state for the Clinton and Bush administrations were almost indistinguishable in their credentials even though they differed by race and gender. President Clinton's first secretary of state was a director of Lockheed Martin, Southern California Edison, and First Interstate Bancorp, a trustee of the Carnegie Corporation, a recent vice-chair of the Council on Foreign Relations, and officially a corporate lawyer at the time of his appointment. President Bush's first secretary of state, a four-star army general who retired in 1993, made millions as a speaker to corporate employees at $60,000 to $75,000 per appearance. He served as a director of Gulfstream Aerospace until its merger with General Dynamics in 1999, where he earned $1.5 million from stock options in exchange for helping the company sell its corporate jets in Kuwait and Saudi Arabia. He was a member of the Council on Foreign Relations at the time of his appointment (and became one of its directors after he left the Bush administration).

The Clinton and Bush appointees to the Department of Treasury also had similar careers. President Clinton's first secretary of treasury inherited millions from his rancher father, founded his own insurance company in Texas, and later became a senator. He was succeeded by the co-director of Goldman Sachs, with an estimated net worth between $50 and $100 million at the time, who was also a trustee of the Carnegie Corporation. The Bush administration's first secretary of treasury was the recently retired chair of Alcoa and a member of the Business Council and the Business Roundtable. The second was the CEO of CSX (a freight transportation company), a director of three other corporations, and a member of the Business Roundtable. The third secretary of treasury was the chairman of Goldman Sachs and a member of the Business Roundtable.

THE FIRST OBAMA ADMINISTRATION

Many of the major appointees in the first Obama administration were different from past appointees in that they were far more likely to have spent most of their careers in government service than business, although several of them worked for corporations or served on corporate boards at various points in their careers. Their educational backgrounds were similar to those of most members of the power elite and they had been involved with organizations in the policy-planning network.

The appointments to five cabinet positions of major importance to the corporate community, along with the two most important White House staff appointments, demonstrate these patterns.

The secretary of state, Hillary Rodham Clinton, a graduate of Wellesley and Yale Law School, worked as a lawyer for the largest corporate law firm in Little Rock and served on the board of directors of Wal-Mart for six years, while her husband was the governor of Arkansas, then became the first lady for eight years and then a senator from New York. The secretary of defense, mentioned in Chapter 4 as a holdover from the Bush administration, sat on several corporate boards before his appointment. The attorney general, the son of West Indian immigrants, whose father was a real estate broker in New York City, graduated from Columbia Law School, did an internship at the NAACP Legal Defense and Educational Fund, and then worked in the Department of Justice for nearly 25 years. In the early 2000s he became a partner in a leading Washington law firm, where his clients included Merck and Chiquita Brands International, earning several million dollars each year and accumulating assets worth $5.7 million by the time of his cabinet appointment. The secretary of commerce, the son of Chinese-American parents of modest incomes, earned an undergraduate degree at Yale and a law degree at Boston University, then won elective offices in Seattle before becoming governor of the state of Washington from 1997 to 2005. After leaving office he joined an international corporate law firm in Seattle, working to develop trade relations with Chinese companies, and served on the board of directors of Safeco, a large insurance company.

The top appointees at the Department of Treasury were as consistently from the Wall Street financial community as in previous administrations. The secretary of treasury, the son of a Ford Foundation official and a graduate of Dartmouth, had been president of the Federal Reserve Bank of New York since 2003, an appointment that is made by a board of directors dominated by New York banks. Previous to his appointment as the bank's president, he had worked first for a corporate consulting company founded by a former secretary of state, next for the International Monetary Fund, and then for the Department of Treasury. He was a senior fellow at the Council on Foreign Relations when he was asked to take the position at the Federal Reserve Bank of New York. He had a central role in structuring the bank bailouts by the George W. Bush administration in 2008. His deputy secretary of treasury was the president of property casualty operations at Hartford Insurance, his chief of staff was a managing director of Goldman Sachs, and his other nine top appointees had affiliations with Wall Street financial firms as well (Foster and Holleman 2010, Table 1).

President Obama's two most important White House staff appointments had direct connections to the corporate community. His first chief of staff worked after his graduation from Sarah Lawrence with a public interest group and then as an aide to elected officials, including six years in the Clinton White House. He joined the private sector for a few years in 1998 as a dealmaker in the Chicago office of a Wall Street banking firm, brokering several lucrative mergers that earned him $16.2 million, including the merger of two smaller utility firms into Exelon, which became the largest utility company in the country (Luo 2008a). The president's other key White House appointment, Valerie Jarrett, was mentioned in Chapter 6 as his friend, fundraiser, and main connection to the middle-class black community in Chicago. In the White House she had numerous liaison duties to communities of color, women's groups, and the Chicago business community, where she had been the CEO of a real estate management firm, a director for USG (a Chicago-based building materials company), the vice-chair of the board of trustees at the University of Chicago, and a trustee of the Joyce Foundation (the 63rd largest family foundation in 2008). She had an estimated net worth between $5 and $15 million at the time of her appointment.

Looking at President Obama's original cabinet and staff appointees as a whole, including the many people that have not been discussed, their previous involvement in government is notable. Overall, 10 of those who served in the original cabinet or on the White House staff had held elective office as governors, senators, or members of the House of Representatives. The absence of any corporate chieftains was also striking. Thus, the members of the first Obama administration, with the exception of the Department of Treasury, were more of a political elite than the kind of corporate-based elite that predominated in previous administrations, including the Clinton administration and all other Democratic administrations after World War II. At the same time, the Obama appointees were a political elite that maintained far closer ties to the corporate community and the policy-planning network than to the liberal-labor alliance.

SUPREME COURT APPOINTMENTS

The Supreme Court has a special role in the American system of governance that is rare among industrial democracies. As the final arbiter in major disputes, it has been imbued with a mystique of reverence and respect that makes it a backstop for the corporate rich on the one hand and for many individual freedoms on the other. While its members are to some extent constrained by legal precedent, there is also a fair degree of discretion in what they decide, as seen in the numerous "great reversals" of opinion. These reversals occurred most dramatically on two issues on which there was general ferment and pressure in the society at large at the times the decisions were made: (1) civil and voting rights for African Americans and (2) rights and protections for labor unions (Ernst 1973). The independent power of the Supreme Court was on display for all Americans in the 2000 elections: The five conservative Republican appointees on the court, who usually decried "judicial activism" and emphasized states' rights, nonetheless found a way to override the Florida Supreme Court and stop the counting of uncounted votes that might have tipped the presidential election to the Democrats. As constitutional scholars heatedly argued about the legal reasoning behind the court's majority, the Democratic Party and most ordinary Americans quietly accepted the decision.

As the court's prevention of the Florida recount shows, Supreme Court appointees and popular deference to their decisions do matter, which is yet another reason why the power elite work so hard to win elections. Biographical studies of court appointees down through the decades support the importance of being able to make court appointments. They conclude that virtually all appointees shared the ideological and political views of the presidents who appointed them, although some appointees voted more liberally than Republican presidents expected (usually concerning civil rights) or more conservatively than Democratic presidents expected. Even with some surprises, the Supreme Court has reflected the range of acceptable opinion within the corporate community on the issues of concern to it (Baum 1998). The appointees were also primarily from the upper- and upper-middle classes, and an "inordinate number had served as corporate attorneys before their appointments" (Carp and Stidham 1998, p. 217). In addition, they also tended to be from elite law schools, to have abandoned the practice of corporate law for lower-level judicial appointments or professorships at prestigious law schools, and to have been active in a political party.

The nine justices during the first Obama administration fit many of these generalizations. Five were graduates of Harvard Law School, including three Republican appointments; three graduated from Yale Law School, and one from the School of Law at Columbia University. Five were millionaires (three Democratic appointees, two Republican appointees) according to estimates by the Center for Responsive Politics that were based on the justices' required annual statements (Cline 2011). However, the nine justices were notable for the fact that none of them had ever held elective office, and collectively they had not spent as many years in private practice as the justices who came before them. Instead, they had been government lawyers and law professors for most of their careers (Barton 2012). Nevertheless, six of the justices practiced with corporate law firms early in their careers. On the other hand, none of them ever did legal work for unions, environmental groups, or consumer groups.

Four of the five justices appointed by Republican presidents had experience as corporate lawyers. Antonin Scalia worked for a corporate law firm for six years after graduation from Harvard Law School in 1960, and then became a law professor. Clarence Thomas's work experience after graduation from Yale Law School in 1974 included two years as a corporate attorney for Monsanto Chemical Company, followed by two years as a legislative assistant to a multimillionaire Republican senator from Missouri, John C. Danforth, an heir to a corporate fortune. Anthony M. Kennedy, the son of a corporate lawyer, practiced corporate law for 14 years after his graduation from Harvard Law School in 1961, then was appointed to the Court of Appeals in 1975 and the Supreme Court in 1988.

Chief Justice John G. Roberts practiced corporate law for 14 years in a Washington firm after graduating from Harvard Law School in 1979 and working in the Attorney General's office during the Reagan administration. He was known as the go-to lawyer for the corporate community in the years before his court appointment, partly because of briefs he wrote in 2001 and 2002 for the National Chamber Litigation Center, a legal center created by the Chamber of Commerce in 1977 to prepare briefs on business-related cases and pressure both parties to appoint pro-business judges (Rosen 2008). Only Samuel Alito Jr., appointed to the court by President Bush in 2007, had spent his entire career as a United States attorney (including positions in President Reagan's Department of Justice from 1981 to 1987) after graduating from Yale Law School in 1975. He became a judge on the Court of Appeals in 1990.

Of the four Democratic appointees on the court in 2012, two had experience with corporate law firms. After graduating from Yale Law School in 1979 and working in the district attorney's office in New York for four years, Sonia Sotomayor worked for a corporate law firm from 1984 to 1992, becoming a partner in 1988. She left the firm after her appointment to the U.S. District Court for the Southern District in New York by President George H. W. Bush. She then became celebrated by sports fans across the nation in 1995 when she ended a lengthy Major League Baseball strike by issuing an injunction against the team owners, which stopped them from unilaterally instituting a new collective bargaining agreement and using replacement players. Republicans later slowed her appointment when President Clinton nominated her for the United States Court of Appeals Second Circuit, but she was eventually confirmed in 1998, and President Obama appointed her to the Supreme Court in 2009. Elena Kagan, appointed to the court by President Obama in 2010, worked for a corporate law firm in Washington for three years after her graduation from Harvard Law School in 1986 and a clerkship with a Supreme Court justice. She then became a law professor at the University of Chicago Law School, a legal counsel in the White House during the Clinton administration, and the dean of Harvard Law School from 2003 until 2009, when she was appointed Solicitor General of the United States.

Corporate law firms still excluded women when Ruth Bader Ginsberg, appointed to the court in 1993 by President Clinton, graduated from Columbia Law School in 1959. She taught law at Rutgers and Columbia and served as the general counsel for the ACLU during the 1970s, which involved her in many women's issues. President Jimmy Carter appointed her to the Court of Appeals in 1980. As for Justice Stephen Breyer, a graduate of Harvard Law School who was appointed to the high court by President Clinton in 1994, he divided his career between teaching at Harvard Law School and working for the federal government in a variety of legal positions before President Carter appointed him to the U.S. Court of Appeals in 1980. He is a multimillionaire through the fortune inherited by his wife, a member of the British aristocracy.

Although the Supreme Court generally defended corporate interests during the nineteenth and twentieth centuries, it also protected and expanded some individual freedoms by taking an expansive view of the Bill of Rights, thereby solidifying the right to privacy and the protection of freedom of speech. It also made decisions that ensured the freedom of the press and insisted that states must obey all provisions of the Bill of Rights, which many states had ignored in the past. Led by Chief Justice Earl Warren, a former Republican governor of California and an appointee to the court by President Dwight Eisenhower, the Supreme Court also played a major role in the civil rights revolution through its 9–0 ruling against school desegregation in 1954. It also made "one person, one vote" reapportionment rulings between 1962 and 1964, which outlawed the thinly populated rural House districts that greatly favored the conservative coalition. Between 1962 and 1966 it outlawed mandatory school prayer, extended the right to privacy into the bedroom, and gave new rights and protections to those arrested for alleged criminal acts. From the point of view of ultra-conservatives and Southern Democrats, the "Warren Court" was an anathema, a hotbed of liberals and radicals who destroyed the country's foundations, but it continued to make rulings that favored corporations over unions in the 1960s (Gross 1995, Chapter 10).

Faced by Southern and ultraconservative anger and bolstered by the appointments made by presidents Nixon and Reagan, the Supreme Court turned in a more conservative direction on many issues after the 1970s. In addition, the corporate community's success rate was improved by the work of the Chamber of Commerce's National Chamber Litigation Center and the specialization of corporate lawyers at several major firms on cases that would be heard by the Supreme Court (Yeomans 2012). After 1980, the Supreme Court became even more pro-corporate by limiting shareholder suits against corporate management, antitrust challenges to mergers, lawsuits alleging securities fraud, product-liability lawsuits, and large punitive-damage awards by juries (Rosen 2008). It also handed down several decisions that made it more difficult for individuals to file lawsuits against corporations, in effect creating a series of blockades that are spelled out in detail in a book by the dean of the law school at the University of California, Irvine (Chemerinsky 2010). In 2010, the National Chamber Litigation Center had a string of successful arguments before the Supreme Court that "read like a top ten" list of corporate wishes: "Its victories included thwarting class-action claims of gender discrimination at Wal-Mart; forcing individuals to have their claims against big corporations settled in arbitration rather than gaining access to the courts; beating back litigation by states and municipalities seeking to regulate greenhouse gases; defeating claims for damages caused by the defective design of vaccines; limiting recovery by whistleblowers; restricting the reach of U.S. law over foreign manufacturers of defective products; and blocking suits by private citizens against brokerage firms for making false statements about securities" (Yeomans 2012, p. 14).

The Supreme Court has been closely divided on the same social issues that divide liberals and conservatives in the general public, with one or two Republican appointees sometimes voting to uphold the rights won by women, the LGBT community, and people of color in the 1960s and 1970s. At the same time, there is almost always a solid majority that sides with business when individuals, unions, or local and state governments challenge the corporate community in any way.

THE LIBERAL-LABOR ALLIANCE AND CONGRESS

Despite the presence of supporters of the liberal-labor alliance in Congress since the 1930s, and the growing percentage of liberal Democrats in Congress between the 1990s and 2010, the alliance's efforts to introduce new economic initiatives and defend union rights met with little or no success between 1939 and 2012. As noted in the Introduction and Chapter 6, most of its victories consisted of increases in the minimum wage, increases in Social Security payments, the addition of disability insurance to Social Security, and improvements in social welfare benefits, some of which were attempts to keep even with inflation, and some of which were not opposed by corporate moderates.

The liberal-labor alliance also can claim some victories for its own initiatives in Congress. For example, the Family and Medical Leave Act of 1993 allows both male and female employees of companies with 50 or more employees to take up to 12 weeks of unpaid leave a year for pregnancy or adoption, or 26 weeks to take care of certain family illnesses. The act covers almost half of American workers if government agencies are included. The fact that the leaves are unpaid limits the number of workers who can take advantage of them, and conservatives were able to exempt small companies and reduce the amount of leave time for pregnancies and adoptions from 18 weeks to 12, but health benefits are still in place during the leave. Between 8 percent and 17 percent of eligible employees made use of the act in 2005, according to a study by the Department of Labor (DOL 2007).

The liberal-labor alliance can also claim some of the credit for the passage of the Civil Rights Act in 1964 and the Voting Rights Act in 1965. However, both of these landmark acts owed far more to the civil rights movement itself, whose African American members had been largely excluded from the bargains that had been struck between the Southern Democrats and the liberal-labor alliance between 1935 and 1960 (Brown 1999). Although most liberals and a few unions supported civil rights legislation, a majority of union members, North and South, opposed the integration of their neighborhoods, schools, and jobs from the outset, as discussed further in Chapter 8. As a result, the liberal-labor alliance was as much a hindrance as help, and it lost the support of many white workers as the civil rights movement pressed forward with its agenda (e.g., Boyle 1995; Quadagno 1994; Sugrue 2008).

The liberal-labor alliance played a major role in the creation of Medicare, but that victory also reveals the limits of liberal-labor power in Congress. The battle for Medicare began in 1949 as a liberal-labor proposal for national health insurance for all Americans, but it was blocked by hospitals, the American Medical Association, and the conservative coalition for the next decade. Progress was not possible until the liberal-labor alliance proposed to limit national health insurance to those 65 and older, which happened at about the same time that hospitals were losing money by treating low-income patients of all ages (Altman 2005, p. 186). Although the focus on the elderly created the potential for a compromise, it did not happen without major organizing efforts by the liberal-labor alliance and increasing financial problems for hospitals, insurance companies, and physicians due to the costs of treating indigent patients. By 1962–1963, most Medicare opponents knew that they were fighting a losing battle. The American Hospital Association concluded that its member hospitals needed some form of major federal support. Similarly, the commercial insurance companies were doubtful that their new attempts to insure the elderly could be profitable, so they began to think in terms of selling supplemental insurance to fill any gaps in a government plan (Quadagno 2005, p. 72). However, the American Hospital Association, the Health Insurance Association of America, and the American Medical Association did not end their opposition to Medicare as conceived of by the liberal-labor alliance.

The large Democratic victories at the presidential and congressional levels in 1964 meant that some form of health insurance for the elderly would be passed in the next congressional session. Adopting the stance advocated by the liberal-labor alliance, the Democrats proposed hospital insurance for the elderly; the Republicans countered through a bill adapted from a plan written by experts at Aetna, the giant private insurer. The Republican plan called for supplementary private insurance, in part subsidized by the government, which would pay for physicians' services as well as hospitalization. At the same time, the American Medical Association tried to stave off the Democrats' proposal by updating past Republican plans for federal subsidies for the purchase of private hospital care. Renamed Eldercare, the physicians' plan also included provisions for payment for their services. Conservatives and liberals on the key congressional committees then decided to include all three proposals in a single package: Medicare A, which provides hospital and nursing home insurance for people over 65; Medicare B, which pays their doctors' bills; and Medicaid, which provides hospital and physician payments for low-income patients (Quadagno 2005, Chapters 3–4).

The extent of the insurance coverage for both the elderly and low-income people was far greater than the leaders of the liberal-labor alliance originally thought would be possible, which made their victory all the more significant. However, the congressional conservatives that made the final bargain with the White House abandoned many of the price restraints and other features to control costs that had been worked out carefully by union experts. As a result, the legislation built a relentless inflationary pressure into medical costs. Hospital costs increased 14 percent and physician fees 6.8 percent a year during Medicare's first five years, far more than most other costs were rising at the time (Marmor 2000, p. 98). In the process, the health insurance companies became a more powerful lobby as they greatly increased their profits. In addition, more for-profit hospitals were able to enter the market and earn high profits, often after buying up or buying out and closing a large number of nonprofit and public hospitals. Medicare and Medicaid were a savior for many individuals, but they were also a bonanza for hospitals, health-related corporations, and physicians.

With the election of Republican Richard Nixon to the presidency in 1968, the liberal-labor alliance lost on everything except the expansion of Social Security benefits and the Earned Income Tax Credit, which had the support of President Nixon and many moderate Republicans as well. The value of the minimum wage declined after 1968 despite a few small increases in it during the 1970s that did not keep up with inflation. There were no further increases between 1981 and 1990, and it was frozen again between 1997 and 2007. By 2012, the minimum wage would have been $10.52 an hour if it had retained its 1968 purchasing power, not the $7.25 to which it was raised in 2007, so it declined in value by 35 percent over that 44-year period. It lost even more value in comparison to the average salary of those who were employed in 1968 and 2012 (Schmitt 2012). This large decrease on a "who benefits?" indicator is further evidence that the liberal-labor alliance gradually lost much of its political power after the 1960s.

It perhaps goes without saying that the liberal-labor alliance had no success with any new initiatives during the Reagan and George H. W. Bush administrations; moreover, it also suffered cutbacks on many social programs, including Social Security (Domhoff 2013, Chapter 12). Except for the Family and Medical Leave Act of 1993, there were no victories for the liberal-labor alliance during the eight years of the Clinton administration either. The social welfare program for low-income and unemployed families, which was created during the New Deal as one part of the Social Security Act and then expanded during the 1960s, was reduced to a shadow of its former self by a welfare reform act in 1996. The reform was the outcome of Clinton's 1992 campaign promise to "end welfare as we know it," but his plan was made more stringent by the Republicans' insistence that his provisions for child care and health insurance for those on welfare had to be eliminated (Quadagno and Rohlinger 2009). Called the "Personal Responsibility and Work Opportunity Act" in order to reinforce the idea that those on welfare had lost moral fiber and needed to look harder for work opportunities, it put time limits on the number of years a person could receive welfare, added a work component, and reduced assistance for immigrants, due to the strong Republican belief that many immigrants came to the United States with the hope of receiving welfare assistance.

The impact of the cuts were not immediately felt because the time limits did not kick in immediately, and the stock-market bubble of the late 1990s took the unemployment rate from 5.4 percent in 1996 to 4.0 percent in 2000, the lowest it had been since the early 1970s. But the full extent of the cuts was made apparent with the arrival of hard times in late 2007, when welfare payments were so few and small that food stamps and the Earned Income Tax Credit had to be the primary supports for the 46.5 million people that lived in poverty by 2012, about 15 percent of the adult population (DeParle 2012; Seefeldt, Abner, Bolinger, Xu, and Graham 2012; WSJ 2012).

The string of defeats suffered by the liberal-labor alliance during the Clinton administration, and in the George W. Bush administration as well, continued during the first Obama administration. To deal with lengthy delays in holding representation elections, which corporations used as a tactic to defeat unionization drives, union leaders made clear to the Democrats that their number one goal was to legislate new ways to overcome this problem. They thought the best remedy would be their Employee Free Choice Act, which would instruct corporations to recognize and bargain with unions if a majority of their employees signed a card expressing their desire to be represented by a union (Greenhouse 2008). As a senator, President Obama had voted for a similar (unsuccessful) proposal in 2007, and he expressed his support for the Employee Free Choice Act during his 2008 presidential campaign.

In anticipation of a congressional vote on the bill in 2009, the corporate community launched a multimillion-dollar media campaign through new lobbying coalitions, with names like Workplace Fairness Institute and the Coalition for a Democratic Workplace, which falsely claimed that the legislation would take away workers' right to vote for or against unionization in a secret ballot. The president of the National Association of Manufacturers, a former Republican governor of Michigan, warned that the unionization of Wal-Mart's 1.4 million workers alone would add $500 million a year in union dues, part of which would be used to support pro-labor Democratic candidates (Greenhouse 2009). "We like driving the car," the CEO of Wal-Mart told stock market analysts in October 2008, "and we're not going to give the steering wheel to anybody but us" (Kaplan 2009, p. 10).

Three Chicago billionaires who had backed President Obama's first presidential campaign, all of them with interests in hotels that unions were trying to organize, let it be known to him that they opposed the bill. One of them was Penny Pritzker, Obama's 2008 National Campaign Finance chair, whose family owned the Global Hyatt. Another hotel investor had raised $160,000 as a bundler. The 93-year-old patriarch of the Crown family, which backed Obama heavily in 2008, spoke out against the pro-union legislation in a published interview. However, even while doing so, he emphasized that he still supported Obama and added, "I think the world of him. This doesn't have anything to do with other relationships" (Lippert and Rosenkrantz 2009). Meanwhile, while all this was going on, the 41 Republican senators remaining in the Senate after the large Democratic gains in 2008 announced they would not support new labor legislation, and three Democrats said they would not support it either. Since only 41 votes are needed to sustain a filibuster, the bill never came up for a vote.

Next, a liberal proposal for raising tax revenues, a 0.05 percent transaction tax on every financial trade by stock and bond brokers, which was vigorously opposed by the financial industry, was dropped. It would have reduced the number of destabilizing speculative trades while raising an estimated $100 billion a year (Pollin, Baker, and Schaberg 2008). Liberal calls to send federal money to states that were running deficits were opposed by Republicans and moderate Democrats in the Senate, which led to layoffs for teachers and other government employees that are paid with state funds, which in turn undercut the impact of the federal stimulus package because the newly unemployed workers now had less money to spend (Krugman 2012).

Then liberal plans for dealing with the mortgage crisis were also cast aside. Congress thereby ignored the precedent set by the creation of the Home Owners

Loan Corporation during the New Deal. Back then it bought underwater mortgages on low-income homes from private financial companies and then provided the homeowners with government mortgages that had lower interest rates and more years to pay off the loan. It was, in effect, a government bailout for both the mortgage lenders and the homeowners, but in 2009–2010 the financial industry was strong enough to reject any government involvement in mortgages that threatened its complete control of mortgage lending. Instead, the various plans that were tried between 2009 and 2011 only helped out the banks, several of which were reaping very large profits from mortgage loans by 2012. The series of mortgage plans did include clauses calling for banks to renegotiate loan payments and interest rates, but these clauses helped very few families. They left complete control of the issue in the hands of the bankers, who had little or no incentive to renegotiate. Nor did a liberal plan that gave indebted homeowners the right to stay on as renters at the market rate go anywhere, although it might have saved several million people from losing their homes and encouraged bankers to negotiate more realistically (Baker 2009).

The Patient Protection and Affordable Care Act ("Obamacare"), which passed in 2010, represented the biggest addition to government health insurance since the passage of Medicare in 1965. Building on the private health insurance industry, it expanded health care coverage to 35 million additional Americans, allowed children to stay on their parents' health insurance policies until age 25, and had the potential to reign in some healthcare costs. However, few members of the liberal-labor alliance greeted it with enthusiasm; most of them preferred the straightforward expansion of Medicare to cover all citizens, a proposal that was also called "national health insurance" or a "single-payer" system.

Ironically, the Obama administration's proposal was very similar to, but more conservative than a proposal put forth 37 years earlier by the corporate moderates in the Committee for Economic Development (CED 1973). Liberal and labor leaders of that era rejected the plan because they thought the time for national health insurance finally had arrived (Quadagno 2005, Chapter 5). In both plans, Medicare would continue for those over age 65, companies had to offer health insurance to their employees, and individuals without coverage would be required to purchase health coverage (through community trusts in the Committee for Economic Development plan, through state-level private insurance pools in the Obama plan). Both plans provided government subsidies for insurance purchases by low-income people that were not eligible for Medicaid. The main differences were that the Obama proposal, by prior agreement with the health insurance industry and the supposed representatives of small business, the ultraconservative National Federation of Independent Business, gave a bigger role to private insurance companies and exempted millions of small businesses from offering insurance plans (Quadagno 2012).

When the campaign for Medicare for everyone received little or no support from elected Democrats in early 2010, the liberal-labor alliance threw its support behind a "public option" plan that would permit the federal government to offer an insurance plan that would compete with private insurers, perhaps thereby assuring that the private insurance plans would hold down prices and costs. But the private insurers that had agreed to support the White House's original legislation said that a public option was completely unacceptable, and the idea had to be dropped (Quadagno 2012). Even with the support of the insurance industry and some parts of the health industry, only one Republican in the Senate voted for it, and all 178 Republicans in the House voted against it.

Overall, then, the liberal-labor alliance did not enjoy much success between 1939 and 2012 beyond what had been made possible by the National Labor Relations and Social Security acts in 1935, and a Fair Labor Standards Act passed in 1938, which established minimum wages and maximum hours for the first time (see Domhoff 2013 for a more detailed analysis of legislation that was passed, modified, or defeated in those decades). Nor can the liberal-labor alliance ever achieve a full measure of success, even if it were to obtain large majorities in both the House and the Senate, as long as Senate rules include the right of a minority of 41 senators to block legislation (through a filibuster) that it finds objectionable. Until such time that there are 60 liberals in the Senate and the Democrats regain control of the House, the corporate rich can hold on to their many gains since the 1970s as long as they maintain their alliance with the great majority of white voters in the southern, Great Plains, and Rocky Mountain states.*

CORPORATE COMPLAINTS OF IMPOTENCE: THEIR REAL FEARS

Despite the strong "who governs?" and "who wins?" evidence that the corporate rich have great power within the federal government on the issues of concern to them, many corporate leaders feel they are relatively powerless in the face of government. To hear them tell it, the Congress is more responsive to organized labor, environmentalists, and consumers than it is to them. They also claim to be harassed by willful and arrogant bureaucrats that encroach upon the rightful preserves of the private sector, sapping them of their confidence and making them hesitant to invest their capital. In 2010 members of the financial industry felt insulted by any criticisms of them by President Obama, despite his administration's support for the bailout passed at the end of the Bush years and their complicity in the financial failures of 2008–2009.

A journalist and a political scientist documented these sentiments when they had the opportunity to observe a series of meetings at the Conference Board during which the social responsibilities of business were being discussed. At a time

---

* The one escape hatch in the face of a likely filibuster is a legislative process called "reconciliation," which allows for a vote after 20 hours of Senate debate on resolutions having to do with the budget. While budget issues may seem narrow, the reconciliation process was used by the Republicans in 1996 to pass welfare reform, by the Republicans to pass tax cuts in 2001, 2003, and 2005, and by the Democrats to pass parts of the Patient Protection and Affordable Health Care Act in 2010.

in the mid-1970s when the Republicans held the presidency and the conservative coalition won 60 to 80 percent of its challenges and did not lose on any major piece of legislation, the corporate leaders at these meetings were convinced that government listened to everybody but them. Government was seen as responsive to the immediate preferences of the majority of citizens. "The have-nots are gaining steadily more political power to distribute the wealth downward," complained one executive. "The masses have turned to a larger government" (Silk and Vogel 1976, pp. 50, 75).

The fear corporate leaders expressed of the democratic majority led them to view mild recessions as a saving grace, because they help to keep the expectations of workers in check. Workers who fear for their jobs are less likely to demand higher wages or government social programs. For example, different corporate executives made comments such as "This recession will bring about the healthy respect for economic values that the Great Depression did" and "It would be better if the recession were allowed to weaken more than it will, so that we would have a sense of sobriety" (Silk and Vogel 1976, p. 64).

The negative feelings these corporate leaders had toward government were not a new development in the corporate community. A study of business leaders' views in the nineteenth century found that they believed political leaders to be "stupid" and "empty" people who went into politics only to earn a living (Silk and Vogel 1976, p. 193). Even in the 1920s, a time when social scientists and historians think that business was unrivaled in its power, there were constant outcries from the corporate rich about a domineering and overbearing federal government (Prothro 1954). These complaints undercut any claims that business hostility toward government stems largely from the growth of effective government programs during and after the New Deal.

Although a few social scientists and media commentators once took these expressions of impotence as evidence for their claim that business leaders do not have sufficient power to be called a dominant class, the emotional expressions of business owners about their lack of power cannot be taken seriously as power indicators. The investigation of power concerns actions and their consequences, not the inner world of subjective feelings. Still, it is useful to try to understand why corporate leaders complain about a government they dominate. There are three aspects to the answer.

First of all, complaining about government is a useful power strategy, a form of action in itself. It puts government officials on the defensive and forces them to keep proving that they are friendly to business so that corporate leaders will not lose "confidence" in economic conditions and stop investing. One of the most insightful political scientists of the twentieth century concluded after 30 years of studying the relationship between business and government that "Whether the issue is understood explicitly, intuitively, or not at all, denunciations serve to establish and maintain the subservience of government units to the business constituencies to which they are actually held responsible" (McConnell 1966, p. 294). "Attacks upon government in general," he continued, "place continuing pressure on governmental officers to accommodate their activities to the groups from which support is most reliable."

The perennial complaints about government by corporate officials also reveal a fear of the American belief system about power that emerged during the Revolutionary War. Since power is in theory in the hands of all the people, as explained in Chapter 1, there is always the possibility that some day "the people," in the sense of the majority, will make the government into the pluralist democracy it is supposed to be. In the American historical context, the great power of the dominant class is illegitimate, and therefore the existence of such power is vigorously denied (Vogel 1978).

However, the most potent reason for the corporate rich's fear of popular control is revealed by their belief that government is the only institution that can challenge corporate domination, particularly in the case of labor markets. Elaborating on comments in the Introduction, the federal government can influence labor markets in five basic ways:

1. The government can hire unemployed workers to do necessary work relating to parks, schools, roadways, and the environment, which would tighten private labor markets and force corporations to compete for workers through higher wages, improved working conditions, and better benefit packages. Such government programs were a great success during the New Deal, when unemployment reached 25 percent and social unrest seemed to be growing. But they were quickly shut down at the insistence of business leaders when order was restored and the economy began to improve (Piven and Cloward 1971/1993, Chapter 4; Smith 2006; Taylor 2008).

2. Although moderate conservatives in the corporate community appreciate the value of old-age, disability, and unemployment insurance, they join ultraconservatives in worrying that politicians might allow these programs to become too generous. In fact, these programs expanded in response to the turmoil of the 1960s and 1970s, but the benefits for low-income people were cut back during the Reagan administration.

3. The government can tighten labor markets by limiting immigration, which is the main reason why the American Federation of Labor opposed immigration from the date of its founding in 1886 until a new law in 1924 reduced immigration to a trickle (Mink 1986). By contrast, corporate leaders and large-scale farmers generally support immigration because they see low-wage labor as essential to their continuing success. When ultraconservative Republicans began to think about passing anti-immigration legislation in the mid-1990s and early 2000s, as called for in their campaign speeches, they were met with a barrage of employer opposition, particularly from leaders in agribusiness, and quickly retreated.

4. Under normal economic conditions, but not in the kind of recession that was generated by the financial collapse in 2007–2008, the Federal Reserve System can reduce unemployment and tighten labor markets by *lowering* interest rates, which increases spending by consumers, homebuyers, and businesses, and thereby stimulates the economy. This fact was made obvious to a large percentage of the public by the way in which the Federal Reserve did just the opposite, increasing unemployment at various times from the 1970s through the early 1990s. It *raised* interest rates whenever the unemployment rate dipped too low to suit the corporate community, which made loans more expensive for businesses and households, and thereby lowered the demand for goods and services. Higher interest rates are justified by corporate leaders in terms of limiting the risks of runaway inflation. However, leaders in the liberal-labor alliance argue that inflation of 1 to 3 percent a year generally helps the great bulk of employees and does not lead to runaway inflation, which they say is due to extreme economic shocks caused by defeats in wars, the doubling or tripling of oil prices by foreign countries, and events of a similar magnitude. In other words, the economics of inflation often involve the politics of labor markets.

5. The government can support the right to organize unions and bargain collectively, as it did when Congress passed the National Labor Relations Act in 1935. As noted several times in this book, the corporate rich oppose this kind of government initiative even more strongly than government jobs and social benefits because unions give workers an organizational base for moving into the political arena, as well as the power to force wage increases through strikes.

Due to the many ways in which the American government could tighten labor markets, and thereby reduce corporate profits and increase the economic and political power of American workers, it is clear once again that structural power, status power, and expert power are not enough to sustain corporate dominance of the economy and government. If it is assumed that the corporate rich want to remain rich and powerful, it makes sense that they would be fearful of the government they dominate, and therefore they would constantly complain about how it treats them.

THE LIMITS OF CORPORATE DOMINATION

Involvement in government is the final and most visible aspect of corporate domination, which has its roots in the class structure, control of the investment function, and the operation of the policy-planning network. If government officials usually did not feel they have to wait for corporate leaders to decide when and where there will be financial investment, and if government officials were not further limited by the general public's acceptance of policy recommendations from the policy-planning network, then power elite involvement in lobbying, policy formation, and elections would matter much less than they do.

This general point is supported by the way in which corporate dominance was momentarily called into question by the failure of the financial system in the summer and fall of 2008, leading to calls from liberals to temporarily nationalize failed banks, force them to fire top management, and limit their size in the future. The need for sudden government bailouts of large magnitudes and the resulting economic anxieties experienced by a large portion of the voting public played a big part in the Democratic Party's victories in the presidential and congressional elections in 2008. Those victories in turn led to a deficit spending program that kept unemployment from growing worse, along with a health insurance program, which extends coverage to most Americans for the first time in the country's history. It triggered several modest reforms in the financial system. Liberal-labor critics noted at the time that the stimulus program was too small to reduce unemployment to a significant degree, and a wider range of critics pointed out shortcomings in the health insurance and financial reform programs, but the fact remains that the corporate-conservative alliance opposed all three of these initiatives to the best of its ability. More generally, it is unlikely that any of these legislative actions, however limited, would have happened without the financial implosion that led worried centrist voters to turn to the Democrats.

Thus, domination by the corporate rich through the power elite does not negate the reality of continuing conflict over government policies or major policy changes in the face of future large-scale economic or military failures. Nevertheless, as this chapter shows, few legislative conflicts between 1935 and 2012 involved liberal-labor challenges to the rules that create privileges for the corporate rich. Most of the numerous battles within the interest-group process, for example, were only over specific spoils and favors; they often added up to contests between competing business interests.

Similarly, conflicts within the policy-making process usually concerned differences between the moderate conservatives and ultraconservatives in the corporate community. Many issues that at first appeared to be legislative defeats for the corporate community turned out to be situations in which the moderate conservatives decided for their own reasons to side with the spending coalition in times of disruption, thereby expanding government social insurance and other support programs, at least until the turmoil had subsided. At other times the policy disagreements involved issues that brought the needs of the corporate community as a whole into conflict with the needs of specific industries, which is what happened on trade policies and also on some environmental legislation.

However, the most consequential loss for the corporate community since it came of age in the 1870s and 1880s, the National Labor Relations Act of 1935, was a major factor in creating a strong labor movement in many states outside the South and Great Plains over the next four decades. This loss occurred in a context of increased labor militancy and a willingness on the part of Southern planters to side with the large number of newly elected non-Southern liberal Democrats in exchange for the exclusion of their own labor force. The defeat, although tempered by later legislation, had a dramatic impact on the nature of the American power structure. The organized labor movement lost all subsequent legislative battles and had been reduced to enclaves in construction, service industries, and government by 2012, due to the tenacity of the corporate rich, but the full history of organized labor during the twentieth century shows that limits can be placed on corporate power under some conditions.

It is now time to put the findings and conclusions in this and previous chapters into a larger theoretical and historical context in order to explain why there is corporate domination in the United States.

8

The Big Picture

The Introduction began with two seeming paradoxes. How can the owners and managers of highly competitive corporations develop the policy unity to shape government policies? And how can large corporations have such great power in a democratic country? The step-by-step argument and evidence presented in previous chapters provide the foundation for a theory that can explain these paradoxes—a *class-domination* theory of power in the United States.

Domination means that the commands of a group or class are carried out with relatively little resistance, which is possible because that group or class has been able to establish the organizations, rules, and customs through which everyday life is conducted. Domination, in other words, is the institutionalized outcome of great distributive power ("power over"). The corporate rich are a dominant class in terms of this definition because the cumulative effect of their various distributive powers leads to a situation in which most Americans generally accept (or acquiesce in) its policies. Even when there are highly vocal complaints, the routinized ways of acting in the United States follow from the rules and regulations needed by the corporate community to continue to grow and make profits.

The overall distributive power of the dominant class is first of all based in its structural power, which falls to it by virtue of being owners and high-level executives in corporations that sell goods and services for a profit in a market economy that is fashioned in good part to benefit the sellers of goods and services, not employees or consumers. The power to invest or not invest and to hire and fire employees leads to a political context in which most elected officials try to do as much as they can to create a favorable investment climate in order to avoid being voted out of office in the event of an economic downturn. This structural power is augmented by the ability to create new policies through the policy-planning network, which it was possible for the corporate rich to develop gradually over many decades because their common economic interests and social cohesion give them enough unity to sustain such an endeavor.

But even these powers might not have been enough to generate a system of extreme class domination if the bargains and compromises embodied in the Constitution had not led unexpectedly to a two-party system in which one party was controlled by the Northern rich and the other by the Southern rich. This in turn reinforced a personality-oriented candidate-selection process that is heavily dependent on large campaign donations—now and in the nineteenth century as well. The system of party primaries is the one adaptation to this constrictive two-party system that has provided some openings for insurgent liberals and trade unionists on one side and social conservatives and libertarians on the other.

Structural power, policies generated in the policy-planning network, and control of the two parties resulted in a polity in which there is little or no organized public opinion on specific legislative issues that is independent of the limits, doubts, and obfuscations generated by the opinion-shaping network. In addition, the fragmented and constrained system of government crafted by the Founding Fathers led to a relatively small federal government that is easily entered and influenced by wealthy and well-organized private citizens, whether through Congress, the separate departments of the executive branch, or a myriad of regulatory agencies.

The net result is that the corporate rich score very high on all three power indicators: who benefits, who occupies seats of government power, and who wins. They have a greater proportion of wealth and income than their counterparts in any other large industrialized democracy, and they are vastly overrepresented in key government positions and decision-making groups through the power elite. They win far more often than they lose on those issues that make it to the government for legislative consideration, although a temporary division between the Northern and Southern rich in the face of worker militancy in the North made it possible for liberals and organized labor to pass the National Labor Relations Act in 1935, which gave union members far more income and power for the next 40 years than they ever had before or after.

Despite their lack of power, many Americans feel a sense of empowerment because they have religious freedom, freedom of expression, the right to vote, and the hope that they can make more money or rise in the class structure if they try hard enough. Those with educational credentials and/or secure employment experience a degree of dignity and respect that allows them to hold their heads high and maintain their sense of self-regard, because elite arrogance and condescension toward average people is rarely expressed publicly. Then, too, liberals and leftists retain hope because they had success in helping to expand individual rights and freedoms—for people of color, for women, and for gays and lesbians.

But individual rights and freedoms do not necessarily add up to distributive power. In the same time period between 1965 and 2000 in which individual rights and freedoms expanded, corporate power also became greater because industrial unions were decimated, the civil rights movement dissipated, and the liberal-labor alliance splintered as part of the resistance to the integration of job sites, neighborhoods, and schools. Thus, class domination actually increased in recent decades in spite of increases in individual freedom. It is therefore possible to have class domination in a society based on individualistic liberal values, as many decisions by the Supreme Court also demonstrate.

WHY ARE THE CORPORATE RICH SO POWERFUL?

How is such a high concentration of corporate power possible? This question can be answered with the insights gained by comparing America's history to the histories of democratic countries in Europe. Very generally, there are two separate but related historical reasons for class domination in the United States. First, the corporate community in America is stronger because it did not have to contend with feudal aristocrats, strong states, and the hierarchy of an established church, all of which had a pervasive influence in Western European history (Mann 1986; Mann 1993). Second, those who work for wages and salaries are weaker as an economic class than in other democratic countries for reasons discussed later in the chapter, and they cannot mold themselves into a social class of freely intermarried families because they discriminate against each other on the basis of race, ethnicity, and religion.

The well-known historical factors leading to a decentralized and relatively powerless federal government are especially important in understanding modern corporate dominance. The prerevolutionary history of the United States as a set of separate colonial territories, only lightly overseen by the appointed governors representing the British crown, left plenty of room for the development of wealthy merchants and slaveholders, primarily because the colonial governments were so small. The Founding Fathers, as the representatives of the merchants, bankers, and planters in the separate colonies, were therefore able to create a government with divided and limited powers that was designed to accommodate the concerns of both Southern slave owners and Northern merchants and bankers. They took special care to deal with the fears of the Southern rich, who rightly worried that a strong federal government might lead to the abolishment of slavery in an industrializing society.

These constitutional compromises failed in that their differences over the expansion of slavery into western territories led to a murderous Civil War, which demonstrates how quickly societies can descend into violence when rival elites cannot compromise on their disagreements (Higley and Burton 2006, pp. 64-68). Nevertheless, the Southern and Northern rich were once again able to work together after they fully compromised their differences in 1877 through extended secret negotiations that resolved disputes over whether the Democrats or Republicans won the presidential elections in 1876. The Republicans were awarded the presidency in exchange for (1) the removal of the remaining federal troops from the South, which conceded a free hand to the planters to do everything in their power to subjugate their former slaves; (2) the appointment of a Southern Democrat to the cabinet in the patronage-rich position of postmaster general; and (3) the promise of continuing government subsidies for rebuilding the South.

The bargain also was supposed to include a gradual switch to the Republican Party on the part of the Southern white rich. However, as briefly noted in Chapter 6, wealthy white Southerners quickly realized that they needed to remain Democrats to make it impossible for a low-income, black-white voting coalition to gain a toehold in the two-party system. This possibility seemed to be a serious risk in the 1870s because populism had begun to develop in the areas dominated by white farmers with small holdings (Kousser 1974; Woodward 1966; Woodward 1973).

Once Northern Republicans abandoned African Americans and agreed to spend federal tax money in the South in disproportionate amounts, the Compromise of 1877 made it possible for Northern industrialists and Southern plantation owners to oppose any federal program or agency that might aid those who worked with their hands in factories or fields, an opposition that came to be known as the conservative coalition during the 1930s. From the 1880s on, however, the Southern plantation owners were the junior partners in the ownership class, although they were able to build up considerable political power through their strongholds in Congress and their alliance with the wealthy ethnic out-groups in Northern cities, which were excluded from social institutions and elite universities by the Protestant white rich.

Despite the federal tax dollars sent to the South after the Compromise of 1877 and in the twentieth century due to the development of the spending alliance in the Democratic Party during the New Deal, the federal government remained small. It did not have to make large expenditures for war preparations, as most European countries did at the time, due to the absence of any dangerous rival nations along the country's borders. In addition, the British navy provided a deterrent against invasion by any other European states throughout most of the nineteenth century, and U.S. involvement in World War I was relatively brief, with no postwar European military obligations. Thus, the United States did not have a permanent military establishment until World War II, when corporate leaders came to Washington (while remaining on corporate payrolls so they did not have to take a pay cut) to oversee military development and ensure control of it (Domhoff 1996, Chapter 6; Waddell 2001). By contrast, the nation-states that survived the severe competition that began among many small states in Europe seven or eight hundred years ago were the ones with strong central governments and large military organizations. These countries came into the modern era with strong states that had long-standing ties with the old aristocracy, so the new business class had to compete for power. The result is a more complex power equation in most European countries (Lachmann 2000; Lachmann 2010; Mann 1993).

Within this context, it is very important that there were big corporations in the United States by the second half of the nineteenth century, well before there was any semblance of a "big government" at the national level. These corporations and their associated policy-planning organizations were able to play the major role in creating new administrative agencies and regulatory bodies that became important in the twentieth century, as overviewed in Chapters 4 and 7. As noted in Chapter 7, efforts within the policy-planning network also led to the establishment of a reorganized Department of Defense, a new National Security Council in the White House, and the Central Intelligence Agency after World War II (Hammond 1961; Huntington 1961).

For all the early divisions between property owners in the North and South, ordinary Americans were even more divided from the beginning—free white farmers and artisans in the North and black slaves and low-income whites in the South. These divisions were exacerbated by the arrival of waves of immigrants from eastern and southern Europe in the late nineteenth century, who were viewed by entrenched skilled workers of northern European origins as a threat to the tight labor markets they enjoyed (e.g., Mink 1986). To make matters more difficult, there was no good way to overcome these divisions because bold activists could not develop strong trade unions in the North, where employers dominated state and local governments. In the South, African Americans were almost completely subjugated between the 1880s and 1965 by a combination of disenfranchisement and vigilante violence.

Despite these problems, the union movement in the Northern United States was very similar to the ones in Britain and France between the 1830s and the 1880s. Then highly organized employers used violent methods to defeat attempts at class-wide union organization. In doing so they had the support of the local and state governments controlled by the political parties they dominated. In that atmosphere, workers could only organize in the few business sectors in which employers were unable to bring in replacement workers for one or more of several reasons, including high skills levels (e.g., typographers, highly trained construction workers, and machinists), the need for fast turnaround in delivery services (e.g., shipping and railroad workers), or geographic isolation (e.g., coal mining, logging, and other isolated extractive industries) (Kimeldorf 2013). These high replacement costs, in turn, made strikes and threats of equipment destruction more effective for workers to utilize. By contrast, and this point cannot be underscored enough, business owners in Britain and France were forced by government, which was still dominated by landed aristocrats and bureaucracies in both countries, to compromise with unions (Hamilton 1991; Voss 1993).

For the most part, few workers in the United States could take advantage of high replacement costs. Most large-scale attempts at union organizing between the 1880s and 1936 were therefore broken up by government troops or the armed private police forces controlled by corporations. More violence was directed against the American labor movement than any other labor movement in a Western democracy. It was not until early 1937, shortly after the landslide reelection of Franklin D. Roosevelt to the presidency, along with the election of liberal governors in Pennsylvania and Michigan, that large industrial unions were able to organize in some Northern states. Braced by their electoral victories and facing highly organized union activists, the president and the two liberal governors refused to send federal troops or state police to arrest workers when they took over factories (Bernstein 1969; Fine 1969).

This refusal to honor repeated requests from corporate leaders for armed intervention—on the grounds that sit-down strikes were a form of trespassing on private property—marked the first time in American history that government force was not used to break a major strike. The result was a victory for union organizers in the automobile, rubber, and other heavy industries. Just a year later, however, state police in Ohio, Indiana, and Illinois helped corporate leaders defeat strikers who were trying to organize the steel industry (Piven and Cloward 1977, Chapter 3). By 1939, the growth in union membership slowed. Only the decline in unemployment beginning in 1940 due to defense spending, along with the need for national solidarity during World War II, made it possible for unions to resume growth, from 9 million in 1939 to 15 million in 1945, with the help of government intervention on their behalf. This sequence of events is often obscured in studies of the union movement by pro-labor authors, who ignore or downplay the role of the government in making unionization possible. They instead focus almost exclusively on the courage of the workers and the skillful leadership provided at the grassroots by leftists. Skillful leaders and militant workers are indeed necessary, but as a historian who specialized in leftist social movements concluded, "the central importance of government mediation, and of the alliance with the Democrats, has been glossed over" in many accounts of the surge in union growth (Weinstein 1975, pp. 80–81).

Despite the development of greater class solidarity, craft and industrial workers could not develop their own political party because the government structure and electoral rules pulled everyone into a two-party system, as explained in Chapter 6. Thus, there was no way for people to come together to create programs that might help to transcend the white/black and old immigrant/new immigrant divisions. They were stuck with the choice of joining a Democratic Party controlled by Southern planters and machine Democrats or creating a third party, which would inadvertently ensure complete government dominance by the anti-union Republican Party. Once again, the situation was different in most European countries, mainly because their parliamentary systems made the development of a labor or socialist party more feasible, even in the face of changes in electoral rules that constrained their potential (Ahmed 2013a).

Lacking an organizational base in unions and a party, which might have formulated and popularized a more communal and pro-government ethos, there was little possibility for the American working class to overcome the strong individualism and the racial, ethnic, and religious prejudices that are widespread in the United States. Thus, these divisive orientations persist among nonunionized white workers and continue to matter in terms of union organizing and voting patterns.

THE TRANSFORMATION OF THE AMERICAN POWER STRUCTURE

With the Northern rich dominating the Republicans and the Southern rich dominating the Democrats between 1877 and the 1970s, and a conservative coalition of Republicans and Southern Democrats controlling Congress on class issues into the 1990s, there was little chance of egalitarian social change through the electoral system. Those who were opposed to class domination or racial exclusion therefore resorted to disruptive social movements outside of the electoral system to try to win new rights, including in some cases the right to vote.

The largest, most sustained, and best known of these social movements, the civil rights movement of the 1950s and 1960s, not only transformed the lives of African Americans in the South and made possible the growth of a black middle class throughout the nation. It also dynamited the power arrangements that persisted from the New Deal to the mid-1960s. As stated in Chapter 6, those power arrangements rested on the acceptance of African American exclusion—10 to 12 percent of the country's population—by the liberal-labor alliance in the North, as well as by the Republicans and Southern Democrats, to ensure the support of white workers, many of them union members. Moreover, as mentioned in the Introduction, the Voting Rights Act of 1965 made it possible for African Americans to help defeat open segregationists and other ultraconservatives in Democratic primaries in the South, thereby hastening their shift to the Republican Party.

Black voters' pressure on ultraconservative and racist Democrats was complemented by the fact that the gradual industrialization of the South since World War II had made the situation of the Southern segment of the ownership class even more similar to that of its Northern counterpart. When the Democratic Party could no longer fulfill its main historical function, namely, keeping African Americans powerless, it was relatively easy for wealthy white conservatives to become Republicans. (Due to the gradual decline in prejudice toward Catholics after World War II ended, it also became easier for wealthy second-generation and third-generation Catholic immigrants to be accepted into upper-class social institutions and become supporters of the Republican Party.)

The changing political economy of the South also made the complete oppression of African Americans less crucial for the white rich, but civil rights did not come easily or simply. The civil rights acts of 1964 and 1965 would not have passed without the social disruption created by the civil rights movement. The conservative coalition in the Senate was not prepared to budge because it had the 34 votes needed in that era to continue a filibuster (Bloom 1987). As a result, the Republicans did not abandon the Southern Democrats on this issue until moderate conservatives in the power elite, confronted with the potential for ongoing social turmoil in inner cities across the nation, decided to move in an accommodating direction to bring the South more in line with practices in the rest of the country. It was only at this juncture that enough Republicans finally broke with the Southern Democrats to end the filibuster.

The enactment of civil rights legislation and the exodus of the Southern segment of the ownership class from the Democratic Party created the possibility that the Democratic Party could be transformed into an organizational base for a nationwide liberal-labor alliance that included African Americans as well as the newly arriving immigrants from Latin America and Asia. But something very different happened instead, short-circuiting the possibilities for progressive economic change.

The problems for the creation of an expanded liberal-labor alliance began when the Southern white ownership class used appeals to long-standing racial resentments and hostility to the federal government to carry a majority of middle- and low-income white Southerners into the Republican Party with them. As already stated in Chapter 6, Republican presidential candidate Barry Goldwater emphasized his belief in state's rights in 1964 to capture the four traditionally Democratic states of South Carolina, Georgia, Alabama, and Mississippi, which have been Republican strongholds ever since. The openly segregationist Democratic governor of Alabama, George Wallace, used race as a wedge issue to win 13.5 percent of the vote nationwide in his third-party presidential race in 1968, thereby taking away enough traditional white Democratic voters in the South and Midwest to give the Republican candidate, Richard Nixon, a very narrow victory over his Democratic opponent with only 43.4 percent of the popular vote (Carter 2000). In 1972 President Nixon solidified the former Wallace voters for the Republicans at the presidential level, especially in the South, paving the way for the Reagan-Bush era from 1980 to 1992 and the Bush-Cheney administration from 2000 to 2008 (Carmines and Stimson 1989; Carter 1996).

As a result of the racial backlash, later supplemented by emotional appeals on other social issues, Republicans held the presidency for all but 12 of the 40 years between 1968 and 2008 and gradually consolidated a nationwide conservative Republican majority that gained control of Congress. The abandonment of the Democrats at the congressional level by Southern whites did not happen at a faster pace primarily because the seniority they enjoyed gave Southern Democrats great power in Congress as long as the Democrats could maintain a majority. Wherever possible, then, southern whites continued to control the Democratic Party at the local level while voting Republican at the national level. The result was a split party system in the South from 1968 to 1994. Once the Republicans took control of Congress in 1994, most of the remaining white Southern Democrats quickly consolidated within the Republican Party, including several elected Southern Democrats in the House and Senate who switched parties.

But it was not just racial conflict in the South that destroyed any possibility of an expanded liberal-labor alliance within the Democratic Party. There was also racial conflict and backlash in the North. The arguments and buzzwords later used by ultraconservatives in the Republican Party to appeal to Northern whites were already being used by trade unionists and machine Democrats in the early 1960s as part of their resistance to renewed demands for greater integration in the North (Quadagno 1994; Sugrue 2008). There were a few notable exceptions, and many leaders of industrial unions supported civil rights legislation, but enough of the rank-and-file and other middle-income white voters resisted integration in housing, schooling, and unions to put the Democrats on the defensive in the North as well as the South. This point is seen most dramatically in the votes for Governor Wallace of Alabama in Democratic presidential primaries as early as 1964—30 percent in Indiana, 34 percent in Wisconsin, and 47 percent in the former slave state of Maryland, where he won 16 of 23 counties, the state capital, and the white ethnic neighborhoods of Baltimore (Carter 2000, p. 215).

Nor was it simply racial conflict that caused many Northern whites to oppose liberals of all colors. Many of them did not like the feminists or environmentalists either, who were seen as threats to their status as proud white males or a danger to their jobs. Moreover, many did not like what they saw as the anti-Americanism of the 1960s antiwar movement. All of these factors contributed to the disintegration of the liberal-labor alliance and made it possible for President Nixon and his ultraconservative allies to attract more and more white middle-income voters (blue collar and white collar, union and nonunion) into the Republican Party, using the same social issues that have been employed by Republican candidates ever since (Edsall 2006; Edsall and Edsall 1992).

For several different reasons, then, just enough white voters switched to the Republicans to solidify its reconstructed corporate-conservative alliance, which created further problems for the weakened liberal-labor alliance. Most white trade unionists did not fully realize that their unions was now at risk because of the renewed corporate attack on them, which were triggered by the issues mentioned in the discussion of the Committee for Economic Development in Chapter 4—union power, cost-push inflation, cost-of-living increases, and wage-price guidelines (Domhoff 2013; Gross 1995). They did not understand that the strong unions they had built over the previous 35 years could be dismantled very quickly by moving production to the South or out of the country at a record-breaking pace. Nor did they imagine that the Republicans that had been courting their votes would aid the corporations in their attack by making antiunion appointments to the National Labor Relations Board.

As also explained in the discussion of the Committee for Economic Development in Chapter 4, the nationwide white turn to the Republicans also made it possible for the moderate conservatives to make a right turn on other policy issues in the 1970s, once inner cities were calm and the corporations were faced with new economic problems due to increased foreign competition, rising oil prices, and inflation. In particular, they focused on raising interest rates through the Federal Reserve Board as the easiest way to dampen inflation by creating unemployment and lowering consumer demand. In the process, they abandoned the moderate ("commercial Keynesian") policies of tax increases, decreased federal spending, and wage-price guidelines they had entertained in the 1960s as alternative ways to control inflation (Domhoff 2013, Chapters 9–10). The result was a "new class war," culminating in the Reagan administration's cutbacks in various social support programs (Piven and Cloward 1982/1985). This renewed class war also led to the step-by-step deregulation of the financial sector by the Reagan and Clinton administrations, which opened the way for the stock market and housing market bubbles that buoyed the economy for most of the years between 1997 and 2007 (Baker 2009; Krugman 2012).

The gradual elimination of unions since the 1970s and the attendant movement of production facilities out of the country played a significant role in the declining share of income that goes to those who work for wages and salaries, as did the declining value of the minimum wage and unemployment insurance after 1968 (Baker 2007; Volscho and Kelly 2012; Western and Rosenfeld 2011). Although economists often focus on the overall economic advantages of the new overseas production practices, including the benefits for people in the low-income countries with new production facilities, these changes also meant a loss in power for average Americans as well as stagnating incomes. For all their faults as bureaucracies that can become fiefdoms for self-serving leaders, as is the risk with any large organization, unions provided a measure of security and dignity to many people's lives, a point that includes people who were not members of unions because their wages were often pulled upward by union wages.

How much has this relatively unique American history mattered in terms of class dominance? The impact is in part revealed by comparing the share of wealth held by the top 10 percent and the amount of income received by the top 1 percent in several large industrialized democracies for which this information is available for slightly different years between 1998 and 2002. These comparisons show that both the wealth and income distributions are more concentrated in the United States than in the other democracies (Alvaredo, Atkinson, Piketty, and Saez 2012; Davies, Shorrocks, Sandstrom, and Wolff 2008). Table 8.1 demonstrates this point by presenting the specific figures for the United States, Germany, and Japan, which show the large contrasts that can exist among highly developed countries. Sweden is also included in Table 8.1 because its highly concentrated wealth distribution (far greater than that for Germany or Japan) is accompanied by the lowest income share for the top 1 percent in just about any country in the world, which is due to progressive taxation.

Based on these two "who benefits?" power indicators, wealth and income, it seems likely that class dominance is greater in the United States than in any other fully industrialized democratic country.

Table 8.1 Wealth Shares for Top 10% and Income Shares for Top 1% in United States, Sweden, Germany, and Japan

Country	Year	Top 10% Wealth	Top 1% Income
United States	2001	69.8%	16.5%
Sweden	2002	58.6%	6.0%
Germany	1998	44.4%	10.9%
Japan	1999	39.3%	8.2%

Note: Sweden is included to show that high wealth concentration need not lead to high income concentration.

Sources: Alvaredo, Atkinson, Piketty, and Saez 2012 on incomes; Davies, Shorrocks, Sandstrom, and Wolff 2008 on wealth.

POWER AND SOCIAL CHANGE

Although there is extreme class domination in the United States, this does not necessarily mean it is inevitable in the future. Power structures change, as demonstrated most dramatically by the relatively peaceful replacement of white rule and a repressive system of apartheid in South Africa in the early 1990s; the forceful but nonviolent replacement of dictators in the late 1980s by broad-based (not class-based) coalitions in Eastern Europe, after the Soviet Union signaled that it would no longer use force to prop up these regimes; and then by the even more sudden and unexpected nonviolent collapse of the Soviet Union itself in 1991. Rather obviously, nothing so large-scale seems likely in the United States, but several events between the 1930s and 2008 that are discussed in this book suggest that unexpected changes sometimes occur.

No social scientist predicted that there would be a Great Depression, or a New Deal in reaction to it, which led to the creation of the liberal-labor alliance. No one foresaw that a massive nonviolent civil rights movement would come roaring out of the Silent Fifties, inspiring antiwar, feminist, environmental, and gay-lesbian (later LGBT) movements. Nor did anyone anticipate the impact the religious right and the rest of the ultraconservative wing of the Republican Party would have during and after the 1970s through their opposition to affirmative action and to the liberal social agenda. In fact, most social scientists, and many liberals and labor leaders, thought that the economic self-interest of white workers and the respect for individual rights in the American belief system would lead to a Democratic majority and integration during the 1970s. More recently, the idea that liberal Democrats would be in a position in late 2008 and early 2009 to even momentarily imagine making major changes in the economic system was unthinkable just before the financial meltdown in early September 2008, after 40 years of setbacks for the liberal-labor alliance and increasing income inequality.

This series of unanticipated crises and opportunities underscores that social scientists and historians can at best outline the structure of power and analyze trends. They can say that social movements often (but not always) emerge in reaction to sudden disruptions of everyday life due to wages cuts, depressions, wars, and cultural shocks. However, the only thing anyone knows for sure is that unexpected conflicts and crises often occur because of the dynamic and constantly changing nature of power structures, which gives rise to the possibility that activists with the right mix of programs, strategies, and tactics might be able to take advantage of new cracks and openings to challenge class dominance. The analysis presented in this book is based on this open-ended view of history, which is explained in theoretical terms in the final section of the next chapter.

9

What Do Other Social Scientists Think?

Although most social scientists agree that the corporate community has had more influence than any other group in American society since 1980, many doubt that the owners and managers of large financial companies and corporations possess the scope of vision, policy cohesion, and degree of power to be considered a dominant class. Since the early 1990s they have tended to favor one of four alternative theoretical perspectives that have led to ongoing research—*pluralism, historical institutionalism, organizational state theory,* or *elite theory*. Each of these views will be explained and critiqued in turn, followed by a section suggesting that the theory of four overlapping power networks utilized in this book provides an overarching framework that does not require any of the other theories to abandon their main insights.

PLURALISM

Pluralism, as the word suggests, is a theory that sees power in the United States as divided among competing interest groups and voluntary associations, which become involved with each other in shifting coalitions to exert influence, depending on the issue at hand. Pluralism does not deny, and even emphasizes, that some groups may have more power on some issues than do others, but it denies that the corporate community has the cohesion to generate common policies and win regularly enough on a wide range of issues to be considered a dominant class. Pluralists point to the successes of nonbusiness groups, such as labor unions from the 1930s to the 1970s or environmentalists and consumer advocates in the 1970s, as evidence for their claim.

203

Pluralism, they continue, is made possible by several factors, including the separation of the ownership and control of corporations, along with the lack of any unifying groups in the corporate community. Corporate leaders in different sectors of the economy tend to stick to their own knitting and to have disagreements among themselves on some issues, so they are too divided among themselves to dominate government. Even more important, citizens are said to have the power to shape the general direction of public policy by voting for the candidates and political parties that are sympathetic with their preferences. Citizens also have the freedom and capacity to create voluntary associations and pressure groups, including unions, to bring citizen influence to bear on elected officials over and beyond elections, who are responsive to citizen lobbying if only to assure that they are not voted out of office.

However, the long-standing pluralist claim that any tendencies toward class dominance have been overcome in part because corporate owners and managers are too divided among themselves to dominate government is first of all refuted by the evidence presented in Chapter 3, which shows that corporate managers are assimilated into the upper class of wealthy owners through a wide range of social occasions and economic incentives. It also ignores the ease with which family offices, private equity funds, and many other financial companies can take over and reshape all but the few very largest corporations in the country. The pluralist conclusion about the separation of ownership and control also ignores the fact that class and organizational perspectives are brought together within boards of directors, as explained in Chapter 2.

The pluralist assertion that corporations are only organized into narrow interest groups that argue among themselves misses the high degree of unity generated through common ownership, interlocking directorships, and participation in the policy-planning network, as demonstrated in Chapters 2 and 4. However, pluralists are right that the corporate rich are not completely unified, as this book also demonstrates. They do have disagreements among themselves, but they are not as divided as their rivals in the more fragmented liberal-labor alliance. Looking at this point from a pluralist perspective with its general emphasis on lack of unity and agreement, perhaps the class-domination view could be rephrased to say that the corporate rich usually win because they are less disorganized than any of their potential rivals.

The pluralist claim that voting in elections has a major influence on legislation is based in good part on theoretical arguments and the experience of other countries, not evidence about elections in the United States. It does not take into account the several factors shown in Chapter 6 to dilute this potential influence. In particular, it downplays the way in which a two-party system leads candidates to blur policy differences as they try to win the centrist voters, leaving elected officials relatively free to say one thing in the campaign and do another once in office. It also takes the major role of the Southern rich in the Democratic Party into the late twentieth century too lightly, as well as the veto power of the conservative coalition in Congress.

Pluralists put great weight on the power of public opinion to influence elected officials, but as discussed in Chapter 5, there are few voluntary associations in which it is any longer considered proper to discuss political issues, thereby decreasing any possibility that they can contribute to the understanding of political issues or develop their members' ability to discuss issues articulately as part of pressure groups that impact government. Furthermore, the evidence pluralists usually present to demonstrate the importance of public opinion is almost entirely correlational, which means that it can tell us nothing about causality. Pluralist claims based on correlations also overlook the role of the opinion-shaping network outlined in Chapter 5 as well as the fact that the public's liberal preferences on a wide range of economic programs never have been fulfilled, as demonstrated in the large-scale study of public opinion surveys that covers the years from 1981 to 2002 (Gilens 2012).

Despite these general findings on the lack of influence of public opinion, an ambitious study using an aggregated indicator of public "mood" concluded that business loses on visible general issues in which public opinion takes a liberal stance (Smith 2000). In this study, the public mood indicator was compared with the stances taken by the U.S. Chamber of Commerce on over 100 "major" legislative issues between 1953 and 1992, leading to the further finding that business does win on narrow issues that are not focused upon by the general public. However, there are serious limitations to the type of indicator used to construct a general measure of public opinion because public opinion has several dimensions that are risky to mix, among several problems (Page 2002, pp. 326–332). As for the Chamber of Commerce as the exemplar of the corporate point of view, it speaks primarily for the ultraconservatives and often takes principled stances on routine issues on which it knows it is very likely to lose. In fact, several of its "losses" in the 1970s were on successful rollbacks of liberal-labor gains by the conservative coalition, but the chamber opposed them because they did not go far enough.

In an analysis of the 56 defeats suffered by the Chamber of Commerce on 107 pieces of legislation that passed between 1953 and 1984, it was found that the chamber lost as often to the growth coalitions on subsidies for downtown development and to agribusiness interests seeking renewal of their agricultural subsidies as it did to the liberal-labor alliance (Domhoff 2013). This finding shows that the chamber is often at odds with its usual allies because of its focus on reducing government expenditures. Nor can the issues on which the chamber lost to the liberal-labor forces be considered major ones, such as raising the minimum wage, increasing Social Security benefits, extending or increasing unemployment benefits, providing rent support, and aiding the homeless. These issues are very important in the lives of average citizens, but most of the liberal-labor successes barely kept up with inflation or fell well behind it, especially after the late 1970s. Nor did they receive much if any opposition from the corporate moderates, which usually supported increased Social Security benefits until the 1980s, including the indexing of Social Security in the early 1970s.

The way in which government leaders ignore public opinion on major foreign policy issues, such as the wars in Vietnam and Iraq, as expressed in national surveys as those wars dragged on, also presents a major problem for the pluralists' emphasis on the importance of public opinion. Even after both exit polls and the electoral outcome in 2006 showed that the American public wanted to wind down the war in Iraq, the Bush administration used a plan proposed by ultraconservatives at the American Enterprise Institute to increase troop strength over the next two years. Although the army was eventually withdrawn from Vietnam in 1975 and Iraq in 2011, this was as much due to mounting casualties and the inability to attain American goals as it was to public opinion. In the case of the Vietnam War, bad morale and racism led to the killing of some officers by enlisted men and the need to rebuild a failed army (Moskos and Butler 1996).

The New Liberalism

One of the recent widely read and cited statements of pluralism suggests a *new liberalism* has arisen in which citizen's lobbies, meaning various nonprofit and voluntary groups, proliferate (Berry 1999). This neo-pluralist view puts great emphasis on the battles between liberals and the religious right over cultural values, concluding that the liberals often won from the 1970s through the 1990s. However, any liberal success on these issues is irrelevant in analyzing corporate power. This new version of pluralism grants that major foundations, especially the Ford Foundation, funded many of the liberal citizen groups and nonprofit advocacy groups at their outset, but claims nonprofits became independent due to money raised through direct mailings and other outreach efforts. In fact, as documented in Chapter 4, most of these organizations, including the advocacy groups for low-income communities of color, were still very dependent on foundation money as of 2010. Even if a few of the nonprofits receive a majority of their funds from other fundraising activities, minimizing the role of foundation grants overlooks a key point made by organizational theorists—the importance of discretionary money in any organization that wants to generate new innovations and continue to grow in membership or impact.

All environmental groups are counted as part of the new pluralism, but as shown in Chapter 2, conflicts between the corporate community and the growth coalitions over clean air in major cities like Pittsburgh and Los Angeles gave environmentalists their first real opening (Gonzalez 2005). And as Chapter 4 documents, the key groups as far as the formulation of environmental policy are still funded by large foundations and are part of the policy-planning network. Grassroots environmentalists that are more liberal than the mainstream environmental groups have had great success in sensitizing public opinion on environmental issues. They have been able to create watchdog groups whose reports receive attention in the mass media. They have developed new ideas and technologies for controlling some forms of pollution, which have been grudgingly accepted by the corporate community. Their activism has been crucial in stopping many specific development projects and in saving old forests. But from 1975 through 2012 they were not able to pass any legislation opposed by the Business Roundtable. The environmental movement as a whole and its liberal wing in particular is more marginal in a power sense than its public reputation would suggest. This conclusion includes their lack of success between 1990 and 2012 in convincing the federal government to take any steps to slow global warming that were opposed by fossil fuel companies and their thousands of lobbyists.

The consumer movement that developed out of the activism of the civil rights and antiwar movements of the 1960s is also held out as evidence for the success of the new liberalism. Inspired in part by the efforts of Ralph Nader, the movement led to the passage of many new consumer protection laws between 1967 and 1974. When Jimmy Carter became president in 1976, he appointed the leader of the Consumer Federation of America as an undersecretary of agriculture and the head of one of Nader's congressional watchdog groups as the chair of the National Highway Traffic Safety Administration. In addition, a respected academic researcher was put in charge of the Occupational Safety and Health Administration and a Senate staff member who helped to draft many of the new consumer safety laws became chair of the Federal Trade Commission.

However, there is less evidence of liberal power in this story than meets the eye because the relevant business groups either agreed with the legislation or forced modifications to make it acceptable. Although the Chamber of Commerce registered its usual protestations, there was little or no business opposition to any of the consumer protection legislation of the 1960s. The important exception is the automobile industry's objections to the National Traffic and Motor Vehicle Safety Act, an effort to force them to make safer cars (Luger 2000; Vogel 1989).

The profound weakness of the consumer movement was exposed in 1978 when it could not win enactment for its cautious plan for an Office of Consumer Representation, due to the efforts of the Business Roundtable and its allies, who worked with the conservative coalition to stop the legislation (Akard 1992; Schwartz 1979). The consumer movement also failed in all its efforts to legislate greater corporate responsibility. Congress refused to consider the idea of federal charters for corporations, leaving them free to continue to incorporate in states with very weak laws governing corporations. Plans to increase shareholder rights and strengthen the laws on corporate crime were rejected. A flurry of new initiatives at the Federal Trade Commission led to a strong reaction by Congress when it was inundated by complaints from the car dealers, funeral directors, and other business groups that felt put upon and harassed. Every reform was lost. In the early 1980s the ultraconservatives tried to abolish the Federal Trade Commission entirely, but it was saved with the help of corporate moderates, who believed it had some uses (Pertschuk 1982).

Surveying the successes and failures of consumer activists from the vantage point of the 1990s, the most detailed study of this movement concluded that pluralists are wrong to claim that the "new" regulation starting in the 1970s, which covers a wide range of companies, such as mandated by the Occupational Safety and Health Act, is different from earlier forms of regulation that focused on a single industry. More generally, its authors conclude that business is the dominant force in the interest-group community despite the increase in nonbusiness interest groups in the 1970s (Maney and Bykerk 1994). Nothing happened between the 1990s and 2012 that alters that judgment.

In conclusion, pluralism provides a reasonable day-to-day portrait of political activity in the United States, with its constant back and forth between the leaders and members of liberal, labor, and ultraconservative groups. But pluralism overlooks or downplays the enduring nature of the corporate-conservative and liberal-labor alliances, and it seldom adds up the record of wins and losses that shows the overwhelming dominance of the corporate-conservative forces on the issues that decide war and peace, the state of the economy, the safety of the workplace, and the quality of the environment. However, it is true that new coalitions are formed when new issues arise and that numerous elections are hotly contested, with liberals and unions winning enough of them to sustain their hope that they can attain some major victories in the future.

HISTORICAL INSTITUTIONALISM

Historical institutionalist theory, which emphasizes the independent power of government, is a useful general starting point because historical and comparative studies suggest that the government indeed has the potential for autonomy (Lachmann 2010; Mann 1986). Historical institutionalists also usefully stress that large formal institutions, including a government's departments and agencies, develop in a step-by-step way in response to the specific issues that confront them, which means that institutional arrangements are different from issue to issue, place to place, and time to time. They emphasize that each policy decision influences and places limits on what can take place at a later time. They add that institutions develop in relation to one another and take one another's actions and likely reactions into account when they contemplate any changes in their own strategies for stability or expansion. The net result is an "institutional environment" that further shapes and constrains any one institution's options in response to new developments. The fact that institutions develop in distinct ways and are embedded in institutional fields means that societies usually change very slowly.

Generally speaking, this overall framework captures what a stable society looks like on a day-to-day or month-to-month basis when everything is functioning normally. But it misses the dynamic nature of any society over a period of months or decades. What historical institutionalists see as established patterns are more often power stalemates in which those outside the top power circles are biding their time until new opportunities to resume the conflict become available. As one organizational theory concluded, institutionalist theory "de-emphasizes power and conflict" and instead "emphasizes routines, imitation, unreflective responses, custom and normative practices, and convergence of organizational forms" (Perrow 2002, p. 19). It is a static theory because it is not alive to the tensions that can develop among the economic, governmental, military, and ideological networks, and because it usually gives only minor attention to classes and class conflict.

Moreover, the theory does not fit well with many empirical findings about key issues in the United States. To begin with, as this book shows, there is little evidence that the potential for government independence manifests itself in the United States. Government autonomy is only possible when a government is unified and relatively impermeable to the employees and representatives of private organizations, but the American government is neither. For historical reasons explained in Chapter 8, it is a fragmented government, completely open to outside agents and therefore vulnerable to domination through the electoral process explained in Chapter 6 and through the appointments from the corporate community and policy-planning network documented in Chapter 7. The movement by members of the power elite between the private sector and government blurs the line between the corporate community and the state, which does not fit with the idea of government independence. Furthermore, one of the three branches of the federal government, the Supreme Court, consisting in large part of corporate lawyers with lifetime appointments, often thwarts the efforts of the other two branches, as it did in the case of the executive branch during the early New Deal and in the case of Congress in the early 1960s, when it declared thinly populated rural congressional districts to be unconstitutional.

This type of empirical critique has been recognized to some degree by historical institutionalists, who have modified their original strong claim about the "autonomy" of the American government to a focus on what they call a "polity-centered approach," which concedes that social movements, coalitions of pressure groups, and political parties must be included in the equation (Skocpol 1992, p. x). They note that the lack of strong government bureaucracies and an established church in the United States leave ample space for voluntary associations and necessitate the creation of "broad, transpartisan coalitions of groups—and ultimately legislators" that have to be "assembled for each particular issue" (Skocpol 1992, pp. 368, 529). This polity-centered approach puts more emphasis on political institutions and the structured nature of the political process than pluralists do, but its concern with voluntary associations, shifting coalitions, and political parties gives the theory much in common with pluralism, especially when it is added that historical institutionalists see business as weak and disorganized in the United States.

Historical institutionalists stress that the institutional structure of a government—for example, whether it is parliamentary or presidential, centralized or decentralized—has an important role in shaping party systems and political strategies (Skocpol 1980; Skocpol 1992). This is a useful point that fits equally well with a class-dominance theory in the case of the United States. As shown in Chapter 6, the existence of an independent executive branch and the election of Congress on a state-by-state and district-by-district basis accounts for the strength of the two-party system. Moreover, the historic lack of large planning staffs in most executive departments made it possible for the private, nonprofit policy-planning network to flourish. Then, too, the division of American government into national, state, and local levels helps to explain why growth coalitions can be so powerful in most cities.

In stressing the importance of how a government is structured, however, historical institutionalists tend to overlook the ways in which those structures are often changed by the corporate rich and the growth coalitions in the United States. As documented in Chapter 6, one of the best example of this point is the way in which the electoral rules were changed by growth coalitions in many cities to off-year nonpartisan elections on a citywide basis in order to dilute the influence of low-income voters. Historical institutionalists also ignore cases that contradict their claim that new agencies are soon accepted as part of the government's routine functioning, but in fact several New Deal agencies set up by the White House or accepted begrudgingly by the conservative coalition because of the severe nature of the Depression were abolished by conservatives during World War II, particularly those having to do with planning or with helping low-income farmers and farm labor. Most of all, the corporate rich continued to oppose the National Labor Relations Board and ultimately reduced its effectiveness. The changes in electoral rules, along with the dismantling or hamstringing of agencies opposed by ultraconservatives, when joined with the fact that the corporate-sponsored policy-planning network created several of the new government agencies celebrated by historical institutionalists as examples of state autonomy, add up to a very large empirical challenge to historical institutional theory.

Historical institutionalists argue that independent experts, those with few or no connections to corporations or labor unions, can be powerful because they have information that is valuable to state officials. They are right that experts provide many of the new policy ideas, but they do not see that the most important experts are selected and sponsored by one or more of the organizations within the policy network and that their ideas are discussed and criticized by corporate leaders before appearing in reports and proposals, as explained in Chapter 4.

Due to their mistaken belief that business lost power during the New Deal and that independent experts helped build state capacity for programs such as the Agricultural Adjustment Administration in 1933 and the Social Security Administration in 1935, historical institutionalists are factually wrong in their analyses of the origins of those two important additions to government (Finegold and Skocpol 1995). Contrary to their account, experts from the policy-planning network, with the backing of the main corporate moderates of that era, created the programs that were the key parts of the Agricultural Adjustment Administration, then gained the support of the Chamber of Commerce, the Farm Bureau, and plantation owners (Domhoff and Webber 2011, Chapter 2). Similarly, as briefly noted in the discussion of the Business Council in Chapter 4 and as fully demonstrated with new archival findings in the document on "How Corporate Moderates Created the Social Security Act" on whorulesamerica.net, it was members of the policy-planning network that created (and implemented) the Social Security Act. Liberals, social workers, independent experts, and government employees played a secondary role, a fact that historical institutionalists ignore (Hacker and Pierson 2002; Hacker and Pierson 2004; Orloff 1993).

Historical institutionalists also have an inadequate analysis of the ultra-conservative turn in government policy during the Nixon administration, which they incorrectly locate in the second half of the 1970s (Hacker and Pierson 2010, pp. 58–58, 127–130). Their analysis is based on the "great 'bulge' of government activism that runs from, roughly, 1964 to 1977," by which they mean the large growth in government domestic spending during that 13-year period (Hacker and Pierson 2010, p. 96). As part of their argument, they use the expansion of social spending programs during the Nixon administration as evidence that the corporate community was "getting its clock cleaned," which would be a remarkable thing for a Republican administration to do to its closest allies and biggest fundraisers (Hacker and Pierson 2010, p. 116). They reject the emphasis in prior explanations of the right turn on the backlash by white voters and downplay the importance of the turmoil and division both within the unions and in their alliance with liberals. They call that widely accepted account a "colorful, easy to tell, and superficially appealing" analysis that "misses the real story" (Hacker and Pierson 2010, pp. 95, 96).

In their alternative view, the right turn began with a new corporate mobilization, epitomized by the founding of the Business Roundtable in 1972, which they describe as the equivalent of a "domestic version of Shock and Awe" in terms of its impact (Hacker and Pierson 2010, p. 118). Weary of being defeated and pushed around, the corporate leaders created a more united, active, and sophisticated lobbying effort with which they could "flood Washington with letters and phone calls" (Hacker and Pierson 2010, p. 121). The result was a level of pressure on Congress that had not been applied before. The corporate community also increased its influence in politics through large campaign donations to PACs, the new avenue for them to fund political candidates made possible by changes in campaign finance laws in the mid-1970s.

In making their analysis, historical institutionalists overlook or ignore evidence, such as that presented in Chapters 2 and 4 of this book, that the corporate community was already well organized before the Business Roundtable was created in 1972 by members of the Business Council and the Committee for Economic Development. They do not realize that its origins were in the renewed conflict with organized labor that began in the 1960s, not in a concern with regulatory agencies or enlarged budgets (Gross 1995, pp. 234–239). Nor do they recognize that corporate moderates were supportive of increased domestic spending in the face of the civil rights movement, rising tensions in the inner cities, and the turmoil generated by the antiwar movement, as seen most clearly in the policy statements and lobbying coalitions put together by the Committee for Economic Development. These efforts by corporate moderates, carried out at the same time that they were working very hard to limit union power, demonstrate that increased government budgets cannot be assumed to be evidence for the power of liberals or the government, as many historical institutionalists do, without understanding the constellation of forces that were for and against those budgets. Furthermore, the defeat of legislation opposed by the Business Roundtable and its corporate allies in the 1970s was not primarily due to their increased lobbying efforts, but to the continuing existence of the conservative coalition (see Domhoff 2013 for detailed evidence on the points in this paragraph).

Contrary to the historical institutionalists' conclusions about the right turn beginning in the second half of the 1970s, the liberal-labor alliance had been losing major legislative battles since 1939, with the important partial exception of Medicare in 1965. Then their alliance began to splinter over racial integration and how to deal with disruption in large Northern cities between 1961 and 1968, as explained in Chapter 8. Even in the case of the largest liberal industrial union of that era, the United Automobile Workers, its hopes for an enlarged welfare state on the basis of a black-white workers' coalition in both the North and the South, with the segregationist Southern Democrats finally displaced, were "little more than ashes" by 1968 (Boyle 1998, p. 230). It lost the confidence of many of its white members, and perhaps even a majority of them in some key elections in which the UAW leadership put its support behind Democratic candidates. It also lost the support of its major allies, including African Americans, antiwar liberals, and the New Left, which saw it and other unions as "a prop for the status quo" (Boyle 1998, p. 231).

From 1968 on, facing an enlarged conservative coalition and a revived ultra-conservative grassroots movement, organized labor went downhill as a legislative and lobbying force, even though many large unions in construction and heavy industry continued to win wage gains during the 1970s. Contrary to the idea that the Nixon administration was "liberal" because it spent money on welfare programs and improved Social Security benefits, it supported an all-out attack on organized labor and had the complete backing of the corporate moderates in all of its policy initiatives (Domhoff 2013, Chapter 9). More generally, President Nixon's narrow election victory in 1968, made possible in part by the defection of white union members to the Republicans and a new segregationist third party, was a major turning point in post–World War II American history.

THE ORGANIZATIONAL STATE PERSPECTIVE

The organizational state perspective begins with an emphasis on organized private groups that have a major impact on government by hiring professional lobbyists who are experts on the specific issues of concern to them. It is "pluralistic" in its emphasis on separate policy areas (called "domains") and in stressing that an organization that is powerful in one domain is usually inactive or weak in other domains. On the other hand, its emphasis on organizations, such as businesses, unions, farm organizations, and organized medicine, as the key forces in their areas of interest makes it more of a "plural elites" model. At the same time, it rejects a class-domination theory because (1) no one set of closely knit organizations seems to control all of the specific policy domains and (2) some of the most important policy issues, such as the functioning of the national economy and decisionmaking on national defense, are outside the purview of any of the specific policy domains (Laumann and Knoke 1987).

The most complete empirical demonstration of the theory provides a detailed look at four policy domains (agriculture, energy, health, and labor). It is based on a large number of interviews and questionnaire responses from the individuals and groups that a large research team found to be influential in one of these policy domains. Network analysis methods were then used to examine the connections within and among the four policy domains, including any adversarial relationships. There were two main results.

First, the business organizations within most of the domains, which were represented by government affairs officers from large corporations and high-level representatives of trade associations, were in one camp, but the representatives and employees of liberal and labor organizations were in another. Further, there were no mediating figures or central cliques between the rival camps. The organizational state theorists interpret their finding as a strike against a class-domination theory, but they overlook the fact that a class-domination theory anticipates the division of each domain into pro-business and liberal-labor subgroups due to the importance of class conflict. Put another way, a class-domination theory does not claim that liberals and union leaders are part of the power elite. Nor does it assume that second-level corporate executives and trade association representatives hired by corporate groups, many of whom are former elected officials or government employees, are central figures in the power elite.

Second, the organizational state theorists discovered that there were few or no people in their overarching network (constructed from their information on the four policy domains) that had any connections outside their own policy domain. They interpret this to mean that there is an empty space, a "hollow core," in the space in which a power elite should be found. Instead, there is just a set of separate policy networks, which form a ring around an empty center. However, the problem with this finding as a refutation of class-dominance theory is that their work focuses exclusively on lobbyists that are part of the special-interest process. When their findings are viewed as part of the special-interest process, in which different corporations and business sectors were already known to look out for themselves, their results are the most rigorous research support there is for one aspect of the theory presented in this book.

As for the higher-level integration between the corporate community and government that these theorists think is missing, it is located in the policy-planning network and the activities that go on within it, as demonstrated by the networks' impact on government through many different avenues, as documented in Chapters 4 and 7. This network is the province of corporate CEOs, specialists with graduate training and doctoral degrees from elite universities, and corporate lawyers that practice in New York and Washington. Thus, major policies are not at all within the purview of second-level corporation executives, trade-association lawyers, former government staffers, or former elected officials, all of whom take orders from the CEOs of major banks and corporations. The policy-planning network and the power elite are a very different realm from that of the hired lobbyists that keep their eyes on congressional committees and government agencies.

The closest the organizational state theorists come to the policy-planning process is through several mentions of the Business Roundtable, even noting that its president was involved in two policy domains and was always on the opposite side from organized labor in the social spaces created by their network analysis technique (Heinz, Laumann, Nelson, and Salisbury 1993, pp. 269, 274, 280). However, they overlook the fact that the Business Roundtable's stated goal is to focus on larger and more general issues of concern to the corporate community and that it did exactly that with great success between 1972 and 2012. It did so through its direct involvement in organizing lobbying coalitions, such as the Clean Air Working Group, and taking the lead on the two key trade policies passed by Congress over the objections of the liberal-labor alliance and the majority of the public, NAFTA in 1994 and permanent normal trade relations with China in 2000 (Dreiling 2001; Dreiling and Darves 2011; Gonzalez 2001, Chapter 6). More generally, organizational state theorists do not trace the connections among the CEOs on the Business Roundtable, which would have led them to the network of foundations, think tanks, and policy-discussion groups examined in Chapter 4 and then to the congressional testimony, federal advisory committees, presidential commissions, and cabinet appointments through which members of the policy-planning network impact government, as shown in Chapter 7.

Organizational state theorists have provided the most sophisticated network-based analyses of the groups involved in the special-interest process, showing their patterns of alliance and opposition in great detail. If they were to examine the equally sophisticated network-based work on NAFTA and permanent normal trade relations for China by sociologist Michael Dreiling (2001; 2011), they might find themselves ready to incorporate the groups and networks that shape government on large-scale issues into their theoretical framework. Dreiling's work shows that organizational variables matter, as organizational state theorists would predict, but he also shows that centrality in the corporate and policy-planning networks matter even more.

ELITE THEORY

Elite theorists begin with the idea that all modern societies are dominated by the leaders of large bureaucratically structured organizations, whether corporate, nonprofit, or governmental. The people who hold these top positions (called *elites*) have the money, time, contacts with other organizations, and authority over lower-level employees to shape political and many other outcomes outside their organizations. Although corporations are one important power base according to elite theorists, they do not see the corporate community as predominant over other organizational leaders in the United States, as class-dominance theorists do (Burton and Higley 1987; Dye 2002; Higley and Burton 2006).

Elite theorists, like the other theorists discussed in this chapter, emphasize the organizational basis of power, thereby contributing important insights to the understanding of modern-day power structures. Organizations are indeed the basis of power because their leaders command great resources, have more information than those below them in the hierarchy, and can reward followers and punish critics. They can shape lower-level jobs so that the flexibility and information available to employees is limited. They can make alliances with the leaders of other organizations to strengthen their own positions. At the same time, elite theorists point out that conflicts between organizational elites often arise and have to be carefully managed if the continuing dominance of the general citizenry is to be maintained. They emphasize that in a country such as the United States, dominance by the corporate community is open to challenge by other elite interests and that average citizens sometimes have the ability to set limits on the actions of elites, especially when the elites are in conflict among themselves.

However, elite theory does not fully appreciate the degree to which corporate-based owners and managers dominate other organizational elites in the United States. As shown in Chapters 4 and 5, virtually all nonprofit organizations in the country, with the exception of labor unions and many churches, are funded and directed by the corporate rich. As demonstrated in Chapter 6, most elected officials at the national level are dependent upon the corporate rich for their initial financial support, unless they are part of the liberal-labor alliance. As shown in Chapter 7, members of the corporate community have been overrepresented in the executive branch of the federal government and have control over military elites through civilian control of the Department of Defense. More generally, elite theory puts little or no emphasis on classes and class conflict. It generally characterizes the general population as "masses," not as a congeries of occupational groupings wearing blue, gray, or white collars. Nor do they stress that "the masses" are often parts of religious subcultures as well. Put another way, the many different types of employees that exist in the United States do not lack for independent power bases that make them more than a "mass." What they lack is the unity among themselves to turn their organizational bases into a more coordinated basis for generating power.

The lack of attention to classes and class conflict also leads elite theorists to underestimate the differences between corporate-dominated organizations and unions. The leaders of unions did work with the leaders of corporate-oriented organizations on some issues from the 1940s to the 1960s, once their unions were established, as some elite theorists emphasize, but many of their objectives remained class-based in doing so (Higley and Moore 1981). Moreover, at the same time as the union leaders were working with the corporate leaders on some issues, their institutional, base was under siege from the corporate community, making them a secondary elite at best until the 1980s, when they lost their organizational base and their standing as an elite to be reckoned with.

The most detailed and sustained attempt to apply elite theory to the United States, by political scientist Thomas Dye (1976; 2002), exemplifies the shortcomings of elite theory and makes many questionable empirical claims not shared by other elite theorists. Unlike most modern-day elite theorists, Dye (2002, p. 1) begins with the assertion that in all societies, both "primitive and advanced," only a few people "exercise great power." This is a highly doubtful claim in the case of both hunting and gathering and tribal societies, which more likely have "inverted power structures" through which members of the group in general are able to exercise control through a variety of means. These methods include the banishment or assassination, if necessary, of any shamans, leaders of the hunt, warriors, or dispute adjudicators who try to dominate based on the limited roles they have been accorded by other members of the society (Boehm 1999).

Dye claims that many institutional elites work their way to the top, thereby ignoring research showing that most leaders come from the top one-third of the society at best. As part of his stress on great mobility in all institutional realms, he asserts that a majority of those on the *Forbes* 400 list of the richest Americans are "self-made, single-generation tycoons," which is contradicted by systematic studies of the people on the list in the mid-1990s and 2011 (Collins 1997; Dye 2002, p. 51; Moriarty et al. 2012). And even when those on the *Forbes* 400 list are not inheritors of great wealth, the majority come from higher levels of society or had wealthy relatives or friends who often give them their start.

Although Dye readily adopted the concept of a policy-planning network first developed by class-dominance theorists in the early 1970s, and then provided further evidence for the involvement of corporate leaders in all parts of it, he concludes that it simply brings together business, government, foundation, and media elites "to reach a consensus about policy directions" (Domhoff 1971; Dye 1976, Chapter 9; Dye 2002, p. 202). There is no acknowledgment that the process serves the interests of the corporate rich, who are just another institutional elite in his theory. In the process, he greatly overstates the role of the media elites in "setting the agenda," and adds the questionable assertion that prime-time television, including entertainment shows, is a way of "socializing the masses" (Dye 2002, p. 110).

Dye (2002, p. 184) claims that the ultraconservative efforts to limit the scope of the Environmental Protection Agency, the Food and Drug Administration, and the Occupational Safety and Health Administration (OSHA) after 1980 "largely failed" because of resistance by the national legal community, which does not fit with most assessments of the success of these agencies. For example, one account concluded that OSHA was a "political prisoner" by 1984 (Szasz 1984). One of President George W. Bush's first decisions when he took office in 2001 was to rescind a new OSHA rule, over 10 years in the making, with origins in his father's administration, that would have reduced repetitive stress injuries for those who work long hours at keyboards (Goldstein and Cohen 2004). More generally, his administration allowed OSHA to do very little during his eight years in office (Smith 2008).

The idea of class and class conflict are completely absent from Dye's account. Class is a matter of "ranking along a superiority-inferiority scale," which collapses the distinction between "class" and "status." That said, Dye misunderstands the use of overrepresentation as an indicator of power when he says that only about 30 percent of the institutional elites he studied had upper-class backgrounds. He concludes this is not enough for class domination, overlooking the point that 30 percent is 30 times what would be expected if everyone had an equal likelihood of being part of the institutional elite (Dye 2002, pp. 150–151). A power indicator is not an analysis of how the corporate rich dominate corporations, which involves family offices, holding companies, the use of Delaware as a home base to ensure control through minority stockholdings, and other means explored in Chapters 2 and 3.

The liberal-labor alliance is never discussed as a political force. Liberalism is portrayed as one current within a general elite consensus, as best embodied in the Ford Foundation and other corporate moderate foundations. Union leaders as institutional elites are never mentioned, despite evidence of their participation in some policy-discussion groups and presidential advisory groups, although unions are mentioned as important donors to the Democratic Party. Nor is the corporate-conservative alliance or the conservative coalition in Congress part of his analysis. Due to the absence of the concept of "class conflict" in his theory, whatever dynamism and conflict the country contains is due to the competition among rival institutional elites and personal competition for higher positions within the various institutional sectors.

As this book shows, it is the combination of insights from class theory and organizational theory that explains the strength of the corporate rich in America, not simply the fact that most organizations are controlled by their leaders. The private-enterprise system creates an ownership class that has great economic resources and the potential for political power, but at the same time generates competition among businesses and the rise of new corporations. It also generates ongoing class conflict over wages, profits, work rules, taxes, and government regulation. But the wide range of nonprofit organizations sponsored by the corporate rich gives them the institutional bases from which they can deploy their class resources for ultimately political ends, making it possible for them to compromise on many of their own differences within the policy-planning network and to contain class conflict through their domination of government. It is therefore the interaction of class and organizational imperatives at the top of all American organizations, including government institutions, that leads to class domination in the United States.

To conclude this discussion of the alternative theories, it should be emphasized that none of them is able to account for the strong findings in this book on all three of the power indicators. They cannot explain why the wealth and income distributions would be so highly skewed if the corporate rich are not

disproportionately powerful. Instead, both pluralists and historical institutionalists have rejected such "outcomes" as valid indicators of power, claiming that the
results of policy battles leading to changes in benefit distributions might be unintended consequences (Dahl 1982, p. 17; Hacker and Pierson 2002, pp. 283–285;
Polsby 1980, p. 132). Nor can they explain why men and women from the power
elite would be overrepresented in key government positions and decision-making
groups, which is another power indicator that pluralists and historical institutionalists tend to dismiss, simply by asserting that such people could be acting in
terms of their government roles while in office. Finally, they cannot explain why
the corporate rich have defeated their main opponents—the unions, the environmentalists, and consumer-protection groups—in most of the legislative contests
in which they engaged between 1939 and 2012.

FINDING COMMON GROUND

The general theoretical framework that informs this book has agreements with
each of the four other theories on some basic concepts, even though it disagrees
with many of their specific claims about the United States. Its emphasis on four
major independent bases of power—the economic network, the political network,
the military network, and the ideological network—generates a dynamic and
open-ended view of the future because these networks interact and come into
conflict in constantly changing ways due to newly created organizational forms,
newly invented technologies, new methods of communication, military innovations, and new spiritual movements. Thus, there is an emergent and constantly
changing quality to social organization that makes the present and future very
different from the past, thereby rendering history an unreliable guide for present-
day actions.

In the ancient past, for example, class domination and class conflict were not
at the center of the power equation. State rulers, not property owners, dominated the
empires at the dawn of civilization, and the military had greater power than owners
in the Roman Empire. The Catholic Church was the most powerful force in Europe
for the 1,000 years after the fall of the Roman Empire, when commercial enterprises
were small, the numerous governments were weak, and its inhabitants knew the area
as "Christendom" (Mann 1986). Coincidentally, the weakness of the many small
states allowed the system of private property to take deeper root without the danger
of state appropriation and for an independent merchant class to develop. The result
was a growing independence for the economic network in general.

As commercial enterprises and markets grew, there was more need for state
regulation, and as merchants increased the scope of their trade into far-flung
regions, they needed greater protection against bandits and the petty rulers of
small territories. Merchants thus quietly encouraged the growth of governments,
lending them the money necessary to raise large armies. From the sixteenth century onward, the first genuinely powerful states in history began to play a major

role, developing the capacity to be more independent (Lachmann 2010). Governments and privately owned companies grew powerful together because they needed and aided each other, and in the process they subordinated the Catholic Church and military leaders. Much of Western history from that time forward centered on the struggle for ascendancy between the owners of commercial enterprises and top government leaders.

The continuing changes in the relationships among the four power networks overviewed in the previous two paragraphs put constant strains on seemingly settled power arrangements, thereby creating fissures within national power structures, which is why Iranian revolutions based in a religious movement arise (1979), Soviet Unions with faltering economic systems collapse (1991), Arab Springs in countries with tyrannical governments seemingly appear out of nowhere (2010), and New Deals and civil rights movements occur in the aftermath of Great Depressions and major world wars. They render past methods of challenging power structures obsolete, turning advocates of the old ways into anachronistic futilitarians, while at the same time creating openings for upcoming generations of activists that are alive to the new possibilities because they are rooted in the here and now, not past social movements.

When applied to the United States, the four-network theory explains how and why the economic network has always had ascendancy over the other three. It explains why the federal government was not very large until the 1940s and never very independent of those that dominated and benefited the most from the economic system. It explains what most Americans take for granted and that most social scientists agree upon, that the military has never had a large or independent role in important government decisions and that the churches and other places of worship have been too divided and fractious to be the kind of power base that the Catholic Church once provided in all of Europe and then in several major nation-states, such as Italy and Spain.

If the dominance of the economic network is given its full due, and if the desire of the corporate rich to limit programs that might help government develop more independence and capacity is fully appreciated, then the country's weak union movement and the late arrival of its government social insurance programs, a major concern of research by historical institutionalists, are understandable as outcomes of corporate dominance. This point about corporate dominance includes the conservative coalition's control of Congress on issues having to do with taxes, labor unions, and business regulation.

Similarly, the prominence of the economic network, in conjunction with the somewhat conflicting needs of Northern business interests and Southern planters from the country's founding until the late twentieth century, helps account for the institutional impediments to majority rule that are stressed by pluralists and historical institutionalists as independent causal factors. They include the nature of the Constitution, the decentralized structure of the government, the weakness of the federal bureaucracy, and the strongholds of committee power within Congress. The American federal government lacks "capacity," except as a military establishment that also provides pensions and health insurance for many of its civilian citizens, because the corporate community wants to limit the independence of elected officials and government employees.

The theory underlying this book encompasses the key insights of the other theories without incorporating their weaknesses, and the evidence presented for a high level of class dominance in the United States calls into question many of their empirical claims.

REFERENCES

ADA. 2010. *The ADA 2010 voting record: A year of accomplishment and frustration.* Washington: Americans for Democratic Action.

AFL-CIO. 2012. "Executive paywatch." Washington: www.aflcio.org/Corporate-Watch/CEO-Pay-and-the-99/.

Ahmed, Amel. 2010. "Reading history forward: The origins of electoral systems in European democracies." *Comparative Political Studies* 43:1059–1088.

———. 2013a. *Democracy and the politics of electoral system choice: Engineering electoral dominance.* New York: Cambridge University Press.

———. 2013b. "The existential threat: Varieties of socialism and the origins of electoral systems in early democracies." *Studies in Comparative International Development* 48: In press.

Ahmed, Azam. 2011. "Soros family office names a new chief investment officer." *New York Times,* September 19, dealbook.nytimes.com/2011/09/19/soros-family-office-names-a-new-chief-investment-officer/.

———. 2012. "Family investment funds go hunting for Wall St. expertise." *New York Times,* March 5, p. F4.

Akard, Patrick. 1992. "Corporate mobilization and political power: The transformation of U.S. economic policy in the 1970s." *American Sociological Review* 57:597–615.

Albert, Bruce. 2011. "Former U.S. Rep. Billy Tauzin was paid millions as a lobbyist, records show." *New Orleans Times-Picayune,* December 6, www.nola.com/politics/index.ssf/2011/12/former_us_rep_billy_tauzin_was.html.

Albrecht, Stephen and Michael Locker. 1981. "CDE Stock Ownership Directory No. 5. Fortune 500." New York: Corporate Data Exchange, Inc.

Alexander, Herbert E. 1971. *Financing the election 1968.* Lexington, MA: Heath Lexington Books.

Alford, Robert and Eugene Lee. 1968. "Voting turnout in American cities." *American Political Science Review* 62:796–813.

Allen, Michael Patrick. 1992. "Elite social movement organizations and the state: The rise of the conservative policy-planning network." *Research in Politics and Society* 4: 87–109.

Almond, Gabriel. 1998. *Plutocracy and politics in New York City*. Boulder: Westview Press.

Alpert, Irvine and Ann Markusen. 1980. "Think tanks and capitalist policy." In *Power Structure Research*, ed. G. W. Domhoff, 173–197. Beverly Hills: Sage Publications.

Altemeyer, Bob. 2006. *The authoritarians*. Manitoba, Canada: home.cc.umanitoba .ca/~altemey/.

Altman, Nancy. 2005. *The battle for Social Security: From FDR's vision to Bush's gamble*. New York: John Wiley & Sons.

Alvaredo, Facundo, Tony Atkinson, Thomas Piketty, and Emmanuel Saez. 2012. "The world top incomes database." In *Paris School of Economics*: g-mond.parisschoolofeconomics .eu/topincomes/.

Andrews, Suzanna. 2003. "Shattered dynasty: Legal wrangling between Jay Pritzker's family members over inheritance." *Vanity Fair*, May 1, pp. 80–97.

Appelbaum, Eileen, Rosemary Batt, and Ian Clark. 2012. *Implications of financial capitalism for employment relations research: Evidence from breach of trust and implicit contracts in private equity buyouts*. Washington: Center for Economic and Policy Research.

Armstrong, Christopher. 1974. "Privilege and productivity: The cases of two private schools and their graduates." Ph.D. Thesis, Sociology, University of Pennsylvania, Philadelphia.

Baer, Kenneth. 2000. *Reinventing Democrats: The politics of liberalism from Reagan to Clinton*. Lawrence: University of Kansas Press.

Bagdikian, Ben H. 2004. *The new media monopoly*. Boston: Beacon Press.

Bailey, Stephen K. 1950. *Congress makes a law: The story behind the Employment Act of 1946*. New York: Columbia University Press.

Baker, Dean. 2007. *The United States since 1980*. New York: Cambridge University Press.

———. 2009. *Plunder and blunder: The rise and fall of the bubble economy*. Sausalito, CA: PoliPoint Press.

———. 2011. *The end of loser liberalism: Making markets progressive*. Washington: Center for Economic and Policy Research.

Baltzell, E. Digby. 1958. *Philadelphia gentlemen: The making of a national upper class*. New York: Free Press.

———. 1964. *The Protestant establishment: Aristocracy and caste in America*. New York: Random House.

Balz, Dan and Jon Cohen. 2008. "The bad economy helps Obama." *Washington Post National Weekly*, September 29–October 5, pp. 13–14.

Barker, Lucius and Ronald W. Walters. 1989. "Jesse Jackson's 1984 presidential campaign: Challenge and change in American politics." Urbana: University of Illinois Press.

Barnes, Roy C. and Emily R. Ritter. 2001. "Networks of corporate interlocking: 1962–1995." *Critical Sociology* 27:192–220.

Barnes, Roy C. and Emily Sweezea. 2006. "Bohemians and beyond: Social clubs and the corporate elite." In *Meetings of the Southern Sociological Society*. New Orleans.

Barrow, Clyde W. 1990. *Universities and the capitalist state: Corporate liberalism and the reconstruction of American higher education, 1894–1928*. Madison: University of Wisconsin Press.

Barshay, Jill and Kathryn Wolfe. 2004. "Special interests strike gold in richly targeted tax bill." *CQ Weekly*, October 16, p. 2434.

Barton, Benjamin. 2012. "An empirical study of Supreme Court justice pre-appointment experience." In *Legal studies research paper series: Research paper #181*, vol. ssrn.com/abstract=2010781. Knoxville: University of Tennessee, Knoxville College of Law.

Baum, Lawrence. 1998. *The Supreme Court*. Washington: CQ Press.

Beckel, Michael. 2012. "Nonprofits outspent super PACs in 2010." In *OpenSecrets.org*: www.opensecrets.org/news/2012/06/nonprofits-outspent-super-pacs-in-2.html.

Becker, Jo and Christopher Drew. 2008. "The long run: Pragmatic politics forged on the South Side." *New York Times*, May 11, p. A1.

Bellant, Russ. 1991. *The Coors connection: How Coors family philanthropy undermines democratic pluralism*. Boston: South End Press.

Belz, Herman. 1991. *Equality transformed*. New Brunswick: Transaction Books.

Benoit, Denise. 2007. *The best-kept secret: Women corporate lobbyists, policy, & power in the United States*. New Brunswick: Rutgers University Press.

Bergthold, Linda. 1990. *Purchasing power in health: Business, the state, and health care politics*. New Brunswick: Rutgers University Press.

Bernstein, Aaron. 2000. "Too much corporate power?" *Business Week*, September 11, pp. 145–149.

Bernstein, Irving. 1969. *Turbulent years: A history of the American worker, 1933–1941*. Boston: Houghton Mifflin.

Berry, Jeffrey M. 1999. *The new liberalism: The rising power of citizen groups*. Washington: The Brookings Institution.

Bloom, Jack M. 1987. *Class, race, and the civil rights movement*. Bloomington: Indiana University Press.

BLS. 2012. "Union membership 2011 USDL-12-0094: Bureau of Labor Statistics." Washington: Department of Labor.

Bluestone, Barry and Bennett Harrison. 1982. *The deindustrialization of America: Plant closings, community abandonment, and the dismantling of basic industry*. New York: Basic Books.

Boehm, Christopher. 1999. *Hierarchy in the forest: The evolution of egalitarian behavior*. Cambridge: Harvard University Press.

Bonacich, Phillip and G. William Domhoff. 1981. "Latent classes and group membership." *Social Networks* 3:175–196.

BondGraham, Darwin. 2011. "Building the new New Orleans: Foundation and NGO power." *The Review of Black Political Economy* 38:279–309.

Bourdieu, Pierre. 1986. "Forms of capital." pp. 241–258 in *Handbook of theory and research for the sociology of education*, edited by J. G. Richardson. Westport, CT: Greenwood Press.

Boyle, Kevin. 1995. *The UAW and the heyday of American liberalism*. Ithaca: Cornell University Press.

———. 1998. "Little more than ashes: The UAW and American reform in the 1960s." pp. 217–238 in *Organized labor and American politics 1894–1994: The labor-liberal alliance*, edited by K. Boyle. Albany: State University of New York Press.

Breiger, Ronald L. 1974. "The duality of persons and groups." *Social Forces* 53:181–190.

Broad, David. 1996. "The Social Register: Directory of America's upper class." *Sociological Spectrum* 16:173–181.

Brown, Michael K. 1999. *Race, money and the American welfare state*. Ithaca: Cornell University Press.

Browne, William, Jerry Skees, Louis Swanson, Paul Thompson, and Lauren Unnevehr. 1992. *Sacred cows and hot potatoes*. Boulder: Westview Press.

Browning, Lynnley. 2004. "Foreign tax havens costly to U.S., study says." *New York Times*, September 27, p. C2.

Brownlee, W. Elliot. 2000. "Historical perspective on U.S. tax policy toward the rich." pp. 29–73 in *Does Atlas shrug? The economic consequences of taxing the rich*, edited by J. Slemrod. Cambridge: Harvard University Press.

———. 2004. *Federal taxation in America: A short history*. New York: Cambridge University Press.

Bruck, Connie. 1988. *The predators' ball: The junk-bond raiders and the man who staked them*. New York: Simon & Schuster.

Bumiller, Elizabeth. 2008. "Research groups boom in Washington." *New York Times*, January 30, p. A12.

Bunting, David. 1983. "Origins of the American corporate network." *Social Science History* 7:129–142.

———. 1987. *The rise of large American corporations, 1889–1919*. New York: Garland.

Burch, Philip. 1972. *The managerial revolution reassessed: Family control in America's large corporations*. Lexington, MA: Lexington Books.

———. 1980. *Elites in American History: The New Deal to the Carter administration*, Vol. 3. New York: Holmes & Meier.

Burris, Val. 1992. "Elite policy-planning networks in the United States." *Research in Politics and Society* 4:111–134.

———. 2005. "Interlocking directorates and political cohesion among corporate elites." *American Journal of Sociology* 111: 249–283.

———. 2008. "The interlock structure of the policy-planning network and the right turn in U.S. state policy." *Research in Political Sociology* 17:3–42.

Burton, Michael and John Higley. 1987. "Invitation to elite theory: The basic contentions reconsidered." pp. 219–238 in *Power elites and organizations*, edited by G. W. Domhoff and T. Dye. Beverly Hills: Sage.

Campaign Finance Institute. 2012. "Independent spending wars fought to a standstill in 2012." In *Campaign Finance Institute:* www.cfinst.org/.

Campaign Finance Institute. 2013. "Money vs. Money-Plus: Post-Election Reports Reveal Two Different Campaign Strategies." Washingon: Campaign Finance Institute.

Carmines, Edward G. and James A. Stimson. 1989. *Issue evolution: Race and the transformation of American politics*. Princeton: Princeton University Press.

Carnes, Nicholas. 2012. "Does the numerical underrepresentation of the working class in Congress matter?" *Legislative Studies Quarterly* 37:5–35.

Carney, Francis. 1958. *The rise of the Democratic clubs in California*. New York: Holt.

Carnoy, Martin and Derek Shearer. 1980. *Economic democracy: The challenge of the 1980s*. White Plains, NY: M. E. Sharpe.

Carp, Robert and Ronald Stidham. 1998. *Judicial process in America*. Washington: CQ Press.

Carson, Rachel. 1962. *Silent spring*. Boston: Houghton Mifflin.

Carter, Dan. 1996. *From George Wallace to Newt Gingrich: Race in the conservative counter-revolution, 1963–1994*. Baton Rouge: Louisiana State University Press.

———. 2000. *The politics of rage: George Wallace, the origins of the new conservatism, and the transformation of American politics*. Baton Rouge: Louisiana State University Press.

Cartwright, Dorwin and Alvin Frederick Zander. 1968. "Group dynamics: Research and theory." New York: Harper and Row.

CED. 1968. *Financing a better election system*. New York: Committee for Economic Development.

———. 1970a. *Improving the welfare system*. New York: Committee for Economic Development.

———. 1970b. *Training and jobs for the urban poor*. New York: Committee for Economic Development.

———. 1973. *Building a national health-care system: A statement on national policy*. New York: Committee for Economic Development.

CEE. 2009. "Campaign for economic literacy." In *Council for Economic Education*. New York: www.councilforeconed.org/.

Celsi, Teresa. 1992. *Jesse Jackson and political power*. Brookfield, CT: Millbrook Press.

Chemerinsky, Erwin. 2010. *The conservative assault on the constitution*. New York: Simon & Schuster.

Chen, Jennifer, Dennis Patten, and Robin Roberts. 2008. "Corporate charitable contributions: A corporate social performance or legitimacy strategy?" *Journal of Business Ethics* 82:131–144.

Choma, Russ. 2012. "Unions gave Democratic super PACs last-minute burst of cash." *OpenSecrets.org: Center for Responsive Politics*. Washington: www.opensecrets.org.

Clausen, Aage R. 1973. *How congressmen decide: A policy focus*. New York: St. Martin's Press.

Clavel, Pierre. 2010. *Activists in city hall: The progressive response to the Reagan era in Boston and Chicago*. Ithaca: Cornell University Press.

Clawson, Dan, Alan Neustadtl, and Denise Scott. 1992. *Money talks: Corporate PACS and political influence*. New York: Basic Books.

Clawson, Dan, Alan Neustadtl, and Mark Weller. 1998. *Dollars and votes: How business campaign contributions subvert democracy*. Philadelphia: Temple University Press.

Cline, Seth. 2011. "Ruth Bader Ginsburg, Steven Breyer wealthiest judges on U.S. Supreme Court." In *Center for Responsive Politics*. Washington: www.opensecrets.org/.

CMD. 2012a. "Nick Nichols." In *Center for Media and Democracy*. Madison: www.sourcewatch.org/.

———. 2012b. "The National Federation for Independent Business: A front group for big business." In *Center for Media and Democracy*. Madison: www.sourcewatch.org/.

Coleman, Richard Patrick, Lee Rainwater, and Kent A. McClelland. 1978. *Social standing in America: New dimensions of class*. New York: Basic Books.

Collins, Chuck. 1997. *Born on third base: The sources of wealth of the 1996 Forbes 400*. Boston: United for a Fair Economy.

Coltrane, Scott. 2001. "Marketing the marriage 'solution': Misplaced simplicity in the politics of fatherhood." *Sociological Perspectives* 44:387–418.

Colwell, Mary Anna. 1980. "The foundation connection: Links among foundations and recipient organizations." pp. 413–452 in *Philanthropy and cultural imperialism: The foundations at home and abroad*, edited by R. F. Arnove. Boston: G. K. Hall.

———. 1993. *Private foundations and public policy: The political role of philanthropy*. New York: Garland.

Confessore, Nicholas and Jess Bidgood. 2012. "Little to show for cash flood by big donors." *New York Times*, November 8, p. A1.

Cookson, Peter W. and Caroline Hodges Persell. 1985. *Preparing for power: America's elite boarding schools*. New York: Basic Books.

CQ. 1996. "Will the rise of 'blue dogs' revive the partisan right?" *Congressional Quarterly*, December 21, pp. 3436–3438.

CTJ. 2012a. "Big no-tax corps just keep on dodging." In *Citizens for Tax Justice*. Washington: www.ctj.org/.

———. 2012b. "Which Fortune 500 companies are sheletering income in overseas tax havens?" In *Citizens for Tax Justice*. Washington: www.ctj.org/.

Cunningham, David. 2004. *There's something happening here: The New Left, the Klan, and FBI counterintelligence*. Berkeley: University of California Press.

Daalder, Ivo and James Lindsay. 2003. *America unbound*. Washington: The Brookings Institution.

Dahl, Robert A. 1982. *Dilemmas of pluralist democracy*. New Haven: Yale University Press.

———. 1961. *Who governs? Democracy and power in an American city*. New Haven: Yale University Press.

Dalzell, Robert F. 1987. *Enterprising elite: The Boston Associates and the world they made*. Cambridge: Harvard University Press.

Daniels, Arlene Kaplan. 1988. *Invisible careers: Women civic leaders from the volunteer world*. Chicago: University of Chicago Press.

Davidson, Chandler, Tanya Dunlap, Gale Kenny, and Benjamin Wise. 2004. "Republican ballot security programs: Vote protection or minority vote suppression—or both?" Washington: Center for Voting Rights and Protection.

Davies, James B., Anthony Shorrocks, Susanna Sandstrom, and Edward Wolff. 2008. "The world distribution of household wealth." The World Institute for Development Economics Research, Helsinki.

Davis, Allison, Burleigh Gardner, and Mary Gardner. 1941. *Deep South*. Chicago: University of Chicago Press.

Davis, Gerald F., Mina Yoo, and Wayne Baker. 2002. "The small world of the American corporate elite, 1982–2001." *Strategic Organization* 1:301–326.

Davis, James K. 1992. *Spying on America: The FBI's domestic counterintelligence program*. New York: Praeger.

Defense News. 2012. "Defense News top 100 for 2011." in *Defense News: Digital edition*. Springfield, VA: special.defensenews.com/top-100/charts/rank_2011.php.

deFigueiredo, John and James M. Snyder. 2003. "Why is there so little money in U.S. politics?" *Journal of Economic Perspectives* 17:105–130.

Delli Carpini, Michael X. and Scott Keeter. 1996. *What Americans know about politics and why it matters*. New Haven: Yale University Press.

Dellinger, David. 1993. *From Yale to jail: The life story of a moral dissenter*. New York: Pantheon Books.

Delton, Jennifer. 2009. *Racial integration in corporate America, 1940–1990*. New York: Cambridge University Press.

DeParle, Jason. 2012. "Welfare limits left poor adrift as recession hit." *New York Times*, April 8, p. A1.

Deutsch, Claudia. 2003. "The revolution that wasn't: 10 years later, corporate oversight is still dismal." *New York Times*, January 26, p. C1.

DiTomaso, Nancy. 1980. "Organizational analysis and power structure research." pp. 255-268 in *Power Structure Research*, edited by G. W. Domhoff. Beverly Hills: Sage.

DOL. 2007. "Family and Medical Leave Act regulations: A report on the Department of Labor's request for information." *Department of Labor, Employment Standards Administration, Wage and Hour Division, Federal Register* 72.

Dolan, Scott V. 2011. "Business as usual: The nonprofit sector in the U.S. national elite network." Ph.D. Thesis, Sociology, University of Albany, Albany, New York.

Dolan, Scott V. and Gwen Moore. 2013. "Elite interlocks between the corporate community, nonprofits, and federal advisory committees." *Meetings of the American Sociological Association.* New York.

Dolny, Michael. 2012. "Think tank spectrum revisited: Conservatives gain within still-narrow spectrum." In *FAIR: Fairness and Accuracy in Reporting:* www.fair.org/.

Domhoff, G. William. 1967. *Who rules America?* Englewood Cliffs, NJ: Prentice-Hall.

———. 1970. *The higher circles.* New York: Random House.

———. 1971. "How the power elite set national goals." pp. 210–219 in *The triple revolution emerging,* edited by R. Perucci and M. Pilisuk. Boston: Little, Brown.

———. 1975. "Social clubs, policy-planning groups, and corporations: A network study of ruling-class cohesiveness." *The Insurgent Sociologist* 5:173–184.

———. 1983. *Who rules America now?* New York: Simon & Schuster.

———. 1987. "Where do government experts come from? The CEA and the policy-planning network." pp. 189–200 in *Power elites and organizations,* edited by G. W. Domhoff and T. Dye. Beverly Hills: Sage.

———. 1990. *The power elite and the state: How policy is made in America.* Hawthorne, NY: Aldine de Gruyter.

———. 1996. *State autonomy or class dominance? Case studies on policy making in America.* Hawthorne, NY: Aldine de Gruyter.

———. 1998. *Who rules America? Power and politics in the year 2000.* Mountain View, CA: Mayfield Publishing.

———. 2005a. "San Francisco is different: Progressive activists and neighborhoods have had a big impact." www.whorulesamerica.net.

———. 2005b. "Who really ruled in Dahl's New Haven?" www.whorulesamerica.net.

———. 2006. *Who rules America? Power, politics, and social change.* New York: McGraw-Hill.

———. 2013. *The myth of liberal ascendancy: Corporate dominance from the Great Depression to the Great Recession.* Boulder: Paradigm Publishers.

Domhoff, G. William and Michael J. Webber. 2011. *Class and power in the New Deal: Corporate moderates, Southern Democrats, and the liberal-labor coalition.* Palo Alto: Stanford University Press.

Dowie, Mark. 1995. *Losing ground: American environmentalism at the close of the twentieth century.* Cambridge: MIT Press.

Draper, Robert. 2012. "The price of power." *New York Times Magazine,* July 8, pp. 20–25, 38.

Dreier, Peter, John Mollenkopf, and Todd Swanstrom. 2004. *Place matters: Metropolitics for the twenty-first century.* Lawrence: University Press of Kansas.

Dreiling, Michael. 2001. *Solidarity and contention: The politics of class and sustainability in the NAFTA conflict.* New York: Garland Press.

Dreiling, Michael and Derek Darves. 2011. "Corporate unity in American trade policy: A network analysis of corporate-dyad political action." *American Journal of Sociology* 116:1514–1563.

Driscoll, Dawn-Marie and Carol R. Goldberg. 1993. *Members of the club: The coming of age of executive women.* New York: Free Press.

Duhigg, Charles and David Kocieniewski. 2012. "How Apple sidesteps billions in taxes." *New York Times,* April 29, p. A1.

Dunn, Marvin. 1980. "The family office: Coordinating mechanism of the ruling class." pp. 17–45 in *Power structure research,* edited by G. W. Domhoff. Beverly Hills: Sage.

Dye, Thomas R. 1976. *Who's running America?* Englewood Cliffs, NJ: Prentice-Hall.

———. 1986. *Who's running America? The conservative years.* Englewood Cliffs, NJ: Prentice-Hall.

———. 2002. *Who's running America? The Bush restoration.* Upper Saddle River, NJ: Prentice Hall.

Dyreng, Scott, Bradley Lindsey, and Jacob Thornock. 2011. "Exploring the role Delaware plays as a domestic tax haven." *Social Science Research Network*: ssrn.com/abstract=1737937 or dx.doi.org/10.2139/ssrn.1737937.

Edison Research. 2012. "Edison Research 2012 exit polls." In *FoxNews Online*: www.foxnews.com/politics/elections/2012-exit-poll?intcmp=related.

Edsall, Thomas B. 2006. *Building red America: The new conservative coalition and the drive for permanent power.* New York: Basic Books.

Edsall, Thomas B. and Mary D. Edsall. 1992. *Chain reaction: The impact of race, rights, and taxes on American politics.* New York: Norton.

Ehrenhalt, Alan. 1991. *The United States of ambition: Politicians, power, and the pursuit of office.* New York: Times Books.

Eliasoph, N. 1998. *Avoiding politics: How Americans produce apathy in everyday life.* New York: Cambridge University Press.

Environmental Working Group. 2012. "Farm subsidy database 2012." In *Environmental Working Group.* Washington: farm.ewg.org.

Erikson, Robert and Kent Tedin. 2011. *American public opinion.* New York: Pearson Education.

Ermann, M. David. 1978. "The operative goals of corporate philanthropy: Contributions to the Public Broadcasting Service, 1972–1976." *Social Problems* 25:504–514.

Ernst, Morris Leopold. 1973. *The great reversals: Tales of the Supreme Court.* New York: Weybright and Talley.

Eulau, Heinz and John D. Sprague. 1984. *Lawyers in politics: A study in professional convergence.* Westport, CT: Greenwood Press.

Ewen, Stuart. 1996. *PR!: A social history of spin.* New York: Basic Books.

FEX. 2012. "About the Funding Exchange." In *The Funding Exchange*: www.fex.org/about.

Fine, Sidney. 1969. "Sit-down: The General Motors strike of 1936–1937." Ann Arbor: University of Michigan Press.

Finegold, Kenneth and Theda Skocpol. 1995. *State and party in America's New Deal.* Madison: University of Wisconsin Press.

Flacks, Richard. 1988. *Making history: The radical tradition in American life.* New York: Columbia University Press.

Food & Water Watch. 2012. *The economic costs of food monopolies.* Washington: Food & Water Watch.

Forbes. 2011. "America's largest private companies." In *Forbes Magazine Online*: www.forbes.com/lists/2011/21/private-companies-11_land.html.

Forbes, Keith. 2012. "Bermuda's many insurance advantages: Offshore policies can have major benefits to clients and beneficiaries." In *Welcome to Bermuda*: www.bermuda-online.org/insuranceadvantages.htm.

Foster, John Bellamy and Hannah Holleman. 2010. "The financial power elite." *Monthly Review*, May, pp. 1–19.

Frederick, William. 1981. "Free market vs. social responsibility: Decision time at the CED." *California Management Review* 23:20–28.

Gallup. 2011. "Americans decry power of lobbyists, corporations, banks, Feds." In *Gallup Politics*: www.gallup.com/poll/147026/americans-decry-power-lobbyists-corporations-banks-feds.aspx.

Gamson, William A. 1992. *Talking politics*. New York: Cambridge University Press.

Gans, Herbert. 1985. "Are U.S. journalists dangerously liberal?" *Columbia Journalism Review*, November–December, pp. 29–33.

Gendron, Richard and G. William Domhoff. 2009. *The leftmost city: Power and progressive politics in Santa Cruz*. Boulder: Westview Press.

Ghiloni, Beth Wesley. 1987. "The velvet ghetto: Women, power, and the corporation." pp. 21–36 in *Power Elites and Organizations*, edited by G. W. Domhoff and T. Dye. Beverly Hills: Sage.

Gilens, Martin. 2012. *Affluence and influence: Economic inequality and political power in America*. Princeton: Princeton University Press.

Goertzel, Ted. 1985. "Militarism as a sociological problem." *Research in Political Sociology* 1:119–139.

Gold, Howard J. 1992. *Hollow mandates: American public opinion and the conservative shift*. Boulder: Westview Press.

Goldstein, Amy and Sarah Cohen. 2004. "The rules that apply: Under the Bush administration, OSHA is friendly with business." *Washington Post National Weekly*, August 23–29, pp. 6–9.

Goldstein, Kenneth M. 1999. *Interest groups, lobbying, and participation in America*. New York: Cambridge University Press.

Golland, David. 2011. *Constructing affirmative action: The struggle for equal employment opportunity*. Lexington: University Press of Kentucky.

Gonzalez, George. 2001. *Corporate power and the environment: The political economy of U.S. environmental policy*. Lanham, MD: Rowman & Littlefield.

———. 2005. *The politics of air pollution*. Albany: State University of New York Press.

Goodstein, Eban. 1999. *The trade-off myth: Fact and fiction about jobs and the environment*. Washington: Island Press.

Gordon, Michael. 1969. "Changing patterns of upper-class prep school college placements." *Pacific Sociological Review* 12:23–26.

Gordon, Stacy. 2005. *Campaign contributions and legislative voting behavior: A new approach*. New York: Routledge.

Grabois, Andrew. 2012. *National directory of corporate giving*. New York: The Foundation Center.

Granfield, Robert. 1992. *Making elite lawyers: Visions of law at Harvard and beyond*. New York: Routledge.

Greenberg, Daniel. 2007. *The perils, rewards, and delusions of campus capitalism*. Chicago: University of Chicago Press.

Greenhouse, Steven. 2008. "Unions look for new life in world of Obama." *New York Times*, December 28, p. A1.

———. 2009. "Bill easing unionization under heavy attack." *New York Times*, January 9, p. A14.

Greider, William. 1989. *Secrets of the temple: How the Federal Reserve runs the country*. New York: Simon & Schuster.

Griswold, Eliza. 2012. "The wild life of 'Silent Spring'." *New York Times Magazine*, September 21, pp. 36–41.

Gross, James A. 1981. *The reshaping of the National Labor Relations Board*. Albany: State University of New York Press.

———. 1995. *Broken promise: The subversion of U.S. labor relations policy*. Philadelphia: Temple University Press.

Guttsman, W. L. 1969. *The English ruling class*. London: Weidenfeld & Nicholson.

Hacker, Andrew. 1961. "The elected and the anointed: Two American elites." *American Political Science Review* 55:539–549.

Hacker, Jacob and Nate Loewentheil. 2012. "Prosperity economics: Building an economy for all." In *Creative Commons*. Washington: Economic Policy Institute and the AFL-CIO.

Hacker, Jacob and Paul Pierson. 2002. "Business power and social policy: Employers and the formation of the American welfare state." *Politics & Society* 30:277–325.

———. 2004. "Varieties of capitalist interests and capitalist power: A response to Swenson." *Studies in American Political Development* 18:186–195.

———. 2010. *Winner-take-all politics: How Washington made the rich richer—and turned its back on the middle class*. New York: Simon & Schustser.

Hamilton, Richard. 1975. *Restraining myths: Critical studies of U.S. social structure and politics*. New York: Sage Publications.

———. 1991. *The bourgeois epoch: Marx and Engels on Britain, France, and Germany*. Chapel Hill: University of North Carolina Press.

Hammond, Paul. 1961. *Organizing for defense*. Princeton: Princeton University Press.

Hartz, Louis. 1955. *The liberal tradition in America: An interpretation of American political thought since the Revolution*. New York: Harcourt, Brace.

Hasen, Richard. 2012. *The voting wars: From Florida 2000 to the next election meltdown*. New Haven: Yale University Press.

Hawthorne, Fran. 2008. "The family office, granting every wish." *New York Times*, March 18, p. H2.

Heard, Alexander. 1960. *The costs of democracy*. Chapel Hill: University of North Carolina Press.

Heinz, John P., Edward O. Laumann, Robert L. Nelson, and Robert H. Salisbury. 1993. *The hollow core: Private interests in national policy making*. Cambridge: Harvard University Press.

Herman, Edward S. 1975. *Conflicts of interest: Commercial bank trust departments*. New York: Twentieth Century Fund.

———. 1981. *Corporate control, corporate power*. New York: Cambridge University Press.

Hewitt, Christopher. 1977. "The effect of political democracy and social democracy on equality in industrial societies: A cross-national comparison." *American Sociological Review* 42:450–464.

Higley, John and Michael Burton. 2006. *Elite foundations of liberal democracy*. Lanham, MD: Rowman & Littlefield.

Higley, John and Gwen Moore. 1981. "Elite integration in the U.S. and Australia." *American Political Science Review* 75:581–597.

Himmelstein, Jerome L. 1997. *Looking good and doing good: Corporate philanthropy and corporate power*. Bloomington: Indiana University Press.

Hirsch, Glenn K. 1975. "Only you can prevent ideological hegemony: The Advertising Council and its place in the American power structure." *The Insurgent Sociologist* 5:64–82.

Hoffman, Paul. 1973. *Lions in the street*. New York: Saturday Review Press.

Hofstadter, Richard. 1969. *The idea of a party system: The rise of legitimate opposition in the United States, 1780–1840*. Berkeley: University of California Press.

Hogg, Michael. 1992. *The social psychology of group cohesiveness*. New York: New York University Press.

Hollingshead, August and Fredrick C. Redlich. 1958. *Social class and mental illness: A community study*. New York: Wiley.

Hoppe, Robert. 2012. *Structure and finances of U.S. farms: Family farm report, 2012 edition.* Washington: Economic Research Division, U.S Department of Agriculture.

Horowitz, Juliana. 2008. "Winds of political change haven't shifted public's ideology balance." Philadelphia: Pew Research Center for the People and the Press.

Horrock, Nicholas. 1976. "Reagan resists financial disclosure." *New York Times,* August 13, p. A10.

Huntington, Samuel. 1961. *The common defense.* New York: Columbia University Press.

IFA. 2012. "Franchise businesses continue to outperform economy." In *International Franchise Association.* Washington: www.franchise.org/Franchise-News-Detail.aspx?id=58317.

Iyengar, Shanto and Adam F. Simon. 2000. "New perspectives and evidence on political communication and campaign effects." *Annual Review of Psychology* 149.

Jacobs, Lawrence and Benjamin Page. 2005. "Who influences U.S. foreign policy?" *American Political Science Review* 99:107–123.

Jacobs, Lawrence and Robert Shapiro. 2000. *Politicians don't pander.* Chicago: University of Chicago Press.

James, Harvey, Mary Hendrickson, and Philip Howard. 2013. "Networks, power and dependency in the agrifood industry." In *The ethics and economics of agrifood competition,* edited by H. James. New York: Springer Press.

Johnson, Stephen. 1976. "How the West was won: Last shootout for the Yankee-Cowboy theory." *Insurgent Sociologist* 6:61–93.

Johnston, David Cay. 2000. "Study finds that many large corporations pay no taxes." *New York Times,* October 29, p. C2.

———. 2003. *Perfectly legal: The covert campaign to rig our tax system to benefit the super rich—and cheat everybody else.* New York: Portfolio.

———. 2007. *Free lunch: How the wealthiest Americans enrich themselves at government expense (and stick you with the bill).* New York: Portfolio.

Johnston, David Cay and Joseph Treaster. 2007. "Insurers want U.S. to curb competitors' fund transfers to Bermuda." *New York Times,* September 26, p. B1.

Jones, Alice. 1980. *Wealth of a nation to be: The American colonies on the eve of the revolution.* New York: Columbia University Press.

Jost, John T. and David Amodio. 2012. "Political ideology as motivated social cognition: Behavioral and neuroscientific evidence." *Motivation and Emotion* 36:55–64.

Jost, John T., Vagelis Chaikalis-Petritsis, Dominic Abrams, Jim Sidanius, and Jojanneke van der Toorn. 2012. "Why men (and women) do and don't rebel: Effects of system justification on willingness to protest." *Personality and Social Psychology Bulletin* 38:197–208.

Jost, John T. and Brenda Major. 2001. *The psychology of legitimacy: Emerging perspectives on ideology, justice, and intergroup relations.* New York: Cambridge University Press.

Kahn, Jonathan. 1997. *Budgeting democracy: State building and citizenship in America, 1890–1928.* Ithaca: Cornell University Press.

Kanter, Rosabeth Moss. 1993. *Men and women of the corporation.* New York: Basic Books.

Kaplan, Esther. 2009. "Can American labor revive the American dream?" *The Nation,* January 26, pp. 10–14.

Kazee, Nicole, Michael Lipsky, and Cathie Jo Martin. 2008. "Outside the big box: Who speaks for small business, July/August?" In *Boston Review:* www.bostonreview.net/BR33.4/kazee.php.

Kendall, Diana. 2002. *The power of good deeds: Privileged women and the social reproduction of class*. Lanham, MD: Rowman & Littlefield.

———. 2008. *Members only: Elite clubs and the process of exclusion*. Lanham, MD: Rowman & Littlefield.

Kerbo, Harold R. 2006. *Social stratification and inequality: Class conflict in historical, comparative, and global perspective*. New York: McGraw-Hill.

Key, V. O. 1949. *Southern politics in state and nation*. New York: Random House.

Keyssar, Alexander. 2009. *The right to vote: The contested history of democracy in the United States*. New York: Basic Books.

Khan, Shamus. 2010. *Privilege: The making of an adolescent elite at St. Paul's School*. New York: Basic Books.

Kimeldorf, Howard. 2013. "Worker replacement costs and unionization: Origins of the American labor movement." Ann Arbor: Department of Sociology, University of Michigan.

Klinenberg, Eric. 2007. *Fighting for air: The battle to control America's media*. New York: Metropolitan Books.

Konigsberg, Eric. 2008. "Advising, and calming, the worried super rich." *New York Times*, October 25, p. A17.

Kopczuk, Wojciech and Emmanuel Saez. 2004. "Top wealth shares in the United States, 1916–2000: Evidence from estate tax returns." *Tax Journal* 47:445–487.

Kousser, J. Morgan. 1974. *The shaping of Southern politics: Suffrage restriction and the establishment of the one-party South, 1880–1910*. New Haven: Yale University Press.

Krugman, Paul. 2012. *End this depression now!* New York: W. W. Norton.

Kubey, Craig. 1973. "Notes on a meeting of the Business Council." *Insurgent Sociologist* 3:48-55.

Kuo, David. 2006. *Tempting faith: An inside story of political seduction*. New York: Simon & Schuster.

Labaton, Stephen. 2000. "Congress severly curtails plan for low-power FM stations." *New York Times*, December 19, p. A1.

Lachmann, Richard. 2000. *Capitalists in spite of themselves: Elite conflict and economic transformation in early modern Europe*. New York: Oxford University Press.

———. 2010. *States and power*. Malden, MA: Polity Press.

Lakoff, George. 1996. *Moral politics: What conservatives know that liberals don't*. Chicago: University of Chicago Press.

Lane, Robert Edwards. 1962. *Political ideology: Why the American common man believes what he does*. New York: Free Press of Glencoe.

Laneri, Raquel 2010. "America's best prep schools." *Forbes*, April, www.forbes.com/2010/04/29/best-prep-schools-2010-opinions-private-education.html.

Laumann, Edward and David Knoke. 1987. *The Organizational State*. Madison: University of Wisconsin Press.

Lazarsfeld, Paul. 1966. "Concept formation and measurement." pp. 144–202 in *Concepts, Theory, and Explanation in the Behavioral Sciences*, edited by G. DiRenzo. New York: Random House.

Lichtblau, Eric. 2012. "Chamber competes to be heard in the fiscal debate." *New York Times*, November 30, p. B1.

Lindblom, Charles. 1977. *Politics and markets: The world's political economic systems*. New York: Basic Books.

Lippert, John and Holly Rosenkrantz. 2009. "Billionaire donors split with Obama on law that may hurt hotels." in *Bloomberg.com*: www.bloomberg.com/apps/news?sid=a6A3G.MZZqIw&pid=newsarchive.

Lipset, Seymour. 1963. *The first new nation: The United States in historical and comparative perspective*. New York: Basic Books.

Lipset, Seymour and Gary Marks. 2000. *It didn't happen here: Why socialism failed in the United States*. New York: W. W. Norton.

Livingston, James. 1986. *Origins of the Federal Reserve system: Money, class, and corporate capitalism, 1890–1913*. Ithaca, NY: Cornell University Press.

Lizza, Ryan. 2008. "Making it: How Chicago shaped Obama." *The New Yorker*, July 21, pp. 49–65.

————. 2012. "The Obama memos." *The New Yorker*, January 30, pp. 36–49.

Lobao, Linda. 2013. "Corporate farms." In *Encyclopedia of Food and Agricultural Ethics*, edited by P. Thompson and D. Kaplan. New York: Springer.

Lobao, Linda and Katherine Meyer. 2001. "The great agricultural transition." *Annual Review of Sociology* 27:103–124.

Logan, John and Harvey Molotch. 2007. *Urban fortunes: The political economy of place*. Berkeley: University of California Press.

Lovejoy, Allen F. 1941. *La Follette and the establishment of the direct primary in Wisconsin, 1890–1904*. New Haven: Yale University Press.

Luger, Stan. 2000. *Corporate power, American democracy, and the automobile industry*. New York: Cambridge University Press.

Luo, Michael. 2008a. "In banking, top Obama aide made money and connections." *New York Times*, December 4, p. A1.

————. 2008b. "Study: Many Obama small donors really weren't." *New York Times*, November 24, p. A12.

Luo, Michael and Karen Cullotta. 2008. "Even workers surprised by success of factory sit-in." *New York Times*, December 13, p. A9.

Luo, Michael and Sarah Wheaton. 2008. "List of McCain fundraisers includes prominent lobbyists." *New York Times*, April 21, p. A17.

Lupia, Arthur. 2010. "Did Bush voters cause Obama's victory?" *PS* 43:1–3.

MacDonald, James and Penni Korb. 2011. *Agricultural contracting update: Contracts in 2008*. Washington: Economic Research Division, U.S. Department of Agriculture.

MacLeod, Margo. 1984. "Influential women volunteers: Rexamining the concept of power." Meetings of the *American Sociological Association*. San Antonio.

Magat, Richard. 1999. *Unlikely partners: Philanthropic foundations and the labor movement*. Ithaca, NY: ILR Press.

Main, Jackson Turner. 1965. *The social structure of revolutionary America*. Princeton, NJ: Princeton University Press.

Malbin, Michael. 2008. "Reality check: Obama received about the same percentage from small donors in 2008 as Bush in 2004." Washington: Campaign Finance Institute.

Mandelbaum, Robb. 2009. "Whom does the NFIB represent (besides its members)?" *New York Times*, August 26, www.boss.blogs.nytimes.com/2009/08/26/whom-does-the-nfib-represent-besides-its-members/.

Maney, Ardith and Loree Gerdes Bykerk. 1994. *Consumer politics: Protecting public interests on Capitol Hill*. Westport, CT: Greenwood Press.

Mann, Michael. 1986. *The sources of social power: A history of power from the beginning to A.D. 1760*, Vol. 1. New York: Cambridge University Press.

————. 1993. *The sources of social power: The rise of classes and nation-states, 1760–1914*, Vol. 2. New York: Cambridge University Press.

————. 2012. *The sources of social power: Global empires and revolution, 1890–1945*, Vol. 3. New York: Cambridge University Press.

————. 2013. *The sources of social power: Globalizations, 1945–2011*, Vol. 4. New York: Cambridge University Press.

Manza, Jeff. 2012. "Elections." pp. 168–179 in *The Wiley-Blackwell Companion to Political Sociology*, edited by E. Amenta, K. Nash, and A. Scott. New York: Blackwell.

Manza, Jeff and Clem Brooks. 1999. *Social cleavages and political change: Voter alignments and U.S. party coalitions*. New York: Oxford University Press.

Marchi, Neil. 1975. "The first Nixon adminstration: Prelude to controls." pp. 295–352 in *Exhortation and control: The search for a wage-price policy 1945–1971*, edited by C. Goodwin. Washington: The Brookings Institution.

Mariolis, Peter. 1975. "Interlocking directorates and control of corporations." *Social Sciences Quarterly* 56:425–439.

Marmor, Theodore. 2000. *The politics of Medicare*. Hawthorne, NY: Aldine de Gruyter.

Marquez, Benjamin. 1993. "Mexican-American community development corporations and the limits of directed capitalism." *Economic Development Quarterly* 7:287–295.

———. 2003. "Mexican-American political organizations and philanthropy: Bankrolling a social movement." *Social Service Review* 77:329–348.

Marsh, Ann. 1996. "The Forbes Four Hundred." *Forbes*, October 14, p. 100(5).

Massey, Douglas. 2005. *Return of the "L" word: A liberal vision for the new century*. Princeton, NJ: Princeton University Press.

Matusow, Allen. 1998. *Nixon's economy*. Lawrence: University Press of Kansas.

Mauss, Marcel. 1924/1969. *The gift: Forms and functions of exchange in archaic societies*. London: Cohen & West.

Mayer, Gerald. 2004. *Union membership trends in the United States*. Congressional Research Service: www.digitalcommons.ilr.cornell.edu/key_workplace/174.

McConnell, Grant. 1966. *Private power and American democracy*. New York: Knopf.

McIntyre, Robert S. 2004. "Corporate income taxes in the Bush years." Washington: Citizens for Tax Justice.

McQuaid, Kim. 1979. "The frustration of corporate revival in the early New Deal." *Historian* 41:682–704.

———. 1982. *Big business and presidential power from FDR to Reagan*. New York: Morrow.

Medvetz, Thomas. 2012a. "Murky power: 'Think tanks' as boundary organizations." *Research in the Sociology of Organizations* 34:113–133.

———. 2012b. *Think tanks in America*. Chicago: University of Chicago Press.

Melber, Ari. 2008. "Obama's iSuccess." *The Nation*, October 27, p. 8.

Mendell, David. 2007. *Obama: From promise to power*. New York: HarperCollins.

Michaels, David. 2008. *Doubt is their product: How industry's assault on science threatens your health*. New York: Oxford University Press.

Miethe, T. D. 1999. *Whistleblowing at work: Tough choices in exposing fraud, waste, and abuse on the job*. Boulder, CO: Westview Press.

Miller, Berkeley and William Canak. 1995. "There should be no blanket guarantee: Employers' reactions to public employee unionism, 1965–1975." *Journal of Collective Negotiations in the Public Sector* 24:17–35.

Miller, Claire. 2012. "Bartz reflects, and offers advice to her successor." *New York Times*, October 8, p. B4.

Miller, John J. 2002. "A third party on the right?" *New York Times*, November 16, p. A27.

Miller, Mark C. 1995. *The high priests of American politics: The role of lawyers in American political institutions*. Knoxville: University of Tennessee Press.

Miller, Norman. 1970. "The machine Democrats." *Washington Monthly*, pp. 70–73.

Miller, William. 1949. "American historians and the business elite." *Journal of Economic History* 9:184–208.

Mills, C. Wright. 1956. *The power elite.* New York: Oxford University Press.

Mink, Gwendolyn. 1986. *Old labor and new immigrants in American political development, 1870–1925.* Ithaca: Cornell University Press.

Mintz, Beth. 1975. "The president's cabinet, 1897–1972: A contribution to the power structure debate." *Insurgent Sociologist* 5:131–148.

———. 1998. "The failure of health care reform: The role of big business in policy formation." pp. 210–224 in *Social policy and the conservative agenda,* edited by C. Lo and M. Schwartz. Malden, MA: Blackwell.

Mishel, Larry, Jared Bernstein, and Heidi Shierholz. 2009. *The state of working America 2008/2009.* Ithaca: ILR Press.

Mitchell, Greg. 1992. *The campaign of the century: Upton Sinclair's race for governor of California and the birth of media politics.* New York: Random House.

Mitchell, Robert. 1991. "From conservation to environmental movement: The development of the modern environmental lobbies." pp. 81–113 in *Governmental and Environmental Politics,* edited by M. Lacey. Baltimore: Johns Hopkins University Press.

Mizruchi, Mark. 1982. *The American corporate network, 1904–1974.* Beverly Hills: Sage Publications.

———. 1996. "What do interlocks do? An analysis, critique, and assessment of research on interlocking directorates." *Annual Review of Sociology* 22:271–298.

Mizruchi, Mark and David Bunting. 1981. "Influence in corporate networks: An examination of four measures." *Administrative Science Quarterly* 26:475–489.

Molotch, Harvey. 2004. "Spilling out (again)." pp. 87–90 in *Enriching the sociological imagination: How radical sociology changed the discipline,* edited by R. F. Levine. Boston: Brill.

Molotch, Harvey and Marilyn Lester. 2004. "Accidents, scandals, and routines: Resources for insurgent methodology." pp. 91–104 in *Enriching the sociological imagination: How radical sociology changed the discipline,* edited by R. F. Levine. Boston: Brill.

Moore, Gwen. 2007. "From Vietnam to Iraq: American elites' views on the use of military force." *Comparative Sociology* 6:215–231.

Moore, Gwen, Sarah Sobieraj, J. Allen Whitt, Olga Mayorova, and Daniel Beaulieu. 2002. "Elite interlocks in three U.S. sectors: Nonprofit, corporate, and government." *Social Science Quarterly* 83:726–744.

Moriarty, Shannon, Mazher Ali, Brian Miller, Jessica Morneault, Tim Sullivan, and Michael Young. 2012. *Born on third base: What the Forbes 400 really says about economic equality and opportunity in America.* Boston: United for a Fair Economy.

Morris, David. 2004. "How to write a prize-winning essay on inequality." Minneapolis: Federal Reserve Bank of Minneapolis.

Morrison, Nan. 2010. "Department of Education recognizes the importance of economic education." In *Council for Economic Education.* New York: www.councilforeconed.org/.

Mosk, Matthew and Sarah Cohen. 2008. "Big donors drive Obama's money edge." *Washington Post,* October 22, p. A1.

Mosk, Matthew and Alec MacGillis. 2008. "Big donors among Obama's grass roots: Bundlers have a voice in campaign." *Washington Post,* April 11, p. A1.

Moskos, Charles and John Butler. 1996. *All that we can be: Black leadership and racial integration the Army way.* New York: Basic Books.

Mueller, John E. 1973. *War, presidents, and public opinion.* New York: Wiley.

———. 1984. "Reflections on the Vietnam antiwar movement and on the curious calm at the war's end." pp. 151–157 in *Vietnam as history: Ten years after the Paris Peace Accords,* edited by P. Braestrup. Washington: University Press of America.

———. 2005. "The Iraq syndrome." *Foreign Affairs,* November/December, pp. 44–54.

Murray, Shailagh. 2008. "In Obama's circle, Chicago remains the tie that binds." *Washingon Post*, July 14, p. A1.

Nader, Ralph, Mark Green, and Joel Seligman. 1976. *Taming the giant corporation*. New York: W. W. Norton.

Nanea (Anonymous) and Yves Smith. 2012. "Private equity: A government-sponsored enterprise." In *The naked capitalist*: www.nakedcapitalism.com/2012/08/private-equity-a-government-sponsored-enterprise.html#ABDS4qRB0w2g1oFv.99.

Nelson, Robert L. 1988. *Partners with power: The social transformation of the large law firm*. Berkeley: University of California Press.

Neustadtl, Alan, Denise Scott, and Dan Clawson. 1991. "Class struggle in campaign finance? Political action committee contributions in the 1984 elections." *Sociological Forum* 6:219–238.

Nieuwbeerta, Paul, Clem Brooks, and Jeff Manza. 2006. "Cleavage-based voting in cross-national perspective: Evidence from six countries." *Social Science Research* 35:88–128.

Nixon, Richard. 1978. *RN: The memoirs of Richard Nixon*. New York: Grosset & Dunlap.

Norton, Michael and Daniel Ariely. 2011. "Building a better America one wealth quintile at a time." *Perspectives on Psychological Science* 6:9–12.

NRDC. 1990. *Twenty years defending the environment: National Resources Defense Council 1970–1990*. New York: Natural Resources Defense Council.

NYT. 2012. "Shrinking corporate tax rates, April 29." In *New York Times*: www.nytimes.com/interactive/2012/04/28/business/Shrinking-Corporate-Tax-Rates.html.

Olsen, Marvin E. and Martin N. Marger. 1993. *Power in modern societies*. Boulder, CO: Westview Press.

Olson, Elizabeth. 2006. "Amassing the troops for political battle." *New York Times*, May 4, p. C7.

OpenSecrets. 2012a. "2012 presidential race." *OpenSecrets.org: Center for Responsive Politics*. Washington: www.opensecrets.org.

———. 2012b. "2012 presidential: Barack Obama's bundlers." *OpenSecrets.org: Center for Responsive Politics*. Washington: www.opensecrets.org.

———. 2012c. "Education: Top contributors to federal candidates, parties, and outside groups." *OpenSecrets.org: Center for Responsive Politics*. Washington: www.opensecrets.org.

———. 2012d. "Blue team aided by small donors, big bundlers: Huge outside spending still comes up short." *OpenSecrets.org: Center for Responsive Politics*. Washington: www.opensecrets.org.

———. 2012e. "Business-labor-ideology split in PAC and individual donations to candidates, parties, super PACs and outside spending groups." *Open Secrets.org: Center for Responsive Politics*. Washington: http://www.opensecrets.org.

———. 2012f. "Revolving door." *Open Secrets.org: Center for Responsive Politics*. Washington: www.opensecrets.org.

———. 2012g. "Top lobbying firms." *OpenSecrets.org: Center for Responsive Politics*. Washington: www.opensecrets.org.

———. 2012h. "Wall Street funds down from Obama's inaugural run." *OpenSecrets.org: Center for Responsive Politics*. Washington: www.opensecrets.org.

Orloff, Ann. 1993. *The politics of pensions: A comparative analysis of Britain, Canada, and the United States, 1880–1940*. Madison: University of Wisconsin Press.

Ostrander, Susan A. 1980. "Upper-class women: Class consciousness as conduct and meaning." pp. 73–96 in *Power structure research*, edited by G. W. Domhoff. Beverly Hills: Sage.

———. 1984. *Women of the upper class*. Philadelphia: Temple University Press.

———. 1987. "Elite domination in private social agencies: How it happens and how it is challenged." pp. 85–102 in *Power elites and organizations*, edited by G. W. Domhoff and T. Dye. Beverly Hills: Sage.

———. 1995. *Money for change: Social movement philanthropy at Haymarket People's Fund.* Philadelphia: Temple University Press.

Overacker, Louise. 1932. *Money in elections.* New York: Macmillan.

Page, Benjamin. 2002. "The semi-sovereign public." pp. 325–344 in *Navigating public opinion: Polls, policy, and the future of American democracy*, edited by J. Manza, F. Cook, and B. Page. New York: Oxford University Press.

———. 2008. *The foreign policy disconnect: What Americans want from our leaders but don't get.* Chicago: University of Chicago Press.

Page, Benjamin, Larry Bartels, and Jason Seawright. 2011. "Democracy and the policy preferences of wealthy Americans." Meetings of the *American Political Science Association.* Seattle.

Page, Benjamin and Cari Hennessy. 2010. "What affluent Americans want from politics." Meetings of the *American Political Science Association.* Washington.

Page, Benjamin and Lawrence Jacobs. 2009. *Class war? What Americans really think about economic inequality.* Chicago: University of Chicago Press.

Page, Benjamin and Robert Y. Shapiro. 1992. *The rational public: Fifty years of trends in Americans' policy preferences.* Chicago: University of Chicago Press.

Palmer, Griff and Michael Cooper. 2012. "How maps helped party keep edge in the House." *New York Times*, December 15, pp. A10, A15.

Palmer, Robert R. 1959. *The age of the democratic revolution: A political history of Europe and America, 1760–1800.* Princeton, NJ: Princeton University Press.

Parker-Gwin, Rachel and William G. Roy. 1996. "Corporate law and the organization of property in the United States: The origin and institutionalization of New Jersey corporation law, 1888–1903." *Politics & Society*, June, pp. 111–136.

Patterson, James T. 1967. *Congressional conservatism and the New Deal: The growth of the conservative coalition in Congress, 1933–1939.* Lexington: University of Kentucky Press.

Pear, Robert. 2009. "House passes two measures on job bias." *New York Times*, January 9, p. A13.

Pederson, Morgens. 1972. "Lawyers in politics: The Danish Folketing and United States legislatures." pp. 25–63 in *Comparative legislative behavior*, edited by S. Patterson and J. Wahlke. New York: Wiley & Sons.

Peoples, Clayton. 2007. "Class dominance and policymaking in the U.S. House." *Meetings of the Pacific Sociological Association.* Oakland, CA.

———. 2010. "Contributor influence in Congress: Social ties and PAC effects on U.S. House policymaking." *The Sociological Quarterly* 51:649–677.

Peoples, Clayton and Michael Gortari. 2008. "The impact of campaign contributions on policymaking in the U.S. and Canada: Theoretical and public policy implications." *Research in Political Sociology* 17:43–64.

Perrow, Charles. 2002. *Organizing America: Wealth, power, and the origin of corporate capitalism.* Princeton, NJ: Princeton University Press.

Pertschuk, Michael. 1982. *Revolt against regulation: The rise and pause of the consumer movement.* Berkeley: University of California Press.

Peschek, Joseph. 1987. *Policy-planning organizations: Elite agendas and America's rightward turn.* Philadelphia: Temple University Press.

Pessen, Edward. 1984. *The log cabin myth: The social backgrounds of the presidents.* New Haven: Yale University Press.

Pettigrew, Thomas. 2008. "Still a long way to go: American black-white relations today." pp. 45–61 in *Commemorating Brown: The social psychology of racism and discrimination*, edited by G. Adams, M. Biernat, N. Branscombe, C. Crandall, and L. Wrightsman. Washington: American Psychological Association.

Pew Research Center. 2012. "Obama gains edge in campaign's final days." in *Pew Research Center for the People and the Press*. Philadelpha: www.people-press.org/.

Phillips, Peter. 1994. "A relative advantage: Sociology of the San Francisco Bohemian Club." Ph.D. Thesis, Sociology, University of California, Davis. Davis, CA.

Piketty, Thomas and Emmanuel Saez. 2003. "Income inequality in the United States, 1913–1998." *Quarterly Journal of Economics* CXVIII:1–39.

PIRG/CTJ. 2012. *Loopholes for sale: Campaign contributions by corporate tax dodgers.* Washington: Public Interest Research Group and Citizens for Tax Justice.

Piven, Frances. 2006. *Challenging authority: How ordinary people change America.* Lanham, MD: Rowman & Littlefield.

Piven, Frances and Richard Cloward. 1977. *Poor people's movements: Why they succeed, how they fail.* New York: Random House.

Piven, Frances and Richard Cloward. 1971/1993. *Regulating the poor: The functions of public welfare.* New York: Vintage Books.

———. 1982/1985. *The new class war: Reagan's attack on the welfare state and its consequences.* New York: Pantheon Books.

Piven, Frances, Lorraine Minnite, and Margaret Groarke. 2009. *Keeping down the black vote: Race and the demobilization of American voters.* New York: New Press.

POGO. 2004. *The politics of contracting.* Washington: Project on Government Oversight.

Pollin, Robert, Dean Baker, and Marc Schaberg. 2008. "Securities transaction taxes for U.S. financial markets." Political Economy Research Institute, Amherst, MA.

Polsby, Nelson. 1980. *Community power and political theory.* New Haven: Yale University Press.

Potter, David. 1972. *The South and the concurrent majority.* Baton Rouge: Louisiana State University Press.

Potter, Wendell. 2010. *Deadly spin: An insurance company insider speaks out on how corporate PR is killing health care and deceiving Americans.* New York: Bloomsbury Press.

Prothro, James. 1954. *The dollar decade: Business ideas in the 1920s.* Baton Rouge: Louisiana State University Press.

Public Citizen. 2011. "12 months after: The effects of Citizens United on elections and the integrity of the legislative process." In *Public Citizen's Congress Watch*. Washington: www.citizen.org.

———. 2012. "White House for Sale." Washington: www.Citizen.org.

O Pusser, Brian, Sheila Slaughter, and Scott Thomas. 2006. "Playing the board game: An empirical analysis of university trustee and corporate board interlocks." *Journal of Higher Education* 77:747–775.

Quadagno, Jill S. 1994. *The color of welfare: How racism undermined the war on poverty.* New York: Oxford University Press.

———. 2005. *One nation, uninsured: Why the U.S. has no national health insurance.* New York: Oxford University Press.

———. 2012. "Interest-group influence on the Patient Protection and Affordability Act of 2010: Winners and losers in the health care reform debate." *Journal of Health Politics, Policy and Law* 36:449–453.

Quadagno, Jill S. and Deana Rohlinger. 2009. "Religious conservatives in U.S. welfare state politics." pp. 236–266 in *Religion, class coalitions, and welfare states*, edited by K. Kersbergen and P. Manow. Cambridge: Cambridge University Press.

Renner, Tari and Victor DeSantis. 1994. "Contemporary patterns and trends in municipal government structures." In *The Municipal Yearbook 1993*. Washington: International City Managers Association.

Riddiough, Christine and David Card. 2008. *Americans for Democratic Action: The 2007 voting record*. Washington: Americans for Democratic Action.

Riley, Charles. 2012. "Oops! Aetna discloses political donations." *CNN MoneyLine*, June 15, pp. www.money.cnn.com/2012/06/14/news/economy/aetna-political-contributions/index.htm.

Rising, George. 1997. *Clean for Gene: Eugene McCarthy's 1968 presidential campaign*. Westport, CT: Praeger.

Robinson, Marshall. 1993. "The Ford Foundation: Sowing the seeds of a revolution." *Environment*, pp. 10–20.

Rosen, Jeffrey. 2008. "Supreme Court Inc.: How the nation's highest court became increasingly receptive to the arguments of American business." *New York Times Magazine*, March 16, pp. 20–26.

Rosenstone, Steven J., Roy L. Behr, and Edward H. Lazarus. 1996. *Third parties in America: Citizen response to major party failure*. Princeton: Princeton University Press.

Rossi, Peter and Robert Dentler. 1961. *The politics of urban renewal*. New York: Free Press.

Rothschild, Joyce and Terance Miethe. 1994. "Whistleblowing as resistance in modern work organizations." pp. 252–273 in *Resistance and power in organizations*, edited by J. Jermier, D. Knights, and W. Nord. New York: Routledge.

Roy, William G. 1983. "Interlocking directorates and the corporate revolution." *Social Science History* 7:143–164.

———. 1997. *Socializing capital: The rise of the large industrial corporation in America*. Princeton, NJ: Princeton University Press.

Ruskey, Frank and Mark Weston. 2012. "A survey of Venn diagrams." In *Department of Computer Science, University of Victoria*: www.combinatorics.org/files/Surveys/ds5/VennEJC.html.

Russell, Bertrand. 1938. *Power: A new social analysis*. London: Allen and Unwin.

Ryan, William. 1971. *Blaming the victim*. New York: Random House.

Saez, Emmanuel. 2012. "Striking it richer: The evolution of top incomes in the United States updated with 2009 and 2010 estimates." Berkeley: Department of Economics, University of California.

Salzman, Harold and G. William Domhoff. 1980. "The corporate community and government: Do they interlock?" pp. 227–254 in *Power structure research*, edited by G. W. Domhoff. Beverly Hills: Sage.

———. 1983. "Nonprofit organizations and the corporate community." *Social Science History* 7:205–216.

Sanders, Jerry. 1983. *Peddlers of crisis: The Committee on the Present Danger and the politics of containment*. Boston: South End Press.

Savage, Charlie. 2008a. "Obama fundraiser knocks down cabinet rumors." *New York Times*, November 21, p. A25.

———. 2008b. "Shepherd of a govenment in exile." *New York Times*, November 7, p. A18.

Schiesl, Martin J. 1977. *The politics of efficiency: Municipal administration and reform in America, 1800–1920*. Berkeley: University of California Press.

Schlesinger, Joseph A. 1966. *Ambition and politics: Political careers in the United States*. Chicago: Rand McNally.

Schmitt, John. 2012. "The minimum wage is too damn low." In *Center for Economic and Policy Research*. Washington: www.cepr.net/index.php/publications/reports/the-minimum-wage-is-too-damn-low.

Schneider, William. 1998. "And lo, the momentum shifted." *National Journal*, October 3, p. 2350.

Schuby, T. D. 1975. "Class, power, kinship and social cohesion: A case study of a local elite." *Sociological Focus* 8:243–255.

Schudson, Michael. 1995. *The power of news*. Cambridge: Harvard University Press.

———. 2011. *The sociology of news*. Second edition. New York: W. W. Norton.

Schulte, Fred, John Farrell, and Jeremy Borden. 2011. "Obama rewards big bundlers with jobs, commissions, stimulus money, government contracts, and more." *1WatchNews.org: Center for Public Integrity*, June 15.

Schwartz, George. 1979. "The successful fight against a federal consumer protection agency." *MSU Business Topics* 27:45–56.

Schweizer, Peter and Rochelle Schweizer. 2004. *The Bushes: Portrait of a dynasty*. New York: Doubleday.

Sciammacco, Sara. 2011. "The downfall of direct payments." In *Environmental Working Group*: www.ewg.org.

Seefeldt, Kristin, Gordon Abner, Joe Bolinger, Lanlan Xu, and John Graham. 2012. "At risk: America's poor during and after the Great Recession." School of Public and Environmental Affairs, Indiana University, Bloomington.

Sellers, Christopher. 2012. *Crabgrass crucible: Suburban nature and the rise of environmentalism in twentieth-century America*. Chapel Hill: University of North Carolina Press.

Sennett, Richard and Jonathan Cobb. 1973. *The hidden injuries of class*. New York: Norton.

Shaiko, R. and M. Wallace. 1999. "From Wall Street to Main Street: The National Federation of Independent Business and the new Republican majority." pp. 18–35 in *After the revolution: PACs, lobbies, and the Republican Congress*, edited by R. Biersack, P. Herrnson, and C. Wilcox. Boston: Allyn and Bacon.

Shear, Michael D. and Jeffrey H. Birnbaum. 2008. "The anti-lobbyist surrounds himself with lobbyists." *Washington Post National Weekly*, March 3–9, p. 13.

Shearn, Ian. 2012. "Whose side is the American Farm Bureau on?" *The Nation*, July 16, www.thenation.com/article/168913/whose-side-american-farm-bureau#.

Shefter, Martin. 1994. *Political parties and the state: The American historical experience*. Princeton, NJ: Princeton University Press.

Shelley, Mack C. 1983. *The permanent majority: The conservative coalition in the United States Congress*. Tuscaloosa: University of Alabama Press.

Sherwood, Jessica. 2010. *Wealth, whiteness, and the matrix of privilege: The view from the country club*. Lanham, MD: Lexington Books.

Shoup, Laurence. 1974. "Shaping the national interest: The Council on Foreign Relations, the Department of State, and the origins of the postwar world." Ph.D. Thesis, History, Northwestern University, Evanston, IL.

Silk, Leonard Solomon and David Vogel. 1976. *Ethics and profits: The crisis of confidence in American business*. New York: Simon & Schuster.

Silver, Nate. 2012. *The signal and the noise: Why so many predictions fail—but some don't*. New York: Penguin Group.

Silver-Greenberg, Jessica and Susanne Craig. 2012. "Citigroup's chief resigns his post in surprise step." *New York Times*, October 17, p. A1.

Silverstein, Ken. 2006. "Barack Obama, Inc.: The birth of a Washingon machine." *Harper's*, November, pp. 14–29.

Sinclair, Barbara. 1982. *Congressional realignment, 1925–1978*. Austin: University of Texas Press.

Skocpol, Theda. 1980. "Political responses to capitalist crisis: Neo-Marxist theories of the state and the case of the New Deal." *Politics and Society* 10:155–202.

———. 1992. *Protecting soldiers and mothers: The political origins of social policy in the United States*. Cambridge: Harvard University Press.

———. 2012. *Obama and America's political future*. Cambridge: Harvard University Press.

Small Business Administration. 2006. "Size distribution of American business in 2006." In *Small Business Administration*: http://archive.sba.gov/advo/research/rs371tot.pdf.

Smith, Jason. 2006. *Building New Deal liberalism: The political economy of public works, 1933–1956*. New York: Cambridge University Press.

Smith, Mark A. 2000. *American business and political power*. Chicago: University of Chicago Press.

Smith, R. Jeffrey. 2008. "Under Bush, OSHA mired in inaction." *Washington Post*, December 29, p. A1.

Sorkin, Andrew. 2012. "Big law steps into uncertain times." *New York Times*, September 25, pp. F1, F3.

Staples, Clifford. 2012a. "Confidential e-mail interview."

———. 2012b. "The Business Roundtable." pp. 100–123 in *Financial elites and transnational business: Who rules the world?*, edited by G. Murray and J. Scott. Northhampton, MA: Edward Elgar Publishing.

———. 2013. "The corporate community, think tanks, policy-discussion groups, and government: Their interlocks and their interactions." Meetings of the American Sociological Association, New York. Also on www.whorulesamerica.net.

Starr, Paul. 2007. *Freedom's power: The true force of liberalism*. New York: Basic Books.

Stauber, John C. and Sheldon Rampton. 1995. *Toxic sludge is good for you: Lies, damn lies, and the public relations industry*. Monroe, ME: Common Courage Press.

Steinhauer, Jennifer. 2008. "Phoenix club expels member over his press interview." *New York Times*, July 31, p. A19.

Stephens, John. 1979. *The transition from capitalism to socialism*. London: Macmillan.

Stewart, James B. 1991. *Den of thieves*. New York: Simon & Schuster.

Stone, Peter. 2000. "A Bermuda brouhaha for insurers." *National Journal*, October 14, p. 3262.

Stowell, David. 1999. *Streets, railroads and the Great Strike of 1877*. Chicago: University of Chicago Press.

Street, Paul. 2008. *Barack Obama and the future of American politics*. Boulder: Paradigm Publishers.

Sugrue, Thomas. 2008. *Sweet land of liberty: The forgotten struggle for civil rights in the North*. New York: Random House.

Szasz, Andrew. 1984. "Industrial resistance to occupational safety and health regulation: 1971–1981." *Social Problems* 32:103–116.

Taylor, Nick. 2008. *American-made: The enduring legacy of the WPA*. New York: Bantam Books.

Tedlock, Philip. 2005. *Expert political judgment: How good is it? How can we know?* Princeton, NJ: Princeton University Press.

Temin, Peter. 1997. "The American business elite in historical perspective." Cambridge: National Bureau of Economic Research.

———. 1998. "The stability of the American business elite." Cambridge: National Bureau of Economic Research.

Tittle, Diana. 1992. *Rebuilding Cleveland: The Cleveland Foundation and its evolving urban strategy.* Columbus: Ohio State University Press.

Tomkins, Silvan. 1964. "Left and right: A basic dimension of personality and ideology." pp. 388–411 in *The study of lives,* edited by R. W. White. New York: Atherton Press.

Unekis, Joseph. 1993. "Blocking the liberal agenda in House committees: The role of the conservative coalition." *Congress & the Presidency* 20:93–99.

Union of Concerned Scientists. 2007. "Smoke, mirrors, & hot air." Cambridge: Union of Concerned Scientists.

Useem, Michael. 1979. "The social organization of the American business elite and the participation of corporate directors in the governance of American institutions." *American Sociological Review* 44:553–571.

———. 1980. "Corporations and the corporate elite." *Annual Review of Sociology* 6:41–77.

———. 1996. *Investor capitalism: How money managers are changing the face of corporate America.* New York: Basic Books.

Useem, Michael and Jerome Karabel. 1986. "Pathways to top corporate management." *American Sociological Review* 51:184–200.

Vaughn, James C. 2006. "The culture of the Bohemian Grove: The dramaturgy of power." *Michigan Sociological Review* 20:85–121.

Vogel, David. 1978. "Why businessmen mistrust their state: The political consciousness of American corporate executives." *British Journal of Political Science* 8:45–78.

———. 1989. *Fluctuating fortunes: The political power of business in America.* New York: Basic Books.

Volscho, Thomas and Nathan Kelly. 2012. "The rise of the super-rich: Power resources, taxes, financial markets, and the dynamics of the top 1 percent, 1949 to 2008." *American Sociological Review* 77:679–699.

Voss, Kim. 1993. *The making of American exceptionalism: The Knights of Labor and class formation in the nineteenth century.* Ithaca: Cornell University Press.

Waddell, Brian. 2001. *The war against the New Deal: World War II and American democracy.* DeKalb: Northern Illinois University Press.

Wala, Michael. 1994. *The Council on Foreign Relations and American foreign policy in the early Cold War.* Providence: Berghahn Books.

Warburg, James P. 1964. *The long road home: The autobiography of a maverick.* New York: Doubleday.

Washburn, Jennifer. 2005. *University, Inc.: The corporate corruption of American higher education.* New York: Basic Books.

Waters, Mary C. 1990. *Ethnic options: Choosing identities in America.* Berkeley: University of California Press.

———. 1999. *Black identities: West Indian immigrant dreams and American realities.* Cambridge: Harvard University Press.

Wayne, Leslie. 2012. "How Delaware thrives as a corporate tax haven." *New York Times,* July 1, p. BU1.

Webber, Michael. 2000. *New Deal fat cats: Business, labor, and campaign finance in the 1936 presidential election*. New York: Fordham University Press.

Weber, Max. 1998. "Class, status, and party." pp. 43–56 in *Social class and stratification: Classic statements and theoretical debates*, edited by R. F. Levine. Lanham, MD: Rowman & Littlefield.

Wehr, Kevin. 1994. "The power elite at the Bohemian Grove: Has anything changed in the 1990s?" *Critical Sociology* 20:121–124.

Weinstein, James. 1967. *The decline of socialism in America, 1912–1925*. New York: Monthly Review Press.

———. 1968. *The corporate ideal in the liberal state*. Boston: Beacon Press.

———. 1975. *Ambiguous legacy: The left in American politics*. New York: Franklin Watts.

Western, Bruce and Jake Rosenfeld. 2011. "Unions, norms, and the rise in U.S. wage inequality." *American Sociological Review* 76:513–537.

Whalen, Charles and Barbara Whalen. 1985. *The longest debate: A legislative history of the 1964 Civil Rights Act*. Washington: Seven Locks Press.

White, Lawrence J. 2002. "Trends in aggregate concentration in the United States." *Journal of Economic Perspectives* 16:137–160.

White, Shelby. 1978. "Cradle to grave: Family offices manage money for the very rich." *Barron's*, March 20, pp. 9–11.

Wikipedia. 2012. "Council for Economic Education." In *Wikipedia*: www.en.wikipedia.org/wiki/Council_for_Economic_Education.

Williams-Derry, Clark. 2001. *Report on Farm Subsidies, 1996–1999*. Washington: Environmental Working Group.

Williamson, Jeffrey and Peter Lindert. 1980. *American inequality: A macroeconomic history*. New York: Academic Press.

Winters, Jeffrey. 2011. *Oligarchy*. New York: Cambridge University Press.

Wolff, Edward. 2012. "The asset price meltdown and the wealth of the middle class." New York: Department of Economics, New York University.

Woods, Tim. 2003. "Capitalist class relations, the state, and New Deal foreign trade policy." *Critical Sociology* 29:393–418.

Woodward, Bob. 2000. *Maestro: Greenspan's Fed and the American boom*. New York: Simon & Schuster.

Woodward, C. Vann. 1966. *Reunion and reaction: The compromise of 1877 and the end of Reconstruction*. Boston: Little, Brown.

———. 1973. "Yes, there was a Compromise of 1877." *Journal of American History* 60:215–223.

Wright, Erik Olin. 1998. "Class analysis." pp. 141–165 in *Social class and stratification: Classic statements and theoretical debates*, edited by R. F. Levine. Lanham, MD: Rowman & Littlefield.

Wright, Stephen C. and M. Lubensky. 2009. "The struggle for social equality: Collective action vs. prejudice reduction." In *Intergroup misunderstandings: Impact of divergent social realities*, edited by S. Demoulin, J.-P. Leyens, and J. F. Dovidio. New York: Psychology Press.

Wrong, Dennis. 1995. *Power: Its forms, bases, and uses*. New Brunswick: Transaction Publishers.

WSJ. 2012. "More than 1 in 7 use food stamps in U.S." In *Wall Street Journal, Real Time Economics*, March 2: www.blogs.wsj.com/economics/2012/03/02/more-than-1-in-7-use-food-stamps-in-u-s/.

Yaqub, Reshma. 2002. "Getting inside the ivory gates." *Worth Magazine*, pp. 10–20.

Yearwood, Pauline. 2008. "Obama and the Jews." *The Chicago Jewish News Online*, www .chicagojewishnews.com/.

Yeomans, William. 2012. "How the right packed the court." *The Nation*, October 8, pp. 14–17.

Yuen, Eddie, Daniel Burton-Rose, and George Katsiaficas. 2001. "The battle for Seattle." New York: Soft Skull Press.

———. 2004. *Confronting capitalism: Dispatches from a global movement.* New York: Soft Skull Press.

Zaller, John. 2006. *The nature and origins of mass opinion.* New York: Cambridge University Press.

Zeller, Shawn. 2000. "Cassidy captures the gold." *National Journal*, October 21, pp. 3332–3334.

Zweigenhaft, Richard L. 2013. "Diversity among interlocking directors and on major policy boards." *Meetings of the American Sociological Association*, New York. Also on www .whorulesamerica.net.

Zweigenhaft, Richard L. and G. William Domhoff. 1982. *Jews in the Protestant establishment.* New York: Praeger.

———. 2006. *Diversity in the power elite: How it happened, why it matters.* Lanham, MD: Rowman & Littlefield.

———. 2011. *The new CEOs: Women, African American, Latino, and Asian American leaders of Fortune 500 companies.* Lanham, MD: Rowman & Littlefield.

Index